P9-CEU-520

PCG (GRG) (MCG) (SDG) (MGG) PTG

Snow, Richard

I invented the modern age: The rise
 of Henry Ford

I INVENTED THE MODERN AGE

Center Point
Large Print

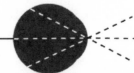

**This Large Print Book carries the
Seal of Approval of N.A.V.H.**

I INVENTED THE MODERN AGE

The **RISE** *of* **HENRY FORD**

Richard Snow

CENTER POINT LARGE PRINT
THORNDIKE, MAINE

This Center Point Large Print edition
is published in the year 2013 by arrangement with
Scribner, a division of Simon & Schuster, Inc.

All pictures are from the collections of The Henry Ford,
except the photo of Ford with Evangeline Dahlinger,
which appeared in *The Secret Life of Henry Ford* by
John Côté Dahlinger.

The text of this Large Print edition is unabridged.
In other aspects, this book may vary
from the original edition.
Printed in the United States of America
on permanent paper.
Set in 16-point Times New Roman type.

ISBN: 978-1-61173-827-8

Library of Congress Cataloging-in-Publication Data

Snow, Richard, 1947–
I invented the modern age : the rise of Henry Ford / Richard Snow. —
Center Point large print edition.
pages cm
Reprint of: New York : Scribner, 2013.
ISBN 978-1-61173-827-8 (library binding : alk. paper)
1. Ford, Henry, 1863–1947.
  2. Automobile engineers—United States—Biography.
  3. Industrialists—United States—Biography.
  4. Automobile industry and trade—United States—History.
  5. Ford Model T automobile—History. I. Title.
TL140.F6S66 2013b
338.7′629222092—dc23
[B]
2013009787

FOR CAROL,

who brightened my explorations of Greenfield Village, just as she has everything else I've done for the last quarter century.

ACHIEVEMENT, *n.* The death of endeavor and the birth of disgust.

—Ambrose Bierce,
The Devil's Dictionary

. . . Yes, Tin, Tin, Tin,
You exasperating puzzle, Hunk o' Tin.
I've abused you and I've flayed you,
But by Henry Ford who made you,
You are better than a Packard, Hunk o' Tin.

—C. C. Battershell, "Dedicated to
the Memory of Car No. 423,"
a Model T ambulance destroyed
on the Western Front in 1917.
After Rudyard Kipling's "Gunga Din."

CONTENTS

In 1913 the Ford Motor Company issued this cross-section of its world-changing creation, assuring the recipient that "the better you know your car, the better . . . you will enjoy it."

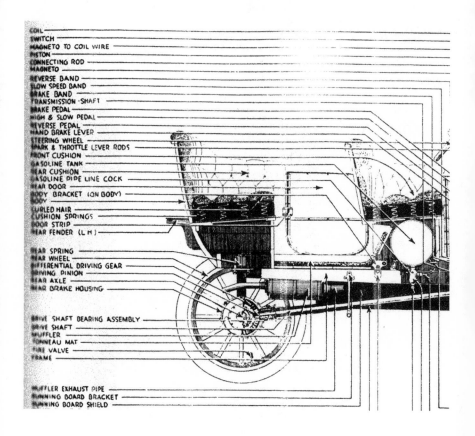

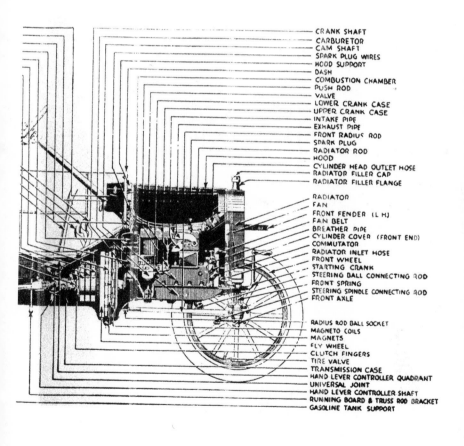

CRANK SHAFT
CARBURETOR
CAM SHAFT
SPARK PLUG WIRES
HOOD SUPPORT
DASH
COMBUSTION CHAMBER
PUSH ROD
VALVE
LOWER CRANK CASE
UPPER CRANK CASE
INTAKE PIPE
EXHAUST PIPE
FRONT RADIUS ROD
SPARK PLUG
RADIATOR ROD
HOOD
CYLINDER HEAD OUTLET HOSE
RADIATOR FILLER CAP
RADIATOR FILLER FLANGE

RADIATOR
FAN
FRONT FENDER (L H)
FAN BELT
BREATHER PIPE
CYLINDER COVER (FRONT END)
COMMUTATOR
RADIATOR INLET HOSE
FRONT WHEEL
STARTING CRANK
STEERING BALL CONNECTING ROD
FRONT SPRING
STEERING SPINDLE CONNECTING ROD
FRONT AXLE

RADIUS ROD BALL SOCKET
MAGNETO COILS
MAGNETS
FLY WHEEL
CLUTCH FINGERS
TIRE VALVE
TRANSMISSION CASE
HAND LEVER CONTROLLER QUADRANT
UNIVERSAL JOINT
HAND LEVER CONTROLLER SHAFT
RUNNING BOARD & TRUSS ROD BRACKET
GASOLINE TANK SUPPORT

CHAPTER 1

A Homecoming

Saving the farm, then saving the entire past; between the steam engine and the Apple; "nobody knew anything about cars"; Fordism.

On a summer day in 1919 a middle-aged man left his Detroit office and drove out to Dearborn, ten miles away, to see the house where he'd been born. It was a farmhouse, long past its best days, and any passersby who noticed him poking around it must briefly have wondered what this visitor was doing there.

He wasn't in any way flamboyant, but he was obviously prosperous, probably wearing one of the neat, quiet gray suits he favored year-round. A little over middle height, he stood so straight that most who met him described him as "tall." He was moderately good-looking, but what might have been an ordinary face had already somehow proved impossible for painters, journalists, and even photographers to capture satisfactorily. Team sports had never interested him although he was athletic and loved to challenge friends to footraces; each time he moved to another vantage point in the farmhouse yard, he did it suddenly and quickly, almost as if he were answering a

19

starting gun. He was not an architect, but he knew how things were put together, and carefully studied the window frames, the chimney, the pitch of the roof. This might be his last chance to see the farmstead, because the house was about to be destroyed.

That was largely his fault. The flow of traffic had grown so heavy in the past decade that the Dearborn city fathers had decided the road bordering the sixty-year-old building needed to be widened. Every second car contributing to that traffic bore the man's name. Henry Ford was making half the automobiles in America.

Few people have the means to defy this sort of progress, but Ford did. He had the farmhouse moved two hundred feet back from the new road. But once the house was safe, it wouldn't let him alone. At first he merely had it restored—some carpentry, fresh paint—but that wasn't enough. He found that he wanted it furnished as it had been in the 1870s, when he was a boy interested in machinery, taking watches apart in his room there.

Now the tenacious perfectionism of the man took over. Representative furniture, typical furniture of the 1860s, wouldn't do. It had to be the same furniture. He'd kept warm in the Michigan winters beside a Starlight Stove in the front parlor. He spent months searching for one, found a near-perfect example—but no, it was a bit too small, it wasn't a Model 25. Then there was the carpeting on the stairs, a faded rusty crimson that he remembered precisely. He had one of the fifty thousand men who worked for him go through antiques shops—local ones, at first, then as far away as Cincinnati—to match it.

The family china: He could remember the stair carpet, but not the plates he had once eaten off. Workers excavated where the dooryard had been, and came up with a ceramic shard large enough to reveal the pattern. Ford had a full dinner service reproduced. Beds, chairs, sofas were found and reupholstered. Ford's agents got the right bureau, and Ford specified exactly what needles and thread should stock one of the drawers. He deviated from utter fidelity with the family organ. It was born with a foot-pump, but Ford had the instrument electrified—nobody could see the difference, after all—and when he stepped back into his youth he would sit at the keyboard for hours, laboriously playing with a finger or two the first songs he'd heard: "Turkey in the Straw," "Flow Gently Sweet Afton."

Upstairs the beds were made with fresh linen; out back stood the stacks of firewood, just as they had in his boyhood; the reservoirs of all the kerosene lamps were full, their wicks trimmed and ready for the match.

Ford had got more things than he'd needed to furnish his farmhouse. He kept the overflow in his office until 1922, when one of his tractor operations moved, leaving behind it an empty building that covered three acres. With this repository available, the carmaker's ambitions expanded beyond the home of his youth to encompass the world of his youth.

Once again his agents went out, this time in their hundreds. They were, said the boss, to bring back "a complete series of every article ever used or made in America from the days of the first settlers down to the present time."

The stream began to flow in: birdcages and settees and patent washboards; carriages, rifles, apple-parers; reapers and binders and the lunch wagon where Ford had grabbed meals when he was working for Detroit Edison back in the nineties. Ford accumulated enough objects, as it turned out, to entirely furnish, from weather vane and lightning rod to mantel clock and furnace, 107 buildings.

At the time, those buildings were living out their lives far from Ford and far from one another. One was a courthouse in Illinois where the young Abraham Lincoln had argued cases; two were Georgia slave cabins, one the brick storefront where Wilbur and Orville Wright sold bicycles while they conducted their momentous experiments.

The homely items Ford had collected still radiated the residual warmth of life from a vanished time, but the signals they sent out were faint, diffuse, cluttered. Put them in a landscape where men and women had used them, though, and their feeble, dissonant notes might become a powerful harmony.

Beyond the airport Ford had just built in Dearborn—it was 1926 now—lay a tract of land where nothing much at all had ever happened. He would, he decided, inject these anonymous acres with history by building on them a monument to the past: a village that would preserve the "American life as lived" of what he called a "saner and sweeter" time.

The man incubating this plan had done more than anyone else alive to annihilate that life; and he found much of its sweet sanity repellent. Everyone today knows his name, but very few could attribute more than one statement to him, which is that history was "bunk." The "bunk" part he perceived in history may have been the sheer mass of it, all those names you had to learn, all those treaties and tariffs and boundary disputes. Ford always liked to see the thing itself. Years later some of his old lieutenants would say he couldn't read a blueprint. He could, and competently, too. But it is perfectly true that he would far rather see the objects encoded in the cool white lines. His sense of what was sound engineering transmitted itself most surely through his fingertips.

So it was with the past. Ford wanted to be able

to handle it, to walk inside it and look around. He bought the Illinois courthouse and moved it to Dearborn, to the town he had named Greenfield Village, after his wife's birthplace. He bought the Wright brothers' cycle shop, and moved it there, too—and, to keep it company, the carpentry Queen Anne house the brothers grew up in. He brought Thomas Edison's laboratory from Menlo Park, New Jersey, along with a dozen freight-car loads of Jersey dirt so it could stand amid the snails and fungi it had always known, and the boardinghouse where Edison's hard-pressed staff hadn't slept enough.

The Edison Illuminating Company and its dynamos took up residence near Noah Webster's home. Toward the end of his life Ford moved his farmstead there, and you can walk right into it today and see that perfectly retrieved stair carpeting.

What you won't see in Greenfield village is a bank, or a law office: Ford had no use for bankers and lawyers. Many of them were Jews, he believed, and all were leeches who lived off the blood of creativity. He had no hesitation—for many years, at least—in sharing this information with anyone who would listen. This was Ford at his most independent and least attractive, tirelessly venting the cranky certainties that had seeped into his character even as he became famous.

All was mixed together as he conjured up his village, and it remains a place of contradictions, at least as far as his first expressed purpose goes. Edison and the Wrights had not worked to preserve the agrarian world of Ford's boyhood. And neither had Ford.

As his village took shape, it turned out to be a wistful tribute not only to the sturdy American small farmer and the one-room schoolhouse where his children absorbed virtue along with grammar from their McGuffey's Readers, but also to the forces that swept that world away, the dynamo and the electricity it conjured, the airplane, and of course the machine that Ford began building in 1903 in his Mack Avenue factory, whose gray-painted board front he carefully re-created.

Once, stopping at a house he was planning to move, where he had spent a good deal of time as a boy, Ford made a discovery. "I found some marbles, put a few of them in the palm of my hand, and as I applied pressure, they disintegrated. Life, change, had gone on."

Not in Greenfield Village. As building after building arrived, as the automobile factory rose near the smithy, it became increasingly clear that this town was a concrete representation of Henry Ford's mind, the things he missed, the things he took pride in, his ability to banish the things he disliked.

It was a monument not only to the agrarian youth of the nation, but also to the vehemently nonagrarian youth of Henry Ford.

Greenfield Village is a place unlike any other because its creator's youth was unlike any other. Walking its streets as dusk fell, or going through the enormous museum he built next to it, Ford could retrieve that youth. And such was the strength of his engaging, elusive, infuriating personality that more than sixty years after his death, so can you and I.

He would have wanted that. His willful egotism only grew stronger as he aged, but it never got strong enough to blind him to the fact that the first half of his life was by far the better half.

Those were the years before an improvident libel suit had brought him into a nationally publicized trial in which the prosecution set out to prove his ignorance; before his bigotry boiled over and he was tormented into making insincere public retractions; before he was scared of his workers; before he got at odds with his only son and, in the view of his grandson Henry II, literally badgered him to death.

No, there's none of that in Greenfield Village. Passing by its yards and alleys its founder would have caught spectral glimpses of his mother, dead when he was thirteen, of his first car jittering triumphantly through the vacant streets of two-in-the-morning Detroit, of the Grosse

Pointe racetrack in 1901, where the pennant of blue smoke from the engine of Alexander Winton's far more powerful automobile signaled Ford that he was about to win a career-saving victory, and of the day not long after his mother's death when he and his father went into town. Their wagon came upon a steam-powered farm engine heading toward a job. There was nothing unusual about that, but rather than attaching it to draft horses, the owner had thought to attach it to itself. Hissing and smoking right there in the everyday road, the engine was moving toward the enchanted boy under its own power.

Every century or so, our republic has been remade by a new technology: 170 years ago it was the railroad; in our time it's the microprocessor. These technologies do more than change our habits; they change the way we think. Henry David Thoreau, hearing the trains passing Walden Pond, wrote, "Have not men improved somewhat in punctuality since the railroad was invented? Do they not talk and think faster in the depot than they did in the stage-office?" And of course anyone over the age of twenty (younger, and it's simply the air you breathe) knows what computers and the Internet are doing to us now.

In between the steam locomotive and the Apple came Henry Ford's Model T. One day toward the end of his life its maker was talking with a local high school boy named John Dahlinger, whose father had helped lay out his village, and they got onto the subject of education. Ford spoke of the virtues of the McGuffey's Reader era, and this sounded pretty fusty to Dahlinger. "But, sir," he protested, "these are different times, this is the modern age and—"

"Young man," Ford snapped, "I invented the modern age."

The claim is as preposterous as it is megalomaniacal. It is also largely true.

Sometime early in 1908 a knot of workmen stood peering up at the ceiling in a building on Piquette Avenue in Detroit. A few years later, these men would have been drenched in daylight in a new factory so lavishly windowed that it was known as the Crystal Palace. But this was just like any other big factory, and the object of their attention glinted dully above them in the perpetual industrial dusk.

A new kind of engine, swaddled in more rope than the task demanded, was inching its way down toward the chassis of a new kind of car.

The descending engine began to swing heavily in its slings, and, accompanied by impotent shouted instructions, started to revolve, slowly and then faster, until it tore loose and plummeted down through the car body to the factory floor.

A worker named James O'Connor remembered

the moment of horrible silence that followed ended when the two men superintending the mounting of the engine got into a heated disagreement about which of them had been responsible for the catastrophe.

"I know more about cars than you will ever know!" one yelled.

His colleague came back predictably with, "I know more about cars than *you* will ever know!"

Henry Ford didn't find this a productive discussion. The slender man in the neat suit stepped forward and gestured them to pipe down. They'd fix the engine and try again. He'd stay around until the job got done. He was annoyed, of course, but not full of fury and blame. There might be time for such indulgences in the years ahead, right now he was building his first Model T and he just wanted to get on with it.

The engine went in the next morning.

Decades later, James O'Connor, looking back on the squabble between the men in charge of the job, said, "I often think about them saying, 'I know more about cars than you do.' Nobody knew anything about cars." That was not entirely true—253 American carmakers were in business at the time the engine fell—but it was true enough.

In 1925 an editor of the *Encyclopedia Britannica*, seeking a contribution on a topic still too recent to have been mentioned in earlier editions, asked

Henry Ford to write an article about "mass production."

The essay appeared over Ford's name. It is a lucid, concise, occasionally eloquent statement that, a little more than a decade later, the historian Roger Burlingame described as "a colossal blurb that begins 'In origin, mass production is American and recent; its earliest notable appearance falls within the first decade of the 20th century,' and devotes the remainder of the article and two full pages of half-tone plates [photographs] to the Ford factory."

Burlingame said Ford's "great one-man show" suggested that mass production had "never existed in the world before." What about Eli Whitney, Burlingame asked, who had pioneered the idea of interchangeable parts for rifles back in the 1790s? What about Oliver Evans, whose fully automated flour mill had prefigured Ford's moving assembly line at almost the same time? And Singer, who had deluged the world with his sewing machines a generation before Henry Ford ever thought of an automobile?

Burlingame's ridicule did not touch on the question of the article's authorship, although the man who actually wrote it, Ford's spokesman and explainer William J. Cameron, said he "should be very much surprised to learn" that his boss had even read it.

Here, for example, is a passage from the

Britannica essay that accurately states a belief Ford held: "The early factory system was uneconomical in all its aspects. Its beginnings brought greater risk and loss of capital than had been known before, lower wages and a more precarious outlook for the workers, and a decrease in quality with no compensating increase in the general supply of goods. More hours, more workers, more machines did not improve conditions; every increase did but enlarge the scale of fallacies built into business. Mere massing of men and tools was not enough; the profit motive, which damaged enterprise, was not enough."

And here is a sample of this essay's putative author writing, just a few years earlier, on the futility of war: "But the people who *profitt* [sic] from war must go. . . . War is created by people who have no country or home except Hadies Hell and live in every country."

Ford wouldn't have cared about Burlingame's criticisms, nor would he have been in the least embarrassed had anyone accused him of putting his name to an article he'd never seen. He would have known he was in the right. He was always sure of that.

Often he was disastrously wrong about things, but he was not wrong about this big one. Mass production, which reshaped America in a decade, and which created our national prosperity in the twentieth century, was Henry Ford's doing.

To a degree, even the phrase itself is. The *Britannica*'s editor asked him to write about "mass production," but it was the "H.F." attached to the article that planted the term in the language forever. Before that, people had called what it described "Fordism."

CHAPTER 2
"My Toys Were All Tools"

The boy who hated farming; McGuffey's "new green world"; steam and clockwork; a house without a mainspring; "the biggest event in those early years"; into Detroit.

This man, who lived to read about the atomic bombs falling on Hiroshima and Nagasaki, was born three weeks after the battle of Gettysburg into a rural America whose routines he disliked as soon as he became aware of them.

The first thing I remember in my life is my Father taking my brother John and myself to see a bird's nest under a large oak log twenty yards east of our Home and my birthplace, John was so young that he could not walk Father carried Him I being two years older could run along with them this must have been the year 1866 in June I remember the nest with the 4 eggs and also the bird and hearing it sing I have remembered the song and in later years found it was a song sparrow.

He would love birds all his long life. Not so the other fauna around him. Unlike most farm boys, he never developed the least fondness for horses, and he detested cows. "The cow must go!" he declared decades later, apparently in complete seriousness. He wrote, "Milk is a mess." Whatever wholesome ingredients it might contain should be counterfeited with soybeans: "We MUST make milk out of something—Heaven can't." As for chickens, he wouldn't even eat one: "Chicken is fit only for hawks."

Not that he disliked rural life itself. He believed it contained inherent virtues—just that they didn't have anything to do with the labor that accompanied them. "I was born on July 30, 1863, on a farm at Dearborn Michigan, and my earliest recollection [after the sparrow, presumably] is that, considering the results, there was too much work on the place. That is the way I still feel about farming."

But despite the considerable task of having to make things grow on it, Henry Ford would always be drawn—sometimes merely wistfully, sometimes with a reformer's zeal—back to the farming world.

Michigan had been a state only for a quarter century when he was born, and much of it was still frontier. Forest stood all about him during his childhood, but his was not the hardscrabble infancy of a cider-barrel cradle in the dooryard of a log cabin.

William Ford, Henry's father, had been born in County Cork to a Protestant family of English ancestry. In 1847, the second year of the potato famine, the twenty-year-old carpenter and his family—his father and mother, John and Thomasina, his brother, and four sisters—followed two of his uncles across the Atlantic to Michigan where, one promoter had written, there was loam "four feet deep and so fat it will grease your fingers."

William Ford ended up in Dearbornville, in Springwells Township, a community eight miles west of Detroit—a site chosen because it was one day's journey by oxcart from the city whose factories and machine shops were already beginning to offer a livelihood that didn't involve hoeing and threshing.

That smoky, young alternative world had no appeal for William Ford. He worked for a while as a carpenter for the Michigan Central Railroad, but his heart was in farming, and he saved what money he could toward getting some land of his own, in his spare time working the eighty acres that his father, John, had bought and paid off.

In the late 1850s, William Ford did some carpentering for a neighbor, Patrick O'Hern, another County Cork man. He and his wife had adopted an orphaned child, a girl named Mary Litogot. Nobody ever knew where she came from, despite Henry Ford's using all his later resources to find out.

In 1858 William Ford paid six hundred dollars for half of his father's acreage and, thus established, married Mary Litogot in 1861. He was thirty-five; she, twenty-one.

The couple moved into the spacious, comfortable frame house that William had built for the O'Herns, with whom they lived harmoniously for years.

In the first week of 1862 Mary delivered a stillborn son. She was soon pregnant again, but the parents passed an anxious few months until, at seven o'clock on a summer morning, Henry Ford was born, full of the vigorous health that would serve him all his days.

He formed a strong attachment to the home he would re-create down to its sewing drawer. In it he was joined by siblings on a precise biannual schedule: John came in 1865, Margaret in '67, Jane two years later, William Junior two years after Jane, and finally Robert, in 1873.

From the start Henry was interested in machinery. "Even when I was very young I suspected that much [farmwork] might somehow be done in a better way. That is what took me into mechanics—although my mother always said I was a born mechanic."

He was to begin school at the age of seven on the second day of January 1871. Rural America valued education, but the necessity of survival dictated it not interfere with the fall harvest. The first week of the year found the Ford family snowbound, and Henry didn't get to the Scotch Settlement School, two miles distant, until the ninth. It was a one-room schoolhouse, and like so many of the architectural surroundings of Ford's youth is now living out the years in Greenfield Village. The curriculum was supplied by an Ohio schoolmaster named William Holmes McGuffey, who in the 1830s had conceived a series of six books: a primer, a speller, and four readers. For these, he received royalties capped at one thousand dollars. By the early 1840s the series was selling a million copies a year, by 1860, two million. Between the year Henry Ford started school and 1890 Americans bought 60 million.

These readers were attuned to the society into which Henry Ford was born. McGuffey intended them to be universal (or at least national, although by 1890 they were instructing children in Tokyo), but the midwestern critic and social historian Walter Havighurst believed them directed toward the trans-Appalachian West—"a new green world," as he put it, "a world of creeks and woods and meadows, of dogs and horses, sheep and cattle, orchards, pastures and farmyards."

The first page of the first speller featured the most indispensable of frontier tools—"A is for Ax"—and as McGuffey's audiences grew older and learned to read, succeeding volumes offered little morality tales mostly set in rural scenes.

They were often far from comforting. One is headed by a drawing of a farmer carrying a boy whose hair is dripping water past another boy about the same age who is standing, hands in pockets, staring abjectly at the ground.

"Look, look, is this not Frank Brown? What can be the mat-ter with him?

"The poor boy is dead.

"He was on his way to school when a bad boy met him and said:

" 'Come Frank, go with me to the pond.' "

Frank protested that he had to get to school, but the bad boy prevailed, and Frank went to the pond and fell in. "He cried 'Help!' 'Help!' A man heard him and ran to the pond. But when he got there, poor Frank was dead.

"What will his pa-rents do when he is ta-ken home dead?"

Not all the stories ended so grimly, and most offered redemption. Although "the idle boy is always poor and miserable," said the *Third Reader*, "the industrious boy is happy and prosperous."

Virtue was espoused for virtue's sake, but had its practical advantages, too. When in the *Second Reader* George breaks a merchant's window with a snowball, he confesses and feels much better. And possibly better still when "George became the merchant's partner and is now rich."

Good boys, boys who would not be seduced by the splendors of the pond, get rich. The books are full of exhortations to hard work, hustle, and enterprise, coupled with homilies urging religious faith (Christian faith, that is: the *Fourth Reader* explains that "Jewish authors were incapable of the diction and strangers to the morality contained in the Bible") and strict obedience to the stern dictates of conscience. In the advanced readers the mandates were softened somewhat by the addition of increasingly sophisticated selections from Longfellow, Hawthorne, Whittier, and Dickens. The frontier memoirist Hamlin Garland wrote in his popular *A Son of the Middle Border*, "I wish to acknowledge my deep obligation to Professor McGuffey, whoever he may have been, for the dignity and grace of his selections. From the pages of his readers I learned to know and love the poems of Scott, Byron, Southey, Wordsworth . . . I got my first taste of Shakespeare from the selections I read in those books."

No schoolchild could escape the books and the freight of their message in those expansive, pious postwar decades. Henry Ford loved the readers, and took their precepts, with the possible exception of piety, to heart. In time, drawing on the determination William Holmes McGuffey had helped instill in him, he tracked down the whitewashed log cabin in which the school-master had been born and moved it near the schoolhouse where Ford had first read his primers.

He went further than that. For those who couldn't make the pilgrimage to McGuffey's transplanted cabin, he reprinted the run of 1857 primers and readers, and sent them out across the country, saying, "Truth, honesty, fair-dealing, initiative, invention, self-reliance—these were the fundamentals of the McGuffey readers and they are as timeless and dateless now as they were when he assembled his texts."

He made friends with Hamlin Garland. William Richards, a Detroit newspaperman who met Ford in 1917, remembered that the two of them "not only shared a common resentment against theoretical farm lovers who painted rural life in rosy color as if the cows milked themselves and crops were self harvesting, but both were McGuffey alumni. Ford would sit on one side of a desk and Garland on the other and try each other's memory on what McGuffey had put in his books. One would recite a line, the other would follow with a second, and they'd go on until one or the other was stumped—then start afresh on other stanzas."

Ford found things to do in school when he wasn't mourning poor drowned Frank. The boys shared two-seat desks, and he was put next to Edsel Ruddiman, a neighbor who was to become his best friend. Edsel was afforded an early glimpse of two traits that would stay with his seatmate all his life: mechanical aptitude and a fondness for practical jokes. Once, when recess had emptied the classroom, Ford drilled two small holes through the seat of the desk in front of him, and set a needle in one threaded through the second with a near-invisible strand that ran to Ford's desk. Later, during a quiet moment, Ford gave the thread a sharp tug, driving the needle up into his classmate's rump. (Ford would have found this prank equally hilarious when he was in his seventies.)

The boy's mechanical ingenuity took forms more constructive than getting a yelp out of a school friend. When Henry was seven, one of William Ford's hired hands opened the back of his pocket watch and showed him how it worked: the jewel bearings, the tiny cogs, the busy mandibles of the escapement. Ford was fascinated, and spent all the time he could during trips to Detroit peering into watchmakers' windows. He began making tools: screwdrivers filed and hammered out of knitting needles, a pair of tweezers fashioned from one of his mother's corset stays. In 1922 he wrote, "My toys were all tools—they still are!" Of course he put the tools to work. A neighbor remarked that "every clock in the Ford home shuddered when it saw him coming," and his sister Margaret remembered, "When we had mechanical or 'wind-up' toys given to us at

Christmas, we always said, 'Don't let Henry have them. He just takes them apart.' He wanted to see what made them go rather than just watching them go."

Once he saw what made them go, he understood it. By the time he was twelve, he could not only take watches apart, but put them back together so that they worked better. At school he dissected them behind the screen of his open geometry book. His teacher must have seen something unusual in Henry Ford, for he fully acquiesced in these explorations, so long as his pupil didn't disturb the class with the rasping of a file.

Ford's interest in machinery ran right across the scale from the balance wheels of watches to the driving wheels of locomotives. On a visit to Detroit, William Ford brought Henry to the yards of one of the ten railroads that were nourishing the young city. In the roundhouse there, an engineer took the delighted boy up on the deck of his locomotive, showed him the levers and gauges in the cab, and explained how the firebox heated the water in the boiler into steam, which, when the throttle was cracked open, made its way to the cylinders and punched the pistons that turned the wheels. Seven decades later Ford still remembered the engineer's name: Tommy Garrett.

The boy left the roundhouse to begin years of steam experiments. For many of these he recruited helpers who were glad to follow his directions.

This gift of swiftly being able to establish a cordial, happily received dictatorship would stay with him all through the time of his greatest achievements. As Margaret put it, "He had the ability of getting his brothers and his companions to work for him."

Occasionally his projects had spectacular results. Once he had his schoolmates help him build a fire beneath some sort of vessel resting on a circle of stones: Ford remembered it as a "turbine." As Tommy Garrett had surely told him, steam is powerful stuff. The vessel exploded, setting the school fence ablaze and, the grown Henry Ford jotted in one of the pocket notebooks he always carried with him, "a piece hit Robert Blake in the stomach-abdomen and put him *out!*"

As for the work he was supposed to be doing, he dodged it. A neighbor said of the young Ford, "You know, that little devil was the laziest bugger on the face of the earth. . . . Henry would work along all right until about ten o'clock in the morning, and then he would want to go to the house for a drink of water. He would go and get the drink of water, but he would never come back."

However adroitly the boy avoided its sweaty particulars, he never lost his fondness for the world he lived in: joking with his brothers, teasing his sisters, nut-hunting in the woods, the twelve-by-sixteen-foot shed his father granted him as a workshop, the family singing around the pump-organ, the ruby glow the stove cast on the parlor rug. He later compressed his youth into one of the hastily scribbled telegraphic messages he sometimes liked to send to his past: "Remember sleigh, wood hauling, cold winters, setting sun, sleighbell, long walks, cold weather, boys and girls."

Mary Ford's first child had been born dead, but the next six came into the world without difficulty. In mid-March of 1876, however, when she was thirty-seven, her eighth child died being born, and twelve days later she died, too.

Henry said, expressing it as accurately as he could, "The house was like a watch without a mainspring."

Ford would ever after speak of his mother with the greatest warmth, in time coming to contrast her understanding and generosity of spirit with what he chose to see as his father's attempts to sway him from his car-building destiny. Yet often he makes her sound sterner than he may have intended: "She was of that rarest type of mothers—one who so loved her children that she did not care whether they loved her. What I mean by this is that she would do whatever she considered necessary for our welfare even if she thereby temporarily lost our goodwill."

However sympathetic she might have been toward her eldest son, that sympathy did not extend to his dislike of milking or plowing: "Life will give you many unpleasant things to do; your duty will be hard and disagreeable and painful to you at times, but you must do it."

On candy: "Let your health, not your diet be your guide. Never eat merely for the pleasure of eating."

Surely McGuffey can be heard at his most minatory in this reminiscence: "Fun we had and plenty of it, but she was forever reminding us that life cannot be all fun. 'You must earn the right to play,' she used to say to me."

Years after she died, Ford said, "I thought a great wrong had been done to me." He was just thirteen at the time, after all, but he never did speak of how his father must have been affected by the death, trying to repair that broken mainspring with the help of a few desolated children.

Four months later, in July, William Ford brought his son to what Henry called "the biggest event of those early years."

They were driving into Detroit when, about eight miles outside the city, they met a steam farm engine laboring toward them beneath a sooty turban of coal smoke.

"I remember that engine as though I had seen it only yesterday," Ford wrote, "for it was the first vehicle other than horse-drawn that I had ever seen. It was intended primarily for driving threshing machines and sawmills and was simply a portable engine and boiler mounted on wheels with a water tank and coal cart trailing behind. I had seen plenty of these engines hauled around by horses, but this one had a chain that made a connection between the engine and the rear wheels of the wagon-like frame on which the boiler was mounted. The engine was placed over the boiler and one man standing on the platform behind the boiler shoveled coal, managed the throttle, and did the steering. It had been made by Nichols, Shepard & Company of Battle Creek. I found that out at once. The engine had stopped to let us pass with our horses and I was off the wagon and talking to the engineer before my father, who was driving, knew what I was up to. The engineer was very glad to explain the whole affair. He was proud of it. He showed me how the chain was disconnected from the propelling wheel and a belt put on to drive the machinery. He told me that the engine made two hundred revolutions a minute and that the chain pinion could be shifted to let the wagon stop while the engine was still running."

And here Ford, so much of whose youth and early development is elusive, makes a clear and plausible statement of the moment his life took a course that would intersect with everyone else's.

"This last"—the engine running in neutral while not driving the wagon—"is a feature which, although in different fashion, is incorporated into

46

modern automobiles. It was not important with steam engines, which are easily stopped and started, but it became very important with the gasoline engine. It was that engine which took me into automotive transportation."

Henry Ford followed that traction engine for the rest of his life.

In 1922 he wrote, "I wanted to have something to do with machinery. My father was not entirely in sympathy with my bent for mechanics. He thought I ought to be a farmer. When I left school at seventeen and became an apprentice in the machine shop of the Drydock Engine Works I was all but given up for lost."

This account is a small miracle of compression and omission.

He did leave home, in 1879, but not for the chances and perils of the road. He made the journey to Detroit, and when he got there moved in with his aunt, Mrs. Rebecca Ford Flaherty. From this haven he could look for a job in a city that could scarcely have offered more promise to a young would-be mechanic.

Once a fur-trading outpost, then a lumber town, Detroit had been phenomenally boosted when the Erie Canal opened in 1825, connecting the Eastern Seaboard with what was then the western frontier. The home to 9,000 people on the eve of the Erie's completion, it had a population of 116,000 by the time Ford got there. The mines to the north produced iron and copper; the timber stood everywhere. Cornish ironworkers got word, and came, and soon Detroit was selling cast-iron stoves, and railroad cars, and any boiler or stanchion a Lakes steamer might need. All that metal and lumber fed close to a thousand companies large and small, ranging from coachbuilders to leatherworks, that would within a generation be turning out automobile components. The city's ties with the East were close enough for Detroiters to have begun the nearly century-long custom of having oyster stew on Christmas, the delicacy's main ingredient arriving alive in casks, packed safely on cushions of Atlantic seaweed.

Ford quickly found a job in the Michigan Car Works—the cars were streetcars—and was just as quickly fired, gone after six days. He never said why. Perhaps he realized for the first time how restive having a boss made him. Perhaps, as seems to be the flattering consensus, he showed such speed and skill in diagnosing and fixing ailing machinery that he made the older machinists jealous.

Whatever the cause, he was fired, and his father stepped in. William may have wanted Henry back on the farm, but he was friendly with James Flower, who, with his two brothers, owned one of the best machine shops in the city. He brought his son by and got him a job there. The pay wasn't nearly as good as it had been at the car works:

48

There Henry got $1.10 a day, and at the new job $2.25 for a sixty-hour workweek. But he loved Flower Brothers.

Fred Strauss, a twelve-year-old floor sweeper at the time, explained why: "It was a great old shop. . . . They manufactured everything in the line of brass and iron—globe and gate valves, gongs, steam-whistles, fire hydrants, and valves for water pipes. There was a great variety of work. Some of the castings on the iron bodies of the large gate valves weighed a ton or more."

> They made so many different articles that they had all kinds of machines, large and small lathes and drill presses. Some of the large lathes stood for months without having been used, but they had to have them to take care of the different jobs.
> They had more machines than workmen in that shop.

This living museum was in effect Ford's college, and he incessantly explored its exhibits, some busy spewing sparks and bright curls of metal, some shadowy and still, all of them increasingly eloquent to him.

He also acquired a friend at Flower Brothers, Fred Strauss, even though the sweeper was four years his junior. "My job was roustabout in the brass shop," Strauss said long after. "Henry was working on a small milling machine, milling hexagons on brass valves.

"They put Henry in with me and he and I got chummy right away. Henry was to do the same work I did. He didn't sweep the floor. I did that because I was more of a worker than he was. He never was a good worker, but he was a good fellow."

However content he might have been at Flower Brothers, the shop put him in a financial squeeze. He had moved from his aunt's into a boarding-house on Baker Street to be closer to his work, and room and board came to $3.50. This left him a dollar short every week.

To compensate, he went to Robert Magill, a jeweler on Michigan Avenue whom Ford had spent hours observing bent over his watches. Magill liked Henry—everybody liked Henry— and gave him $3.00 a week: fifty cents for six hours of work a night.

Ford was full of bouncy stamina—an old friend remembered that he seemed to be "made of springs"—and the sixteen-hour days didn't wear on him. But he looked young, even for sixteen, and Magill would smuggle him through a side door of his shop and into a back room lest the customers think their watches had been entrusted to a child.

Ford liked his work at the jeweler's, too, and so, sure enough, Robert Magill's shop is now in

Greenfield Village, complete with the display cases, Mrs. Magill's needlepoint, and the side door where Ford used to slip in.

He stayed at Flower Brothers for nine months—just about the span of an academic year—and then decided he'd learned all it had to teach him. He went home to help his family with the harvest, and in the fall of 1880 returned to the city and machinery, this time at the Detroit Dry Dock Engine Works, a larger operation than Flower Brothers.

He stayed friends with Fred Strauss, who said, "Henry always wanted to make things. The first time I ever saw him spend any money (he usually got the other fellow to spend it) he bought a set of castings for $1.25 . . . castings of a little steam engine. . . .

"Henry always had another idea. We never did get that machine finished. He always wanted to have something else."

As it turned out, he needn't have finished that steam engine, because he was about to be given charge of a full-size one. By 1882 one of William Ford's neighbors, John Gleason, had done well enough to buy a portable steam engine. Nowhere near as large as the Nichols & Shepard that had astounded Henry half a dozen years earlier, it was nevertheless a sturdy, capable machine that generated almost the same amount of power. Manufactured by Westinghouse, Number 345 had its engine in front beneath a tractor seat, a vertical boiler in back, and, like the Nichols & Shepard, it could drive itself. "The power was applied to the back wheels by a belt," Ford recalled. "They could make twelve miles an hour on the road even though the self-propelling feature was only an incident of the construction."

Number 345's primary function was not to roll across the landscape, but to plant itself next to a job and thresh clover, grind feed, and saw planks, all of which Ford was about to make it do.

Gleason had hired an operator, but "the man knew little about it," said Ford, ". . . and he found himself in trouble. I have an idea he was afraid of his machine. The little high-speed, quick steaming thing made him nervous, and he did little work with it that first day."

Gleason had heard that William's boy Henry was good with machinery, and early the next morning he showed up at the door of the Ford farmhouse. "I was about as proud as I have ever been when he asked if I might run the engine while it was on his place."

William Ford was hesitant. "He was afraid, I am sure, to let me have anything to do with an engine that had proved too much for a professional engineer. . . . He asked me if I felt certain of my ability and his tone showed that he doubted.

"To tell the truth, I was frightened myself. . . . But I was unwilling to be beaten by an engine and

I solemnly assured my father and the farmer that I was sure." William and Gleason talked it over. Henry's younger brothers had grown big enough so that he was not necessary to bring in the harvest, and it was indisputable that he had a bump for machinery. "They finally decided to let me try."

He approached the machine with as much seeming nonchalance as he could muster. He called it a "little engine," but its stack stood a good six feet taller than he did, and it had already scared away a pro. Still, he fed the firebox and adjusted valves and "it was not long before my doubts entirely disappeared, and getting a grip on the engine, so to speak, I got a grip on myself.

"At the end of the first day I was as weary as I had been nervous at its beginning, but I had run the engine steadily, inducing it to stand up nicely to its work, and I forgot my grimness and weariness in the consciousness I had actually accomplished what I had started out to do."

For eighty-three summer days, richer by three dollars at the close of each one, Henry Ford steamed about the local fields and woodlands. "It was hard work. I had to fire [345] myself and the fuel most generally was old fence-rails, though it would burn coal the few times coal was to be had." Coal, imported from Pennsylvania or Ohio, was something of a luxury in that heavily forested world.

"I became immensely fond of that machine," and by summer's end was its "complete and expert master. I have never been more satisfied with myself than when I guided it over the rough country roads of the time."

Ford's amazing magpie memory preserved the fact that 345 had eventually been sold to somebody in McKean County, Pennsylvania. So when, in 1913, he decided to go after it, at least he had a place to start. He found it, too, derelict on a Pennsylvania farm, only its builder's plate, which bore the 345, still in active service as a patch on the farmhouse stove. The farmer wanted ten dollars for it. Ford thought this was pretty stiff for some rusted-out plumbing, and stipulated that he must get the builder's plate, too. The farmer complied, and Ford paid over the ten. Then he sent the man a new Model T.

CHAPTER 3

Clara

"He's a thinking, serious person"; winning a dead man's job; electricity; a baby and a seventh home; the Christmas Eve engine.

Ford had many reasons to feel closely connected with 345. For one, during his summer labors, he apparently fell for its owner's daughter, Christine Gleason. Her contemporaries described her as a "beauty queen," and her brother said that Ford asked her to marry him. Instead, she chose Joseph Sheffery, who was both older and richer. Sheffery owned a blacksmith shop, and maintained horses and a carriage. Did Ford, who developed an increasingly powerful vindictive streak as he aged, ever take satisfaction in his career's having extinguished his old rival's job along with his equipage? Perhaps not, since 345 also brought Ford into contact with John Cheeney, the Westinghouse road agent in southern Michigan. Cheeney came and watched Ford at work and hired him to repair and run Westinghouse engines throughout Michigan and northern Ohio. This kept him happily and profitably busy during the summer months. He was in the farming country that he liked, and using machinery to make benign the chores that he loathed.

When winter and its snows put an end to the seasonal labor, Ford would return to the farm and his workshop there. Clouded accounts survive of his trying to build self-propelled vehicles during the cold, short days, but although he would later sometimes insist that they ran, it is all vague. Not time wasted, though, for his efforts seem to have persuaded him that steam power would always involve mechanisms too heavy to propel the vehicle he was beginning to envision.

In early December of 1884 he left his workbench for Detroit once again, this time not to tend a lathe but to enroll in Goldsmith's Bryant & Stratton Business University, in a substantial-looking building on Griswold Street.

All we know of the school's influence on Ford is that for a little while it had him producing clear, even elegant handwriting. That didn't last, and Ford's notes and letters have always frustrated his biographers. Sidney Olson, a shrewd, witty, clear-eyed chronicler of Ford's early years, said that when "the Goldsmith influence wore off . . . his handwriting lapsed into an illegibility that almost rises to grandeur, a magnificent nonpenmanship in which every simple-looking word can be construed in ten different ways." By way of example, Olson cites the entries in the "jotbooks" (Ford recorded the fate of his school fence in one) where he noted everything that caught his interest. Music often did and, Olson says, "In over thirty-odd years of jotting down 'Tales of the Vienna Woods,' he never spelled the title the same twice, and never once correctly."

No record survives of what courses he took at Goldsmith's, and he wasn't there very long—back with his steam engines by summer—but it is interesting to speculate whether he might have brushed up against some unsung Carnegie or Rockefeller there. Whatever happened to him at the school was the only formal business training this supremely capable businessman ever got.

Amid all the steam engines that came his way in 1885, he received one prophetic assignment. Back when he had been cutting metal at Flowers', a brass fitter recently arrived from Britain loaned him a copy of a magazine called *English Mechanic and World of Science*. In it he read that a German named Nikolaus August Otto had developed a "silent gas engine." Ford recalled, "It ran with illuminating gas, had a single large cylinder, and . . . as far as weight was concerned it gave nothing like the power per pound of metal that the steam engine gave, and the use of illuminating gas seemed to dismiss it even as a possibility for road use. It was interesting to me only as all machinery was interesting." He kept up with the Otto in the technical magazines, though, and "most particularly the hints of the possible replacement of illuminating gas fuel by a gas formed by the vaporization of gasoline."

So he was not wholly unprepared when the Eagle Iron Works in Detroit called him to repair an Otto, even though it was the first gas engine he had ever seen. "No one in town knew anything about them. There was a rumor that I did and, although I had never been in contact with one, I undertook and carried through the job. That gave me a chance to study the new engine at first hand."

An equally consequential encounter had taken place on the first day of 1885. Ford had begun to get interested in dancing—"There were no teachers in those days," his sister Margaret said, "he just learned at the parties"—and he went to a New Year's Night celebration at a hostelry called Martindale House.

In the dance hall a fiddler was calling out instructions like, "Last gentleman lead to the right, around that lady with a grapevine twist," and Ford joined in. During a quadrille he found himself next to a second cousin, Annie Ford, and across from a graceful dark-haired girl. Annie introduced them: Her name was Clara Jane Bryant.

Clara would have seen a slender young man a couple of years her senior, with wide-set blue-gray eyes. He stammered out a few common-places, so obviously fascinated and distracted that his cousin mildly scolded him once a partner had taken Clara off into the crowd.

The girl had pretty much the same effect on Ford as that self-propelled traction engine did. He spent futile months going to other dances hoping to meet her. Nearly a year passed before he managed to track her down. It was Christmastime again, and they ate oyster stew together and later Ford gravely demonstrated a watch he'd acquired that simultaneously told the newly instituted standard railroad time with steel hands, and the locally observed "sun time" with brass ones. This disquisition went over better than he had any right to expect. When Clara got home she told her parents that she liked Henry Ford: "He's a thinking, serious person—serious minded."

That quality might have appealed to Clara because she shared it, and not all of her large family did. She had nine younger siblings. Her two sisters were smart and pretty, but mercurial, somewhat random, and one of them, Eva, was already known for her bad temper.

As so often in his life, Ford went after what he wanted. He at once bought a sleigh so he could drive Clara about the winter landscape. By Valentine's Day of 1886 he could write her a confident letter (the script still tidy from Goldsmith's, the orthography a bit uncertain): "I again take the pleasure of writing you a few lines.

It seems like a year since i seen you. It don't seem mutch like cutter [sleigh] rideing to night does it but i guess we will have some more sleighing. . . . i think as the weather is so bad you will not expect me tonight, but if the weather and roads are good you look for me. . . . Clara Dear, you can not imagine what pleasure it gives me to think that i have at last found one so loveing kind and true as you are and I hope we will always have good success."

He pursued that success so vigorously that, a few days after Clara's twentieth birthday, the two became engaged on April 19. But Clara's mother believed, engagement notwithstanding, her eldest daughter was too young to get married.

Months passed by while Ford remained something of a permanent suitor. The long courtship followed the rituals of the time and place: quadrilles at Martindale House, summer picnics at one or another's family farmstead, moonlight husking bees where the shucker who uncovered a red ear earned a kiss. This all sounds sweet with Currier & Ives placidity, but of course it was a molten, yearning, anxious time for Henry Ford.

The uncertainty came to an end when William Ford offered Henry the use of an eighty-acre tract he had bought from a neighbor named Moir who lived three-quarters of a mile to the west. Half the land was cleared, the other half still thick with timber.

Henry's first job would be to cut down the trees, but once that was done his father hoped he might take up the prosperous farming life William Ford found so miraculous an improvement over his early years on a few acres of Irish soil owned by somebody else.

Henry saw an opportunity here, if not quite the one his father did. He could clear the forest—behind a steam engine, not a plow—and sell the lumber. The old Moir residence was Spartan but perfectly habitable. He would have land, and an income, and a house a few miles from where his fiancée had grown up.

Surely Mrs. Bryant couldn't further postpone the wedding now. She didn't. Clara Bryant and Henry Ford were married in the Bryant home on April 11, 1888.

They seem to have been at ease with each other from the start. Margaret thinks that a turning point, or at least a profound deepening of her brother's feelings, came before the engagement when William Ford asked his son to get rid of some stumps that were still stubbling already cleared land. Henry borrowed John Gleason's engine—345 back again in his life—and urged the girls to come see it at work.

Margaret and Clara did, and jolted with Henry across the fields, looked on while he and steam power wrenched obdurate stumps out of the ground. Number 345's flashing metal and occasional spew of sparks did not intimidate Clara in the least. Margaret wrote that her brother "was so enthused at that time with this way of taking so much hard work out of farming that he could talk of little else. Clara and I were 'good listeners,' but, I must confess, all the talk meant little to us at the time. I am sure, however, that Clara's willingness to ride on this engine and to go into the field, and watch Henry at his work further convinced him she was the proper girl for his wife."

"All the talk" may have made a deeper impression on Clara than Margaret realized. Clara had listened to her beau's explanation of his dual-purpose watch and gone home to tell her parents about it. She saw the casual expertise with which he ran 345, and knew he was the only man in Detroit who could be trusted to fix the near-occult Otto engine. She came to trust his mechanical judgment so completely that Ford happily began to refer to her as "the Believer." But so did he trust her: He was a Believer, too.

When, after a few months together in the Moir house, the two were speaking about building a better residence, Clara wrote a note:

Kitchen 12 x 18
Sitting-room 14 x 14
Parlor 18 x 14
Bedroom 10 x 14

"Henry, the above figures are the best that I can do. But use your own judgment about it."

He used hers, and at once started cutting and drying lumber for what they were calling the Square House. With the help of an expert carpenter, the little house, thirty-one feet on a side, a story and a half high, took shape. It was a wonderfully amiable-looking building, with almost a postmodern feel to its chipper symmetry—a cube for the first floor, a mansard roof above it punctuated by a single emphatic dormer window, and graceful with ample porches and three tiers of lathe-turned balustrades. Some Ford family members thought it was the most appealing home Clara and Henry ever owned.

They moved in during the spring of 1889, and stayed long enough for Clara to have established an herb garden and acquire the impressive domestic accessory of a pump-organ by the time her husband was summoned to Detroit to heal another Otto engine.

This one, in a bottling works, was smaller and suppler than the first Ford had seen, and he returned home distracted. He sat and brooded over some technical magazines. After a while he interrupted Clara, who was at the organ, mentioned the engine he'd spent the day with, and said he believed it could be used to power a horseless carriage. Clara was puzzled, and Henry took a piece of sheet music and sketched the vehicle while he explained it (in his magisterial biography, Allan Nevins remarks, "To judge from other drawings made by him, there was probably more explanation than sketch"). As soon as Clara understood what her husband was talking about, said Margaret, "She had complete confidence that he could do it."

There was more. Ford knew all about forging and turning metal, he knew all about steam. But the Otto engine was fired by an electric spark, and he didn't know much about electricity. To learn, he would have to move to Detroit and get a job with a power company—he told Clara he hoped that it might be at the Edison Illuminating Company.

This was disingenuous. Ford already had the job. He'd gone into Detroit a few days earlier and enjoyed the following brisk transaction from those robust days before HR departments.

He went up the steps of Edison Illuminating—which, founded five years earlier, was now feeding power to one thousand homes and five thousand streetlights—and ran into an "elderly man" who was just leaving.

"Who's in charge here?" Ford asked him.

Charles Phelps Gilbert said, "I am. What can I do for you?"

"I'm an engineer. Have you any work I can do?"

"How much do you know about the work?"

"As much," Ford boldly replied, "as anyone my age." Half true: He had enough understanding of electricity to know that the generators that produced it were spun by steam engines, and there was nothing about a steam engine he couldn't handle.

That was the interview. Phelps said, "Well, I do think we have a place for you. A man was killed last week down at our substation and we need someone in his place right away." Hours, 6:00 p.m. to 6:00 a.m.; salary, forty dollars a month.

Clara was horrified. Henry may not have told her he was leaping into the shoes of a dead man, but she saw clearly enough what his plan meant. She'd be leaving her family, the countryside she had lived in her whole life, the house she had helped design, the garden. Margaret said, "It almost broke her heart."

She was the Believer, though. The Fords left the Square House on the morning of September 25, 1891, and Henry started his job at Edison Illuminating that same day.

Gone with the couple was William Ford's last hope of seeing his son settle down and work the family acres. Henry summed up his final departure in a sentence that, although just six words long, is spacious enough to show he had never for a moment intended to make the transition from working his engines to farming: "The timber had all been cut."

Clara and Henry Ford rented the right half of a double house at 618 John R Street, ten blocks from the substation where Ford was replacing the killed worker. Detroit would have seemed more alien to Clara than the Edison substation did to Henry, for it contained a one-hundred-horsepower Beck steam engine that he knew well. On the other hand, the familiar Beck stood in company with two total strangers: a Rice dynamo and an Aldington & Sims generator, machines that generated the electricity about which Ford had yet to learn. It was his good fortune that the Beck broke down first, less than a month after he'd arrived.

Detroit Edison had managed to win contracts for supplying the city's churches. Demand was, naturally, heaviest on Sundays, and at the end of one of them the Beck collapsed under the strain. Ford immediately knew the damage was bad: a piston rod snapped, a broken valve, a hole in the cylinder block. Charles Phelps Gilbert, looking over the wreckage with his new hire, saw a trying and costly future of experts called in from everywhere, and dark churches that might well seek out rival power companies.

Ford surprised his boss by saying he could fix the engine himself. Phelps didn't believe it, but said to go ahead and try. Ford made on his own a pattern from which to cast a new cylinder block, took care of the valve and the piston rod, and rearranged the engine's vitals so that it could withstand the pressures of future Sundays. During this there was no sign of the winning slacker who got his friends to do his work and disappeared after going for a drink of water. Ford was at the engine all the time, and by the following Sunday the Beck was in good shape and the Detroit churches had all the electricity they needed.

Gilbert gave Ford a five-dollar raise immediately, and another one shortly after.

Clara Ford would have been gratified by this victory, but even as her husband was getting his second raise from Detroit Edison, the couple was moving to Washington Boulevard and, shortly after that, to Cass Avenue. During the coming decades the Believer would pack up and soldier forward into ten different rental houses.

They were in one on Forest Avenue when their son and only child was born.

The doctor attending was named David O'Donnell. He was a year out of medical school and there because Clara's brother Harry had met him in a Detroit cigar store and thought he might do a good job with Harry's wife's impending childbirth. He had, and so, on November 6, 1893, the Fords called him to their home on Forest Avenue. Still so new to his practice he couldn't afford the horse and buggy that was a professional necessity for physicians in those days, O'Donnell arrived with his doctor's bag dangling from the handlebars of a bicycle.

"I didn't run into any difficulty," he said. "Mrs. Ford didn't give me any trouble at all. She never complained. Mr. Ford was in the house. He didn't get excited and he didn't bother me. Most young fathers bother the life out of a doctor."

If the doctor liked the father, the father liked him. Once there was a Ford automobile company, and once Dr. O'Donnell could afford a car, the Ford company repaired it free for the rest of his life.

The visit's outcome couldn't have been more satisfactory. The couple named the boy after Henry's school friend and Clara's family: Edsel Bryant Ford.

Henry Ford had been promoted from the sub-station to the Main Station of the Edison Illuminating Company less than a week before his son was born. Edsel was ten days old when Detroit Edison nearly doubled his father's salary, to ninety dollars a month, and in December raised Ford to an even hundred and made him chief engineer. This meant he was on constant call, around the clock. Many would have hated this; Ford did not. He had managed to climb to a place he wanted to be, and would stay there for the rest of his life. The fact that he could be summoned to the now familiar dynamos at any hour also meant that he had no fixed hours. In the absence of a crisis, he could appear and leave when he chose. He was good at the latter, having mastered what Sidney Olson termed "the art of the short call": stopping by, taking an interest in this armature or that condenser, joking easily with the men who'd be doing the actual fixing, and then—gone. "He always seemed to be leisurely," said Olson, "and he always seemed to be leaving."

He might be leaving for yet another evanescent appearance at one of the dozens of machine shops that supplied his continuing education.

Mostly, though, he would go to 58 Bagley Avenue, where the Fords had relocated—the seventh move of their marriage—on December 15. This was a solid, comfortable two-family brick house. The twenty-five-dollar-a-month rent included use of the woodshed out back, which was more substantial than that sounds: It was a good-sized outbuilding, also of brick, that Ford shared with his neighbor.

The neighbor was Felix Julien, and nobody ever had a better one. A calm, amiable older man, retired from the coal business, he soon noticed that the newcomer was not storing wood or coal in the shed, but rather had set up benches and machinery to begin building something.

Julien moved his own coal into his house, took down the brick wall that divided the two areas, and said Ford was welcome to the whole shed:

Clearly he had a better use for the room than fuel storage. Julien's only request was that he be allowed to look on sometimes; he found this metalwork fascinating.

A few days after he'd moved his family to Bagley Avenue, Ford was at the Edison plant watching a boilermaker—his name has come down to us, as it happens: James Wolfenden—cutting and brazing some pipes in the engine room. His repairs finished, Wolfenden found himself with a length of leftover tubing too awkward to carry around on the Christmas errands he was eager to get to. He was heading toward the scrap pile that disfigured every industrial establishment in those days when Ford told him to leave the pipe there; he'd take care of it.

In Wolfenden's rubbish, Ford had seen a cylinder for his gasoline engine.

Over the days that followed, he bored out the pipe to a one-inch diameter, made a piston to slide in it, and scavenged other parts: a discarded handwheel from a lathe could serve as a flywheel. Cam, exhaust valve, cloth-wrapped stub of wire to ignite the spark necessary to fire these elements into life. . . . He put them all together, and presented the result to his wife as what may have been 1893 Detroit's least agreeable Christmas surprise.

On the evening of December 24, Clara Ford was getting ready to entertain the cascade of Bryants the holiday always brought when her husband stepped into the kitchen with his new machine. It was not imposing. He had mounted the piece of pipe on a board, and from this cylinder a frail-looking steel rod connected the piston inside it to a crankshaft a few inches away. A second rod—again, not much thicker than a wire coat hanger—reached back to the side of the pipe. When the first rod moved, so would the second, opening and closing an exhaust valve. Both rods would be kept in motion by the lathe handwheel that had been promoted to flywheel status.

Here was Henry Ford's first gasoline engine. But it was an engine in barely fetal form, and that's why it had appeared in the kitchen. If the device was to work at all, it needed two people to tend it, one to feed fuel into the narrow throat of the intake, the other to spin the flywheel to get it started. Most of all, it needed electricity, available in the kitchen but not in the shed. Ford had run a wire into the cylinder; as the piston moved, it brought another wire, embedded in it, into contact with this one. When the piston kept moving the wires would draw apart and, given the application of an electric current, a spark would jump between them, igniting the gases that had been squeezed out of the fuel by the pushing piston.

Edsel was asleep in the next room; family was looming; it was likely the busiest evening of Clara Ford's year. If ever the Believer had justified her husband's epithet it was now, as she stood aside while Ford fastened his engine to the kitchen sink and wormed the other end of the cylinder wire into the ceiling fixture that held the kitchen's overhead light.

He handed his wife an oilcan full of gasoline, and issued instructions: She was to squirt the gas into the thimble-sized cup that stood on top of the machine's intake, and then adjust a screw that would let the gasoline into the cylinder quickly or slowly, depending on the virgin engine's thirst.

Henry put a hand on the wheel, and Clara upended the oilcan. As the clear fluid dribbled into the little cup, the kitchen filled with a smell that would have puzzled and alarmed almost every American alive in 1893, and that within a generation would be familiar as the scent of woodsmoke. Henry rotated the wheel, the piston sucked in air and gas from the cup, and the kitchen light dimmed in protest as the spark jumped and the cylinder emitted a sharp little bark.

Ford spun the wheel again, and his engine exploded into strident life. The flywheel spun, the cam did its job, spikes of blue flame jetted from the exhaust valve. The sink shook on its moorings, exhaust further dimmed the kitchen light, and surely the racket disturbed Edsel.

But not for long. After thirty seconds of clamor Henry indicated to Clara that she could move away from the sink. The engine drank off the cup and went silent. It never ran again. "I didn't stop to play with it," Ford said years later. His assemblage of cast-off metal oddments had taught him what he had needed to know.

He was thirty years old, far from young to be gambling his and his family's future on a raucous novelty he'd improvised in time stolen from a respectable and promising job.

Clara knew that was what he was going to do, though. She rinsed the gasoline off her hands and returned to her holiday cooking.

CHAPTER 4

Working from the Ground Up

Making a car in a world without any; "a colorless, limpid, innocent-appearing liquid"; the Bagley Avenue woodshed; America's first car race; Henry Ford's first car.

The Christmas Eve engine was the seed from which Ford's first car grew, but the growth was a slow one, because every screw and bracket needed to be thought through, and many made for the first time. Ford was working in a world that contained no automobile parts.

When he had to consider so basic an element of his engine as a carburetor, the all-important device that blended fuel with the proper amount of air before breathing it into the engine, he couldn't draw on literature discussing float valves and chokes. He had to figure out the entire mechanism for himself: how to get just the right mix of air and gas to cause the strongest combustion in the cylinder; and how to get the fuel flowing (from wherever it was going to be kept) to the carburetor; and how to adjust that crucial fuel-air mixture so it would work equally well in winter and summer, on dry days and wet ones; and how to connect the future carburetor to the future driver, who would have to control it to control the vehicle. Ford probably didn't have even the word "carburetor" to help sustain him: It would not appear in print in an automotive sense for another two years.

In 1922 when, with Theodore Roosevelt gone, Henry Ford was the most famous living American, he published an autobiography called *My Life and Work*. This was written, the title page says, "in collaboration with Samuel Crowther." A capable journalist, Crowther found himself almost alone in the lopsided collaboration. If it had been hard to keep Henry Ford standing still in the Detroit Edison days, it was all but impossible a quarter century later. The book needs to be read with caution, for what information Crowther did manage to snatch from his subject on the fly was often wrong (Ford asserts, for instance, that he got his first car on the road three years earlier than he actually did). Nevertheless, there are many passages where one does seem to hear the actual voice of Henry Ford, astringent and direct.

About his Bagley Avenue days he says, "I had to work from the ground up—that is, although I knew a number of people were working on horseless carriages, I could not know what they were doing."

Despite the demands of his Detroit Edison job, the up-from-the-ground automaking didn't wear on him. "I cannot say that it was hard work. No work with interest is ever hard." Then he adds, engagingly, "But it was a great thing to have my wife even more confident than I was. She has always been that way."

He says next to nothing about the actual work he was doing. Here, in its entirety, is his description of two and a half years of unremitting effort: "The hardest problems to overcome were in the making and breaking of the spark and in the avoidance of excess weight. For the transmission, the steering gear, and the general construction, I could draw on my experience of the steam tractors."

One can get a clearer idea of what was going on in the Bagley Avenue woodshed from a contemporary of Ford's named Hiram Maxim, who was struggling with his own self-propelled vehicle in equal isolation in West Lynn, Massachusetts. Neither man had heard of the other (although Ford may have been familiar with the name Maxim, because Hiram's father had already become well known in technical journals for developing the modern machine gun), but both were groping their way through the same labyrinth.

Maxim had been lured into it by a woman. Late on a summer night in 1892, pedaling his bicycle along a country road the five miles between West Lynn and Salem, which was home to "an attractive young lady" who had him "pretty much up in the clouds," he was struck by a thought: "It would be a wonderful thing if a little engine were to be devised which would furnish the power to drive a bicycle." Creating one "did not appear to be a serious problem," because he wasn't "expending more than a sixth or a quarter of a horsepower, and that would not mean much of an engine."

Forty years later, Maxim recounted what followed this revelation in a delightful, detailed memoir called *The Horseless Carriage Age.* Maxim was six years Ford's junior, an easterner, and unmarried, but their situations were similar. Maxim, too, was superintending a substantial industrial operation—an armaments factory—and like Ford he had decided that gasoline should drive his vehicle.

"At the start," Maxim said, "I knew engines pretty well but I did not know much about gasoline. That it was bought in paint shops, that it was about as temperamental as dynamite, was very volatile, would remove grease spots from clothing, and was a petroleum derivative was about the total of my knowledge."

He started out by going to a paint shop and buying an eight-once bottle. "It was a colorless, limpid, innocent-appearing liquid," and Maxim studied it fondly: "Gazing at the bottle and its fascinating contents, I saw in my mind's eye thousands of drops. Each one of these little drops, vaporized and mixed with air, could develop ten times the thrust against my bicycle pedals that I could develop with my legs. The contents of that bottle could develop enough power to take me to Salem."

Maxim brought his magic fluid back to the factory and began to experiment with it. He got a brass artillery shell casing—there were plenty at hand—a couple of inches across and a foot high. In it he put a single drop of gasoline and shook the cartridge to mix the gas with air. Then he stood back and tossed in a match.

After a brief pause, there came a "terrifying explosion, fire shot up out of the cartridge-case, and the match I had thrown went hurtling to the ceiling. It was evident that there was about a thousand times more kick in a drop of gasoline than I had pictured in my wildest flights of imagination."

Maxim tried it with two drops, then three, and was surprised to find that the more gasoline he put in, the slower and weaker the explosion.

Thus educated, he went in search of a vehicle to carry the engine that would live on the unpredictable liquid, and found, in Salem, a secondhand tandem Columbia tricycle. Despite the sound of its name, it had been designed for husky adults. With great trepidation—"thirty dollars was a lot of money"—Maxim bought it.

After he'd wrestled his tricycle back to Lynn and put it in a room next to his office in the factory, it silently urged him on: "There it stood, ready to take to the road. All I needed was an engine to drive it."

This he worked on every spare hour, from six o'clock quitting time until midnight on weekdays, Saturday afternoons, Sundays: "I strove mightily at first to design the general layout—the chain drive, the clutch, its operating mechanism, a change-gear system, gasoline tank and support, engine mounting and engine. But every effort resulted in something that would require an express wagon to contain it."

So he turned to the engine, which seemed to him an altogether easier proposition. "I laid out a light three-cylinder, four-cycle, air-cooled machine, three inches bore by three inches stroke, with mechanically actuated exhaust and automatic inlet valves . . . I passed up the carbureting arrangements, muffler, manifolds and lubricating systems, as minor details, the designing of which could be tossed off at any convenient time!"

The engine turned out to devour his convenient and inconvenient time alike. "It required months of night-work to finish the . . . design and make all the working drawings. It took months more to get the patterns, castings, and machine work done here, there, and everywhere."

Maxim finished the engine late in 1894, and thought it "the most ravishingly beautiful bit of machinery the hand of man had ever created." But what he called his "little darling" needed some of the fundamental things he had earlier shrugged off designing.

He improvised a carburetor from a kerosene can and tried to start it. Nothing doing: "The whole future looks black and forbidding after spending a week unsuccessfully cranking a cold engine." He worked and worked on "the beautiful creation that seemed perfect in all particulars except its prime object." At last, after hooking the recalcitrant machine up to the "electric-light system in the factory"—at almost the same time his unknown co-revolutionist was doing the same thing in a kitchen eight hundred miles away—and fastening it to one of the shop's lathes to turn it over, he was ready to try again.

A colleague wondered "if it were necessary for a self-propelled road vehicle to carry around an electric factory lighting system and a lathe and the power to run the lathe, did it not appear that the thing would become a bit top-heavy?"

This is only research, Maxim replied—nervously, because an audience of his fellow weapons-makers had gathered to watch the demonstration.

Maxim started the lathe; the engine turned, gasoline smell filled the room—so the fuel was flowing properly—but the little darling lay silent. Maxim stopped the lathe and closed off the gas supply to the engine. Perhaps the same thing was happening that had with the cartridge experiment: the more gas, the less bang. By starving the engine of gas, Maxim was also cutting down what the future would know as a "rich mixture"—a heavy ratio of gas to air.

He started the lathe again. It "turned a few times when, without the slightest warning, what seemed like the most frightful machine-gun fire cut loose. I had never heard such a terrible clatter. Noise came from everywhere. Something was buzzing around under my nose at tremendous speed, fire was spitting out of everything, and smoke, smell, and confusion reigned supreme."

His coworkers were frightened by this clamorous glimpse into the next century, and so was Maxim. He had expected his prodigy to sound like "a sweet-running little sewing machine," not a battle. He was discouraged for a few days, then he began to think about a muffler, exhaust pipes, a carburetor, and the necessity of putting some sort of load on the engine so it wouldn't race until it thrashed itself apart.

The big tricycle would provide the drag he needed. He mounted the engine on it, and liked the way it looked. It would probably be a good idea to have a clutch, he thought, but that could come later. For the moment, he connected the engine directly to the wheels with a bicycle-like chain-and-sprocket arrangement, happy in the thought that he could pedal it into life without any tedious hand cranking, let alone a lathe.

After a while, he summoned the nerve to attempt a road test. Wanting no onlookers this time, he took the tricycle (or automobile; it was surely more than a tricycle now) out into the streets of West Lynn just after sunrise.

He found that with the engine yoked to the wheels, it was too cumbersome to pedal. Maxim disconnected the chain, pushed his creation to the brow of a hill, and reattached the chain. Even pedaling downhill was stiff, slow progress with the wheels turning the silent engine, and the road was about like any other one in America at that time: a stretch of parallel troughs dug by wagon wheels and filled with stones.

Maxim set the gas-air mixture rich and pushed along; then, beginning to run out of hill, shifted it to lean, just as it had been in the artillery shell on his very first try. Immediately "there came a terrific snapping noise and what seemed to be a rear-end collision. . . . The tricycle gave a lunge ahead and started for the bottom of the hill hell-for-leather, regardless of loose stones, rocks and gullies, at a speed nothing less than horrible . . . I suppose the run lasted ten seconds. It seemed to me ten minutes."

The front wheel locked itself in a rut, and when Maxim tried to steer free shed its tire and collapsed, flinging the tricycle and its driver into the air.

Maxim landed a life-saving distance from the overturned machine and got to his feet to assess the damage. He was abraded but intact; the tricycle looked a total wreck, emitting a few final hiccups of blue smoke and "the smell which goes along with all new gasoline engines." But "to my astonishment, nothing was damaged beyond repair excepting my trousers."

Maxim spent the last days of 1894 trying to devise a clutch. The next summer he went to Hartford, Connecticut, and visited the Pope Manufacturing Company, the nation's foremost bicycle producer, whose owner, Colonel Albert A. Pope, was beginning to be intrigued with the idea of horseless carriages. So were many Americans at the time, but Pope was in a position to do something about it, and he hired Maxim to be in charge of a department that would build a horseless carriage named the Columbia (which would have four wheels; Maxim was through with tricycles). This new operation was to be called the Motor-Carriage Department. The forward-looking Colonel Pope felt that even the word "horseless" was beginning to sound antiquated.

Hiram Maxim and Henry Ford had spent 1894 engaged in nearly identical tasks. Maxim had made mistakes that Ford avoided, mostly in the latter's approach to his work. Ford had figured out how to control his engine before trying to take a ride with it. "I draw a plan and work out every detail in the plan before starting to build," he said, "for otherwise one will waste a great deal of time in makeshifts as the work goes on and the finished article will not have coherence. It will not be rightly proportioned. Many inventors fail because they do not distinguish between planning and experimenting."

The similarities between the two inventors, however, were greater than the differences. Maxim had risked his life trying to prove his machine. Ford was to do that. Both shared the frustrations that came from the fact that in the automobile's earliest days, there was little difference between experimenting and planning. Most of all, Ford would have sympathized with Maxim's ceaseless search for parts and castings. "The largest building difficulties that I had," Ford said, "were in obtaining the proper materials. The next were with tools. There had to be some adjustments and changes in details of the design, but what held me up most was that I had neither the time nor the money to search for the best material for each part."

Money was a problem, but not a misery. Ford was drawing a good salary, and his wife was an excellent manager. The Strelinger hardware store gave him a credit of fifteen dollars a month—not an enormous sum but, considering Maxim's worry over committing thirty dollars to his tricycle, not negligible. And at Bagley Avenue the Fords were able to buy a player piano, the single most expensive domestic machine before the advent of what Ford was trying to create.

Ford worked all that late winter and spring, often under Felix Julien's fascinated gaze. His neighbor had become so interested in the project that he sometimes would sit alone in the woodshed, waiting for Ford to return from Detroit Edison. Others visited the shed: Ford had several friends who were willing to help him and capable enough actually to be helpful. One was James Bishop, who worked at the Edison plant, and who liked Ford even though he'd been the butt of one of his practical jokes. This form of humor was far more prevalent a century ago than it is now, but even by the standards of the day Ford relished it to an unusual extent. When another Edison employee left his work shoes in the middle of the room, Ford jimmied up a floorboard, fixed the shoes to it with spikes driven through the soles, hammered the points of the spikes to a right angle on the bottom of the plank to make sure the marriage was solid, and then nailed the board back in place.

Ford's joke on Bishop was equally subtle. His colleague was repairing an engine in one of the plant's older buildings when Bishop and the other men on the job began to have difficulty breathing. What air they could draw in was vile. Bishop discovered his superintendent outside, with a small bellows and a shovelful of glowing coals. He was dropping sulfur on the coals and pumping the resulting stench into the room through a knothole.

It says something about Ford's personality in those days that despite this sort of thing, Bishop was fond of him. So, too, was a man five years his junior who would have a decisive effect on his work.

At about the time Ford moved to Bagley Avenue, Charles B. King rented space in a new building on St. Antoine Street that housed the Lauer Brothers machine shop—one of the best in the city—in which he hoped to develop an automobile of his own. The son of an army officer, Charles King first came to Detroit, his mother's hometown, when his father retired as a general. He spent two years studying science at Cornell before his father's death brought him back to Detroit and into a draftsman's job at the Michigan Car Works. His tenure there was happier than Ford's had been.

King invented a brake beam that was adopted by the entire railroad industry, and a pneumatic hammer, which won him a high award at the 1893 Chicago World's Fair. When he moved into the Lauer building he planned to develop, along with his automobile, the pneumatic hammer and marine engines. Lauer, just one floor below him, would do his manufacturing.

Ford knew the Lauer Brothers shop well; he often came there on Edison business. On one of his visits he met King and discovered that they were both interested in building a motorcar. King was friendly, enthusiastic, and possessed formal training and real patents. Ford wanted to know whether his new friend might help him. "He asked me to give him a hand," King said decades later. "Of course, I was willing."

Soon after opening his office, King hired as his assistant a seventeen-year-old named Oliver Barthel. He had been born in Detroit, but raised in Germany, where his father represented a stove company. His mother brought him back to Michigan to study engineering in high school, but like King he had to break that off and go to work when his father died. Despite his truncated education, his new boss found him a first-rate engineer. Moreover, his complete command of the German language could get Lauer's largely German-American workforce to hurry King's projects along. For his part, Barthel adored King—"I never worked so well with anyone"—and he, too, became close friends with Henry Ford.

So King, Barthel, and Bishop often stopped in at the woodshed to help with the engine. Seventy years later a handful of elderly men in Detroit still remembered as schoolboys sneaking down the alley by 58 Bagley to catch a glimpse of Mr.

Ford and his friends and the thing they were making.

The woodshed was by no means open to all comers. Clara was highly protective of her husband and his work. When, early in 1894, her sister Kate and niece Nettie, both in their early twenties, came for a weeklong stay, she neither showed them the shed nor let them in on what was happening there. All she would say was, "Henry is making something and maybe someday I'll tell you."

"Well," Nettie said tartly long after, "she didn't tell us."

Clara's secretiveness about the project reflected her husband's. The affable, gregarious Ford, welcome in any machine shop in the city, was always closemouthed about what exactly he was doing there.

Fred Strauss had by now opened a machine shop on Shelby Street where he made gasoline engines for boats. Ford liked to drop by, give him a hand, and even sold two engines for him. He also got Strauss to help him build a crankshaft. It was not until years later that Strauss learned that it had been destined to be part of an automobile.

But if the busy inventor chose not to show his visiting in-laws what was going on in the woodshed, he did manage to find the time one day to smear butter on all the doorknobs in the house. A few days later, as they were tiptoeing quietly up to their room after a late party, the sisters were alarmed by a vaguely human-looking thing flapping and thumping toward them down the darkened staircase. It was a bundle of clothes, weighted with bricks and flung, of course, by their host. (Henry Ford would change in many ways during his life, but not in this one: Thirty years later, he'd be garnishing Harvey Firestone's soup with wooden croutons.) The girls got their own back by filling Henry's shoes with finely ground pepper, which so discomfited the wearer that he had to come back in the middle of the day from Detroit Edison to wash off his feet and change his footwear.

There were few practical jokes in the woodshed, though, where Ford was pushing his way through the thicket that has entrapped most inventors, a thorny place of false leads, real setbacks, and will-o'-the-wisp successes.

A decade later, Ford described his routine in those days: "Most of the iron work was got from a firm by the name of Barr & Dates; they were located at that time on the corner of Park Place and State Street, Detroit. The wheels I made; the seat I got from the Wilson Carriage Company, and from C. A. Strelinger & Co. bolts and screws and nuts; I made the handle myself; I don't know where I got the balance wheel from; I made the pattern and got it cast; I made the braking device; the springs from the Detroit Steel and Spring Co."

When he says he made things like the wheels and handle himself, he almost always means that he supervised their making. Ford was a fine machinist, but he had a rarer skill than that, the one his sister noticed so early, which was his ability to draw work out of friends and keep them happy while they did it. For the most part, other hands than his fitted the spokes to the wheel rims. "I never saw Mr. Ford make anything," said one of his Bagley Avenue helpers. "He was always doing the directing." And the helpers he found, first-rate engineers like King and Barthel, always took the directing gladly. Fred Strauss said of Ford that in those days "he had the magnet."

There was plenty to direct. His cylinders—he'd decided to have two—were easily gotten, born like their little predecessor in a length of scrap pipe. This pipe, which had once served as the exhaust for a steam engine, was larger. Ford, working with the close tolerances that internal combustion demanded, increased its bore from 2.5 inches to 2.565 inches. He made the cylinders eleven inches long; their pistons would have a six-inch stroke. He fretted over the flywheel, trying to find the right recipe of weight (to keep the pistons moving) and lightness (to keep them as free as possible in their motion). This all went well enough, but he had little luck with the ignition, and none at all with the valves.

• • •

Eighteen ninety-four passed in filing and fitting, cutting and testing. Edsel's first birthday came and went and not long afterward so did Christmas—this time with no combustive visitor to the holiday kitchen—and then it was 1895.

Two things that were to have powerful consequences for Henry Ford's life happened that year. Of one he knew nothing; of the other, a great deal.

The former was not spectacular. A Rochester, New York, man named George B. Selden moved forward on a long-pending patent claim, and on November 5 was issued U.S. patent No. 549,160.

"Long-pending" understates the case. Selden had first submitted his claim on May 8, 1879. It was for a horseless carriage.

Selden had been trying to build an internal combustion engine. He hadn't had any great success, but he could imagine his unfinished motor placed in some sort of vehicle—he never did try to build that—and he wanted his patent to cover what he might one day achieve.

Neither Selden nor anybody else in America was prepared to build such a thing in 1879, but Selden knew the law—he was a patent attorney—and he knew how to use it to put time on his side.

Under the existing statutes, having submitted his claim Selden could postpone the beginning of its seventeen-year life by making amendments to it. These he scrupulously filed at regular intervals.

Some were substantive, others as finicking as changing a "the" to an "a" in the wording of his application, but they kept the claim alive. The law let him spend seventeen years on such refinements; then he had to accept the patent or withdraw it.

Selden evidently did want to build an automobile, but he had a haughty, rebarbative nature that drove away investors. At the end he had no investors, no car, and only a few months left him.

Eighteen ninety-five was a far more promising year for automobile making than 1879 had been. Selden finally pulled the trigger and got his patent for "the production of a safe, simple and cheap road-locomotive light in weight, easy to control, and possessed of sufficient power to overcome any ordinary inclination." It would have a steering mechanism, he said, either one or several cylinders, a clutch, passenger seats, a brake, and so forth. None of these was described in any great detail, and didn't need to be. Selden had sought—and, amazingly, got—a patent on the *idea* of the automobile.

Although Henry Ford had no inkling of this, if he wanted to build a motor carriage, United States law now said he would have to get George Selden's permission.

If Selden's patent made not a ripple in the embryonic American automotive world, another event that same November transformed it.

In the summer of 1894 the motorcar had progressed sufficiently in Europe—nurtured by roads that had been good since Roman times—for a race to be run the eighty-odd miles between Paris and Rouen. Reports of the contest inspired a young newspaperman named Frederic Adams to approach his boss, Herman Kohlsaat, the owner of the *Chicago Times-Herald*, and suggest that he sponsor a similar race in their town.

Kohlsaat resisted. Surely there couldn't be enough vehicles in America to hold such a race. There will be in a year, Adams said, and Europeans will send some machines if the prize is sufficiently enticing. Kohlsaat thought it over. He was monitoring a confident city in an era that liked machinery, and he decided to put up a five-thousand-dollar purse. The race would be held on the inevitable date of July Fourth. Once committed, Kohlsaat sent Adams off around the country to scratch up possible contestants.

Adams did well. Thirty entries came in from Chicago, six each from Indiana and Pennsylvania, five from New York. Just one came from Detroit. Charles King filed it.

Many were from widely scattered places where one might not have expected to find mechanics capable of building automobiles from scratch doing just that: Skowhegan, Maine; Sisterville, West Virginia; Center Point, Iowa; *two* from Pine Bluff, Arkansas. Clearly Adams was fanning isolated sparks that were heating toward a general blaze.

But as spring came to Chicago and no cars did, the July Fourth date began to seem too optimistic. The *Times-Herald* moved the race back to November.

In France that June there was another automobile race, this one from Paris to Bordeaux, eight hundred miles, ten times the distance of the Paris–Rouen contest of less than a year earlier.

The meet reignited interest across the Atlantic. By September Americans had filed five hundred automotive patents. The *Times-Herald* set the date of its race for Thanksgiving Day, and as autumn blew in from the lake, entrants began to show up in Chicago. Adams put their cars on public display in a store on Wabash Avenue, and people turned out to see the automobiles—without, it occurred to Adams, knowing exactly what to call them.

Reassured that he really did have the makings of a race, Kohlsaat let his paper announce another automotive prize: five hundred dollars for giving the horseless carriage a horseless name. Hundreds of entries came in, endless reiterations of "motor" and "auto," "wagon" and "carriage." The prize was divided among three entrants who, visited by the same muse, offered up: motocycle. The *Herald* gamely stuck with the word until the race was done and then, along with the rest of the English-speaking world, abandoned it.

Adams had drummed up nearly ninety entries for the race itself, but by mid-November the list of those who promised to be there had dwindled to eleven. Kohlsaat, already stung by the merry sarcasm of the *Herald*'s rival newspapers, wanted to cancel the event. Adams prevailed, and for his pains got to spend a miserable Thanksgiving Eve watching an early snowfall deliver eight heavy, wet inches before turning to sleet.

The race was scheduled to set out at 7:30 from the 1893 fairgrounds, ghostly and radiating no festivity whatever in the gray, stormy morning. By 8:30 six motocycles had managed to make their way to the starting line: two electric-powered ones, the Sturges and the wonderfully named Electrobat, what a reporter described as the "Benz, a gasoline wagon of German make entered by H. Mueller Manufacturing Company," two other Benzes, one entered by Macy's department store, and "the Duryea, a gasoline wagon of Duryea Manufacturing Company."

The Duryea company had been founded in Springfield, Massachusetts, by two brothers, Frank and Charles, and they had made a good machine. Frank would drive; Charles would follow behind with a team of horses to offer whatever support he could.

The automobiles faced a course from Jackson Park to Evanston and back, and what even today would not be an easy drive: fifty-two miles over bad roads heavily drifted with snow and glazed with ice.

Charles King was aboard the Mueller Benz. Like so many other hopeful entrants, he hadn't finished his machine on time. He had, however, been chosen as one of the umpires assigned to accompany each contestant, and would be sitting beside the driver, Oscar Mueller, son of the Mueller company's owner. King's friend Henry Ford had wanted to enter, too, but knew he had no chance of getting ready by Thanksgiving. He stayed behind in Detroit, confident in getting a full report from King.

The race got under way an hour late: The Duryea was waved off at 8:55, the Mueller Benz eleven minutes later. The electrics made a brave start, but the cold and the course soon drained their batteries. The Duryea churned along steadily for the first hour, and then the steering gear broke. "The rules forbid outside help," Charles reported, "but did not forbid borrowing facilities. Being a holiday the [blacksmith] shops were closed and it took a good deal of looking to find any open, but finally one was found and the damage repaired in short order. . . . Fifty-five minutes after the stop, the wagon was off again with a steering that steered, even if it was not perfect. In the meantime the Macy wagon had passed us and gotten thirty-five minutes ahead while a third wagon [no "motocycle" for the Duryeas] had rolled into sight several blocks back." Frank Duryea left it behind and overtook the Macy Benz at Evanston.

All this in gray, gloomy weather, but in mid-afternoon the sun showed itself and the sudden onset of a fine winter day brought the Chicago gentry out in their sleighs to enjoy the first snowfall of the year. They heard an unfamiliar crackling noise and reined their horses aside to let the Duryea pass, and to get a good look at it. Here was the nineteenth-century equine world at its most appealing, the horses' breath steaming in the clear air, the sparkle and chime of sleigh bells, men and women waving from beneath blankets and furs above the hiss of the runners, all of them in orbit around the dour nucleus of the noisy little motor carriage.

The sky clouded over, and the cheerful allegorical scene dissolved. The day again turned cold and drab, and the sleighs headed for home. Duryea couldn't: He had to keep his wagon banging forward through the snowy dusk.

He crossed the finish line at 7:18. The Mueller Benz, the only other competitor still running, got in an hour and a half later. Charles King was driving, holding the tiller with one hand and supporting his fellow motorist with the other. The rigors of the day had made Oscar Mueller pass out.

Shortly afterward, Charles Duryea wrote about the race in *Horseless Age*, a magazine just founded in response to the excitement over Paris–Bordeaux. "We had run the first road contest in America. We had proven the motor wagon to be superior to the horse on roads decidedly unfavorable to wheels. We had forever answered the objections of the *ultra* conservative people to the effect that the motor wagon could not be of use except on good roads; we had opened a new era; we had let forth a new type of vehicle. No contest or trip over summer roads, or under pleasant skies could have demonstrated our claim for our vehicle as did this trip."

This none too modest assessment was premature. Bellamy Partridge, a pioneer motorist who years later wrote spirited popular histories of the American automobile, pointed out that although in its reporting of the event, the *Times-Herald* "could not have spread itself any more had Chicago been the target of an invasion from Mars," the eastern press was restrained: four column inches in the *New York Herald*, even fewer in the *Times*.

Yet in the end, Duryea was more right than wrong. That race, the wretched conditions under which it was run, the victory of an American car over European competitors, and a sense of the motor carriage leaving horses behind in the winter twilight seeped through the national consciousness.

A Chicago man who had run his sleigh beside

the Duryea for a few minutes said something that kept being passed from newspaper to newspaper: "No horse on earth could have made those fifty-four miles."

Less than three months later, the Duryea brothers made a sale, thereby becoming not only the first American carmakers to capitalize on a racing success, but the first to sell an automobile.

Later on, when Henry Ford liked to toss out provocative and extravagant statements, he sometimes said that he had built the first automobile seen on the streets of Detroit.

The closest this approached the truth was that he had *seen* the first automobile ever seen on the streets of Detroit.

Charles King had made it. He'd returned from his adventure in Chicago to go back to work on his car and had got well along—the engine finished, the chassis taking shape—when the United States Rubber Company let him down: The three-inch pneumatic tires he'd ordered failed to appear.

In their absence, he accepted an offer from Emerson & Fisher, Cincinnati wagon builders who, like so many of their competitors, were beginning to sniff out the promise in the horseless carriage.

Emerson & Fisher, King said much later, "had been considering self-propelled vehicles without arriving at any practical result, and in the hope of getting somewhere loaned me an incomplete, experimental, iron-tired wagon with full privileges to reconstruct it for testing." King transplanted his nearly completed engine into this body. "That wasn't a car," said Barthel, "it was a testing wagon. We merely built it to have something to test the engine in."

Nevertheless, in early March the *Detroit Free Press* reported, "The first horseless carriage seen in this city was out on the streets last night." A newsman from the *Journal* added that "when in motion, the connecting rods fly like lightning, and the machine is capable of running seven or eight miles an hour."

Another witness was Henry Ford, who rode behind his friend's machine on a bicycle, carefully noting the behavior of the first gas-driven vehicle he had ever seen moving under its own power.

Ford went back to his shop. If he felt at all crestfallen that King had beaten him to the street, he has left no record of it. King had strong patents to his name, and the Duryeas were starting to build cars: They were to sell twelve of them that year, America's first automotive production run.

But Ford had a steady job; he had a steady wife; and he seems to have had a steady faith that no matter what the automotive world might serve up, he could better it.

He also knew he was doing something different

from King. As Barthel pointed out, King's machine had been given a chassis that King had not chosen. Still, King's inaugural car was a true horseless carriage—or, more accurately, wagon. It weighed thirteen hundred pounds.

The automobile would descend not from the horse-and-wagon, but from the bicycle: lithe, supple, mechanically sophisticated, and, above all, light. "The most beautiful things in the world," Ford said a quarter century later, "are those from which all excess weight has been eliminated." The car he was working on would weigh five hundred pounds.

The engine, the thing that would actually replace the horse in the equation, was Ford's most urgent concern, and the one that made the greatest demands on him.

He had decided on a four-cycle engine. The first gas motors, following the example of their steam predecessors, were two-cycle. In the steam engines of the day, every stroke of the piston was a power stroke. That is, the steam, fed in from outside the cylinder, entered under pressure and pushed the piston from one side and then, once the piston drove its distance, gave it a second punch from the other.

This turned out not to be good enough for the gasoline engine. As it began to reveal its properties, the gas engine demanded that the power come from an explosion inside the cylinder—rather than being pumped in from the outside—and that driving the piston on every stroke fouled the mechanism. The two-cycle system didn't allow enough time to exhaust the burned gas, or to draw in a fresh mixture of gas and air.

Everything happens so quickly with gasoline. As Maxim had discovered, it's a powerful elixir, vigorous enough to give the piston a push that would carry the crankshaft to which it was connected around twice before the next push had to come.

Henry Ford explained this economically and well: " 'Four-cycle' means that the piston traverses the cylinder four times to get one power impulse. The first stroke draws in the gas, the second compresses it, the third is the explosion or power stroke, while the fourth exhausts the waste gas."

But how to ignite the compressed gas without the help of a ceiling fixture? That would mean a battery, which could be bought from the outside rather than designed—like the doorbell Ford would mount on the front of his vehicle to warn of its approach (although considering how noisy the engine was likely to be, this seems a redundant precaution).

For the ignition mechanism itself—the "sparking device," Ford called it—he drew on two more of the helpers he so easily recruited. An electrician named George Cato came up with an "ignitor" that would explode the gas, and helped

Ford build two of them. Edwin S. Huff, who went under the irresistible nickname of "Spider," helped him on other parts of the engine—and would stick by Ford in some scary places in the years to come.

The ignition was difficult. The transmission was difficult, finally evolving into a combination of belts and a chain drive to the rear wheels. Everything was difficult. But the work went forward.

Valves proved particularly vexing, until King gave Ford four steam valves that he'd been working on, and Ford figured out how to adapt them to serve a gasoline engine. He avoided the problems of inventing a carburetor by not trying. Instead, he mounted the gas tank above the engine, so that gravity would do the job of getting the fuel to the intake where it blended with the air.

He took his car body off the sawhorses that had supported it for months; he had the machine on its wheels. He had eliminated so much excess weight that he could lift the front or rear end by himself until he put the engine in. Even then, the thing was easy to push back and forth, and needed to be because it had no reverse gear.

It never would. In May the Indianapolis Chain and Stamping Company delivered an order—put in for Ford by Charles King—for ten feet of $1^1/8$-inch "bright" at twenty-five cents a foot. This was what would finally transmit the power to the wheels.

Ford threaded it into place, fitting the sprocket teeth between the pins that held the links together, and tightened it, and that was that. What he was already calling his Quadricycle was finished. There was nothing left to do except take it for a drive.

Gleaming with promise and moody with its capacity to wreck its builder's highest plans, the Quadricycle stood in its brick shed. Ford's benevolent witness Felix Julien had probably gone to bed; it was after two o'clock in the morning. Clara was there carrying an umbrella, for it was June now—most likely, the fourth of June—and a spring rain was falling.

Henry Ford almost never expressed anxiety, but he was frank about having not been able to sleep for the last two nights.

There is another indication of his worry, as well as of the intensity with which he had pursued his project. Only when he began to push the Quadricycle toward the door did he realize it was too wide to fit through.

The man who had spent so much painstaking time with small, cunningly cut pieces of metal took up an ax in the woodshed, and in a few minutes had splintered the doorframe and knocked a gap-toothed opening through the brick wall that surrounded it. He and Bishop pushed the car out into the alley.

Clara went back into the house to bring a sleepy Edsel to the front steps so the three-year-old could see his father carry off the triumph in which her faith had never lagged.

Ford and Bishop got the car pointed in the right direction. Ford set the current running from the battery and spun the flywheel. The engine took: The Quadricycle transformed itself from plumbing into creature.

Ford climbed up on it. The small carriage seat he'd ordered either hadn't arrived or had gotten there too late. He perched on a bicycle seat.

Bishop wheeled out in front of him—he'd be cycling ahead to warn any horse-drivers that might be out so late that drizzling night. Ford pulled back on the lever that tightened the driving belt. The Quadricycle ran along the alley to Bagley, and then Ford turned onto Grand River Avenue, moving forward into his future and ours.

CHAPTER 5
What Edison Said

Ford's first sale; "There's a young fellow who has made a gas car"; Ford's first company; a winter drive with "civilization's latest lisp"; dissolution: "Henry wasn't ready."

Ford had just started up Washington Boulevard on his maiden voyage when a metallic snap and a clatter on the wet cobbles told him something had failed. The car rolled to a stop. Bishop cycled back and Ford figured out that a nut holding the spring on a valve stem had jumped off. The Edison plant was a few hundred yards away. The two men pushed the car over to it and Ford got the needed part from his colleagues. Watched by a few night owls from the nearby Cadillac Hotel, who were grateful for such a diversion at this hour, Ford, working in the spill of light from the plant's tall windows, screwed on the new nut and got the Quadricycle started again. Then, Bishop preceding him, he made his way back to Bagley Avenue.

The two men got a couple of hours of sleep, and Clara made breakfast. Despite his successful trial run, Ford was worried about the shed. He drew again on the bounties of the Edison plant and persuaded two bricklayers to come restore the mutilated door.

They had barely begun when Ford's landlord, a prosperous wholesale meat dealer named William Wreford, stopped by to collect the June rent and demanded to know what was going on with his shed.

Ford said it was being repaired, and in a couple of hours would be good as new. Wreford was not placated. "What did you do it for?"

Ford explained that he'd had to get his motor carriage "out to see if it would run."

Wreford immediately saw that this was more interesting than anything his other tenants might be up to. "You ran it?"

"Yes, sir."

"Let me see it."

Ford at his most engaging explained his car to the landlord, who concluded his visit with a thought that possibly had not yet occurred to the inventor. "Say! If these fellows put the wall back up, how are you going to get your car out again? I've got an idea. Tell the bricklayers to leave the opening and then you can put on swinging doors. That will let you in and out."

By the end of the day William Wreford owned what was almost certainly the first purpose-built garage in America, and Ford was back at work on his car.

The Quadricycle ran, but its brief nocturnal trial

had revealed a host of weaknesses. "The original machine was air-cooled—or to be more accurate, the motor was simply not cooled at all," Ford said. The engine ran so hot that after a while it began to bleed silvery drops of solder, "striking the ground and looking like dimes." Ford took care of this: "I very shortly put a water jacket around the cylinders and piped it to a tank in the rear of the car over the cylinders." But the chassis was all wood, and that wasn't going to serve.

A few weeks after his first drive, Ford made an opportune—indeed, opportunistic—hire at Detroit Edison. A Scottish-born mechanic named David Bell came to the chief engineer and said he was looking for work as a blacksmith.

"What kind of blacksmith are you?"

"A carriage blacksmith."

"You come to work," Ford said.

Bell reported for duty, and discovered that most of it involved the Quadricycle. He fabricated sturdier wheels, a better steering arrangement, substituted iron piping for wood throughout the body, with at least some help from his boss (Bell is the recruit who said, "I never saw Mr. Ford make anything").

The buggy seat replaced the bicycle seat, and Ford began to take Clara and Edsel for rides. One autumn day, he felt confident enough to try a run out to the family farm in Dearborn.

His sister Margaret remembered his arrival there

for the rest of her life: "My first sight of the little car was as it came west along what is now Ford Road. The wheels on one side were deep in the rut made by the farm wagons while the wheels on the other side were high in the center of the road. Henry had built the car in such a way that the distance between the wheels was less than that of the wagons and carriages, thus it was driven in this way on a road which had ruts. Clara and Edsel were with him and all of them were sitting on the slanted seat. . . .

"Henry took all of us for rides during the day, and I well remember the peculiar sensation of what seemed to be a great speed and the sense of bewilderment I felt when I first rode in this carriage which moved without a horse. Henry particularly enjoyed explaining the mechanical details to his younger brother, and I am sure that he enjoyed scaring the life out of his sisters."

Henry's father, Margaret said, "was as interested as all of us in the fact that here was the horseless carriage about which we had been hearing. He looked it all over and listened with interest to Henry's explanation of it, but he refused to ride in it." Nevertheless, "Father was very proud of Henry's achievement. He talked to us at home and he told his neighbors about it."

Charles King has left a more somber account of that first ride out into the country. "I could see that old Mr. Ford was ashamed at a grown-up man like Henry fussing over a little thing like a quadricycle. We'd gone and humiliated him in front of his friends. Henry stood it as long as he could, then he turned to me and said, in a heartbroken way, 'Come on Charlie, let's you and me get out of here.'"

This bleakly satisfying picture of the inventor as solitary visionary, scorned even by those closest to him, seems in Ford's case to be untrue. Margaret flatly denied it. "I do not believe the story which has been told of a visit of Henry and Mr. King to the homestead and of their talks with Father. Neither my brother William nor myself can remember any such incident. We are both sure that if any such incident had occurred, Father would have talked about it at home. Clara also did not recall any such visit." If William Ford was too cautious to take a ride that day, the reason was not shame about what Henry was up to. Once a week or so William liked to go into Detroit, stop at Jimmie Burns's saloon for some whiskey and a sirloin steak (he never shared his son's strong views about the evils of drink), and then seek out Henry and ask him how the car was coming along.

Coming along fine, Henry would have answered, for he kept improving and testing it. He drove it, he said, about a thousand miles around the streets of Detroit. In the beginning, he remembered, it caused such a stir that if he stopped it "anywhere in town a crowd was around before I could start up again. If I left it alone even for a minute some inquisitive person always tried to run it. Finally I had to carry a chain and chain it to a lamppost whenever I left it anywhere."

Not one of those curious bystanders had ever driven a car, so it is hard to see how they could have started it running, let alone motored off in it. But Detroit was a city full of able mechanics and engineers, and perhaps just a few moments looking at the trim, cleanly designed four-horsepower engine—for the first months of the car's life fully exposed to view—would have revealed its secrets to them.

In time Ford covered the engine and completed all the improvements he thought his Quadricycle could bear. Then he was through with it. His first car, the object of years of steady work, had served its purpose and, as with the Christmas Eve engine, Ford "didn't stop to play with it." He sold it for two hundred dollars. "That was my first sale. I had built the car not to sell but to experiment with. I wanted to start another car. Ainsley [actually, Charles Annesely, a wealthy Detroit friend of those days] wanted to buy. I could use the money and we had no trouble in agreeing upon price."

By the time the Quadricycle left its builder's hands it had become an impressively capable automobile, as Ford learned in the spring of 1899 when he got a letter from a bicycle dealer named

A. W. Hall, an acquaintance of his who had bought the car from Annesely.

> Friend Ford—
> . . . You will be surprised when I tell you that the little carriage is still doing its usual duty. I disposed of it this spring and the little rig was still in fair shape after all the banging around that it has had and I guess you know that was considerable; I ran it almost two years as you know and about the only trouble I had was that one tire and the springs on the sparkers working loose, but you know how they were fastened and there was nothing to prevent them from doing so, until I put on a binding bolt and after that I never had any more trouble with it. . . .
> I was out in Chicago all last fall and looked over the few horseless rigs there and among them all I did not see one I would of rather had had than that little rig for when it comes right down to simplicity they were not in it. . . .

Hall could not know it, but his praise for the car's "simplicity" was powerfully prophetic.

Henry Ford bought the Quadricycle back, for sixty dollars, probably in 1905. By then he had made himself known, had founded a motorcar company, and possibly was beginning to believe that his experimental gas buggy might someday be a historical artifact that could stand alongside the frigate *Constitution* and the Liberty Bell.

Less than a month after his trial run, Ford got a new boss. The highly competent Alexander Dow had given up running Detroit's municipal lighting system to become manager of the Edison operations in the city. He soon learned that his superintendent had a second job that he carried on in a number of satellite workshops: the Bagley Avenue woodshed, a basement across the street from Detroit Edison that he had rented for the friendly tariff of seventy-five cents a month (the magnet at work again), and any Edison plant machinery that happened to be idle at the time he needed it.

These arrangements would not have pleased every new employer, but Dow thought highly of Ford, as is evidenced by the manager's immediately asking him to come to New York for the seventeenth annual convention of the Association of Edison Illuminating Companies. Only one other Detroit employee, the company's attorney, got invited.

The convention was held on Coney Island—or, as the report of its proceedings made clear, "Manhattan Beach, Brooklyn." Manhattan Beach was on the island's eastern end, where three immense frame hotels stretched their verandas along hundreds of yards of Atlantic shorefront. Their operators were careful to emphasize the location's distance, in tone at least, from the raffish district to the west where, amid jovial violence, the modern amusement park was busy being born.

Henry Ford would not have visited the district's ample offering of saloons, but surely he would have enjoyed its amusements: for instance, that mechanical incarnation of the practical joke, the roller coaster, invented here a decade earlier.

There is no record that he rode one, but he did encounter something that interested him more than any roller coaster, and perhaps even more than the automobile itself: Thomas Edison.

Henry Ford's career is so thoroughly brined in myth—much of it tended by the carmaker himself—that his meeting with Edison might seem like folklore, but in fact that August he spent three days with the man who played much the same role in the nineteenth century that Ford would in the twentieth.

The conference took place beneath the confection of vaguely pagoda-like towers that complicated the roof of the Oriental, classiest of the hotels. The delegates heard papers read through several sessions—Dow spoke on "The Selection of Alternating-Current Apparatus for Central-Lighting Stations"—and then gathered together again for dinner.

Dow had much faith in Ford, but little in the internal combustion engine. He was an electricity man. Edison had set up his Pearl Street Station, the first central power plant in the country, in Manhattan just thirteen years earlier, and that was modern enough for Dow. On the second night, August 12, he and Ford were seated at Edison's table. The group had been discussing batteries that day, and the talk turned to their use in powering automobiles.

Dow pointed across to Ford and said loudly—everyone spoke loudly around Edison, because he was half deaf—"There's a young fellow who has made a gas car!"

Ford believed the perfectly accurate statement contained a barb of mockery. Possibly Dow hoped that here, next to the man who might as well have invented electricity, Ford could be laughed out of his fixation on gasoline.

Dow went on to tell how he had looked out his office window one day to see his superintendent, wife, and little boy "pop pop popping" past beneath. He made fun of the engine noise because electric cars ran silently.

Servants of electricity though they all were, everyone at the table turned to Ford with interest, including Edison himself, who was clearly struggling to hear. Noticing this, the man next to him got up and gestured Ford into his chair.

"Is it a four-cycle engine?" Edison at once

asked. Ford said it was. What ignited the gas in the cylinder?

"I told him that it was a make-and-break contact that was pumped apart by the piston and drew a diagram for him of the whole contact arrangement." He was going to improve this on his next car, Ford said, and went on to draw "what today we would call a spark plug; it was really an insulating plug with a make-and-break mechanism, using washers of mica. I drew that too."

Edison kept asking questions, and Ford kept drawing, "For I have always found that I could convey an idea quicker by sketching it than by just describing it."

When he was finished Edison banged a fist on the table so hard "that the dishes around him jumped," and said, "Young man, that's the thing; you have it. Keep at it."

He went on to dismiss the competition: "Electric cars must keep near to power stations. The storage battery is too heavy. Steam cars won't do either, for they have to have a boiler and fire. Your car is self-contained—carries its own power-plant—no fire, no boiler, no smoke and no steam. You have the thing. Keep at it."

Edison finished by telling Ford "that for the purpose any gas motor was better than any electric motor could be—it could go long distances, he said, and there would be stations to supply the cars with hydro-carbon. That was the first time I ever heard this term for liquid fuel."

Remembering the evening some thirty-five years later Ford said, "That bang on the table meant the world to me." He went on with an extremely rare mention about having entertained doubts: "I had hoped that I was headed right, sometimes I only wondered if I was, but here all at once and out of a clear sky the greatest inventive genius in the world had given me a complete approval."

While Ford made his way back from New York, Clara waited for him with her family in Greenfield, where she'd taken Edsel to get away from the city, simmering in a bad August. "The heat was so great we could hardly stand it," she wrote her husband the day after his talk with Edison. ". . . And then the dreadful storms. I thought surely we would have a Cyclone that day. . . . It is 5 PM now and the baby is having a glorious time on the lawn . . . I asked him if he would like to send Papa a kiss and he said yes paper him over one. Just like one of his speeches. . . . I suppose you have seen great sights. . . . I hope things will be all right at the Station so that you can come out. For I want you awful bad."

Things were fine at the station, and Ford went out to Greenfield. He told Clara: "You are not going to see very much of me until I am through with this car."

Ford recounted this remark decades later with

117

the implication that Edison had inspired him to persevere. Although of course he was pleased to have had his project so magnificently anointed, he would surely have kept pursuing it even if Edison had delivered a sermon on the primacy of the horse. And his wife had long ago learned not to count on seeing him too much.

Ford started on his second automobile. The work went slowly, because he kept improving the car while it took shape—something more easily done with, say, an oil painting than a transmission. Years later Bell remembered making the handrails for the seat and the radius rods and "a small device to form the spokes for the four wheels." But "I made many other things which were not used—because Mr. Ford had some other thought in mind that might work better. He was still experimenting."

Bishop helped, and so did Spider Huff, who had a more intuitive and inventive grasp of electrical systems than Ford. He also had a host of interests his friend did not share: tobacco, hard liquor, serial divorce (Huff would marry seven times). He was no roisterer; he was always quiet and thoughtful. Always dependable, too, except when some internal spur would drive him into an unannounced exile in his native Kentucky. Ford paid the bills he left behind, and always welcomed him when he returned.

On April 7, 1897, Ford filed a patent application

for a carburetor. Forty years later a man named R. W. Hanington still had a clear memory of speaking to him about it, and wrote to tell Ford so in 1939.

Hanington, an engineer, had come east from Denver to work with Charles Duryea, who was building cars on his own in New Jersey. Not long after their Chicago triumph the brothers had squabbled and split up, and for the rest of their lives would be running separate operations, thereby very possibly robbing themselves of standing in history with Chrysler, Ford, and General Motors. Hanington found the factory a disappointment—indeed, "a total failure"—and after a few months decided to go home. Along the way, though, he ambitiously set out "to see every motor wagon that was being attempted."

Half a lifetime later he told Ford that "the last stop was Detroit where . . . I had the pleasure of an hour's interview with you in the engine room of a large electric plant. . . . You were working on an ingenious device for feeding gasoline into the cylinder."

During his visit, Hanington also conducted a bit of industrial espionage, sending a highly detailed confidential report on Ford's second car to a friend who was interested in the new industry.

Ford never knew of this document, but he would have been pleased by what it contained: "The design of the motor is excellent . . . similar to that of the Springfield Duryea's [Charles's brother Frank] wagon. The sparker is better, however. . . . The carburetor is good. . . . The design of the gearing is compact and well-balanced. . . . The whole design strikes me as being very complete, and worked out in every detail, and . . . the carriage should be the equal of any that has been built in this country."

Hanington was obviously a capable and observant engineer. The conclusion of his report is a succinct summary—still sound today—of what would, in little more than a decade, enable Henry Ford to sell more cars than all the rest of the American automakers combined: "It is apparently a first-class carriage, well thought out and well constructed, but embodying no *novel* feature of great importance. Novelty, rather than good design, has been the idea of most of the carriage builders.

"Simplicity, strength and common sense seem to be embodied in Mr. Ford's carriage, and I believe that these ideals are essential ones for a successful vehicle."

Hanington sent off his report shortly after the Christmas of 1898. The next July, on a bright Saturday that promised good weather, Ford drove his second car into a prosperous Detroit neighborhood and parked in front of a house there. He went up to the door and spoke to the owner, William H. Murphy. "I am ready to take you on that ride," he said.

Murphy was ready to go on it. He got into the car, and Ford set off. They drove through the summer afternoon to Orchard Lake, and then returned to Detroit by way of Pontiac. All during the eighty-mile excursion Murphy made notes in his lurching seat about how much gasoline the car was consuming, how it behaved on good roads and bad. The car did well throughout, bringing them back to Murphy's house in three and a half hours—a lightning run, considering the roads of the era and the capriciousness of any motor carriage that traveled them.

Murphy climbed down from his seat. "Well," he said to his driver, "now we will organize a company."

Murphy was a rich man. Lumber had made him rich. Born in Bangor, Maine, when there was still first-growth timber to cut down there, he had both followed and helped push what loggers called "the big clearing" west to Detroit. Henry Ford found the time, while bringing his genial presence to welding shops and metal turners, to cultivate people like Murphy, the people who ran Detroit.

Later, cleaving to the familiar inventor myth, Ford liked to suggest that he kept his flame burning despite the indifference of the mighty, and even in the face of their efforts to extinguish it. In fact, he had been careful to make friends with them. He used the same techniques that worked in the foundries—Henry's here! He's lively; he's helpful; oh, he's gone—perhaps to greater effect in the turn-of-the-century years that followed the completion of his second car than ever again. His habits, says Sidney Olson, who has tracked him with the most scrupulous care through that time, "are the despair of biographers." Ford was then "a real slippery creature. He is elusive, baffling, protean; submerged, he slides along for a month or two and then pops up in a dozen places at once, like a whole school of dolphins."

He's getting Fred Strauss to machine the mysterious camshaft, he's making himself agreeable to James McMillan, who gave him his first job in the Michigan Car Works, and who has joined his brother Hugh to establish the Detroit Car Wheel Company to make sure the cars have a steady supply of something to move on. The brothers command the largest industrial operation in Michigan, as is suggested by the spacious name of the railroad they own most of: the Duluth, South Shore & Atlantic.

He's making friends with a younger McMillan, William, who not only supervises his father's and uncle's finances, but sits as secretary and treasurer on the ten boards, four of their names beginning with "Detroit": Iron Mining Company; Iron Furnace Company; Railroad Elevator Company; Transportation Company.

William C. Maybury, the city's popular new mayor, likes the motor carriage enthusiast. He amiably gives Ford an official "chauffeur's license"—as official, that is, as an orally issued license can be.

These were some of the people Henry Ford had been making himself agreeable to when he wasn't busy thinking through a new flange or bolt to replace one that his shop helpers believed was already perfectly satisfactory.

To whatever Goldsmith's business school had taught Ford, his duties at Edison had added knowledge about how corporations work, how a big enterprise is organized and how capital gets fed into it. Alexander Dow thought his employee had learned a great deal, and at about the time of Ford's drive with Murphy, Dow recorded in his notebook that he'd "had a talk with Henry as to what part he cared to play in some big plans we were about to carry out."

The plans included Ford: He would become general superintendent of the Detroit Illuminating Company, with a nearly doubled salary of nineteen hundred dollars a year. But it was a demanding job, and would not allow time for automotive experimentation. Dow was friendly and conciliatory: "I offered him the best I then had, in the work upon which my heart was set." Dow's heart, though; not Ford's.

"I had to choose between my job and my automobile," Ford said. "I chose the automobile, or rather I gave up the job—there was really nothing in the way of a choice. For already I knew that the car was bound to be a success. I quit my job on August 15, 1899, and went into the automobile business."

The automobile business was waiting for him. Ten days earlier the papers for the Detroit Automobile Company had been filed: It was capitalized at $150,000, with $15,000 in actual money already put up by a dozen solid Detroit citizens. Henry Ford was superintendent, had some stock in the company, and a salary of $150 a month. Ford and his backers had been shown a suitable factory building, on Cass Avenue, earlier that spring.

Here is Henry Ford the planner working at his shrewdest. When he left Detroit Edison, writes Olson, "We watch Henry leap from security to security. The new job is well in hand before he quits the old; everything is carefully set, with artillery preparation laid on, before he moves."

True enough, but so is what Ford said about his new job. "It might be thought something of a step, for I had no personal funds. What money was left over from living was all used up in experimenting. . . . There was no 'demand' for automobiles—there never is for a new article."

That his move actually was a tremendous gamble is suggested by the fact that not one of his Detroit Edison friends, these men who thought nothing of staying up all night long milling and welding on Ford's behalf, would risk joining his new concern.

He urged Bell, rebuilder of the Quadricycle, to come along: "Dave, Dave, you'll go with the business."

Bell said, "Henry, I've got a wife and family and I can't take the chance."

Ford said he couldn't pay Bell "wages, but he would keep a record. He'd give me a paper for it."

Decades later, Bell said with matter-of-fact rue, "It would have made me rich."

In the end, of all Ford's old friends, only Fred Strauss joined him. Strauss had come with Ford to see the Cass Avenue factory, and only then discovered that Ford was interested in automobiles.

One associate followed without hesitation: "My wife agreed that the automobile could not be given up—that we had to make or break."

Clara Ford's first two decades with her husband seem a study in unassuming courage. In 1897 they'd moved from Bagley Avenue to an eighth home, and now—with the seven-year-old Edsel just starting out in public school—they'd be moving again, to Second Boulevard near the Detroit Automobile Company.

The backers were far more confident than the Edison Illuminating crew. They signed a three-year lease on the factory, and announced that the first cars would be finished by October first.

Frank Alderman, secretary of Detroit Automobile, said, "We have several new devices in connection with the construction of our automobiles, on which patents are now pending, which will make them as near perfect as they can be made. We have solved the problem of the bad odor [of half-burned fuel] by securing perfect combustion, and with our improved method of applying power to the rear axle and keeping all the machinery hidden from sight, we will have a fine motor carriage. We expect to have 100 to 150 men employed before the year is past."

October came and went, and so did November and December, and no motor carriage left the gates of the Detroit Automobile Company. It was not until mid-January that the first car emerged.

It wasn't a car; it was a "delivery wagon," perhaps chosen by Ford to demonstrate the versatility of internal combustion: Here was no toy; this can take an honorable place in the working world.

The delivery wagon, a glossy cube riding high above four pneumatic tires, could not have had a more auspicious advent. Just a little over a month into the new century Henry Ford took a reporter from the *Detroit News-Tribune* for a ride. The man was fascinated by his adventure and wrote an account of it that took over the front page of the paper's second section on the first Sunday in February.

"Swifter Than a Race-horse It Flew Over the Icy Streets," the headline ran. The text beneath offers a glimpse of Ford as promoter, and a feel of the tug of his magnet.

The reporter came into the factory out of a bitter day when, the story's subhead says, "Mercury hovered about zero." Inside was the wagon, "smooth-covered, box-topped, with black enamel sides, red wheels, and running gear, nothing but the absence of the proverbial horse revealed that the motive power was to come from within."

Ford said hello, and filled the tank with three gallons of gasoline—enough, he explained, to "run the automobile 100 miles or more at the rate of a cent a mile."

He yanked the engine into life, a worker pushed open a factory door, and "with incomparable swiftness the machine picked up its speed and glided into the wind-blown street. . . .

"The puffing of the machine assumed a higher key. She was flying along at about eight miles an hour. The ruts in the road were deep, but the machine certainly went with dream-like smoothness. There was none of the bumping common even to a streetcar."

"Hold on tight," Ford told his passenger. "When we strike the asphalt we will have a run."

"How fast?"

"Twenty-five miles an hour."

"Hold on!" yelled the reporter in delighted mock-terror. "I get out."

Instead he spotted an approaching milk wagon whose "horse shivered as though about to run away."

"Ever frighten horses?" he asked Ford.

"Depends on the horse." Which might have seemed answer enough during a freezing ride along a busy street, but which Ford eagerly expanded: "A low-bred, ignorant horse, yes; a high-born fellow, no. There's as much difference between horses as between dogs. Some are wise, some otherwise. The other day I was passing down in front of the Majestic building in the big crush; along came a man with a speeding cart and racer. Alderman, who was with me, told me to slack down, as there would surely be trouble. The racer came flying right by us and merely gave a side glance. He was too wise to show any emotion."

In return, the reporter embarked on a meditation on the aural forces of history.

"Whiz! She picked up speed with infinite rapidity. As she ran on, there was a clattering behind—the new noise of the automobile.

"There has always been, at each decisive period of the world's history, some voice, some note that represented for the time being the prevailing power."

Once "the supreme cry of authority" had been the lion's roar. Then came the "hammering of the stone axe" and "the slapping of oars in the Roman galleys." Wind against sails next, and the all-transforming concussion of gunpowder and then, for generations, "the shriek of the steam whistle has been the compelling power of civilization."

But now the reporter is hearing "in the streets of Detroit the murmur of this newest and most perfect of forces, the automobile, rushing along at the rate of 25 miles an hour.

"What kind of a noise is it?

"That is difficult to put down on paper. It was not like any other sound heard in the world. It is not like the puff! puff! of the exhaust of the gasoline in a river launch; neither is it like the cry! cry! of a working steam engine; but it is a long quick mellow gurgling sound, not harsh, not unmusical, not distressing; a note that falls with pleasure on the ear. It must be heard to be appreciated. And the sooner you hear its newest chuck! chuck! the sooner you will be in touch with civilization's latest lisp, its newest voice."

Ford's visionary passenger watched a couple of horses hearing the "new voice" for the first time, but before it could register on them, "the auto had slipped like a sunbeam around the corner."

At one point during this perfect jaunt Ford pointed out a storefront to the reporter. "See that harness-maker's shop? His trade is doomed."

Not yet, though, and not by the Detroit Automobile Company's delivery wagon.

It ran well enough that cold day to light the flues of the reporter's imagination, to give him a taste of the exhilaration that would seize so many people in the next ten years. Here was an engine of liberation, an epochal break with the past.

Many of the men who worked on the delivery wagon, however, said that far from cornering like a sunbeam, it could barely crawl around the block. In a tone quite different from that of Ford's passenger, Fred Strauss remembered, "We did get one of the engines to run on this car, but we had an awful time doing it." Its flywheel was too heavy; all of it was too heavy; and it took far too long to build.

Ford was looking toward quantity production, but didn't yet know how to do it. Every day in the factory was a frustrating lesson in stasis: Engines stood inert on sawhorses until they were tapped and filed and worried into completion, then moved to a chassis. That is, if the components of the chassis had arrived. Almost everything came from outside manufacturers. Meanwhile bodies were being built at the rate of violins, cosseted in every stage of their development.

Nobody knows how many cars came out of the Detroit Automobile Company. Perhaps no more than a dozen; possibly fewer than that.

Part of the problem was the scattered state of an enterprise that was still too nascent to properly be called an industry. Part of it was

Ford's perfectionism. But there seems to have been something else that was holding back the best-financed automobile company of its day. Ford disliked working for backers, even though he understood the necessity of having them, and this may have slowed his pace, though by all accounts during that time he was working steadily and hard. Surely he would have felt an increasing frustration at being unable simply to will speedier production.

One gets a sad glimpse of this in Fred Strauss's summary of the sinking Detroit Automobile Company. "Henry wasn't ready. He didn't have an automobile design ready. . . . Henry gave me some sketches to turn up some axle shaftings. I started machining these axle shafts to show them we were doing something . . . but they didn't belong to anything. We never used them for the automobile. It was just a stall, until Henry got a little longer into it."

But busy pointless machining and, later, gears laid out in gleaming patterns on worktables could not forever divert the backers from seeing that none of this enterprise was coalescing into cars.

A few months after his confident predictions, Alderman glumly observed, "You'd be surprised at the amount of detail about an automobile."

By the summer most of the directors were beginning to get disgusted with Ford, although Murphy remained loyal to him. At one point the backers convened a meeting that Ford, who by now had managed to persuade himself that he was being ill-used, refused to attend. "If they ask for me," he told Strauss, formulating a fib he would use again and again down the years, "tell them that I had to go out of town."

The day after the meeting, Alderman told Strauss the company was going to move out of the big factory and lay off most of its workers. Strauss could keep a few of them to run a much smaller experimental shop.

The show table of pretty machinery would have to go, said one particularly hard-nosed director. "Throw all that stuff out, bury it, get rid of it."

Strauss was especially saddened by the condemnation of four truck bodies that "were as elaborately built, designed, painted and finished as are pianos." There was no reprieve. "We put them in the boiler room. Charlie Mitchell our blacksmith, and I took sledge hammers and busted all those beautiful bodies. Then we burned them under the engine-room boiler."

To this desolate scene, said Strauss, "All at once Henry came in one morning and came into the experimental shop." He had Spider Huff with him and they got right to work on what Strauss called a "little car."

If Ford felt any grief for his fast-as-a-racehorse delivery wagon and its beautiful woodwork, he never said a word about it.

The little car—which seems to be what the directors wanted from him in the first place—was a regular automobile and, according to Strauss, "It ran pretty good."

Not good enough for its creator, who kept making improvements while autumn turned to winter and the stockholders fretted and then began to pull out. Mayor Maybury, now running for governor, stood by Ford, and even bought more shares, bringing his holding up to five hundred. So did Murphy, who continued meeting the bills. He had met eighty-six thousand dollars of them before the Detroit Automobile Company filed notice of dissolution in January 1901.

Still Murphy stuck. The lumberman and a handful of the original shareholders bought up the remnants of the company at a receiver's sale and kept financing Ford.

No record remains of how generously they were backing him, but perhaps there is a hint in the fact that in January Henry and Clara moved into their tenth home, with Henry's father and sister Jane, who themselves had recently left the family farm to spend the winter in the city. William Ford paid the rent.

His son wasn't there as much as Clara would have liked. The diary she kept for a few months at that time is full of entries like the one in which she recounts her surprise and pleasure at having "met Henry on the crowded streetcar coming home."

On February 1 she "spent half hour with Henry, then took the train to Kate's"—her sister, in Jasper, Michigan, who was about to have a baby. On February 3, "Snow all day. Wrote a letter to Henry. Felt pretty lonely."

Her husband must have, too. He was spending nights on a cot he'd set up in the small patch of the Cass Avenue factory that his backers had saved for him. But the shadowy galleries around him, hired for a production run that never materialized, seemed to depress him not at all. He and Spider Huff and Oliver Barthel were working steadily. So, too, was a twenty-two-year-old newcomer with the Byronic name of Childe Harold Wills (he never used the Childe, but did pass it on to his son).

Wills's father was a master mechanic. His son wanted to be a painter—when he was seventeen the *Detroit City Directory* listed him as an "artist boarding at home"—but the next year he was working as an apprentice toolmaker while studying metallurgy in night school. Within three years he had not only gotten a job in the engineering department of what would become the Burroughs Adding Machine Company, but was its superintendent.

Automobiles interested him more and more, and he sought out Henry Ford. The two men discovered an instant affinity that went beyond Ford's ability to charm good people into working for him.

Like Ford, Wills was happy to work two jobs, or at least indifferent to the pressures of doing so. Unlike Ford he was a brilliant draftsman. Where the former could instinctively know the strengths and weaknesses of any machine he could look at and touch, the latter could envision the machine, put it on paper, and see whether it would work well or not, all without going near a lathe.

What they—Ford, Wills, Huff, Barthel—were trying to make that spring of 1901 had nothing to do with the "little car" that, if ever produced, might sell to a public that was growing more confident in the future of the automobile. In fact, it was that car's antithesis.

CHAPTER 6

"Glory and Dust"

"We had to race"; Smiling Billy's World's Championship Sweepstakes; Ford vs. Winton: "A thin man can run faster than a fat one"; the Henry Ford Company; "The materialization of a nightmare."

I never thought anything of racing," Ford said long afterward. This seems true: He had grown up without once seeing that then ubiquitous American diversion, a horse race. But now he was building a race car.

Ford later explained that he'd had no choice: "The public refused to consider the automobile in any light other than as a fast toy. Therefore we had to race."

It is true that the public had become interested in auto racing. Rich Americans were buying heavy, expensive European machines. William K. Vanderbilt, an early and loyal enthusiast, brought over the "Red Devil," a thirty-five-horsepower Mercedes so costly he had to pay seven thousand dollars on it just in customs duties. He raced it, and won, and generated headlines across the country. There was prize money to be made as well: The Chicago races run the September before had offered a purse of ten thousand dollars.

Still, there seems something disingenuous in Ford's insistence that this spectacular road was the only one open to him. He was still getting support to build a motorcar for regular folks, not moneyed daredevils, and if only he could bring the "little car" to a point where he could say: There; that's it; this is how we'll build it, he had a far better chance than most would-be car builders of getting into production.

He couldn't say it. Possibly he sensed launching his car on the seas of trade as some final surrender of control. Perhaps he still was not confident he could produce cars in any quantity. The great advantage of a race car was that you could enjoy a famous success making only one.

The drawback was that it had better *be* a success. Once Ford had committed himself to the racer, he was quite right about the importance of racing, at least as far as Henry Ford was concerned. If his car failed, that was the end of even tenuous financial support for his automaking ambitions. He could try to get his Edison job back, and then tinker with the little car as a hobby for the rest of his days.

Ford put into the racer all the energy his backers urged him to devote to the car they wanted to produce. The one they didn't diverted Ford from his love of lightness. It took shape at sixteen hundred pounds, which was not heavy for racing cars of the day, but three times the weight of the Quadricycle. Barthel worked closely with Ford—so closely that, fifty years later, he claimed to have "designed the car from the ground up," and its engine, too. The latter had two seven-inch cylinders, lying horizontally, mounted beneath the driver. This was the traditional place, but out ahead of the engine coils of thin copper cooling tubes serving as a radiator were strung across a sort of maw in the front of the hood. For, unlike most automobiles and any that Ford had yet built, this car *had* a hood: It looked like a car. Its machinery was not encased in the shell of a horse-drawn carriage (some of the first automakers were so respectful of tradition that they mounted sockets for buggy whips on their machines).

Scientific American admired the completed car in an article not about technology but aesthetics called "Style in Automobiles." The author, a motoring enthusiast named Hrolf Wisby, complained that "comparatively little is being done by the automobile makers toward guiding the public taste." Instead, they were pandering to "horsey people" with "horseless carriages of a horsey style." This is "a silly combination. An automobile is not merely a vehicle bereft of horses."

Only the racing car, said Wisby, "is progressing toward a definite style," and is showing "a distinct improvement over the most graceful French patterns."

And "the latest American racing automobile, the Ford, possesses features entitling it to credit as being the most unconventional, if not the most beautiful, design so far produced by American ingenuity.

"It is a model that commends itself strongly to the automobile experts because of the chaste completeness and compactness of its structure. In this rarefied type of racer, the . . . chauffeur seat has been shaved down to a mere toadstool perch . . . the carriage arrangement so detrimental to a clear, unsophisticated style, has been avoided. . . . No matter how we may choose to view this machine, it is an automobile first and last."

But this tribute appeared in November, when the car had become a celebrity. In the early spring it was still a half-furtive, half-finished cipher.

As always, Ford was grasping for things to improve it even as he was building.

One day a Norwegian immigrant entered the much-dwindled Cass Avenue factory and introduced himself. He was Peter Steenstrup, he said, and he represented the Hyatt Roller Bearing Company of Newark, New Jersey. He didn't speak English very well, but he spoke it well enough to tell Ford why Hyatt's were the roller bearings he needed.

Of course Ford knew what a roller bearing was. Together with ball bearings, they made the automotive industry possible. On a nineteenth-century wagon the turning axle would be supported by a housing that was kept from sawing through it only by the lavish application of grease. This wouldn't work with cars; their axles turned too swiftly.

But if between the hole in the mounting and the axle there is a circle of steel balls, the friction is so radically reduced that it might as well have disappeared. That's how ball bearings work.

Roller bearings do the same thing, and provide far more support. Roll a marble between the flat of your hand and a tabletop, and you'll instantly feel what a tiny amount of surface the ball is touching at any time. That's a "point" bearing. Now roll a pencil between your hand and the table: that's a "line" bearing.

Roller bearings are line bearings, clustered in a ring like the ball bearings, but each—at least the ones Steenstrup was promoting—perhaps five inches long. They circle the axle and let it turn freely. Even if a machine won't actually ruin itself without them, Steenstrup told Ford, the savings in energy are tremendous. And there was more: Hyatt made roller bearings not just out of solid metal cylinders, but out of strips of cold steel twisted into a tube like a long spring, and cut to length. Given their flexibility, they adjusted themselves to any irregularities in either the turning axle or its housing.

Steenstrup was a salesman. He had begun his American career as a bookkeeper at Hyatt, but when a big machine tool company in Providence, Rhode Island, had turned down Hyatt's salesman, he had begged to go and try himself.

This not surprisingly annoyed his superiors, and his boss said, "We can't have fresh guys around this plant. Since you're so smart, Steenstrup, you can go to Providence. Don't come back unless you get an order."

He came back with the order, explaining with some pride that he'd finally gotten it by bursting into tears.

He didn't have to cry for Ford, who liked him, and was sold. The racer would have ball bearings on its front axle, and roller bearings—Hyatt roller bearings—on its rear.

The axles carried thirty-six-inch wire wheels and four-inch tires. The ignition, as always, was a problem. Huff and Barthel talked it over and decided that an igniter might be far more effective if it were insulated by porcelain, which, along with glass, was used to make insulators for power and phone lines. But who knew anything about porcelain? Barthel suggested Dr. Sanborn, his dentist, who fashioned replacement teeth out of it. Huff and Barthel drew up a spark coil, and Barthel took it to Dr. Sanborn, and a few days later emerged from his offices with the first modern spark plug. This morning time of the industry could bring forth something new and tremendous at any moment.

By summer, the car was ready to try out. The engine was so loud that Ford thought it prudent to have a team of horses pull it to the outskirts of town before opening it up. When he did, on West Grand Boulevard, he claimed he burned through a half mile at seventy-two miles per hour. This would have broken every record of the day. Who knows? Barthel said the car was capable of that speed.

In any event, the machine was done. Ford wanted to go east and challenge Henri Fournier, the French driver—the most famous of the time— who had won a Paris–Berlin race in his Mors, and was now knocking down speed records in America. But as it happened, Ford's opponent turned out to be an American, and came to him.

In 1901 Alexander Winton was the best-known carmaker in America. Part of his reputation came from publicity, but most rested on the fact that, unlike Ford, he was actually building and selling automobiles, and racing them, too.

Born in Scotland in 1860, he trained as a marine engineer on the River Clyde before following a married sister to Cleveland, where he established first a bicycle repair shop and then, in 1892, a bicycle factory. His business did well enough to finance the interest in automobiles that overtook him almost immediately. By July 1897 his brand-new Winton Motor Carriage Company had produced a car capable enough to carry its maker from Cleveland to New York. This considerable feat—eight hundred miles in slightly less than seventy-nine hours—attracted some mild interest in the press but to Winton's annoyance nothing more. He decided he would have done better had he brought with him a publicist instead of Bert Hatcher, his shop superintendent.

Still, he sold twenty-two cars in 1898. One of the first went to a customer who didn't think much of it. After some attempts to soothe the man, Winton—who had a temper—told him that if he thought he could build a better car, then he should go do it. The customer was James Packard, and he did just that.

In 1899 Winton made the Cleveland–New York run again, this time in the company of Charles B. Shanks, a correspondent for the *Cleveland Plain Dealer* recently returned from the Spanish-American War.

Shanks knew his business. He declared at the outset that the trip was the result of a bet he'd struck when he'd heard Winton boast that he could accomplish the journey in less than fifty hours' running time. Shanks telegraphed reports from every stop along the way. He sent a self-deprecating but scary account of him and Winton being thrown from the car when it hit a boulder, and followed it with some humor about rural folk being terrified by the approach of the horseless apparition. ("It appeared to them no doubt as the sight of a brick block leaving its foundation and chasing up the street would appear to us.") By the time he and Winton were approaching Manhattan, the whole country was following them.

If there had actually been a bet, Winton won it, arriving after forty-seven hours. That year he sold over one hundred cars, more than any other American manufacturer. And Shanks's vigorous promotion had finally settled the issue raised by the *Chicago Times-Herald* in the ballyhoo for its race. "Motocycle" had gone down, but the leading car magazine of the day, *Horseless Age*, was pushing for the machine to be universally known as a "motor carriage." Shanks throughout his journey used the French word "automobile," and it took hold.

In the spring of 1901 the automotive press reported that Winton was building "heavy racing carriages," iron-framed, seventy-horsepower machines that weighed half a ton more than Ford's racer. Winton built four of them, sold three, and kept one for himself.

During the autumn, Ford and Huff kept testing the racer, once as far away as Dearborn, where

William Ford took time off from husking corn to get his neighbors to help plane off the pocked top of the old Scotch Settlement Road to give his son a place to set a speed record. But even with the improvements, the road wasn't up to it.

Ford would have a chance to prove his car soon, though. Three promoters had announced their plans to mount Detroit's first car race. With the huckstering solipsism of the era, they called it the "World's Championship Sweepstakes." One of the backers was Daniel Campeau, a political rival of Maybury's; one was "Smiling Billy" Metzger, owner of a bicycle store and, as his name suggests, a fixture in local organizations and parades; and the third was Charles Shanks, whose accounts of his Cleveland–to–New York trip had been so successful that he was now Alexander Winton's sales manager.

There was little doubt that Winton would take the world championship. Along with announcing a thousand-dollar prize for the main event—a twenty-five-mile race—Shanks chose a supplementary award, an elaborate cut-glass punch bowl with a diadem of accompanying cups that he thought would show particularly well in his boss's bay window back in Cleveland.

The race was to be run on October 10, out on the mile-long Grosse Pointe horse track, made ready for the mechanical interlopers by having its curves banked with earth.

If Ford liked to keep his choices open to avoid giving the final Let's Go, there was no chance of evading this one. The strain of preparations told on him and his wife in opposite ways: "I think Clara is awfully fleshy," her sister Kate wrote that August, "but Henry is awfully thin."

He did not pay in his entrance fee until the night before the race.

The three promoters had sold the city on their spectacle. "The event is the talk of Detroit's smart set," wrote the *Free Press*. "The boxes are almost engaged and the display of feminine finery is expected to attract quite as much attention as the speedy machines.

"One of the most promising contesters is the Detroit chauffeur, Henry Ford."

The day started with what the press called, and what almost certainly was, the largest parade of automobiles ever seen in "the West." "There were more than 100 machines in line and not a horse in sight!"

Grosse Pointe was a summer resort then, and already buttoned up for the empty winter months, but even there automobiles crowded the track. "The horse was forgotten. All around the horse were other things, large, small, white, black, red, yellow. . . . Outside along the fences where usually are found tally-hos and coaches with their gay parties, were long rows of these things instead."

The event was a sellout, the mile-long track's grandstand full and, said the *Free Press* reporter, "A crowd on the lawn in front and a row of railbirds clear down past the three-quarter pole."

Rain had been forecast, but instead it turned out to be a fine tall blue October day.

Unfortunately the race was boring. At the start, anyway. The five preliminary events before the main one, contests of steam cars, electrics, and so forth, were all wan: The one-mile race for the electric cars was won by Walter C. Baker of the Baker Motor Vehicle Company at 4:49, more than thirty seconds slower than the record for the mile run by a human on foot.

Responding to the crowd's rumblings of jocose disgust, the flexible Smiling Billy immediately improvised a "special event." Alexander Winton would "try to break the world speed record."

The obliging Winton got behind his wheel and took three turns around the track, in one of them clocking a mile at $1.12^{2}/5$. This indeed was a new world record. But even while Winton was setting it in Detroit, at the Empire City track in New York Henri Fournier was warming up his Mors to run the mile in $1:06^{4}/5$. The next day the *Evening News* headline ran, "Glory Soon Gone."

This casual demonstration of the Winton's ability cannot have been encouraging to Ford. It perked up the onlookers, though, and prepared them for the climactic event of the day, the

World's Championship race. This was open to all comers, and Smiling Billy had said there would be twenty-five contestants.

Three made it to the starting post: Ford, Winton, and a Pittsburgh sportsman named William Murray, who had bought one of Winton's heavy racers. At the last moment Murray's car started bleeding oil from a cracked cylinder, and its owner had to withdraw.

The earlier events had consumed far more time than had been allotted them. This (and perhaps the desire to avoid a grisly and tiresome embarrassment in which the world's speed record holder lapped the failed local carmaker time after time) caused the promoters to trim the twenty-five-mile race back to ten.

Ford started his car. Spider Huff, who would ride with him, crouched down on the narrow running board, taking hold of a pair of brackets that looked about as substantial as filing cabinet pulls. Charles Shanks, publicist, sales manager, and punch bowl advisor, apparently as versatile and daring a man as Huff, would serve as Winton's riding mechanic.

Ford knew his car was fast. What he didn't know was how it would corner on the track's turns. He'd not yet put it through a turn at all. And the car had no brakes.

Winton's car vibrated next to his, potent with seventy horsepower and its newly won speed record. Ford's engine could put out twenty-six horsepower.

"A fat man cannot run as fast as a thin man," Ford had said. Nevertheless, Winton's physical and moral advantages immediately made themselves clear: He took the lead at once, and easily held it for the first five miles.

The turns frightened Ford. He did fine on the straightaway, but lost ground when he backed off on the gas to skid into another of the endless successions of hard lefts. At each one, Spider Huff would coolly swing himself out from the body of the car, acting as a counterweight, and then crouch back down. The two men, who had never done anything like this before, began to develop a rhythm. Ford got through the turns more quickly. The gap between the cars narrowed.

Now Ford's care with every aspect of the mechanical showed its value. His engine did not begin to pump out smoke, and Winton's did. A reporter wrote that Spider Huff "hung far out in his effort to ballast the car. After three miles Winton was a fifth of a mile to the good. . . . Then Ford on the sixth lap shot up perceptibly. A thin wreath of blue smoke appeared at the rear of [Winton's] machine and it gradually increased to a cloud." Winton pushed hard, and so did Shanks, who squirmed around on the bucking car to pour oil on the running gear, but it did no good.

Clara Ford, watching in the stands, wrote her

brother, "Henry had been covering himself with glory and dust . . . I wish you could have seen him. Also had heard the cheering when he passed Winton. The people went wild. One man threw his hat up and when it came down he stamped on it, he was so excited. Another man had to hit his wife on the head to keep her from going off the handle. She stood up in her seat & screamed 'I'd bet fifty dollars on Ford if I had it!' "

Afterward, Ford stood exhausted by his car while it cooled down in the October dusk. He told one of his hundreds of new fans, "Boy, I'll never do that again! That tight board fence was right here in front of my face all the time! I was scared to death."

The punch bowl eventually shed its anomalous splendor on a landing in Clara Ford's new rented house on Hendrie Avenue—a modest place, but one she did not have to share with in-laws.

A little more than a month after the race Clara Ford wrote her brother Milton, "We are keeping house again and are very happy to be alone. We have a very nice cozy little house. We did not build on account of Henry building the racer. He could not see anything else. So we will have to put up with rented houses a little longer. We got Edsel a bicycle for his birthday. He rides it to school and thinks it fine. He and Henry have raglan overcoats."

These luxuries—bicycle, raglan coats, in-lawless home—all happened because however reckless Ford had been to gamble everything on winning the first race he'd ever seen, he had redeemed himself thrillingly and publicly.

His backers saw this. Murphy had been at the race, and immediately began preparing to form another carmaking operation, this one wearing the new celebrity's name: the Henry Ford Company.

Murphy had already spoken to Ford about this when Henry, feeling flush, went to New York City in early November to have a look at the second Madison Square Garden automobile show (the first had been held the November before).

Ford paid the fifty-cent entrance fee and walked into a barking, fuming, boisterous arena.

The early auto shows were far more strenuous for their stars than the modern ones are. This exhibition was more like the horse shows that had preceded it, because the cars were not merely on display: They had to prove they could move around nimbly under their own power.

Automobiles banged into noisy life and circled the arena, ran obstacle courses, bumped over little bridges, and did everything their sellers could devise to show the machines' abilities. Up on the roof of the Garden, promoters of the Mobile Steamer had built a tall, moderately steep ramp that led to empty sky so that people could watch the Mobile hiss up it, then complacently roll back down.

Henry Ford wasn't intimidated by busy machinery, but there was a lot to take in, and he was getting tired when he heard someone call his name.

He turned to see Peter Steenstrup waving to him from the railing of the stand behind the Hyatt Roller Bearing exhibit. Ford went over, shook Steenstrup's hand, took off his derby, and wiped his forehead with a handkerchief.

"Come in," said Steenstrup. "Where could you find a better place to rest? Sit down at the railing and see the show from a box seat."

Steenstrup introduced Ford to his partner, a young engineer named Alfred Sloan. He and Steenstrup had been spending the day watching from their perch to see which cars drew the most attention from the crowd: the Lane, the Lozier, Col. Pope's Toledo Steamer, the Autocar, the Stearns, the Locomobile, and the Oldsmobile, Ransom Olds's popular little one-cylinder runabout, which was the closest existing exemplar of what Ford's backers wished he would build.

Sloan wrote, "So we three sat and watched the cars go round in the show ring below and talked, for hours I guess." He remembered his guest in a pose that would be characteristic of the man for the rest of his life: "Mr. Ford was tilted back in a

152

chair, his heels caught in the topmost rung, his knees at the level of his chin."

Sloan liked his partner's client, but had little idea that "much was to come from our association with Mr. Ford: fabulous orders for roller bearings." Even less did Sloan "suspect that I was talking with a man who was to take a foremost place among the industrial leaders of all times."

Nor did Ford suspect, as he waded back into the melee of exercising cars and the fog of exhaust, that he had met, in this agreeable twenty-seven-year-old, his Nemesis.

On November 30, 1901, Murphy and several of his original investors filed incorporation papers for the Henry Ford Company. Ford was named chief engineer, and given a sixth of the stock. The company acquired a factory on Cass Avenue where Ford was going to create the car that it would produce. Ford and Barthel began working on a two-cylinder runabout.

And then the company's namesake began to make himself scarce. Barthel, who had joined the firm as a designer, soon discovered where Ford's true enthusiasm lay. "He did not seem inclined to settle down to a small car production plan. He talked mostly about wanting to build a larger and faster racing car. This, together with some dissatisfaction as to the amount of interest he was to share in the company, led to a considerable amount of dissension between himself and Mr. Murphy."

Surely the tone of grievance in a letter Clara wrote her brother Milton just two days after the incorporation papers were filed belongs at least as much to her husband as it does to her: "Henry has worked very hard to get where he is. That race has advertised him far and wide. And the next thing will be to make some money out of it. I am afraid it will be a hard struggle. You know how rich men want it all."

Ford had nothing to say about a small-car production plan in his own letter to Milton, written on imposing new stationery headed "HENRY FORD COMPANY" and bearing, next to the hopeful legend "BUILDERS OF HIGH-GRADE AUTOMOBILES AND TOURIST CARS," a portrait of the victorious racer that is as crisp and authoritative as the engraving on a stock certificate.

In his note, Ford speaks of his continuing desire to get Henri Fournier to race against his car. "If I can bring Mr. Fournier in line there is a barrel of money in this business . . . I don't see why he wont fall in line if he don't I will challenge him until I am black in the face. . . . My Company will kick about me following racing but they will get the advertising and I expect to make $ where I can't make ¢s at manufacturing."

He was quite right about his management

kicking. Murphy told Barthel that if he helped Ford with his race-car designs he'd be fired. The dutiful Barthel continued to work surreptitiously on the racers at night.

Not for very long, though. A little over four months after its formation, Henry Ford left the Henry Ford Company.

His backers had finally grown sick of what could be seen as six straight years of procrastination. For his part, if Ford thought his sixth share in the enterprise too meager, he may also have been vexed by the appearance at the factory of a gaunt, white-bearded man who looked like an El Greco saint, only less jolly.

This was Henry Leland, grim, acerbic, deeply pious, and one of the finest machinists in America. His shop, Leland and Faulconer, could cut parts to $1/100,000$ of an inch. Now he was making engines for Ransom Olds, and Murphy wanted his opinion on what Henry Ford was doing.

Leland's opinion wasn't high. Having played a crucial part in the success of the one-cylinder Oldsmobile, he advised that the two-cylinder engine Ford had been working on was needlessly complex. The company should drop it: Leland had just developed a greatly improved motor that could squeeze ten horsepower out of its single cylinder.

Leland asked the directors to keep the factory alive for long enough to try out his engine. Such was his reputation that the discouraged men agreed to give it one more shot. Leland's engine went in the prototype body that Ford and Barthel had built.

In his autobiography Ford groused about his time at the company. "I could get no support at all toward making better cars to sell the public at large. The whole thought was to make to order and get the largest price possible for our car. And being without authority other than my engineering position gave me, I found that the new company was not a vehicle for realizing my ideal but merely a money-making concern—that did not make much money. In March 1902, I resigned, determined never again to put myself under orders."

Despite Ford's insistence on their venal obtuseness, once Leland gave the backers something to sell, they produced it quickly, and in increasing volume.

Ford left with nine hundred dollars, the half-done plans for his new racing car, and the assurance that the enterprise would cease using his name. The firm chose a new one: the Cadillac Automobile Company.

All that remains today of the Henry Ford Company are a few sheets of its handsome stationery. And, of course, the Cadillac.

What of Ford, carrying nine hundred dollars and his sheaf of unfinished plans out into the raw

Detroit March? As when he left Edison, his quitting was not quite as reckless as it might seem. A photograph of a family picnic he took a few weeks later shows a relaxed and smiling Clara Ford, the stress-gained "fleshiness" her sister had written of melted away. Nine hundred dollars sounds skimpy today, but it could support Ford and his family for half a year. More important, in jumping, he had carefully chosen where he was going to land.

Among the spectators at the October race were two professional bicyclists. During one of the event's many longueurs, Smiling Bill Metzger had urged them out onto the track, but the crowd was interested in automobiles that day, and paid little attention.

They were named Tom Cooper and Barney Oldfield, and they were famous. Bicycle racing was for a while as big a sport as prizefighting or the horse track, and offered purses just as fat. But the "bicycle craze"—and it really did approach the dimensions of a craze for many years—had in 1897 begun to shrink with a suddenness as unexpected as it was inexplicable.

Hundreds of thousands of bicyclists remained, of course, and always would. But Cooper and Oldfield, not long before the objects of fervid national attention, felt themselves drifting toward irrelevancy while still in their early twenties.

Like the bicycle industry itself, they were drawn

toward the motorcar. The Grosse Pointe race fascinated them, and Tom Cooper spoke with Ford during that day.

Then, while Ford was working erratically with his second round of backers, Cooper and Oldfield invested in a coal mine and went to Colorado to run it. This is slightly less surprising than if they had gone west to found a literary magazine, but it was an odd enough choice. What is not surprising is the speed with which they discovered they detested the work.

In February 1902, Cooper was back in Detroit, and talking to Ford again. He wanted a racing car, and he'd done so well at bicycling that he had something like a hundred thousand dollars set aside to invest in it. This was more than sufficient, as Ford's first race car had cost about five thousand dollars. The bicyclist and the mechanic struck a deal: Cooper would pay the bills; Ford would build two racing cars; and one would belong to his partner.

Ford rented a modest workshop on Park Place and Oliver Barthel came to help. He was still working for what was now Cadillac, and later said that Ford offered him 10 percent of all his future profits if Barthel would come on full-time. Barthel agreed to help in odd hours, but he was too cautious to leave Cadillac, and thus joined the many who were brushed by the tail of Henry Ford's comet but failed to take hold of it.

Harold Wills did, apparently working free in exchange for a share of whatever would emerge. And Spider Huff, between bouts of the remorse or whatever it was that occasionally drove him back to Kentucky, was there, too.

Wills and Ford worked together fluently and without friction that season. Although Wills could draw up a plan with a speed and precision that Ford never approached, the two men were similar in temperament. Both liked to discover whether things would work by building them. When told there was a book that offered clear instructions on a project he was attempting, Wills said, "If it's in a book, it's at least four years old and I don't have any use for it."

These men spent the cold spring of 1902 (Ford and Wills would sometimes pull on gloves and box just to warm up) building the two biggest, most powerful automobiles yet made in America.

The machines, all but identical, were well over ten feet long, with a wheelbase of nine feet nine inches, and the yard-high wheels set more than five feet apart. The chassis rode low on the wheels, probably at Cooper's suggestion. The cars carried absolutely nothing that wasn't essential to their being able to move.

In September, with the racers nearly finished—in good time for the second annual Grosse Pointe race, to be run on October 25—a *Detroit Journal* reporter wrote, "All the machinery is exposed.

Oilcups and polished wheels gleam alongside of black wires which lead to entirely exposed batteries. Being racing autos they are 'stripped.'" They were nothing but chassis: The engine, whose four cisterns of cylinders displaced eleven hundred cubic inches, was bolted directly to a suspensionless frame made of two long planks fortified with steel.

The *Automobile and Motor Review* reported, "Built for speed and speed alone, the two new racing machines . . . are first-class examples of how an automobile may be simplified by the 'leaving off' process. This most recent addition to the ranks of racing monsters has power and means to apply it; it has few conveniences, no luxuries and not the slightest indication of a frill or decoration. Not even an attempt has been made to hide the machinery, for a motor-bonnet is not necessary to speed, and no other considerations matter."

Another magazine account, in the *Automobile*, was harsher. "Technically [the racer] . . . is an automobile, practically it is an engine on wheels, a machine in which brute strength and disregard for all the essentials of modern automobile construction are embodied."

Ford had one of the cars painted red, and one yellow. The red one he named the *Arrow*, the yellow the *999* after the New York Central locomotive whose tall driving wheels had carried it to a world speed record of 112.5 miles per hour in 1893.

That paint required plenty of maintenance. The reporters weren't exaggerating about the cars' being stripped down, nor about their being primitive even by the automotive standards of 1902.

Not only did the cars lack a hood over the engine, but every single piece of running gear—valves, flywheel (all 230 pounds of it), and transmission—was unshielded. The cars boiled along in a thunderstorm of their own making, a cloud of flung oil at whose heart blue lightnings of exhaust flickered. The noise alone, said Ford, was "enough to half kill a man."

The *999* was finished first, and on September 17 Ford drove it around the Grosse Pointe track, although not against any competitors: He'd said he'd never do that again, and he never did. A reporter from the *Journal* was there and told how the car treated its driver. "Mr. Ford was a daub of oil from head to foot. His collar was yellow, his tie looked as though it had been cooked in lard, his clothes were spattered and smirched, while his face looked like a machinist's after 24 hours at his bench."

Ford had wanted a fast car, and he got one. The *999*, propelled by perhaps as much as one hundred horsepower, had come awfully close to the automotive grail of a mile a minute on an oval track—1:08—but the car had scared its builder: "I cannot quite describe the sensation. Going over Niagara Falls would have been but a pastime after a ride in one of them [the two cars]. I did not want to take the responsibility of racing the *999*."

Neither did Tom Cooper, once he'd spent some time at the throttle. But, as the year before, Ford *had* to race.

Cooper thought of his friend Barney Oldfield who, after his brief, joyless immersion in the mining business, had moved to Salt Lake City. "He lived on speed," Cooper told Ford. "Nothing would go too fast for him."

Cooper sent a telegram and Oldfield came to Detroit. He was tough, sanguine, and good-natured. He'd never driven a car, but he was philosophical about the risks. "I may as well be dead as dead broke," he told Spider Huff.

Still, he was startled when he first saw the racers.

"We didn't build these for looks," Cooper said.

"You sure as hell didn't. They're ugly as sin!"

A lot of contemporary observers felt the same way. One British reporter said the racers were "the materialization of a nightmare."

In fact, the *999* is an example of Ford's dictum about the most beautiful things: They are "those from which all excess weight has been eliminated."

The massive block of an engine up front, the

low frame, the gallant confidence of its single ("one life to a car was enough," Ford said) bucket seat, the big, wire-spoked wheels—all combine to give the 110-year-old *999* a look of sculptural modernity. And, for all its essential brutality, of lightness: "Weight may be desirable in a steam roller but nowhere else," Ford said. "Strength has nothing to do with weight. The mentality of the man who does things in the world is agile, light, and strong." It is the *999* and not the previous year's racer that most closely approaches the *Scientific American*'s description of being the first automobile truly to look American.

Nevertheless, Cooper and Ford were wise to be wary of it. Oldfield, though, expressed no qualms, even when Ford told him why the car was steered not by a wheel, as his first racer had been, but rather by a fork-shaped tiller a little like a vertical pair of bicycle handlebars. Oldfield didn't record what Ford said, but another racing driver who asked about the steering did: "You see, when the machine is making high speed, and for any reason the operator cannot tell at the instant because of dust or other reasons, he is going perfectly straight, he can look at this steering handle. If it is set straight across the machine he is all right and running straight." Grosse Pointe was, of course, an oval track. If Oldfield recognized the absurdity of the anodyne explanation, he didn't say so.

"It took us only a week to teach him to drive,"

Ford wrote. "The man did not know what fear was. All that he had to learn was how to control the monster. Controlling the fastest car of today was nothing as controlling that car. . . . On this car I put a two-handed tiller, for holding the car in line required all the strength of a strong man."

Oldfield remained confident. Ford apparently did not. Here, at another point that could have made his career, he withdrew. The cars were proving fussy; sometimes they wouldn't start. In the middle of October Ford in effect shut down his new business by selling both of them to Cooper (or, more accurately, selling one, since the cyclist already owned the other by the terms of their agreement). Cooper paid eight hundred dollars, which sounds like a small price until one considers that he had covered all the expenses, and that Ford was leaving with enough money to support his family for another half year.

But if Ford had wished to shield his reputation from the caprices of the untried automobiles by shedding his ownership of them, he failed. The press was greatly interested in the cars, and invariably referred to them as the "Ford racers."

Whatever strains may have accompanied his break with Cooper, Ford said he was there at the Grosse Pointe racetrack on October 25. Indeed, he fired up the *999* for Oldfield that day: "While I was cranking the car he remarked cheerily, 'Well, this chariot may kill me, but they will say afterward that I was going like hell when I hit the bank.' "

There were four contestants in the five-mile race: Oldfield; Alexander Winton, back with a bigger, more advanced race car that he called the Bullet; a driver named Buckman; and the doughty Charles Shanks in another Winton.

It was Oldfield's race from the start. Winton kept up for a while, but the speed of Ford's car, coupled with its driver's swashbuckling indifference to the laws of physics, dominated. Oldfield wrenched the "steering handle" from side to side, but kept it hard left on the turns, which he slewed through like a motorcyclist, the rear wheels cutting arcs in the dirt before they again dug in.

Winton's old trouble returned: His car started misfiring, and he had to withdraw after the fourth mile. Oldfield lapped Buckman, then Shanks. He boomed past the finish line having devoured the five miles in 5:28, a record he topped the next spring when he circled a mile track in a third of a second under a minute.

Cooper took his cars, and Oldfield, and together they campaigned around the Midwest staging exhibition matches. When Oldfield won at Grosse Pointe the crowd had pulled him from the car and carried him around. His fame only grew, and even today strikes a faint chord in the national memory, the only name from the heroic age of American auto racing to hold that residual power.

Everywhere he and Cooper appeared, the press spoke of the "Ford machines."

Cooper was killed in New York City—a car accident in Central Park—in 1906, but Oldfield kept on going. By 1910 he was able to charge four thousand dollars for an appearance.

Toward the end of his life (long, for a racing driver of those days: He lived until 1946), Barney Oldfield liked to tell people, "Henry Ford said that we made each other." Then, his victories and prize money far behind him, he'd add, grinning, "I guess I did the better job of it."

CHAPTER 7

The Seven-Million-Dollar Letter

Malcomson's gamble; from a toy printing press; the Dodge brothers; the Ford Motor Company; "This business cannot last"; the (first) Model A; "BOSS OF THE ROAD."

After Clara Ford died, on the last day of September 1950, somebody inevitably asked, "I wonder if Mr. Ford left any papers."

He had. He'd left virtually every piece of paper he'd ever handled. Nineteen-fifties industrial archaeologists entered Fair Lane, his last, big house in Dearborn, with the same wonder and surprise that Howard Carter and Lord Carnarvon had entered Tutankhamen's tomb thirty years earlier.

As Henry and Clara Ford had aged, they'd given over one after another of the house's fifty-six rooms to stacks and drifts of memorabilia, and papers, papers, papers. Today the Ford Archives, among the greatest of all such American repositories, hold ten million of Ford's papers: a newsboy's forty-five-cent bill for delivering a month of the *Detroit Evening Journal* to 58 Bagley Avenue in 1894; receipts for the payments the couple kept up on that player piano; a 1919 telegram from Henry Ford to the Chase National Bank releasing $175 million to the company's stockholders.

There with all the other paper—the letters from Franklin Roosevelt and Calvin Coolidge and a relative who had made a ten-dollar deposit on a toupee and couldn't come up with the thirty-five-dollar balance (Ford sent it to him)—is a bill for five dollars' worth of coal, which Ford paid on May 28, 1895, to Alexander Young Malcomson. This may have been the day Ford first met Malcomson. If so, it was one of the most important days of his life.

Alexander Malcomson, a short, powerfully built man in his midthirties, had been born in Scotland and immigrated at the age of fifteen to Detroit, where he found a job as a grocery clerk. Within five years he not only owned a grocery store but had gotten bored with it. Energetic himself, he became interested in the nation's prime source of energy, and sold his store to enter the coal business.

He began with a single wagon and zeal, like so many entrepreneurs of the day. But he also had an idea about the industry: The real money lay not only in selling the product, but in its speedy delivery. The zeal before long got him 110 wagons and a half dozen coal yards. The idea made him Detroit's leading coal supplier.

Most coal wagons were heavy, laboring along

behind six-horse teams. Malcomson hitched three horses to lighter wagons and lesser loads and got faster and more regularly to his customers. These grew to include housewives and steamship lines and factories. He was scrupulously fair: He never took advantage of the occasional coal strike and its accompanying fuel scarcity to gouge his clients. The whole city knew his company's motto "Hotter than Sunshine" (it may have sounded catchier to the 1900 ear).

The coal business seems steady, even stolid; but Malcomson had a restlessness of spirit evident in the quick, darting raptor's glances with which he raked every conversation. He was, as his son would put it, "the plunger type, a man who did not hesitate to take chances."

He was fascinated by the plunger's favorite machine, and he owned a Winton. He had probably seen Ford's Grosse Pointe racing victory; if not, he knew about it within hours.

The two men struck up a friendship when Ford was buying coal from Malcomson for the Detroit Edison boilers. During early 1902 Ford talked with him about how they could start a motorcar company.

Ford was still involved with his racing behemoths then, but once again, despite the seeming recklessness of abandoning them, he had carefully cleared the way for his next step.

He didn't talk to Malcomson about racing cars:

He wanted to build the will-o'-the-wisp that had lured on his previous investors, a low-priced runabout.

On August 20, 1902, the two men went to the offices of Malcomson's lawyers, John W. Anderson and Horace H. Rackham, and signed a partnership agreement. Ford would contribute his tools, plans, and experience, and henceforth concentrate on building a prototype of the new car. Malcomson would give him five hundred dollars right away to get things started, and pay what was needed as the project went forward. The prototype, Ford assured him, would cost no more than three thousand dollars. Once it was finished, the two men would form a manufacturing corporation in which their combined shares, split evenly between them, made them the majority stockholders.

The enterprise, Ford and Malcomson, hired one significant employee, Childe Harold Wills. Although he would be a bulwark of Ford's success, and become the nation's foremost metallurgist, Wills made one early contribution that everyone recognizes today. The company was trying to come up with what we would now call a logo, and nobody liked the various blocky FORDs that draftsmen offered. Wills remembered that when he was in his teens he had a toy printing press from which he made some money by striking off business cards for neighbors.

He still had the set, and his type case yielded up

a script *FORD* with a little break in the O and the top of the F sweeping confidently toward the D. This looked pretty good to everyone back then, and you'll see it if you go outdoors today.

Malcomson was true to his word, and Ford would get his money, but somewhat on the sly. In building his business the coal dealer had stretched himself to the limit. He didn't want his bankers to know he was veering into a risky and wholly unconnected enterprise. Before long, Detroit banks would be notorious for shoveling money toward almost anybody who was able to say "car company," but not now, not in 1902.

To keep his credit intact, Malcomson paid Ford through an account he had set up in the name of his office manager, James Couzens. Though Ford could have no idea of it at the time, this was another tremendous stroke of good fortune for him.

It is almost unnecessary to say that the prototype didn't cost three thousand dollars. By November Ford had gone through seven thousand dollars and Malcomson was feeling badly pressed. In August he'd had the sunny idea that once he started selling cars, the influx of money would take care of the overhead, and the business would pay for itself. But in November, Malcomson—in charge of business matters, as Ford was of technical ones—decided he had to form the company. It would issue 15,000 shares of stock, at ten dollars each. Ford and Malcomson would split 6,900 shares as compensation for their efforts thus far, and pay cash for 350 more. That left 7,750 shares, which, once sold, would bring in plenty of working capital.

Sold to whom, though? Nineteen oh three had dawned, and the year would see fifty-seven new automobile companies struggling to get born, all of them thirsting for capital. Ford had already mined out the richest strata of Detroit investors. He tried his old boss Alexander Dow, who received him cordially, but had not changed his mind about the gasoline automobile. Years later, he said, "I didn't know then, of course, that he was going to make millions of the blame things."

It was left to Malcomson, then, to badger his friends and associates as winter turned to spring.

Two early believers were the lawyers who had helped draw up the original agreement, John Anderson and his partner, Horace Rackham. They were different in many ways: Rackham, forty-five, was a stern prohibitionist; Anderson, some years his junior, liked a drink and a cigar and a noisy restaurant. But both men shared qualities that, however appealing in many human beings, are not entirely helpful to lawyers. They were timid, shy, and gentle.

Their little office was struggling. Unable to afford either a secretary or a typewriter, they spent their pinched days writing longhand letters either gingerly inquiring whether clients might be interested in paying the fees they'd incurred, or mildly rebuking the people the clients were sore at.

But on June 4, John Anderson sat down and wrote a long letter that turned out to be well worth the wrist-cramping amount of effort he put into it, for it eventually netted him $17,435,700.

The letter was to his father, a Civil War surgeon who was now the mayor of La Crosse, Wisconsin, asking him for five thousand dollars to invest. It is clear, persuasive, and largely honest—a fine selling letter. It is also the best firsthand account we have of the birth of the Ford Motor Company.

"Dear Father," John began, "Horace and I have an opportunity to make an investment that is of such a character that I cannot refrain from laying the details before you for consideration.

"Mr. Ford of this city is recognized throughout the country as one of the best automobile mechanical experts in the U.S." There follows a summary of Ford's racing history and (this is as close as the writer came to fantasy) a wonderfully benign account of his dealings with Leland: "Several years ago he designed, perfected and placed on the market a machine. A Co. was organized, but not long after, desiring to devote his attention to a new model entirely, he sold out his patents and interest, and retired. The machine is known as the 'Cadillac' (you will see it advertised in all the magazines). . . ."

He then turned his entire attention to the designing and patenting of an entirely new machine. Mr. Malcomson, the coal man, backed him with money and the result is they have now perfected and are about to place on the market an automobile (gasoline) that is far and away the best of anything that has yet come out. . . .

Having perfected the machine in all its parts, and demonstrated to their complete satisfaction and to the satisfaction of automobile experts, and cycle journal representatives from all over the country who came here to inspect it that it was superior to anything that had been designed in the way of an automobile, and that it was a sure winner, the next problem was how to best and most economically place it on the market. After canvassing the matter thoroughly, instead of forming a company, with big capital, erecting a factory and installing an extensive plant of machinery to manufacture it themselves, they determined to enter into contracts with various concerns to supply the different parts and simply do the assembling themselves.

So, they entered with the Dodge Bros. here to manufacture the automobile complete—less wheels and bodies—for $250. apiece, or $162,500, for the 650 machines, which were to be delivered at the rate of 10 per day, commencing on July 1st. if possible, and all by Oct. 1st. I drew this contract, so know all about it.

So the Dodge brothers came into Henry Ford's life, and he could scarcely have found two colleagues more different from himself.

Alfred Sloan once wrote, "I saw nothing of the mining camps of the West and nothing that happened when oil was struck, but I did see Detroit." The gasoline engine and its myriad promoters, from gifted engineers to "manufacturers representatives" living out of their suitcases, were giving the long-established city something of the feverish evanescence of a boomtown. Into this volatile brew of hope and money and opportunism, John and Horace Dodge brought a whiff of the all-but-vanished violence of the frontier.

Now in their late thirties, the Dodges had been born to a blacksmith in southeastern Michigan, and gone to Detroit in the 1880s to become expert machinists. Horace worked two years with Henry Leland and then the brothers went across the river to Canada and set up a bicycle factory. It prospered enough for them to move back to Detroit, open a machine shop, and win the contract to make engines for Olds.

As against this admirable rising professional arc, they were both loudmouth saloon brawlers. The brothers were inseparable: They dressed even more identically than men of business usually did in those days, and shared the red hair that folklore ties to a quick temper. Horace was the slightly less aggressive of the two, and his wife always blamed John for the scrapes they got into. But Horace clearly needed little encouragement. One time they smashed all the light bulbs in the chandeliers of the Cadillac Hotel; once, in a scene truly reminiscent of Tombstone days, John pulled a pistol on a saloon keeper and made him "dance" on top of his bar while using his free hand to fling glasses against the mirror. There must have been a lot of glasses, because this particular spree cost John Dodge thirty-five thousand dollars in damages.

But to continue with John Anderson's pitch to his father, what he wrote next is also true: "Now Dodge Bros. are the largest and best equipped machine plant in the city. They have a new factory, just completed and it is not excelled anywhere. . . . Well, when this proposition was made them by Ford and Malcomson, they had under consideration offers from Oldsmobile, and the Great Northern automobile Co. to manufacture their machines, but after going over Mr. Ford's machine very carefully, they threw over both offers and tied up with Mr. F. and Mr. M.

"Now in order to comply with this contract, which was made last Oct. Dodge Bros. had to decline all outside orders and devote the entire resources of their machine shop to the turning out of these automobiles. They were only paid $10,000/on account, and had to take all of the rest of the risk themselves. They had to borrow $40.000., place orders for castings all over the country, pay their men from last October (they have a large force) and do everything necessary to manufacture all the machines before they could hope to get a cent back."

Most of the car accounted for, Anderson enumerates the rest: bodies and cushions from the C. R. Wilson Carriage Company (suppliers of the seat to the Quadricycle); the wheels from a firm in Lansing at twenty-six dollars per set of four; the tires "by the Hartford Rubber Co. at $46.00 per set (4 wheels)."

Where would the wheels from Lansing join with the Hartford tires and then with the Dodges' chassis and the Wilson company's cushions? "They found a man from whom Mr. M. rents a coal yard on the belt-line R.R., with a spur track running into it. He agreed to erect a building designed by Mr. Ford for their special use, for assembling purposes (which will cost between

3 & 4 thousand dollars) and rent it for three yrs. to Mr. F. and Mr. M. at $75. per month. This building has been all completed and is a dandy. I went all through it today. It is large, light and airy, about 200 feet long by fifty ft. wide, fitted up with machinery necessary to be used incidental to assembling the parts, and all ready for business."

Amid all that light and air "the workmen, ten or a dozen boys at $1.50 per day, and a foreman fit the bodies on the machine, put the cushions in place, put the tires on the wheels, the wheels on the machine and paint it and test it to see that it runs 'o.k.', and it is all ready for delivery. Now this is all there is to the whole proposition."

It might not sound like much of a proposition: a "dozen boys" in a seventy-five-dollar-per-month wooden factory patching together parts pulled in from various works around the countryside and offering the result as an automobile. But given the immense amount of capital necessary to create a factory that could accommodate the whole job of building a car under one figurative roof, the independent supplier and his piece-work were almost inevitable. For a while, budding car companies even argued for the system's superiority: The Cole, one of the hundreds of hopeful automotive brands that lived its mayfly life in those years, boasted about the clear advantage its "assembled" cars enjoyed over "manufactured" ones. With the former, the fortunate motorist was drawing on the long-refined skills of any number of different machinists; the latter was by necessity a sloppy and hastily improvised orchestra of metalworkers doing many things a little beyond their abilities.

There is some truth to this with the Dodge brothers. They had all the business that they could handle with Olds, but Ford's two-cylinder engine that Leland had thought excessive evidently sold them on the idea that Henry Ford was the man to go with. The shift involved a good deal of expensive retooling on their part, but in the end they were willing to bet their company on it.

Anderson sided with the short-lived Cole and the now 110-year-old Ford operations. His letter continues: "Now, as to the investment feature. You will see there is absolutely no money, to speak of, tied up in a big factory."

He goes on to speak about product. The "tonneau" he mentions is actually a backseat. The basic model car was a two-seater, with a sloping rear. If the plunger wanted the tonneau, he would pay another hundred dollars. Tonneaus are described in the literature of virtually all cars of the day with words like "effortlessly attached with seven latches." Fat chance.

Here's where Dr. Anderson will get his returns: "The machines sell for $750., without a tonneau. With a tonneau $850. This is the price of all medium priced machines and is standard. It is what the Cadillac and the Great Northern sell for here, and what other machines elsewhere sell for. Now the cost, figured on the most liberal possible estimate, is as follows."

Machine	$250.00
Body	52.00
Wheels	26.00
Upholstering	16.00
Tires	40.00
Cost of Assembling	20.00
Cost of Selling	150.00
Total cost	554.00
Cost of tonneau	50.00
	604.00
Selling price with tonneau	$850.00
Cost price	604.00
Throwing off $46 (for any possible contingency)	46.00
	$200.00

Anderson adds a couple of notes to his triumphant summary: Even without the tonneau, the car will net $150; and the rather stiff-looking "cost of selling" includes "advertising, all salaries commissions, etc. 20% on each automobile (it will really be nearer to 10 or 12)."

And now the money will flow in: "On the seasons output of 650 machines it means a profit of $97,500 without a tonneau, and more in proportion to those sold with tonneaus, and of course the latter is almost always bought, as it adds to the capacity of vehicle."

Now, the demand for automobiles is a perfect craze. Every factory here (there are 3, including the "Olds"—the largest in this country—and you know Detroit is the largest automobile [manufacturer] in the US.) has its entire output sold and cannot begin to fill their orders. Mr. M has already begun to be deluged with orders, although not a machine has been put on the market and will not be until July 1st. Buyers have heard of it and go out to the Dodge Bros. and inspect it, test it, and give their orders. One dealer from Buffalo was here last week and ordered twenty-five: three were ordered today and other orders have begun to come in every day, so there is not the slightest doubt as to the market or the demand. And it is all spot cash on delivery, and no guarantee or string attached of any kind.

Mr. Malcomson has instructed us to draw up articles of incorporation for a $100,000.00 limited liability company, of which Mr. Ford will take at least $51,000 (controlling interest) and the balance he is going to distribute among a few of his friends and business associates, and is anxious that Horace and myself go in with him. Mr. Couzens is going to leave the coal business, for the present at least, and devote his entire time to the office and management of the automobile business— and he is a crackerjack. He is going to invest, as he expresses it, "all the money he can beg, borrow or steal" in stock. Mr. Dodge, of Dodge Bros, is going to take 5 or 10 thousand, and two or three others, like amounts. Horace is going to put in all that he can raise, and I do want to do the same if I can, because I honestly believe it is a wonderful opportunity, and a chance not likely to occur again. Mr. M. is successful in everything he does, is such a good business man and hustler, and his ability in this direction, coupled with Mr. Ford's inventive and mechanical genius and Mr. Couzens's office ability, together with fixed contracts which absolutely show what the cost will be, and orders already commencing to pour in, showing the demand that exists, makes it one of the very most promising and surest industrial investments that could be made. . . .

I went into the Dodge Bros. plant and the assembling rooms today, and even into the room where the half dozen draughtsmen are kept under lock and key, (all the plans, drawings and specifications are secret you know) making drawings and blue-prints of every part, even to the individual screws, and was amazed at what had been accomplished since last October. Not another Automobile Co. has started and got its product on the market inside of three years before this.

Dr. Anderson read his son's letter and headed for Detroit, spurred on not by enthusiasm but by caution. John had once gotten him involved with a Chicago fire-sprinkler company that had eaten a good deal of Dr. Anderson's capital before expiring as though poisoned by it.

What he found in Detroit did not reassure him. His first stop was at the "large, light and airy" new plant.

I came to see the factory which I had heard so much about. It was nothing prepossessing . . . just a little building on Mack Avenue in which the cars were being assembled from parts made elsewhere.

James Couzens was at the plant when we were there, and he offered to drive us to town in his first Ford car. On the way he attempted to drive through a small park, but the car stalled on a small hill. After frequent attempts to cross the little hill, Mr. Couzens was forced to detour around the block. That was my first auto ride.

Dr. Anderson could have saved himself some trouble and anxiety simply by staying put in La Crosse after receiving his son's lengthy plea. He was evidently a fond father for, after having looked with dismay upon the Mack Avenue factory and gotten stuck in the park in its sole product, he gave his son the five thousand dollars he'd asked for.

All the fund-raising went like that—slowly, the money arriving in painfully extracted dribs and drabs.

Despite his dismal ride with Dr. Anderson, James Couzens remained convinced that this was the one great chance of his life. As he'd told John Anderson, he was going to put all the money he could "beg, borrow, or steal" into it, but this came to $400. His schoolteacher sister Rosetta had managed to save $200 over her lifetime. Couzens, now every bit as much a believer as Clara Ford, told her to throw all of it in with Ford. She said she couldn't do that without asking her father's advice. This would have vexed Couzens; he deeply disliked his father. But instead of saying something like "don't you dare gamble a dime on those devil wagons," the elder Couzens reasonably suggested she halve the risk by putting in $100. This she did, and by 1919 had cleared $355,000 on her gamble.

Charles Bennett, president of the Daisy Air Rifle Company, was combining two errands when he stopped in at his tailor's to order a new suit while on his way to buy an Oldsmobile. He was chatting with the tailor about his future car when another customer peered out through the curtains of the adjoining booth.

"Pardon me," said Alexander Malcomson's cousin Frank, "I couldn't help overhearing your conversation. Have you heard about the Ford car?"

Bennett had not, and amiably allowed himself to be hustled over to Mack Avenue to see the prototype and its builder.

He met Henry Ford at his most charming, and the car on its best behavior, and forgot about the Oldsmobile. For a heady few days it looked as if this industrialist might combine his highly successful company with Ford, but his board pointed out that Daisy's bylaws did not permit it to merge with another enterprise. Still, Bennett said he was good for a five-thousand-dollar investment.

The most cash came from the banker John S. Gray—$10,500. He was Malcomson's uncle, and it was the family tie alone that brought him in. "This business cannot last," he told friends, and refused to ask anyone he knew to invest in Ford, even when, three years later, he had gotten back his ten thousand and fifty thousand on top of it.

The Dodge brothers were in a position to drive a hard bargain, and they did. It was their demands that pried the $10,000 loose from the deeply reluctant Gray.

As John Anderson pointed out, they'd agreed to abandon their other automotive business to make Ford's cars. They gave promissory notes for $10,000, thus acquiring fifty shares of stock each. Then they said they had to have $10,000 in cash, too. Gray supplied it and mournfully added an extra $500 for operating expenses.

On a humid, unseasonably warm Saturday night in mid-June of 1903, the shareholders got together in Malcomson's ramshackle office, which looked more like the domain of an 1880 small-town depot master than the crucible where the twentieth century was being born.

The eleven men there (Gray was evidently too mortified to attend) gave over their money or their promises of money. Couzens had scrambled successfully enough to be able to pledge $2,500. The Ford Motor Company—the name was Malcomson's suggestion—started in business on June 16. Two days later it absorbed what had been the Ford-Malcomson limited partnership.

John Gray was president, Henry Ford vice president and general manager—at $3,600 a year—Couzens treasurer. The company had issued $100,000 in stock. $28,000 had been paid in. Or, its pledgers assured, soon would be.

The Dodges started delivering in July, the chassis pulled from their Monroe Street shop by dray horses. Ford's dozen workers would put on the wheels, thread some wiring to the batteries, test the engine, clean it up, fix it to the body, and send the machine out to an eager public.

So John Anderson had envisioned the process, but it didn't go that way.

The sanguine view of "assembled" cars, in which each contributor does his best work on his own specialty, might have made perfect sense with steam locomotives or windmills or anything else that had been around for a while. Automobiles hadn't.

The Ford car was nothing like the Olds the Dodges had been working on. The chassis the brothers had signed up to deliver was composed of scores of parts that had never before existed in quite the same form.

This meant that every intricacy of the car—which may look like a naïve little antique to us today, but was one of the most complicated things in the world in its time—had to be designed and, most important, drawn perfectly so the Dodge mechanics would know what to do.

Here Ford's career depended on Wills. Ford knew what he wanted, but he couldn't draft a plan.

Wills could, superbly, and he turned out hundreds of them.

Nobody could have done it better, but still it was all new. Further complicating the process was that the Dodges paid by piecework—that is, the more engines you make in a day, the more money you get. The result was reflected in an encounter between Ford's tester, a man named Fred Rockelman, and the Dodges. Rockelman had a fierce temper—all his life Ford attracted bad-tempered associates—and when Rockelman found that the flywheels coming in did not fit tightly enough on the crankshafts, he went to the Dodge works and expressed his dissatisfaction in such a manner that John Dodge told him to get the hell out of his shop and stepped forward to slug him.

"Go ahead!" shouted Rockelman. "Throw me out! But that won't make us accept engines with loose flywheels!" Rockelman grabbed up a finished crankshaft from the shop floor, and easily slid it into a nearby flywheel.

The Dodges, demonstrating the frontier ability to leap from fury to camaraderie, laughed, said the joke was on them, and promised they'd do better. Everyone shook hands, and the Dodges did do a little better.

Still, the problems seemed to multiply them-selves even as the cars came together.

The car was given the name Model A, with its

hopeful suggestion of being the progenitor of a long run of alphabetical successors. Wills had done an immense amount of the work that brought it into being, but it was wholly the product of Henry Ford's mind.

It was light. Later he said "it was lighter than any car that had yet been made." He knew better than that: At 1,250 pounds it weighed 400 pounds more than the Oldsmobile. But in a way, Ford was justified in his hyperbole, because the Model A was a great deal of car for the money. Ford had hoped to sell it for $500, but in the end the cost came to $750—and another hundred with the tonneau. That was nonetheless a very good price for an automobile that had an eight-horsepower, two-cylinder engine that pushed it along at thirty miles an hour while running more smoothly than any single-cylinder could.

The body contributed to the car's relative lightness. One of those first dozen workers, Fred Wandersee, who had been hired to sweep the floors of the place, described fitting it to the chassis. "The body came on a hand truck and they picked it up and put it on. The fellows could lift a car body easy enough. After the car was assembled one fellow would take hold of the rear end and one the front and lift the whole thing up." It had been painted a single color: crimson.

Final fitting included the attachment of vestigial fenders. One of the workers said, "You could wear them as a luck charm, they were so small."

The car itself was small—a wheelbase of just six feet. Clearly this disturbed its creator's sense of proportion. When shown an accurate rendering of the car in profile for his company's first advertising efforts, Ford told the illustrator to "stretch it out. It looks too short."

The Model A appeared at a slightly more dignified but still plausible length in magazine ads that July: "BOSS OF THE ROAD," read one that ran in *Frank Leslie's Popular Monthly.* "This new light touring car fills the demand for an automobile between a runabout and a heavy touring car. It is positively the most perfect machine on the market, having overcome all drawbacks such as smell, noise, jolt, etc., common to all other makes of Auto Carriages. It is so simple a boy of fifteen can run it."

"Always ready, always sure," another ad said. "Built to take you anywhere you want to go and back again on time. Built to add to your reputation for punctuality; to keep your customers good-humored and in a buying mood. Built for business or pleasure—just as you say."

It could go fast, "without acquiring any of those breakneck velocities which are so universally condemned." This from the father of the *999*, and somewhat contradicted by another advertisement: "It is your say, too, when it comes to speed. You can—if you choose—loiter lingeringly through shady avenues or you can press down on the foot-lever until all the scenery looks alike to you and you have to keep your eyes skinned to count the milestones as they pass."

Finally, always, the company promoted the Model A's "exceedingly reasonable" price, "which places it within the reach of many thousands who could not think of paying the comparatively fabulous prices asked for most machines."

All these virtues—simplicity, reliability, dependability, cost—were portents of what would make the Ford Motor Company the Ford Motor Company, and they struck a chord with potential car buyers below the Vanderbilt level.

The *Leslie's* ad finished with a mildly preposterous claim—"for beauty of finish it is unequalled" (at the time the body was being painted by a couple of guys in what Wandersee described as "a barn down the alley")—followed by a bravely preposterous one: "—and we promise IMMEDIATE DELIVERY."

There were no cars to deliver when the advertisements were written. Ford's handful of workers struggled heroically ten hours a day to rectify this as soon as the Dodges sent the first of the 650 chassis mandated by the initial order. Working two or three to a car, some adjusted the carburetors, some made sure the brakes gripped, some pulled out faulty valves and ground them on one of the few machines in the Mack Avenue factory. One of them remembered, "We used to try to get out fifteen cars a day. We would work our hearts out to get out fifteen cars a day."

Getting out even fifteen cars a day cost money, and none was coming in. The company was struggling before the first chassis appeared.

On June 26 the Ford Motor Company had $14,500 on hand. The next day John Anderson turned over his (father's) money, and now there was $19,500. Ten thousand of that went at once to the Dodge brothers. Then $640 was sent to Hartford to buy the tires. Five thousand more to the Dodges; $7 for the charm-bracelet fenders; $22 as per order of C. H. Wills for "sundry bills." By July 10, after being in business for less than a month, the Ford Motor Company had a bank balance of $223.65.

Five days later the starving newborn received sustenance in the form of a check drawn on the Illinois Trust & Savings Bank. A Chicago dentist named Pfennig became the company's first customer. As Anderson had optimistically predicted to his father, Dr. Pfennig had ordered the tonneau, so the check was for $850.

By summer's end, the Model A had proven itself a success. "The business went almost by magic," Ford said. "The cars gained a reputation for standing up." During its first fifteen months, the Model A found seventeen hundred buyers.

Not all of them thought that the Boss of the Road deserved any reputation for standing up. Those early models could set their radiator water on a boil when the car was running through a cool day in high gear on a good road. The brakes were serviceable, but not if the Dodge workers had hurried the job, and rectifying their sloppiness meant tearing apart the rear axle. The carburetor, originally a Dodge contribution, was bad, and continued to be until Ford and Wills designed a better one. The spark plugs fouled. Even when the brakes were properly adjusted, their fragile cast-iron drums often shattered.

A very early dealer sent from Los Angeles a sheet of urgent recommendations that can be read as a sort of free-verse summary of the state of the Model A—actually, of the entire automotive industry—in 1903:

Make brakes more sensitive and powerful
    by shortening and adjusting eye-bolt.
See that the lubricator glasses have large
    enough hole.
Put in Schebler carburetor.
Get the valve in the gas tank out of the way
    of carburetor.
Make strut rod end adjustable for wear.
Put battery terminals outside battery box.
Front wheels turn wrong. Steering knuckles
    should be bent differently.

Radiator too small; more radiator tubes needed.

Steering rod eye-bolt wears out too quickly.

Cast iron in which plug is screwed is too long.

Pins in steering wheel should be upset at each end.

Henry Ford was every bit as sensitive to the faults of his car as was his most angry customer.

Had William Murphy been in the room when Ford told the illustrator to make the Model A longer, he might have given a sour grin of recognition and thought: "It's going to happen again." Ford was perfectly capable of deciding to make not only the portrait of his car longer, but the actual car, too. That might hold up production for a month, and then Ford could decide to tackle the carburetors once they'd revealed their shortcomings, and then the brakes would need attention . . .

That Henry Ford didn't follow this all too familiar pattern is due to the combative persistence of one man.

CHAPTER 8

Ford Finds His Greatest Asset

"Who in hell are you?"; Couzens bosses the boss; the cars get shipped; the importance of dealers; an earthquake proves the Model A; parasites; who was Malcomson?

Early in the negotiations between Malcomson and Ford and the Dodge brothers, John Dodge suggested—probably too mild a word—certain changes in the contract.

A dough-faced but sturdy-looking young man scarcely out of his twenties, wearing over hostile blue eyes round wire-rimmed glasses that were at least a decade too old for him, said, "I won't stand for that."

John Dodge looked at him in astonishment. "Who in hell are you?"

"That's all right," said Malcomson, trying to hurry past a potentially ugly impasse, "Couzens is my advisor on this."

James Couzens had not particularly wanted to advise his boss on this Ford Motor Company, but he'd been with Malcomson long enough to know how swollen and thin-stretched the Malcomson coal enterprises were. If Ford failed, so would they. But if Ford could be made to succeed,

Malcomson would handle its business and the coal operations would fall to Couzens. This interested Couzens greatly.

James Joseph Couzens, Jr., seemed to have been looking for an important job all his life. He had been born in the small town of Chatham in Ontario, Canada. His father—who for some reason could not manage to get along with his own father—was heading to America but ran short of money four hundred miles shy of the border and Detroit. He got off the train in Chatham equipped with a grocery clerk's training and the peculiar vein of arrogance that would show up pure in his son.

The senior Couzens did not seek a lofty job—he found work as a handyman in a hardscrabble general store—but he spoke with a studied elegance that would have made his neighbors think he was "above himself."

Chatham, municipal nonentity that it was, had an interesting history. Its citizens played a large part in capturing Detroit during the War of 1812, and half a century later abolitionists decided it should be the last stop on the Underground Railroad. John Brown convened a meeting there in 1858 calling for an invasion of the United States. By the time John Couzens arrived, the town was still so predominantly black that once he'd married a woman he'd brought over from

England and the two produced a baby, neighbors liked to joke that James Joseph Couzens, Jr., was "the first white child born in Chatham."

Before the boy was in his teens he had dropped the Junior—he wasn't going to be anybody's junior—and the Joseph, because he had already established another generation of paternal hostility in the Couzens family.

The father in time had been accepted by Chatham townsfolk as a cheerful and polite neighbor despite his airs, and charmingly deferential to his wife. To his son, he was savage. "I have been panned ever since I was born," Couzens said once.

The results showed up early in James. In elementary school he yanked the principal's beard for no good reason, getting himself suspended. Later he said he "guessed" he did it because to him the principal's beard represented "authority."

A surprise fifteen-hundred-dollar inheritance allowed Couzens Senior to move from the job he'd gotten working in a soap factory to establishing the "Couzens Steam Soap Works, James J. Couzens, Prop."

The consequent change in family status that his son perceived helped convince him you gained manhood by making money, and he set about doing so. He pumped the organ in his father's Presbyterian church for ten cents a week, bolstering this with a dollar a month lighting Chatham's four gas streetlamps every evening.

His personality solidified early. The mother of one of his classmates, a neighbor, complained to Mrs. Couzens that when her daughter called hello to James from across the street, he "deliberately snubbed" her. Chided for his unsociable behavior, the schoolboy explained that "if a girl wishes to speak to me, she should come across the street and do it properly."

He wasn't a schoolboy for long. At the age of twelve he found an ad in the *Chatham Planet* seeking a bookkeeper for a flour mill. High school would be a waste of time, he decided, and applied for the position and (although the circumstances are almost impossible to imagine) got it.

Over his father's vigorous objections he went to work, and did about as well as could be expected from a preadolescent with no training whatever. He was fired and found he didn't like failing one bit. He went back to high school for two years and then, still stinging from his short-lived career, entered a local business college to study bookkeeping.

By 1890 he'd run out of patience with business school and Chatham, and went to Detroit where, just eighteen, he got a job as a car checker on the Michigan Central Railroad at forty dollars a month. Couzens had to note down the numbers on the freight cars that entered the yards, check the seals on their doors, and tack a confirmatory card to the side of each car. This was merely tiresome work in August, but in December, when the cars might roll in carrying a couple of inches of ice on their sides, it was a true ordeal. During bad weather his fellows often glanced at an encrusted seal and simply wrote down "indistinct." Couzens never shirked, always chipping away the ice until the seal yielded up its secrets to his kerosene lantern. Bundled against the Michigan winter, he couldn't fumble in his pockets for tacks, so he held them ready in his mouth, where sometimes the searing cold froze them to his tongue.

All the time, even in the stormy midnight yards, he dressed like a banker. He made few friends in his ramshackle boardinghouse, and his eyes already looked, as they would for the rest of his life, forbidding as gun sights beyond those round lenses.

Railroad bureaucracy rarely moved swiftly, but the car checker's superiors saw what sort of worker they had in Couzens, and when he turned twenty-one and asked for a promotion, they jumped him over several men who'd been with the road years longer to make him the head of the freight office.

Couzens was not a popular boss. Stern, distant, and always cross—his employees began to say that his sole annual smile signaled the spring breaking of the ice on Lake Erie—he nonetheless was grudgingly regarded as a fair one. "He never tried to shift responsibility upon others to shield himself," said a man who worked for him in the freight office. "If he made a mistake, he would own up regardless of what the result might be."

And if Couzens was intemperate with his underlings, he was every bit as abrupt with his superiors, and even with his customers. "The way Jim Couzens talked with these patrons on the telephone," another employee remembered, "giving them holy hell, was just astounding."

He had plenty of opportunity to dispense holy hell because the Michigan Central had just imposed demurrage charges on its clients, which were in effect fines for taking too much time unloading one of the railroad's cars. This angered virtually everyone who used the road, but Couzens had a bottomless capacity for returning anger with more anger.

One of the customers who often got the sharp side of his tongue was Alexander Malcomson. He had plenty of temper himself, but a few bouts with Couzens left him more impressed than annoyed by the man's utter devotion to the interests of the Michigan Central Railroad.

Wouldn't so implacable an advocate be of use to the Malcomson Coal Company?

In 1897 Alexander Malcomson offered Couzens the job of managing the coal company office, including—which surely would have pleased Couzens—all the bookkeeping responsibilities. Given the grandeur of the opportunity, he would be working for fifty-six dollars a month, only four dollars less than the Michigan Central paid for its humdrum duties.

Couzens accepted. A year later he was earning a hundred dollars a month and scrupulously saving enough to have accumulated his four-hundred-dollar hoard when his boss got together with Henry Ford.

Couzens knew nothing about motorcars, and that was fine with him. He remembered going out with Malcomson in his Winton: "Frequently he turned something on the dash board, explaining that he was changing the mixture." Couzens believed his boss meant he was fortifying the gasoline with water, "and I continued to think so for a long time."

He got more interested in automobiles when his employer told him how consumed he expected to be by the Ford operations. While Malcomson was away discussing engine compression and fly-wheels, he'd give Couzens greater responsibility in the coal business, a raise, and a bonus, too.

As it turned out, Couzens never got near the coal business again. During a meeting of the Ford stockholders-to-be, Malcomson explained his plan to John Gray, reluctant president of the new company. Gray was having none of it. Malcomson knew coal best, he said.

No, no, said Malcomson—no need for that: Couzens here is a wonderful manager; he can easily run our coal operations. That's fine, Gray replied: "If Couzens is so good then you can send him to the automobile business. He can watch that for you."

Malcomson protested again, but Gray shut down the debate: "I am putting up my money on you because you are a good coal man. You must stay in the coal business."

Thus Henry Ford was assigned a partner. He offered to drive Couzens home from the incorporation meeting on that close, muggy June night. In the welcome breeze generated by his car, Ford started discussing salaries with his new business manager. He said, "What do you think we should ask from those fellows?"

The simple question was heavily freighted. He and James Couzens were going to be together at Mack Avenue doing work. "Those fellows" were going to benefit from their efforts simply because they'd been able to write checks. The "we" and "those fellows" shine a light forward along the whole track of Ford's life.

In time, Ford would become consumed by his resentment of "those fellows," but in the first months of manufacturing what worried him most were the complaints of the fellows who had bought his cars. Each one stung him. Perhaps it was a shattered brake drum, perhaps one more cavil about the teakettle radiator. Whatever the particular goad, Ford started once again to voice his conviction that the customers were right, that the car wasn't quite ready yet, and had to be improved before it was sent out in the market. Another month or so should suffice.

Such scruples had already wrecked two promising companies, but those operations hadn't had James Couzens's infinite reserve of stubbornness and resource to draw on.

Couzens told Ford no. Couzens would, he said, be willing to dispatch a mechanic to anywhere in the country to fix an ailing Model A, "but stop shipping, and we go bankrupt."

Ford kept shipping. Couzens would accompany him down to the yards—and no man knew his way better around a railroad yard than James Couzens—to make sure that the automobiles were actually aboard the freight cars, and the car doors sealed shut.

Couzens exercised the same fierce vigilance over every aspect of the company's operations. He got to his office in the Mack Avenue plant at seven in the morning, and stayed there until eleven most nights.

Everything that Ford couldn't do, he did. He took care of the books, of course, he kept a constant intimidating eye on the shop floor, and he wrote lively and seductive advertising copy. He made no friends, above or below him. When Alexander Malcomson sold a close acquaintance a

Model A at a discount (a practice forbidden by Couzens), the founder of the company found himself so flayingly berated that he made up the difference to the company out of his own pocket.

A few years later, managers who had authority over groups of workers the size of army divisions would sneak off into the men's room to open a communication from Couzens, so they could absorb in privacy whatever devastations it might contain.

The only people who didn't live in fear of Couzens were his family. When he was still working for the railroad, Couzens had further enraged his stringently Presbyterian father by marrying Margaret Manning, a Roman Catholic. Couzens treated his father's protests as he did those of any agitator about a Michigan Central freight surcharge. The match seems to have been a remarkably solid and happy one. He was a tolerant, even pliant father to his children, and then to his grandchildren. A decade ago his grandson Frank Couzens, Jr., wrote, "We loved him. We knew him as Daddy Jim." The harshest remonstrance he remembers receiving from the scariest man in Detroit came when Daddy Jim "observed me trying to cut my meat with my elbows up in the air. He asked, 'Are you trying to fly, Frank?'"

In the shop, though, one of the workers from the early days said, "He was a manhandler. We went in enthusiastically and he opened up the hydrant on us and chilled us off." Another colleague put it more succinctly: "I called him 'Sunny Jim' because he was so God damned mean."

Couzens was far more than just a hectoring bully. Ford R. Bryan, a historian and descendant of the Ford family, writes that "Ford by himself could not have managed a small grocery store, and Couzens could not have assembled a child's kiddie car. Yet together they built an organization that astounded the world."

The Model As came off the line—or, rather, their sawhorses—and were tuned and shined to the best of the small factory's ability, and sent out into the world to fare as well as they could despite all their imperfections. Behind them came the Ford mechanics, dozing in the smoking cars of trains that were taking them ever farther from Detroit, stepping down and checking in under the stained ceilings of railroad hotels, seeking out exasperated owners and jollying them into a better mood, fixing the cars, of course, and then reporting the problems back to Mack Avenue where Ford and Wills were quick to address them.

The steering rod eyebolt was strengthened, the eggshell brake drums made thicker, the carburetors replaced. When Ford's friend Peter Steenstrup wrote an anguished letter beginning, "You have broken faith with me!" because he found that the new cars contained ball bearings and not the Hyatts Steenstrup had promised in his advertisements, the roller bearings came into the recipe. Bit by bit, gear by bolt, Ford and Wills and their workers improved the Model A on the fly. Each month saw a more reliable product shipped forth on the implacable tides of Couzens's schedule. The Model A that went to customers in early 1904 looked identical to its predecessor sent six months earlier, but it was a different car. It had, under the steady and heeded hectoring of salesmen and customers and Wills and Ford and Couzens, been entirely reworked; even, in Allan Nevins's word, "reborn."

The Model A had grown up to be an excellent car, worthy now of the premature praise with which Couzens had varnished it. Couzens, who understood everything about the car business except how a car worked, looked at the books and they told him that during the two months ending on September 30, 1903, 215 cars had been built and (here he surely would have hazarded a rare smile) 195 of them shipped. Moreover, as Anderson had assured his father, 159 of them went out capped with the desirable and profitable tonneau.

On November 21, Couzens had the company pay its shareholders a 10 percent dividend. Ford contracted with the Dodges for 725 more chassis, wanting them at the rate of 7 a day. The Mack

Avenue plant grew a second floor, another five thousand dollars' worth of faith in the company.

Henry Ford practiced none of his random disappearances during these months. He was always there, always accessible, always willing to lend a hand. One of the men working on the chassis remembered, "If there was a dirty job and he had a good pair of trousers on, he wouldn't hesitate a minute in those days to tackle any job."

His peppery tester Fred Rockelman said, "At the time we looked upon Mr. Ford as our great godfather or benefactor. We were always able to go to his office because he would have an open door and we felt he had a great sense of understanding of mechanics."

Ford's bonhomie had thorns in it, though, even then. One of those first dozen he hired was a mechanic named Dick Kettlewell, a young man whose long, grave, innocent face was so trusting that it made him the object of practical jokes. Most of them were on the exploding-cigar level, but here is one that Ford and the famously dignified Wills (well, he was in his twenties, but still . . .) worked out together. The two men fixed a live wire to the metal urinal in the shop's men's room, and waited until Kettlewell paid it a visit. Judging the proper moment, one of them threw a switch and the punch of wattage flashed up the stream of urine. A fellow mechanic, Fred Seeman, said, "Dick just gave out one yell and came running out of the toilet before buttoning his pants," while Ford could barely stand for laughing.

This is a harsher practical joke than buttering doorknobs, and far more elaborate than nailing somebody's shoes to the floor. For all the goodwill Ford shed on his Mack Avenue operation, it suggests a coarsening in the man, a nascent cruelty.

The workers who tormented the invincibly gullible Kettlewell would no more have thought of playing a practical joke on Mr. Couzens—which is what Ford himself called the man—than they would have on President Roosevelt. Indeed, they might have picked TR first as the mark, guessing, rightly, that he was better natured.

If Mr. Ford and Mr. Couzens kept a certain distance from each other—and no photograph of the two together betrays the slightest sense of mutual geniality—at first they worked in complete mutual trust.

Couzens believed from the start in the necessity of establishing reliable dealerships at a time when many would-be automobile sellers would display several different machines, knowing that one of the makers would be gone by the spring and that another one's cars wouldn't start. Couzens was pushing for a strictly organized group of dealerships before the first Model A sold, and Ford agreed with him.

Fred Rockelman remembered, "Mr. Ford was always a great believer in service. He always said that a car was never complete, that it was 75 per cent complete when it left the factory, and 25 per cent of the completion was done by the dealers. It needed gasoline, it needed tires, it needed tire repairs, it needed washing, and it needed tuning up. . . . A Ford car as manufactured plus the dealers' service made it 100 per cent in the hands of the public. Mr. Ford from the very early days pressed that the dealers should be able to give service to their cars. That was uppermost in his mind constantly."

Ford himself said, "A manufacturer is not through with his customer when a sale is completed. He has then only started with his customer. If the machine does not give service, then it is better for the manufacturer if he never had the introduction, for he will have the worst of all advertisements—a dissatisfied customer. . . . A man who bought one of my cars was in my opinion entitled to continuous use of that car, and therefore if he had a breakdown of any kind it was our duty to see that his machine was put into shape again at the earliest possible moment."

Ford went on to say that in the days when he was starting out, "The repair men were for a time the largest menace to the auto industry." If "an unscrupulous mechanic [had] an inadequate knowledge of automobiles and an inordinate desire to make a good thing out of every car that came in his shop for repairs, then even a slight breakdown meant weeks of laying up and a whopping repair bill. . . . Even as late as 1910 and 1911 the owner was regarded as essentially a rich man whose money ought to be taken away from him. We met that situation squarely and at the very beginning. We would not have our distribution blocked by stupid greedy men."

The very beginning was William Hughson, a San Franciscan who earned his living by representing eastern manufacturers on the West Coast. In 1902 he went to a bicycle show in Chicago and there was puzzled to come upon a four-wheeled bicycle. He was examining this anomaly when a well-dressed man standing next to him asked, "Interested?"

"What is this thing?"

Hughson wrote that "the man introduced himself as Henry Ford, and the 'thing' as a motor carriage. He hadn't said five words before I began to feel he was the most interesting man I'd ever met. He was a dreamer, too. He talked about the future of his automobile, how it would help people, particularly how it would ease the farmer's burden of heavy toil. A lot of that stuff was over my head, but I felt a complete confidence in this man."

Ford asked Hughson if he might be interested in representing his cars in California. Hughson said sure: "It didn't cost money to be a representative."

That was true, but Ford told his new friend that he'd need about five thousand dollars to buy a stock of cars. This seemed not to bother Hughson in the least: "He agreed to let me know when they would be in production, and I agreed to come back with the money. We shook hands and that was the deal."

Half a year later Hughson showed up in Detroit with five thousand dollars of borrowed money. This was in that hot June when the company was forming. Ford greeted him, said that although he was soon to begin production, there were as yet no cars. Why not invest the money in the company? This seemed like a fine idea to the apparently endlessly optimistic Hughson, but not to his investors, who wired back, "You went to Detroit to buy automobiles. Now buy automobiles."

So the investors, all unknowing, said good-bye to about $35 million and hello to the dozen Model As that eventually arrived—and sat on Hughson's shelf. He "hardly sold one in three years. My partner, George Emmons was a drayman, and we'd rent one out occasionally with a driver. But no sales."

William Hughson and his wife were shaken out of bed on the morning of their fourteenth wedding anniversary, April 18, 1906, by the San Francisco earthquake.

"My cars were in a warehouse on Market Street.

I started to drive there from my office at the other end of town. As I passed the Call Building, the corner fell off it. Before I got to the warehouse, flames were meeting across Market Street like a canopy."

Some of his cars were stuck in the basement, but he managed to wrestle six or seven off the main floor and turned them over to General Frederick Funston, who was in command of the riven, blazing city.

"The United States Army had marched in . . . I went to see General Funston and he assigned every automobile to Red Cross work or helping with the Army. Cars could go where horses balked. My Fords could climb hills, and kept going when others broke down."

Two hundred private automobiles were drafted into service. That it was a hard and steady service is shown by their consuming fifteen thousand gallons of gasoline donated by the Standard Oil Company. When the incandescent streets exploded their tires, the cars clanged uphill and down on their rims, steering around the bodies of dray horses dead from heat and exhaustion.

Ten days later, the *San Francisco Chronicle* wrote, "That the automobile played an all but indispensable part in saving the Western part of San Francisco and at the same time had proved invaluable in the serious business of governing the city through its greatest stress is conceded by every man who has had his eyes open. . . . Old men in the bread lines who had previously occupied much of their time on supper-table denunciations of the whiz-wagons now have nothing but praise for them. Men high in service . . . go even further and say that but for the auto it would not have been possible to save even a portion of the city or to take care of the sick or to preserve a semblance of law and order."

"It was a terrible time," said Hughson. "I lost my voice from inhaling the brick dust; that's why I still talk in this husky whisper. But you know, that was the beginning for the automobile in the West.

"It took an earthquake to show people the soundness of Henry Ford's idea."

General Funston appreciated Henry Ford's idea, and showed his gratitude by having his soldiers knock together a plywood shack at 318 Market Street right in front of the still-warm embers of Hughson's office. "We were the first business to resume on Market Street," Hughson said. "And from then on the automobile business began to grow. Cars became the workhorses in the job of rebuilding San Francisco."

Remembering back across half a century, Hughson said, "Henry Ford came out to the West Coast personally to see if he could help. He said, 'If you need anything, we'll send it out. You pay for it when you can.' Insurance companies were going broke and money was awfully tight. But Ford shipped us carload after carload of cars until we got back on our feet. I never forgot that."

If the Ford visit to the ruined city gives a vibration of the apocryphal, Hughson's feelings toward the man at that time are clearly genuine.

The dealer was, in a way, able to return the favor five years later. In 1911 someone came upon a heap of picturesque wreckage in a West Coast junkyard and recognized it as the *999*, which had campaigned its way to the Pacific and died there. Oldfield went to take a look and said it was scrap, beyond repair. Hughson didn't think so. He bought it and restored it, and today it stands in all its old pugnacious bravado in the Dearborn museum.

Perhaps Henry Ford didn't come personally to visit Hughson, but there's a good chance that Couzens did. He met all the dealers he could, and sized them up with his cold, shrewd gaze. (He clearly approved of Hughson, who eventually was responsible for 120 western Ford dealerships.) Within a decade the requirements for a Ford dealer had been codified, and were strictly enforced: twenty thousand dollars' worth of spare parts on hand; the facilities and willingness to repair any Ford car no matter where it had been purchased; at least one immaculate new model there at all times to show potential buyers; and the strong suggestion that if a disabled Ford had to be taken in to the shop, the towing should take place after dark so as not to draw attention to the car's plight.

While Couzens was building this unprecedented network, Ford's old rival Alexander Winton's advertisements boasted, "Write us direct—WE HAVE NO AGENTS." The Winton Motor Carriage Company built its last car in 1924.

In the spring of 1905 James Couzens could tell the *Detroit Journal*, "We are now turning out twenty-five machines a day on average and giving employment to three hundred men."

His city was enjoying the same boom. That year a *Journal* headline read, "Eight Thousand Men Build Autos." Henry Ford said that the New York Automobile Show should change its name to the Detroit Automobile Show, since Detroit contributed half a dozen times more cars than any other American town. Thanks to its pool of skilled machinists, that year Detroit turned out 11,180 cars. Every part of an automobile was being made there except tires, and that changed in the spring when the Rubber Goods Manufacturing Company started building a plant on the riverfront. The company's president said, "The great industry of today is the manufacture of automobiles, and soon Detroit will be the center of the world in that business." The *Journal* fretted about the coming

"Auto Famine" and said "manufacturers are swamped with orders."

Ford was, and had moved from the Mack Avenue plant to a new three-story building on Piquette that had ten times as much floor space. Here he built the Model A's successors, the B, C, and F (the D and the E disappeared with the experimental models they designated). The C and the F were essentially improved Model As, a little heavier, a little more powerful. The B was a different animal altogether. It was an imposing touring car—the term was just coming into wide use—with a twenty-four-horsepower, four-cylinder engine that could spur it along at forty miles an hour. The Model B weighed seventeen hundred pounds, and cost two thousand dollars. It was Malcomson's baby, and Ford didn't like it.

Malcomson wanted the Ford Motor Company to build expensive cars. In 1906 an Apperson two-seater sports car (although that phrase was still forty years in the future) cost $10,500, and a nice suburban house might go for $2,000. Work out that calculation today: If prices had stayed relative the house would cost $1.2 million, and a Dodge Viper would cost $6 million. Of course it was more desirable to sell something that cost thousands of dollars than something that cost hundreds.

Henry Ford believed exactly the opposite. Make the car cheaper, not more expensive; you'll do better selling lots of low-priced cars to farmers and shop clerks than you will a few lavish ones to millionaires.

In later years Ford suggested that this light-weight, inexpensive everyman's car had been his lifelong goal. In fact it is difficult to discover just when the idea took hold with him, but it was fully formed by the time he founded the Ford Motor Company. In the middle of that year, he told John Anderson, "When you get to making the cars in quantity, and when you make them cheaper you can get more people with enough money to buy them. The market will take care of itself. . . . The way to make automobiles is to make one automobile like another automobile, to make them all alike, to make them come through the factory just alike; just as one pin is like another when it comes from a pin factory, or one match like another when it comes from a match factory."

As his convictions hardened, his friction with the board increased. Couzens, who by now was siding with Ford on virtually everything, just wanted a car that he could sell for more than it cost to build. The Dodge brothers were for an expensive car, but disliked Malcomson and didn't fight on his behalf when he demanded one.

As a leading investor, Malcomson had the clout to get what he wanted. Late in 1905 the Model K came on the market: six cylinders, ten-foot wheelbase, twenty-four hundred pounds and costing more than a dollar a pound, all brass and lacquer and fragrant leather.

At the same time, Ford was feeling his way toward his vision with the Model N. Three feet shorter than the K, and weighing a third as much, it nonetheless had a four-cylinder engine, an unprecedented feature at Ford's asking price: "I believe that I have solved the problem of cheap as well as simple construction. Advancement in building has passed the experimental stage, and the general public is interested only in the knowledge that a serviceable machine can be constructed at a price within the reach of many. I am convinced that the $500 model is destined to revolutionize automobile construction, and I consider my new model the crowning achievement of my life."

Despite this ambitious, even messianic, pronouncement, the crowning achievement did not yet exist. He sent the car to the 1906 New York automobile show with nothing but vacant air under the hood, because the engine wasn't ready. His agents were forbidden to lift that hood no matter what, but the price made the ambitious little car an immediate hit nonetheless.

The Model N's success meant that it *had* to be put on the market for $500, which in turn demanded the most stringent economies at Piquette Avenue. Ford wangled the body maker down from a unit cost of $152 to $72. Some of the savings were fortuitous. One of Ford's associates remembered, "Painting the wheels was considered a highly skilled job, for stripes on the spokes gave a star effect to the center of the wheel. It was quite an expensive operation until the day we refused the painters' demand for more pay per wheel. They went on strike. That settled stripes on wheels. We gave them up, so, in a way, the painters helped us lower costs."

After the Ford Motor Company had squeezed all the excess it could out of the car, and put it on sale for the promised price, the dealers couldn't get enough of them. So eager were they for Model Ns that they meekly swallowed Ford's demand that for every ten Ns they accept one Model K.

Malcomson's ideal car wasn't selling. Ford, a quiet but dedicated gloater, likely gloated about that. He also did a great deal more than gloat.

Even as the Model A was sprinkling prosperity on everyone involved in its creation, friction grew among the shareholders.

Most of the discord came from the different aims of Ford and Malcomson. There was more than that to the acrimony, though. As he had back in the Detroit Automobile Company's brief day, Ford was beginning to resent not being his own man. That Malcomson's faith and capital had made possible his success meant less and less to Ford. He was surely thinking of his chief investor when he said, "Anyone who did not have a part in the manufacturing of the company was actually not contributing and was a parasite."

For his part, Malcomson thought Ford was being both stubborn and perverse. The trend throughout the industry was toward expensive cars. In 1906 half the automobiles sold in America went for between three and five thousand dollars. Why stake your business on sales a tenth this magnitude? A decade later, such cars would command less than 2 percent of the market. But during fractious and hostile board meetings, Ford alone foresaw that.

When the tussling grew from shouted disagreement to an actual corporate fight, it was Malcomson who started it.

He said, truly enough, that the original arrangement had stipulated that Couzens would handle the car business while Malcomson got his coal dealership in order, and then the two men would swap positions. This had been all Couzens wanted when he joined up with Ford a couple of years earlier. But back then he'd believed a car could run on water. His hard-earned success with his partner made him refuse his boss. So did Henry Ford: "I told Malcomson that I did not want him but that I wanted his man Couzens."

Malcomson then seems to have tried to get Couzens fired. Ford in turn persuaded the board to double his business manager's salary from four to eight thousand. This was in part a provocation, and like most deliberate provocations, it worked. Malcomson protested violently at the next shareholders' meeting, despite the fact that the Ford Motor Company had enjoyed a net profit that year of nearly thirty times his initial investment.

As the claustrophobic meetings bickered on, Ford and Couzens decided on a strategy at once sly and forthright.

The Ford Motor Company had advanced to a maturity where it was no longer desirable, and possibly even dangerous, for the company to rely on a single supplier for the heart and muscle of all its automobiles. Henry Ford announced the incorporation of the Ford Manufacturing Company, which would make chassis, but only for the Model N. The Dodges would continue to build them for the big Model K. The brothers had nothing to kick about because they automatically became shareholders in the new company and recipients of all the dividends it would generate.

Malcomson, on the other hand, did not: He retained his shares in the Ford Motor Company, of course, but would get profits only on the sale of the finished cars. And who knew how much the new, housebuilt chassis would cut into that profit. They were to be supplied at an "unspecified" cost. The price ratio would make no difference to those who held shares in both companies; it would make plenty of difference to Malcomson.

He sent an angry letter to the board denouncing the "Ford Manufacturing Company [which is] comprised and controlled by the holders of the majority both of stock and directorships of the motor company, and designed . . . to sell its products to the Motor Company, presumably not without profit." The new company's allocation of shares ensures "the prospect of participating in the profits and confining the injury to those stockholders of the Motor Company on the outside.

"I consider this scheme as unwise as it is unfair."

This was a position difficult for anyone to argue against. But then the gambler's audacity that had given birth to the Ford Motor Company, intensified by indignation and bruised feelings, prodded Malcomson into taking an unwise step.

On December 5, 1905, the *Detroit Free Press* announced the establishment of a new auto plant in the city. The Aerocar Company, capitalized at four hundred thousand dollars, was building a factory on Mack Avenue that would turn out five hundred air-cooled touring cars in 1906. The company, which would be making "The Car of Today, Tomorrow, and for Years to Come," was owned by Malcomson.

That the treasurer of the Ford Motor Company would now be competing with it shifted the sympathies of the entire board to Ford. The directors demanded Malcomson's resignation, and after a few months of quarrelsome negotiations, Malcomson sold his one-fourth interest to Ford.

He got $175,000, hardly a bad return on an investment of $10,000 three years earlier. But if he'd stuck it out for a decade longer he would have gotten $100 million.

Bennett, the Daisy air rifle magnate, disgusted by the maneuver and wanting no more to do with those who had planned it, got out, too.

Ford had found that despite all his squeezing, he could not keep the Model N on the market for five hundred dollars. He raised the price by one hundred dollars. At six hundred dollars the N was not really a cheap car, but with its four-cylinder engine it was more powerful and reliable than anything close to its price. Up until September 1906, when Ford was able fully to back the N, the company had offered many models—among them, of course, the sumptuous K—and sold 1,559 cars altogether. By the end of the following September, selling only the Model N and very minor variations (one of them forthrightly described in his sales literature as "more pretentious"), Henry Ford sold 8,243.

His bruised partner Malcomson had been in earnest about his challenge, and a few Aerocars got built. Then the operation, like so many hundreds of other carmakers in those years, disappeared.

Forty years after the death of the Aerocar company in 1908, the journalist John Gunther came to Detroit to do research for the book that would become his bestselling *Inside USA*. Reading about the original Ford Motor Company stockholders, he spotted an unfamiliar name and got curious: "I would like very much to know about a man named Alex Y. Malcomson. He too had 255 shares in the original company, an amount equal to Ford's, and he was its first treasurer. It seems that he was a coal dealer, and Couzens was a clerk in his office. Ford must, of course, have bought him out many years ago, as he bought out Couzens. I was unable to find anybody in Detroit who knew further about Mr. Malcomson."

CHAPTER 9
Inventing the Universal Car

Who wanted it?; Sorensen's locked room; steering wheel on the left—forever; new experts, new engine, new steel, new car; "Without doubt the greatest creation in automobiles ever placed before a people."

When the struggle was over, Henry Ford was the majority stockholder in the company that Malcomson had paid for and to which he had given Ford's name. In the summer of 1906 heart trouble killed John Gray, and Henry Ford moved up from vice president to president of the Ford Motor Company. Nobody would ever again be in a position to tell him what kind of car he had to build.

Clara Ford's household records suggest that she was beginning to realize that her family was on the way to becoming rich. For the first time she began to buy food from catering firms: chicken salad sandwiches at ten cents each, and lobster salad for a hefty $1.50 a quart. She subscribed to magazines: the once famous children's publication *St. Nicholas*, *Good Housekeeping*, and *Munsey's*, a high-level general-interest monthly. Her husband seemed to be having a good time—

he enjoyed going to the theater with Clara and playing with Edsel—but he was fretting.

The Model N was doing more than well. Yet every time Ford looked at one, he was goaded by the specter of a better car hidden somewhere within it.

On the evening of the day he bought out Malcomson, he asked Fred Rockelman to give him a lift home. Like the time he'd driven with Couzens after the formation of the company that was now wholly and indisputably his, he was rolling through an oppressively hot summer dusk.

"Fred," he said, "this is a great day. We're going to expand this company, and you will see it grow by leaps and bounds. The proper system, as I have it in mind, is to get the car to the people. . . . If you can get people together so they get acquainted with one another, and get an idea of neighborliness, the car will have a universal effect. We won't have anymore strikes or wars."

How to get the car to the people, though? That segment of the people who lived in the cities were already comfortable with it, and those heavy four-thousand-dollar machines went almost entirely to them. When the owners decided to take a spin in the country, they often angered their rural counterparts. Bouncing and banging down dirt lanes at fifty miles an hour, they'd leave behind a cloud of ill will, along with dust settling on lines of drying laundry and terrified livestock.

Some counties passed ordinances that verged on the bizarre. One mandated that if motorists spotted a distant team coming their way, they were to stop and fire off warning flares, like shipwreck survivors in a lifeboat. (It is difficult to see how this measure would reassure the horses or oxen.)

Actually, things were trending in the other direction. More and more farmers wanted cars. Not, of course, the heavy ones that cost more than a farm, and whose weight would often immobilize them on the dire byways of the day. A 1909 census of American roads determined that only 8.66 percent of America's highways were "surfaced," which could mean covered with gravel, or possibly "corduroyed" with logs laid side by side like touching railroad ties that put the traveler in an endless purgatory of violent jouncing. The rest went where wagons had gone for year after year, cutting two ruts with a tall hummock of shale or mud or rocks between them.

These roads were the farmer's thoroughfares, and early in the century a new sort of automobile arose to carry him along them. It was called a "high-wheeler" or "western buggy"—"western" because these vehicles were born in the Midwest; "buggy" because that's what they basically were. To the buggy's frame, which rode on wheels more than a yard high, was fastened a single-cylinder engine. These cars were in a way more primitive than Ford's Quadricycle, but they were light, cheap (starting at $250), and their high freeboard let them scramble over some of the roughest ground. But their lightness and their wooden skeletons meant they could shake themselves into dilapidation in a matter of months, and the single cylinder could never give them quite enough push.

Yet for half a decade they sold well enough to support a score of companies. One farmer spoke for thousands when he explained why, for all its shortcomings, he liked his high-wheeler: All his life his horizon had been "bounded by the ten- or twelve-mile circle that my horses could go in a day and get back in good shape. I now make exploring trips of five times the distance. I can call on friends living thirty miles away who have been asking me to come for twenty years."

Henry Ford understood this. He wanted a car tall enough to successfully attack the worst roads, and strong enough for them not to crack its frame after a season. Most of all, it had to be cheap enough for the landlocked farmer to afford it.

On a winter morning early in 1907, Ford walked into the pattern department of the Piquette Avenue plant and went over to a tall, handsome man in his midtwenties who looked, and was, both tough and dour. He stopped what he was doing and Ford said, "Charlie, I'd like to have a room finished right here in this space. Put up a wall with a door big enough to run a car in and out. Get a good lock for the door, and when you're ready, we'll have Joe Galamb come up in here. We're going to start a completely new job."

Charlie was Charles Emil Sorensen. He would be the longest lasting of Ford's high lieutenants. Most of them had a length of tenure similar to that of Stalin's marshals, but Sorensen could truthfully title his memoir *My Forty Years with Ford*.

He was born in Copenhagen in 1881, and came to America five years later. His father, a skilled woodworker, emigrated from Denmark because of his admiration for a professional runner named "Little Sorensen." The athlete wasn't a relative—"the name Sorensen is as common in Denmark as Smith is here," Charles wrote—but no family tie could have been more binding. Little Sorensen went to compete, with great success, against American runners, and when he wrote his fan, "This is a great country. Come on over," Soren Sorensen immediately complied. Little Sorensen eventually settled in Buffalo, and so it was there that Charles Sorensen spent a decade in public schools before leaving to become a patternmaker for a company that manufactured stoves. By the turn of the century he had moved with his family to Detroit.

Nineteen oh four was a pivotal year in Sorensen's life: He married Helen Miller, a young book-keeper for the Sun Stove Company, and Henry

Ford hired him at three dollars a day as an experimental patternmaker for his new car company.

In choosing Sorensen, Ford again ratified his affection for hard-handed, easily infuriated colleagues. Sorensen's temper was every bit the equal of that possessed by Couzens and the Dodge brothers. So was his ability.

It is not surprising that Ford should have approached a patternmaker to take the first steps toward the automobile he envisioned, for the patternmaker's work was a bridge between the blueprints of Wills and the blades of the machine tools.

Years later, and still proud of what he had mastered by 1906, Sorensen wrote, "Pattern-making is neither a profession nor a trade but an exacting, highly skilled craft which requires understanding of both."

The patternmaker would look over the drawing of the gear or cylinder, and then "translate" it—Sorensen's word—into a woodcarving. He had to be a bit of a "clairvoyant," Sorensen's word again, because he "must be able to read the most complicated blueprints, and he must have more than a cabinet-maker's meticulous skill and infinite patience to saw and plane, sandpaper and glue together an accurate representation of what the designer or draftsman had in mind." It had to be accurate because it made the mold into which was poured the molten metal that, once cooled and machined, would be the part itself.

Ford appreciated the patternmaker's skill more than he did the draftsman's; although he wasn't the blueprint illiterate a few of his colleagues later claimed, he always felt most comfortable with something he could handle rather than something he had to read.

"It was apparent," wrote Sorensen, "that Ford never quite understood what a design looked like until it was put into a three-dimensional pattern. I also discovered that he was not a draftsman and couldn't make a sketch that was any too clear."

Sorensen found out, too, that he almost always understood what his boss was looking for: "I began making sketches of his ideas and final drawings, and when I couldn't finish them on Piquette Avenue, I took them into the pattern shop." Eventually he got so he didn't need drawings. Ford would explain what he wanted, and Sorensen would pick up a piece of wood and make it ("We had the most beautiful white pine in those days," he remembered wistfully, "straight and clear").

From the shop he would bring Ford a model of the part, an accurate prophecy worked in wood. Ford would turn it over in his hands, squint along its curves and notches, and know exactly what needed doing: Shave a few millimeters off here; I think we're a little too thin here; no need for this flange.

So it was Sorensen Ford sought out when he wanted his chamber of invention, and in a few days he had it. The place wasn't much: twelve by fifteen feet, two blackboards, a drafting table at which Joseph Galamb was promptly and almost continuously installed, a few power tools, and a rocking chair imported from Ford's house; it had been his mother's, and he hoped it might bring him luck.

As in the Quadricycle days, access here was severely limited: Galamb, Wills, a machinist named Jimmy Smith who had been with Ford for years, Sorensen (although perhaps not so freely as he suggests in his memoir), and the fourteen-year-old Edsel. Spider Huff was back, too, no longer in his role as the man hanging out over the streaming track to keep the race car from tipping over, but as a brilliant electrical engineer who would give the new car one of its most crucial components.

Ford came every day to sit in the rocking chair, sometimes for hours at a stretch, while Galamb chalked on the blackboard sketches of his ideas and refinements of his drawings. Before being rubbed clean for the next session, the boards were photographed, both for future patent protection and to have some kind of record of the swift progress they recorded.

In this secret room, Ford's genius—and for what was going on here "genius" is not too inflated a word—played as strongly and steadily as it ever would. He deployed his inherent contradictions only toward a creative end. Contradictions, because the car he was building would be at once as simple as he could make it, and yet immensely sophisticated.

For example, it would have four cylinders, like the Model N. But then, not like the Model N. The engines in almost all the multicylinder cars of the day, even the grandest, were essentially a bundle of thick-walled pipes, strapped and bolted together. Even the Model N's four cylinders were a marriage of two different castings.

Fussy, complicated, unsatisfying, said Ford: We must machine our engine out of a single block of metal. While Sorensen was puzzling out how to do this, Ford had another thought: Slice off the top. That is, have the engine be a single casting, its cylinders wholly accessible and thus easy both to build and to repair, and fit a cylinder head on top of the four of them like a hat and bolt it down. And that is how car engines are built to this day.

This left Galamb struggling to find a gasket that could seal the engine to its new head without leaking the power of the endless inferno of little explosions that propelled the car. Ford rocked back and forth in his chair, radiating the calm and friendly conviction that Galamb would come through. Galamb always did.

Couzens was not calm and friendly. "Ford was always relaxed," Sorensen remembered, "whereas

Couzens drove himself to the limit." Yet "Ford's patience, perhaps more than Couzens' driving, inspired the rest of us to work long hours to clear away problems."

At first, the castings made from Sorensen's patterns were mounted on a Model N chassis rolled in through the door Ford had said should be made large enough to accommodate a car. The Model N had run further through the alphabet by now, and new customers could buy the Model S, a grown-up-looking car whose hood and fenders collaborated to flow into a real running board, and that offered such refinements as umbrella holders. This car was not going to be a Model N, though, or even a Model S. It was going to be the Model T.

By the fall of 1907 two of its chassis were ready for the road. A thousand ever-shifting calculations went into the new car. Many of its components had been tried and found satisfactory on the Model N. Others were new. Wills, pondering how to keep both engine and transmission properly lubricated, settled into his bathtub and, like Archimedes, suddenly saw the solution to the problem: Encase both together and let gravity promiscuously bathe the two of them in oil.

What kind of transmission should enjoy this bath? Most cars of the day used the sliding gear that has come down to us, or at least to those of us who have ever used a stick shift. The stick shift was harder to maneuver then than now, for it demanded the driver pick exactly the right moment to shift gears, and then step on the clutch and force the shift to the next speed without breaking their teeth.

Ford tried the system out. Or, rather, he had a worker named Charles Balough try it out. Balough drove into the thick of Detroit one busy weekday evening and found himself confronted by three streetcars. Stamping on the clutch and wrestling with the gearshift, he tried to swing around them and recalled some fifty years later, "The experimental model was completely wrecked, crushed between the street car and a telephone pole."

Balough went back to the office worried about what his boss would say, which turned out to be: "Charley, that's the best job you ever did for this company."

Ford had been willing to try the sliding gear, but he preferred the planetary transmission he had in the Model N. There was no shift lever for the driver to grapple with, because all the gears were always meshed in constant motion around the crankshaft—hence the "planetary"—and engaged by floor pedals that would tighten a band on one while releasing the band on another.

Ford at first wanted a three-speed transmission. Balough tried it out for him on the streets. This time he managed to avoid trolley cars, but the system wouldn't work. Again Ford smiled his driver's worries away: "The gear that gives you no trouble is the one you never use." The T would have two forward gears, and they had to be sturdier than their predecessors on earlier cars. He and Sorensen worked the problem through with a succession of carved wooden disks that Ford insisted—rightly, always, in those glowing days—could get much smaller.

Sometime during the deliberations a decision was made that would soon affect every American. Ford put the steering wheel on the left. He was defying the towering precedent of the railroad, where the locomotive engineer always sat on the right-hand side of the cab. Ford thought this made no sense on American roads.

Those roads also demanded considerable nimbleness. Most cars rode on springs set parallel to their bodies. Ford had his front and rear springs arch across the axles at the front and back of the car nearly from wheel to wheel. He balanced the machine on two sturdy triangles formed by radius rods that ran from close to the wheel hubs to the engine, which was fixed to the car's frame at only three points. Most cars of the day had the engine fastened to the frame at four places, and when the frame bent, the engine might shed its bolts and open like a purse.

Ford developed a chassis that could carry its engine almost anywhere, twisting over the broken, crooked roads supple as a cat scuttling under a fence.

Weight: Ford said that while attending a race at Ormond Beach, Florida, he'd gone over to look at the carcass of a wrecked French car and "I picked up a little valve strip stem. It was very light and very strong . . . I asked what it was made of. Nobody knew." He handed the stem to an assistant. "Find out all about this. That is the kind of material we ought to have in our cars."

This vivid incident may be one of the picturesque promotional fictions Ford manufactured almost instinctively. When he was in his seventies, a reporter noticed a bandage on his ankle and asked about it. Oh, Ford said casually, I was playing football with some kids. In fact, it was a blister.

"I sent to England," Ford wrote, "for a man who understood how they make the steel commercially. The main thing was to get a plant to turn it out."

Actually, he sent to Canton, Ohio, but there *was* an Englishman involved. The metal was real enough, too. It was a steel alloy called vanadium, which Wills first heard about at an engineering conference in 1905. A British metallurgist named J. Kent Smith was a strong proponent and went to the Piquette Avenue factory in 1906 to speak with Ford about it. Smith had a laboratory in Canton, which Ford visited, and came away persuaded:

"Until then we had to be satisfied with steel running between 60,000 and 70,000 pounds tensile strength. With vanadium, the strength went up to 170,000 pounds." That meant "the strength of an automobile axle or crankshaft may be doubled without increasing the dimensions or weight."

Vanadium was strong, light, and easier to machine than nickel steel. It had been used in the Model N, and would be the backbone of the Model T.

Once Ford had decided on it, Wills told him that the company needed its own metallurgy laboratory, and they should hire a professional to establish it. Ford didn't like professionals. "No, make an expert of Wandersee," he told Wills, so a man who had been hired to sweep the factory floors went off for three months of tutelage at the United Steel Laboratory, and by late 1907 he had a laboratory of his own on Piquette Avenue and was ordering vanadium steel for the new car.

What with the vanadium steel and the general paring down of every part, the car would weigh only eleven hundred pounds. The engine could generate twenty horsepower, which might sound pallid now, but in 1907 American cars tended to weigh some eighty pounds per horsepower. The Thomas Flyer that in 1908 won an extraordinary race from New York to Paris (west, of course, across all North America and the Bering Straits and along the tracks of the Trans-Siberian railroad) weighed sixty-four pounds per horsepower. The Model T would weigh sixty pounds for every horsepower, and would cost just a little over a tenth as much as the Thomas six-cylinder limousine. Ford put the difference in engineering terms, and there is clearly no bluffing here: "With the Ford there are only 7.95 pounds to be carried by each cubic inch of piston displacement." He added, more accessibly to the average reader, "That's why Ford cars are 'always going' wherever and whenever you see them—through sand and mud, through slush, snow, and water, up hills across roadless plains."

In the meantime, Spider Huff was figuring out what might be the single most revolutionary component of the Model T. Almost all the cars of the time carried batteries, and these were costly, feeble, and in near-constant need of replacement. But you couldn't do without them, for they gave the spark of fire that ignited the gas in the cylinders.

Huff was going in another direction. For three-quarters of a century engineers had known that when a coil of wire passed close by a magnet, it picked up a charge of electricity. Ford and Huff thought about this. The car's flywheel spun all the time the engine was running: Why not stud it with magnets—sixteen was the number the two men settled on—and face it against a circle of sixteen stationary wire coils? As the flywheel whirled past these, the magnets embedded in it would spit electricity into the coils, and the car would generate its own power to fire the engine. And all of this could be contained in Wills's oil bath.

Always, through every technical decision, Ford was searching for beauty in his machine. Once the car was covered with its superstructure, which had to accommodate the driver and up to five passengers, it might not be an object to inspire aesthetic regard. But the chassis—its proportion, its confidence, its forthrightness—most certainly is.

The first factory-built Model T was finished on September 24. Henry Ford got into it and set off for what he described as a hunting trip up to northern Wisconsin. Jimmy Smith was along to do much of the driving. Smith was nervous about the magneto, and brought a storage battery just in case it didn't do its job. After about eight hours, while they were heading to Chicago, the storage battery tipped over and spilled acid all over the floor of the car. Ford made Smith throw it away. They pushed on, and without the help of the battery made it to Chicago over bad roads at an average speed of more than twenty miles an hour, then headed to Milwaukee, up to Iron Mountain, back through Milwaukee, and got home to Detroit on October 2. The Model T came in looking pretty ratty, caked as it was with a thick impasto of

Michigan mud. But it had gone 1,357 miles and suffered nothing worse than a single flat tire.

Time to put it on the market, for $850. Couzens's dealers were close to rapturous. Some actually hid the early brochures so they could get rid of their stock of Model Ss before the messiah arrived. A Detroit representative wrote, "We have rubbed our eyes several times to make sure we were not dreaming," and one in Pennsylvania declared that the Model T "is without doubt the greatest creation in automobiles ever placed before a people."

The road lay shining ahead. Half of America seemed ready to buy this car. If, that is, Henry Ford was allowed to sell it.

CHAPTER 10
The Man Who Owned Every Car in America

Selden files a patent on all gas-powered automobiles and sues their makers; the court finds for him; most carmakers give in; Ford won't pay "graft money"; a second trial; "One of the greatest things Mr. Ford did . . ."

S o many stories about Henry Ford that sound apocryphal may not be.

It is quite possible that while he was in the freight yard in his shirtsleeves sending off his first Model As under Couzens's stern gaze, a messenger really did pick his way across the tracks to give the men the news that the sixteen-year-long fuse George Selden lit in 1879 had just burned down to the main charge.

On October 23, 1903, Selden filed suit against the Ford Motor Company for infringement on the patent he claimed gave him authority over every gas-powered automobile in America. Selden seems truly to have believed this even though he'd never built an automobile based on his patent, but he didn't have enough money to hire lawyers to act on it. Now, though, he came with a powerful partner, for he had filed his suit in alliance with the Electric Vehicle Company.

As the name suggests, the Electric Vehicle Company was not enthusiastic about the internal combustion engine. When Hiram Maxim gave up trying to build a gas-powered car on his own and accepted the job Colonel Albert Pope offered him in his Hartford factory in 1895, he worked on both gasoline and electric cars, though always favoring the former. This put him somewhat at odds with George H. Day, who was in charge of automotive development for Pope, and who thought gas buggies far too noisy and oily.

Colonel Pope was doing nicely selling both kinds of cars in April 1899 when the financier William C. Whitney came up from New York to Hartford to have a look at his shop.

Whitney liked electric cars, too, and already had a fleet of taxicabs gliding almost noiselessly around Manhattan, built by the Electric Vehicle Company. Now he wanted more cabs—a lot more—and, backed by solid investors, he proposed that the Pope automobile efforts merge with the Electric Vehicle Company. Colonel Pope was delighted: The new company would be capitalized at $3 million.

Before he closed the deal, though, Whitney thought he'd better check and see if there were any lurking patents that might cause problems down the road. Pope had a diligent man in charge of patent matters, and he tracked down Selden.

When Maxim—who by this time knew as much about cars as anyone alive—saw the patent, "I snorted my derision. I pointed out that the engine shown in the patent was utterly impractical and a joke. . . . The claims were so broad that they were ridiculous."

Whitney didn't think so; he gave the fortunate Selden ten thousand dollars for the rights to his patent and offered him 5 percent of any royalties it might generate. In June the Electric Vehicle Company's lawyers started sending a letter out to American carmakers: "Our clients inform us that you are manufacturing and advertising for sale vehicles which embody the invention of the Selden patent. . . . We notify you of this infringement, and request that you desist from the same and make suitable compensation to the owner thereof."

These demands drew the responses that could have been expected—either hostile or non-existent—and the Electric Vehicle Company began to sue.

Alexander Winton was the main target. The patent holders figured that if they could get a judgment against the best-known automaker in the country, the smaller-fry would fall into line.

Winton, by nature a fighter, let his company's treasurer speak for him: "The Selden patent is preposterous, and should never have been granted. . . . It does not have a leg to stand on."

Winton joined in a loose confederation of other carmakers that stood against the claim. The confederation would turn out to be too loose.

In September 1900 Winton's attorney filed a writ of demurrer. This instrument held that although the alleged facts in a complaint may be true, they do not add up to a legal cause for action, and thus the defendant is free to ignore it (today this is known as a motion to dismiss). The Selden car, Winton's lawyer argued, was no invention at all: The substitution of a gas engine for the steam ones that inventors had been mounting on their road vehicles for nearly a century was nothing more than common sense.

Judge Alfred C. Coxe disagreed. "The patentee's contributions to the art should not be considered from a narrow point of view," said Coxe in an impressively eloquent ruling issued that November: "His work should not be examined through an inverted telescope; the horizon of invention should not be contracted to the periphery of a sixpence." Selden "must be regarded as the first to construct a road-locomotive provided with a liquid hydrocarbon gas-engine of the compression type."

The weakest part of the ruling is the word "construct," as Selden had never constructed any road-locomotive, hydrocarbon or otherwise. Beyond that, despite the more than one hundred changes the would-be inventor had appended to his patent during its interminable gestation, the car it described was like nothing on the road in 1900. But in what was still the dawn of a fast-flowing technological revolution, courts tended to look kindly on sweeping claims for basic patents. Everything was moving so swiftly, and flinging off new and complex puzzlements, that judges were reluctant to summarily dismiss an idea a couple of decades old just because the pace of the dawning century might make it seem archaic.

Nor did Judge Coxe's ruling ratify the validity of the patent; it only meant there was no quick way for Winton to resist it, so the case would have to be tried in the courts.

Not that this brought Winton much comfort, for at the time patent struggles were the most complex and time-consuming of all litigation. There would be few sharp, brisk courtroom exchanges, even though there was a great deal of testimony. That testimony had to be gathered by attorneys in the field, painstakingly transcribed and with no judge presiding to stifle irrelevancies or hurry things along. Winton knew that his defense could take years.

Moreover, the patent holders were making plenty of noise about Coxe's decision, promoting it as a complete victory. The companies opposing the patent were lackadaisical in defending their position, and when two small operators, Ranlet

Automobile and Automotive Forecarriage, facing the legal fees inevitable in challenging what had swiftly grown to be an $18 million consortium, folded and accepted the patent, the entire industry began to get nervous.

Winton persevered. He hired a leading New York City patent law firm and sent associates across the country and to Europe to gather evidence refuting Selden. In February 1901 the lawyers filed their answer to Coxe: thirty-two separate defenses unfurled across 1,400 pages and backed by 126 patents—American, British, French—awarded beginning in 1794.

The Selden interests brought the case to trial. The trial lasted two years, during which Winton's confederation fell apart, and he found himself alone responsible for the legal fees. In the autumn of 1902 Winton discovered that some of his old allies had applied for Selden licenses. He approached the Electric Vehicle Company and asked about terms. They were generous. The EVC badly wanted Winton, and immediately waived any royalties accrued before a settlement while offering to deduct all the expenses of his suit from his future payments.

What would those payments be? This was determined by a group of automakers that would form the organization of companies that had agreed to honor the patent. Ten of them were based in Detroit. They were prepared to deal with Selden, but chafing from the coercion, and not warm to the Electric Vehicle Company's demand for a 5 percent royalty on every car sold. They established a miniature organization of their own, and each contributed twenty-five hundred dollars to it before sending five representatives off to New York in March 1903 to take in the auto show at Madison Square Garden and, more important, to negotiate with William Whitney.

The financier invited them to what he meant to feel like an informal meeting at his Fifth Avenue mansion. Whitney was a famously gracious host, but he had made a tactical blunder here. Frederick L. Smith, the treasurer of the Olds Motor Works, wrote, "Neither the urbanity and courtesy of Mr. Whitney nor his evident sincerity and straight-forwardness could offset the bad effect of proposing to shear us sheep in a New York drawing room. Straightaway we became rams, mules, lions, if you like, charging bulls, with $25,000 real money."

The committee put its negotiations in the hands of Elihu Cutler, a pragmatic New Englander who owned the Knox Motor Company in Springfield, Massachusetts. Cutler took a simple approach to the proceedings. He had written his terms on the back of a frayed blue envelope and whenever Whitney or one of his colleagues raised a point, he would pull it out and read aloud:

"First.—We will pay one and one-fourth per cent royalty, three-fourths of one per cent to the Electric Vehicle Co., one-half of one per cent into an association of our own.

"Second.—This association shall say who shall or shall not be sued under the patent.

"Third.—It shall say who shall be licensed and who shall not be licensed under the patent."

Cutler's recitation never varied and it never ceased. In time, the EVC fell beneath his relentless pecking, Winton agreed that Selden's patent was valid, and the wrangling ended with its sometime opponents delighted by the brand-new organization they had founded: the Association of Licensed Automobile Manufacturers.

The ALAM was born plump with good intentions, among them keeping slipshod and shoddy automakers from tarnishing the reputation of the industry it now controlled.

Like many of the ALAM members themselves, Ford thought Selden's claims ludicrous. He was not by nature a man to fall in easily with plans formed by others, and this particular situation must have infuriated him. But he had a car company to launch on a paid-in capital of twenty-eight thousand dollars, and he knew that litigation could lap that up in a matter of months.

In the summer of 1903 he went to Fred L. Smith, who was president of the new organization. Looking back on the meeting across a quarter century, Smith said, "Henry Ford called on me on a morning long ago and wanted to know if, in case application were made, membership in the association would be granted then. Not as the exalted president of A.L.A.M., but as one man to another, I told him I did not think that an application from the Ford Motor Co. at that particular moment would be considered favorably . . . I remember telling Henry Ford that his outfit was really nothing but an 'assemblage plant'— poison to the A.L.A.M. and that when they had their own plant and became a factor in the industry, they would be welcome, because, among other reasons, the type of car they were making was not being turned out by any of the A.L.A.M. members."

This "one man to another" talk would have grated on Ford for several reasons. First, Smith was applying to Ford the same suave ingratiations that had so rankled Smith when he had been on the receiving end of them from Whitney. Then there was the scorn of the "assemblage plant," although most of the ALAM members built their cars that way, and not one of them was wholly independent of outside suppliers. The delicate reference to the fact that the type of car Ford was making "was not being turned out by any of the A.L.A.M. members" meant that it was too cheap.

The ALAM didn't like cheap automobiles. The organization favored the heavy, expensive cars that Malcomson was eager to build. Most of the makers that had gathered under the Selden patent produced cars that sold for three to six thousand dollars. The weeks-old association had already become as haughty as any ancient guild that made breastplates or tableware for the nobility.

Still, Ford went to another meeting with the ALAM, most likely at the urging of John Gray, who lived in a state of perpetual worry about the automobile business, and the usually sanguine John Anderson, whom the ALAM had succeeded in frightening.

The Ford shareholders met for lunch with ALAM representatives at the Russell House, which was—or said it was—"the most complete and elegant hostelry in Michigan." Smith once again tried to be emollient, even though he had the uneasy feeling of being in a slightly false position. During the meal John Gray talked about what the Ford Motor Company hoped to accomplish, and wondered why its aims did not suit the ALAM. Smith recalled, "Mr. Gray put their case so fairly and simply that I had a guilty feeling of 'sassing' my elders and betters when I, in turn, tried to state the A.L.A.M. policies and purposes . . . I was conscious of cutting a rather sorry figure before a group of friendly men who put me personally in the wrong by dealing with me officially."

The friendliness did not outlast the lunch. When Smith had finished making his case, and sat down, James Couzens said, "Selden can take his patent and go to hell with it."

Smith looked unhappily around the room. Ford, his chair tilted back against the wall, had silently been taking in the proceedings. Now he spoke.

"Couzens has answered you."

"You men are foolish," said Smith. "The Selden crowd can put you out of business—and will."

Ford clacked his chair's front legs back to the floor and stood. "Let them try it," he said, ending the lunch and the negotiations.

The ALAM began taking out newspaper ads warning readers that if they bought a Ford car, they were buying a lawsuit, too.

Couzens replied with a defiant letter to the *Cycle and Automobile Trade Journal* saying in part, "So far as our plan of action is concerned for the future it is extremely simple. We intend to manufacture and sell all the gasoline automobiles of the type we are constructing that we can. We regard the claims made by the Selden patent as covering the monopoly of such machines as entirely unwarranted and without foundation in fact. We do not, therefore, propose to respect any such claims."

This was meant to provoke, and it did. The ALAM sued Ford.

Ford and Couzens hired the best patent lawyer in Detroit, Ralzemond A. Parker. A sixty-year-old Civil War veteran—he had fought at Antietam—Parker was on the verge of retiring. But he had early gotten interested in automobiles and thoroughly understood them, he thought the Selden patent absurd, and he admired Ford's opposition to it. So he took a job that turned out to consume him for years.

Soon after Ford retained Parker, the Detroit newspapers carried a "NOTICE To Dealers, Importers, Agents and Users of Gasoline Automobiles. We will protect you under any prosecution for alleged infringements of patents." The advertisement named Parker, and quoted him: "The Selden Patent is not a broad one, and if it was, it is anticipated [that is, people had the idea before Selden did]. It does not cover any practicable machine, no practicable machine can be built from it, and never was."

The copy goes on to make the strong but false claim that "our Mr. Ford made the first Gasoline Automobile in Detroit and the third in the United States," then swerves back to the truth: "Our Mr. Ford also built the famous '999' Gasoline Automobile, which was driven by Barney

Oldfield in New York on Saturday a mile in 55⁴/₅ seconds on a circular track, which is the world's record. Mr. Ford, driving his own machine, beat Mr. Winton at Grosse Pointe track in 1901. We have always been winners."

The fight continued in the papers, with Ford more and more using a word that had appeared in Couzens's opening sally: "monopoly." In an era that had become deeply suspicious of "trusts," Ford was drawing on a widespread public antagonism that was shared by—and fed by—President Theodore Roosevelt.

By 1905 the Ford company was referring to the ALAM simply as "the Trust" in its ads. One of them shows a man (inexplicably wearing a gleaming opera hat) standing, his hand on a Ford, looking with calm disdain at a scarecrow who is tottering toward him blowing a tin horn.

"Watch for Him Whenever the Automobile Show is in Town, that pretty, straw stuffed Bogie Man—the official mouthpiece of the Trust—is equipped with a new supply of wind, straw, and springs—1905 model." The ad concludes by assuring "purchasers of 'Ford' cars . . . as before, that we will protect them absolutely.

"So don't let the Trust, by vigorous agitations of its straw man's arms, scare you into paying $1,000 to $2,000 more than you need for an automobile."

Parker was traveling the country, taking down

evidence in the same way his Winton predecessors had done back when they were still on Ford's side: an examiner or notary public on hand to ensure an accurate record, but no judge to stanch the flow of testimony, which eventually came to a stupefying fourteen thousand pages containing five million words.

More tangible evidence was being offered. The Electric Vehicle Company underwrote the construction of Selden's car, a quarter century after its conception, to demonstrate that it would run. Some citizens of Rochester, where it was built, said they had seen it perform, but when it was introduced into the case as Exhibit 89, Parker, who was not at all pleased that no one on the defense had been told of the exhibit's existence, said, "Personally I don't believe that Exhibit 89 . . . ever ran ten rods in Rochester."

Meanwhile, Charles Sorensen got an assignment that must have surprised him. "Mr. Parker tracked down a description in a French technical magazine of a vehicle driven in 1862 by a gas engine made by a Belgian, Jean Lenoir. It was decided to build an engine according to Lenoir's specifications; if it worked, it might upset Selden's claim. From drawings in the Ford drafting room, I made patterns, produced the castings, and brought them into the plant. Mr. Ford delegated Fred Allison [one of the company's electrical experts] to build the engine and set it up on a Ford chassis.

This took a year and a half and many tests before the contraption ran."

Parker had requested, and been granted, a public test of the Selden car, which bore the date 1877 emphatically painted on its side. It didn't do well: After hours of being fussed over, it ran 1,309 feet. Finally, in September 1907, it was tormented into covering 3,450 feet of Manhattan pavement.

Ford's exercise in automotive archaeology did far better. The company had retained Charles Duryea, as ancient and knowledgeable an automobile veteran as the young industry possessed, to serve as a witness. Riding in the Ford-built Lenoir from the Ford office at Fifty-Fourth and Broadway up around Columbus Circle and back, Duryea reported that "the vehicle started with certainty when wanted, ran when wanted to the limit of its ability, which I should say was as high as 12 miles an hour on some occasions when the streets were good, stopped, started, slowed up, accelerated, reversed and otherwise handled in a satisfactory and practical manner."

In the end, neither of the brand-new antiques had a decisive effect on the case, but their highly public trials fascinated first the New Yorkers who witnessed them and then their countrymen who read about them. The reports showed that this strident newcomer, the automobile, already had a venerable past and thus possibly a greater future than many imagined, and that an issue was being decided that would shape that future.

As the dispute wore on, the public also became more and more aware of Henry Ford. A photograph of his Piquette Avenue plant taken in 1906 shows a sign running the length of the building that reads, "HOME OF THE CELEBRATED FORD AUTOMOBILES." The adjective is misleading: The cars and their maker were known, but hardly celebrated. The company's founder had gained attention with his racing, and his Model A was selling well enough to allow him to defy the ALAM—before long he would be paying six dollars per car to defend his case—but his was just another company in the general ruck of automakers. As he held out against a $70 million consortium, however, more and more Americans began to see in him a brave incarnation of the antimonopolist spirit of the times.

Ford took shrewd advantage of this moment when his business instincts were in perfect harmony with his beliefs. "We possess just enough of that instinct of American freedom," he said, "to cause us to rebel against oppression or unfair competition.

"It goes against the grain of Americanism to be coerced, or bluffed, or sandbagged; and men who will not fight in such circumstances do not, in my estimation, possess the highest degree of self-respect or even honesty—for I protest it is dishonest to bow to expediency in such a case, and thereby not only become contributors of graft money, but subject the entire automobile industry and buying constituency to a tax that is unjust and uncalled for."

The ALAM was equally determined. It sent "patent sleuths" out onto the streets checking automobiles to see whether they carried the proof of having paid the demanded levies, which was a three-inch-wide brass plaque stamped with an image of Selden's theoretical car.

The agents could be thorough. When a young New Yorker named William J. Moore bought an unlicensed Swiss-made Martini, the ALAM found out and sued him. He failed to appear in court, and had an injunction issued against him. This scared him enough to drive him underground after he persuaded the New York Martini dealer to announce that his customer had gone to Texas and died there. Moore stayed in the East under an assumed name, but the ALAM's men tracked him to Albany, where they got a federal marshal to hand him an injunction while he was trying to steady his nerves at the bar of the Ten Eyck Hotel.

Parker kept taking his testimonies, and he was good at it. He looked a little like General William Tecumseh Sherman; photographs of him give the same sense of a tight-skinned face charged with tenacity. Here he is dismantling Hugh C. Gibson, an engineer hired as an expert witness by the ALAM. The issue is the "flame ignition" Selden specified in his patent, which had been universally superseded by electrical ignition (even in Exhibit 89). Parker asked Gibson to explain it.

A. I have no knowledge in my present capacity of flame ignition.

Q. What do you mean by "in my present capacity"?

A. I mean that as an ordinary individual without special knowledge I have no knowledge of pure flame ignition.

Q. Have you any knowledge of "purely flame ignition" as applied to that engine [the one put into Exhibit 89]?

A. As an ordinary individual I do not, nor could I possibly.

Q. What do you know as an expert?

A. I cannot tell what I know as an expert.

Q. You mean you can't or won't?

A. I mean I can't as I say.

Q. Why can't you?

A. I don't know.

Formidable interrogator though he was, Parker could make no headway with Selden himself. The inventor sat facing his questioner, his cravat held in place with a pin crafted in the shape of his car, its wheel hubs and headlamps sparkling with diamonds, full of calm certainty about being the father of the automobile. Yet Selden offered sly evasions if questioned on specifics. When, for instance, Parker asked, "Have you given the public any information whatever in your patent as to which ratio of speed of the crankshaft relative to that of the propelling wheels they must have in order to secure the new and useful results which you have specified . . . ?" Selden replied, "As my invention is a pioneer in the art, my understanding is that my patent on it under existing decisions is to be liberally construed."

Pressed on one detail after another, Selden would instead speak at length of his lonely struggles as a young inventor, or about the ever-growing importance of his invention. When Parker asked him to "answer yes or no," Selden replied with unruffled hauteur: "You have tried several times to dictate my answer to me, and so far as I know you have not yet succeeded, and I really doubt whether you will."

There was no cordiality whatever in these exchanges. At one point Parker asked, "Did you intend to tell the truth?" and Selden replied, "Your question is an insult, sir, and I refuse to answer it."

Parker kept coming at Selden, but he never made a dent.

The case went to trial in the spring of 1909 before the Circuit Court of the Southern District of New York, in the old Post Office Building at the southern end of City Hall Park. Although years had passed since Parker began working on it, he had written Ford, "I wish the case could be delayed a little . . . [and not come] before Judge Hough. Now Hough is said to be cranky and I *know* he is *not* a patent Judge."

That was true, but Judge Charles Merrill Hough took the case anyway. Although Hough was energetic and diligent, and familiar with the fundamentals of patent law, he knew nothing about automobiles or their history. He tried to be fair, but Parker, so effective in taking testimonies, made the mistake of overpreparing. He had spent years absorbing all that testimony, and he had an unfortunate tendency to tell all that he had learned. He bored and irritated Judge Hough. The Selden lawyers were crisp and precise in their arguments.

Hough went off to a dismal summer of reading through the immense record. On September 15 he delivered his opinion. He acknowledged that

Selden had contributed virtually nothing to the development of the automobile, but said that his "patent represents to me a great idea, conceived in 1879, which lay absolutely fallow until 1895, and then concealed in a file wrapper, and is now demanding tribute from later independent inventors . . . who more promptly and far more successfully reduced their ideas to practice.

"But the patent speaks from the date of its issue, and unless Selden did something unlawful during his sixteen years' wrangle with Examiners . . . he is within the law, and his rights are the same as those of the promptest applicant."

Judge Hough found for Selden.

What the magazine *Motor World* called "by far the most momentous and vital decision ever affecting the automobile industry" held that by law no car could be built in, imported to, or driven in America without the permission of the ALAM.

Alexander Winton, his own resistance to Selden's claims far behind him, said with satisfaction, "Nothing now remains but to exact from all trespassers a share of that income they have enjoyed for years without letters patent."

Ford thought plenty remained. The day of the decision he sent a telegram to a fellow carmaker in Indianapolis: "Selden suit decision has no effect on Ford policy—we will fight to the finish."

He would be fighting an increasingly solitary

battle. Within a month of Judge Hough's decision eight independent carmakers came into the ALAM fold, and the organization was suing the holdouts. On October 19, William C. Durant, head of the year-old General Motors, surrendered.

The defections troubled Ford, of course, but by now his stand had made him a national figure. The *Detroit Free Press* ran an editorial under the heading, "Ford, the Fighter," and, in case the reader might have found that too vague, opened with the line, "Ford, the fighter, salute!"

The public stuck by Ford. He wrote that when "some of my more enthusiastic opponents . . . gave it out privately that there would be criminal as well as civil suits and that a man buying a Ford car might as well be buying a ticket to jail," he pledged that his company would indemnify every new owner with a bond. "We thought the bond would give assurance to the buyers—that they needed confidence. They did not. We sold more than eighteen thousand cars—nearly double the output of the previous year—and I think about fifty buyers asked for bonds—perhaps it was less than that."

On November 22, 1910, the contestants were back again in the Post Office Building. Parker had told Ford that clearly he wasn't the one to carry on this fight in the courtroom, and recommended a well regarded New York patent attorney named Edmund Wetmore, who came aboard with an equally capable colleague, Lawrence Gifford. They argued the appeal before three seasoned judges, the youngest of whom, the forty-five-year-old Walter Chadwick Noyes, was already known for his grasp of patent litigation.

Wetmore and Gifford made almost the same case Parker had, but far more succinctly. The judges retired with the testimony, and given the quantity of it Henry Ford and everyone else involved thought they'd take months to come to a decision. They took six weeks.

On January 9, 1911, Judge Noyes read the decision. "Every element in the claim was old, and the combination itself was not new." So much for Selden's insistence that he alone had thought up the automobile. Therefore, the case came down to the engine Selden had named, a two-cycle Brayton. The court upheld the patent where a two-stroke engine was concerned, but of all the cars in America, only the Ohio-built Elmore was still using one. "We can see," Noyes concluded, "that had [Selden] appreciated the superiority of the [four-cycle] Otto engine and adopted that type for his combination, his patent would cover the modern automobile. He did not do so . . . and we cannot, by placing any forced construction upon the patent or by straining the doctrine of equivalents, make another choice for him at the expense of these defendants, who neither legally nor morally owe him anything."

During the next few hours Ford received a thousand telegrams, one from his old friend Charles King: "Hurrah for Henry Ford." Hurrah for Henry Ford was the general response. The *Detroit Journal* echoed scores of other editorials when it wrote, "It would have been considerably to Mr. Ford's personal advantage, in dollars and cents, had he compromised with or capitulated to the Selden patent holder years ago. But for more than seven years now he has fought on, almost alone, against huge odds—for a principle. He believed that his own rights were imperiled and the rights of every American citizen who is entitled to the rewards of his enterprise, industry, and brains."

Although Charles Sorensen had many sour and equivocal things to say about his boss in the memoir he published in the mid-1950s, he was still as much on Ford's side against the ALAM as he had been while he was carving the patterns for the Lenoir car put up against Exhibit 89. "The Ford fight against the Selden patent is a milestone in the history of the automobile industry. I believe it is one of the greatest things Mr. Ford did not only for Ford Motor Company but for everybody in the auto-making business. All of us around him took only minor parts in this long-drawn-out case. He carried full responsibility for success or failure on his own shoulders with little or no encouragement from members of his board."

Henry Ford himself was reticent about his victory. "Whatever I'd say now might sound like boasting. I think the decision speaks for itself."

The day after it came down, he and Edsel drove over to Royal Oak, where Parker lived, to congratulate him and wish him well at the outset of the retirement he had postponed for the better part of a decade. Parker lived to enjoy it until 1925.

Selden was unshaken. "Morally the victory is mine," he said on his deathbed in 1922.

The ALAM dissolved, leaving behind it a few valuable legacies, among them the reform of the patent laws that had so protracted the long case, and a patent-sharing arrangement among car-makers that prevented perpetual litigation, and that exists in the industry to this day. Henry Ford, who never joined any trade association, nonetheless shared his patents with the industry all his life.

Alfred E. Reeves, the ALAM's last president and surely one of the least sore losers in history, said, "Henry Ford is the greatest man in the automobile world; the Ford plant is the greatest automobile plant in the world; the Ford organization is the greatest automobile organization in the world."

In that victorious year of 1911, the organization sold 34,528 Model Ts.

The Dearborn, Michigan, farmhouse where Henry Ford was born in 1863 as it looked one wintry day three years after he revisited it in 1919 and decided to save it.

In 1886: This is the twenty-three-year-old Clara Bryant first saw when she met him at a dance.

Ford stands at the far right in the engine room of the Detroit Edison Illuminating Company. It is 1894, and he still understands those big, immaculately maintained steam engines far better than the electric generators they drive.

Clara and the infant Edsel. Henry took the snapshot in their Bagley Avenue home in 1894, and . . .

. . . Clara took this picture of her husband and son in their backyard two years later.

The substantial "woodshed" behind Ford's house, where he conducted his experiments with internal combustion. The door on the right has been widened—with an ax in the middle of the night—to let his first car out for his first drive.

An early offering from the woodshed: Ford's first gasoline engine. He had put it together from scavenged pieces of scrap metal, and on a busy Christmas Eve in 1893 fastened it to the kitchen sink so Clara could help him with a trial run.

The interior of the Bagley Avenue woodshed as Ford re-created it in Greenfield Village. The Quadricycle stands at the rear, up on blocks.

Ford sits at the wheel of his first race car in 1901, while his indomitable colleague Spider Huff mans the perilous post of the "riding mechanic." *Scientific American* magazine said this was the first car truly to look American.

The enormous *999*: Ford was a bit scared of it, but Barney Oldfield, who is holding the brutal steering mechanism, wasn't scared of anything, and his racing successes helped make Ford's name.

The 1903 Model A, the Ford Motor Company's first car, proved its mettle in the San Francisco earthquake.

Ford turns a cartwheel during a trip to Atlantic City in 1905. He is forty-three now and a success. Clara sits behind him, and Edsel is digging in the sand at her side.

Ford and his indispensable partner James Couzens, the former looking wary, the latter characteristically grim, with a good two feet of chilly air between them, in about 1910.

ASSEMBLY LINE
FINISHED CARS AND STARTER
THIRD FLOOR

By 1913 the company was turning out finished Model Ts in Oklahoma City.

Workers fit wheels to hubs at Highland Park in the mid-1920s.

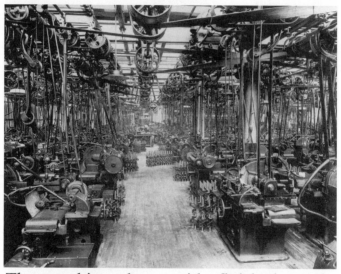

The machine shop—with finished crankshafts—at Highland Park appalled at least one journalist, who wrote that the racket it made was like that of ". . . a million monkeys quarreling, a million lions roaring, a million pigs dying, a million elephants smashing through a forest of sheet iron . . . [and] a million sinners groaning as they are dragged off to hell."

A thousand Model T chassis, here marshaled outside the plant, represented the production of a single nine-hour shift at Highland Park in 1913.

Fair Lane, the Ford estate. Charles Sorensen said it gave him "the creeps" to visit there.

Henry and Clara bird-watching, he more intently than she, in 1914.

One of the none-too-festive executive lunches, in 1933: Edsel sits to his father's right, Sorensen to his left (by the window), and Peter Martin to Sorensen's left.

Edsel and his father take a final ride just before the end of the Model T's two-decade run.

Ford with Evangeline Dahlinger. His confidante for more than three decades, she kept him up-to-date on what was happening in Greenfield Village and in return received such gifts as a Tudor manor house, a summer place on Lake Huron, a herd of cattle, and a Curtiss flying boat.

The "signed photograph" Edsel requested in return for sending Franklin Roosevelt a new Model A in 1929.

The Rouge was the largest industrial plant on earth. The docks in the foreground took in 850,000 tons of ore and 2.5 million tons of coal each season.

Ford has a word with Thomas Edison in 1925; the inventor was very nearly deaf.

Henry and Edsel sit by the hearth at the Plympton Family Home, one of Greenfield Village's hundred-odd buildings. It is late in 1941, and Edsel has less than two years to live.

B-24 Liberator bombers come down the assembly line at Willow Run, Sorensen's last achievement at the Ford Motor Company and, he thought, his greatest.

Henry Ford sits beside Clara at the tiller of his Quadricycle in June 1946 on the fiftieth anniversary of its inaugural run. The car is on a quiet street in Greenfield Village; beyond the farmhouses and their picket fences, a remade world clamors along the thoroughfare its inventor built.

CHAPTER 11
The Model T Takes Over

New York to Seattle on thin ice; learning to drive the Model T; birth of a dealer; the farmer and the car; caring for your Model T; the perils of starting it; "Funny Stories About the Ford"; five thousand accessories; remaking the nation in a decade: "I'll go without food before I'll go without my car."

R alzemond Parker had begun his futile argument before Judge Hough on June 1, 1909.

During recesses that morning everyone in the court went over to the grimy windows of the Post Office Building to watch what was going on a few stories below.

A continent away, the Alaska-Yukon-Pacific Exposition, celebrating the development of the Northwest from the almost frivolously close vantage point of the gold rush that had started twelve years earlier, opened that day in Seattle. Robert Guggenheim, who had a mining fortune and liked cars and was still in his thirties, thought a coast-to-coast automobile race would be a good way to publicize the fair, and he sponsored one.

No car had yet driven from the East Coast to

Seattle, and most of the three-hundred-odd automakers active in America that year didn't want to publicly test their products in mountainous country where roads were always poor, and often nonexistent. Moreover, the ALAM opposed the race, which further discouraged many manufacturers, but made Henry Ford the more eager to take part.

In the end, just five cars got to the starting line; two of them—awarded the designations No. 1 and No. 2—were Model Ts. The other three were far heavier and more powerful: a six-cylinder, 48-horsepower 3,500-pound Acme; a 50-horsepower Itala—the only foreign entrant—weighing 2 tons; and the 45-horsepower Shawmut, which was half a ton heavier than the Itala.

Despite the thin field, Guggenheim's race attracted all the publicity he could have hoped for. In the White House, that June 1, President William Howard Taft opened the fair by putting his forefinger to a gold telegraph key. At the moment of the presidential spark, Mayor George B. McClellan fired a pistol (like the telegraph key, gold plated), and the cars left City Hall Park, bound for Seattle. Henry Ford had gone down from the courtroom to wish his drivers well. After he got back, a member of the defense counsel turned from the window to call in mock astonishment, "Your Honor, there is something that puzzled me. I don't see a Selden car. I see a Ford car, two Ford cars, but I see no Selden car!" This amused even Judge Hough.

It hardly seems credible that these goings-on in lower Manhattan should change the life of a Washington State farm boy, but that's how the Model T went about its business.

Roscoe Sheller lived in the Yakima Valley town of Sunnyside, incorporated six years earlier with 314 residents. He had recently gotten his first job, which was doing everything in Charles Amundson's hardware store that Charles Amundson didn't want to do: sweeping, plumbing, some tinsmithing, keeping the books.

Guggenheim's racers were going to be coming up the Yakima Valley along the wagon road that followed the newly built high-tension line, and everyone in town knew it. Publicity had been growing since the cars left Boise, Idaho, with a Ford nine hours ahead of the costly heavyweights.

After word came that Ford No. 2 had crossed the Columbia River the evening before and was now in the valley, townspeople, skeptical but interested, began to make their way down to the foot of Sixth Street to mill about under the new power line. Roscoe Sheller didn't ask his boss for permission to leave the hardware store, fearing it would be denied, but he joined his neighbors anyway.

The crowd was still gathering, Sheller wrote,

"when dust was sighted far down the pole line. Whatever stirred it was driving faster than a wagon, or even a spirited team and buggy."

"Here she comes!" And Bert Scott and Jimmy Smith jolted into Sunnyside, their car pumping indignant gouts of steam from its radiator. Scott, at the wheel, climbed down and asked, "Can we have water?" He and Smith pulled off their goggles, leaving pale ovals in faces otherwise, Sheller remembered, "plastered with many-hued mud. . . . They appeared like an eerie something from another world, which to us they were."

Sheller looked at their car, and saw it nearly as Henry Ford had first envisioned it, for it was "a skeleton," he said, stripped almost to the bare chassis. This Model T had shed nearly a third of its normal weight, and was down to a little over nine hundred pounds. The battered hood, flailed by the road detritus of twelve states, had a blocky numeral "2" painted on its side.

Number 1, driven by Frank Kulick, had been enjoying a nine-hour lead out of Boise before a local had led it astray with confusing instructions. The other cars were either hours or days behind.

The water came, and Smith and Scott drank before No. 2 did, simultaneously gulping it down and washing their faces. The small platform behind the Model T's two seats was stacked with tied-down tires in various states of distress. Smith leaned over and pulled from this rubber nest a can of motor oil. As the crowd pressed closer he poured it into the engine.

"Sure takes a lot of oil," said a bold young boy out in front. Smith glanced at him. "You would too, if you'd been through what this car has."

"A horse wouldn't." The little reactionary got a laugh from the crowd.

During this back-and-forth, Scott pulled on heavy driving gloves and gingerly unscrewed the radiator cap. He gave it a final turn at arm's length, and stepped back as "belching steam and boiling water blew the cap from Scott's hand, showered Scott and christened front-row spectators with an 'I-was-there' souvenir, about which they might boast to unborn grandchildren."

The driver retrieved the cap and fed a thin stream of water into the radiator, which alternately protested with spitting fury and sighed with relief. Before the bucket was empty the machine had calmed down.

"Say, mister," the boy asked the driver, "is oil and water what makes her go?"

"It helps, kid." Scott got back in his seat. "Ready, Smitty?"

"Ready," said Smith. While Scott manipulated a couple of levers on the steering wheel, his partner went to the front of the car, took hold of a crank beneath the importunate radiator, and gave it a jerk. The still-warm engine instantly came to life—a busy threshing sound. The car was already moving when Smith dodged around the right front wheel and vaulted into his seat.

The Sunnyside townspeople watched until No. 2 was out of sight. Only a couple of hundred miles stood between it and Seattle, but they ran across the Cascades and even now, in late June, the mountains might still be deep in snow.

Sheller returned to the hardware store consumed with thoughts of No. 2, and of someday owning a car himself.

His boss was there. "Late, aren't you? Been down to see the racer?"

Sheller said yes, sir, he had, certain his sixty-dollar-a-month salary was about to evaporate.

Mr. Amundson went over to the window. "Why waste your time on that tin pipedream, when there's something *really* nice to see right here?"

"What do you mean?"

"Look there—across the street."

"*Whew!* Who—who—who is *she?*"

"Don't know her name. She's the new clerk at Moore's drug store."

Her name was Iva Benjamin, and a year later the hardware store clerk married her. All in all, it had been quite a day for Roscoe Sheller.

Smith and Scott did find snow in the Cascades, deep but frozen so hard on top that No. 2 could make its way along the crust for miles. But when the sun got high in the sky the fickle paving weakened and broke, dropping their Model T hub-deep in immobilizing powder. The two men struck out in search of help, and soon came upon the familiar cursing and clanging of a track gang at work. The railroaders obligingly freed the automobilists from their final obstacle.

Smith and Scott were on their way down the last western slope of their journey, ninety miles from Seattle, when they came upon the boss waiting for them, in a Model T touring car, with his Denver and Seattle branch managers.

On June 23 they drove into the Seattle fairgrounds to the cheering of fifteen thousand spectators. As No. 2 passed through the gates, Guggenheim thumbed his stopwatch. Smith and Scott had covered 4,106 miles in twenty-two days and fifty-five minutes. A record, of course, since no other car had ever made that particular trip before.

The Shawmut got there seventeen hours later, and Frank Kulick in No. 1, unlucky ever since he'd left Boise, nonetheless finished third, on June 25. The Acme came in days after Kulick. The Itala arrived in a freight car: Its team had given up in Cheyenne.

Robert Guggenheim awarded the prize with a speech that could not have pleased Henry Ford more had he and Couzens drafted it themselves: "Mr. Ford's theory that a light-weight car, highly powered for its weight, can go places where heavier cars cannot go, and can beat heavier cars, costing five and six times a much, on the steep hills or bad roads, has been proved. I believe Mr. Ford has the solution to the popular automobile."

Ford left an identical Model T in Seattle to absorb the admiration of the fairgoers, and, having given the car a complete overhaul and Scott and Smith five days of rest and sightseeing, sent No. 2 on a leisurely six-thousand-mile trip back to Detroit by way of Los Angeles. The victors stopped at Ford dealerships on the way, while all along their route newspaper advertisements drove home their missionary message: "A duplicate of the winner with a five-passenger touring car body costs you $850. No other car was entered that cost less than five times as much. The winner was a stock car. Any Model T could do as well. It's the one reliable car that does not require a $10,000 income to buy, a $5,000 bank account to run and a college course in engineering to keep in order. Better order now if you want August delivery."

After five fruitful months of this campaign, the judges of the race discovered that Henry Ford had offered his drivers more than moral support. The Ford Motor Company's unrivaled network of dealerships had everywhere been on hand to help them. Somewhere along the punishing route, Ford mechanics replaced No. 2's entire engine, a violation of Guggenheim's rules so egregious that the judges took the prize away from the Ford and awarded it instead to the Shawmut.

As the high-spirited Wall Street buccaneer James Fisk had remarked a generation earlier about one of his exploits, "Nothing is lost save honor." People were no longer interested in details of the race, but they remembered the rich harvest of publicity that it had brought in. They remembered the Model T. The Shawmut had already gone to eternity's garage, where the poor old two-stroke Elmore would soon join it.

Roscoe Sheller remembered the Model T; in fact, he thought about it every day. Automobiles became something of an obsession with him in 1912, when his father died and left him the family farm. Sheller turned out not to like farming any better than Henry Ford had: "Why should I nestle my head in the hairy flank of a squeamish, sad-eyed bovine twice every day, and yank away at her dangling appendages, to her profound disgust—and mine, when a coming motor-age could use my help?"

The coming motor age had little interest in Roscoe Sheller, though: no work at Aub Webber's Studebaker agency, nor at Speck and Roland, which had just started selling Buicks.

One day the squeamish cow summoned enough spirit to give her milker a powerful kick behind the ear, and followed it with a second that emptied the pail on him where he lay.

Sheller was leaning against the barn wall collecting himself when his friend Bob Barnett stepped inside.

"Hello, Farmer, I—" He spotted Sheller. "Haw-haw-haw," was his immediate reaction, followed by some sketchy expressions of concern.

Sheller fingered the growing bump on his head and Barnett said, "Maybe I've brought you the medicine you need."

He'd come to offer his friend a job: "I've just been made manager of a branch Ford agency Fred Chandler is opening in Sunnyside. I'll be needing a helper, and of course I immediately thought of you."

Sheller raised the reasonable objection that he didn't know how to drive.

"I'll teach you in a little while," Barnett said. "Nothing to it."

The job paid sixty dollars a month, which Sheller had been earning at the hardware store three years earlier. He had to start Monday. He jumped at the chance.

Barnett showed up at the farm in a Model T at six-thirty Monday morning, and Sheller began the initiation so many millions of Americans would be undergoing year after year for decades to come. His tutor slid across the seat so Sheller could get behind the wheel. The first thing the novice discovered was that the car had no door on the driver's side. His momentary confusion might not have been as amusing to Barnett as his friend getting kicked in the head by a milk-cow, but it drew several haw-haws.

Sheller squirmed over the sill, dropped onto the shuddering seat—the car was running—and looked down at the floor to see three pedals. Perhaps it was to his advantage that Sheller had never driven a car before, as not one of them was an accelerator. If he had a lot to learn, at least he had nothing to unlearn.

He put his hands on the wheel and looked over to his instructor, who said, "Now rest your left foot—*left* foot, I said—on the left pedal. Hold it exactly where it is now, while you shove the hand lever as far ahead as it will go. Understand?"

The lever, next to the nonexistent door, looked like an emergency brake, and in fact was called one, although it was almost useless for stopping the car, nor could it reliably hold it on a grade. The brake's real job was to take the car out of gear: once it was set, the Model T was in neutral.

Barnett told Sheller to "give her a little gas, like this." He pushed a small lever on the steering column, just behind the wheel. That was the throttle. "The motor *buzz-z-z-ed,* fenders quivered in fevered excitement and rattled a noisy, 'Let's go!'"

Sheller pushed the hand lever but forgot all about keeping his left foot on the pedal. The car stuttered forward a few feet and died.

Barnett climbed out, told his student to set the brake and then not touch anything, and spun the crank. The car started, and Barnett jumped back in, reaching across Sheller to fiddle with the throttle lever and its counterpart on the other side of the steering column, which regulated the spark. The engine relaxed into the businesslike grumble that every Model T owner sought. "See what happens when you do things right?" Barnett asked, but the novice was confused. When Barnett told him to push that left pedal down slowly and feed in a little gas gradually, Sheller remembered, "I was generous with both."

The car took off with a jerk that made Barnett scream, "Hell's fire!" Sheller lifted his foot from the pedal as if it had scalded him. This put the Model T into high, and "we plowed down the lane, hopping from rut to rut, like a panicked jack rabbit." Faced with a sharp turn, Sheller shouted a hopeless, anachronistic, and wholly sincere "Whoa!"

Barnett seized the wheel, cut off the gas, and stamped on the rightmost pedal, which was the actual brake. Then, cursing, he sent Sheller out to crank the car back into life.

During the course of what had come to seem an eternal morning, Sheller learned that after pushing the far-left pedal to the floor and releasing the brake he had the Model T in low. At about ten miles an hour he was to lift his foot, and the transmission would slip into high gear, which could take the car up to forty miles an hour if the road permitted. When he wanted to back up, Sheller had to push the left pedal halfway in, putting the car in neutral, adjust the throttle with his right hand, and, with his right foot, step on the middle pedal, which was stamped with an R for "reverse." The band collaring the forward speed drum would loosen while the one on the reverse grabbed hold. As Sheller's tutorial amply demonstrated, Henry Ford's planetary transmission could take an awful pounding and still continue to function.

Sheller ran off the road, flung himself through impossible turns, alternately enraged and terrified Barnett—and ended the day a competent driver.

That fall Barnett sold enough Model Ts to keep Mr. Eidelberry at the bank at bay, and then the winter of 1915 came down hard. Car buyers disappeared with the first frosts, but the Ford men kept their shop open.

Early one December morning Sheller glanced at the Carter's Little Liver Pills advertising thermometer "that had hung for years beside the post office entrance" and saw it "cuddled its red fluid low in the glass, as though striving for what warmth it might find there." The seasons had scoured away the instrument's numerals, but everyone knew that when that red dropped below the *v* in "Liver" it was destroyingly cold.

Sheller opened the garage, fired up the stoves, and then set about following Barnett's standing orders to start a Model T as soon as he got there and drive it out front. People had to see that this workhorse stood ready to help no matter what the weather.

Sheller strained at the crank, but Spider Huff's ingenious magneto was useless if the engine wouldn't turn in the first place, and this morning the freezing oil had coagulated about the planetary transmission and glued its gears into a solid lump. Sheller couldn't budge the crank with his right arm, and even when he jumped on its handle his two hundred pounds merely got it to give him a creeping ride floorward.

Hoping to melt the oil, he pushed the car over to a stove, which turned out to be hot enough to blister the paint on the nearest fender. Sheller knew he'd catch hell for that, but when he next took hold of the crank the oil had relaxed, and he was able to start the engine and drive the Model T through the big door to stand on the street proclaiming its hardihood.

Barnett arrived in the office minutes later and immediately berated him for bringing the car out on such a cold day. Sheller muttered about orders; Barnett said, "Get it back in here—*now!*"

Sheller went outdoors, reached through the side curtains to set spark and throttle, and tried the crank. Nothing doing. Once again he stood on it, "hoping to wear a channel through the congealed oil."

Despite the freezing morning, a small crowd gathered to watch Sheller cope with his dilemma. Apparently taking pity on him, Sunnyside's blacksmith, a man named Morrow, came forward. "Let me twist 'er tail."

The blacksmith was almost invariably the strongest man in any turn-of-the-century community. Morrow was able to move the crank without standing on it, but he couldn't get a snort of life from the engine. After the smith had the crank loosened enough for an average human to turn it, Barnett emerged from his office and said with Olympian disingenuousness, " 'Smatter boys? Can't start her, eh?" He made some adjustments to the spark and throttle, then took hold of the crank. Despite Morrow's having drilled a path for him, the Model T stood mute.

After a while Barnett stood and said, "You guys have flooded the carburetor." He opened the hood, poked ostentatiously at some fixtures beneath it, and turned back to his audience with an I-thought-as-much "Humph."

He went back to the crank, and gave it a confident spin, then a less confident one, and then kept churning it while his hands grew raw and his vanity bled.

John Steinbeck would write that the Model T was always a shrewd judge of its driver's patience: It would tease you every chance it got, but never more than you could take; and it always came through for you in the end.

Not this time.

At last Barnett stood up, red-faced with effort and fury, and shouted at Sheller, "Go write Chandler a letter. Tell him that I'll not crank MY life away for him, Henry Ford, or any damn man on this earth! Tell him that I'm through!" He strode magnificently off toward the frigid horizon. Morrow helped Sheller push the Model T back inside.

Seated in Barnett's abruptly vacated manager's chair, Sheller immediately began to write a dignified letter to the Ford agent in North Yakima.

> Dear Mr. Chandler,
>
> Mr. R. N. Barnett, your Sunnyside Branch Manager, has resigned, effective today, and has directed me to so inform you.
>
> I hereby make formal application for the position formerly held by Mr. Barnett. . . .

The letter was going out by the night mail, which left on the first morning train, but that evening, talking things over with his wife, Sheller realized that he'd better go up with it. After all, he'd never even met Mr. Chandler.

So he rode on the same train as his letter, and got

to Chandler first. He found the agent to be "a kindly man, well-fed and jovial." Chandler was surprised by Barnett's sudden defection, but evidently not too troubled by it. Sheller told him how badly he needed the job: He'd sold off all his farm equipment and rented out the farm itself to come work with Barnett. He had, he admitted, yet to sell a car, but Mr. Chandler knew that.

Chandler didn't exactly offer Sheller the job, but said he could try it on for a month and see how it fit. Emboldened, Sheller asked if he could have a car.

Chandler pointed out that he had one down in Sunnyside already, the recalcitrant Model T that had driven—or, rather, not driven—Barnett into another line of work. The way the agency worked then was that once Sheller sold a car, he would take the train up to North Yakima, forty miles away, and pick up another one.

Sheller argued that bringing a car back that morning would save the cost of him having to come back up on the train a few days later.

"We sell no cars in the winter," Chandler said. "What makes you think *you* can?"

"Maybe I can't, but I'm going to try harder than I've tried anything before."

Chandler led him down into the garage and told the crew there to get a new Model T ready. Sheller thought he saw him wink at the shop foreman as he called out, "Put the side curtains on good and tight. We want to take good care of our new *branch manager*."

Sheller drove home in a stew of elation and terror. He had a spanking new Model T. He was a branch manager of the Ford Motor Company. And if he didn't sell that new T in an impossible season, he most likely wouldn't be any kind of manager after thirty days.

He reached Sunnyside in the middle of the afternoon, to receive surprising news from an assistant who had been watching the garage: "There's a man in the office, been waiting to see you. Couldn't find anything else to read, so I gave him a Model T instruction book."

Sheller hurried in to find a farmer in a heavy sweater and a denim jacket—a dairy farmer, given the amount of dried milk on his overalls.

"I kinda figured I'd look over one of them thar autos," the man said, and asked if Sheller would teach him to drive.

"Nothing to it," the branch manager replied as airily as Bob Barnett had to him a few months earlier.

While Sheller showed him the Model T, the farmer said he'd been reading the book, and it looked easy. The car, its engine still warm, started with the merest twitch of the crank. Sheller got it out on the road, nervously issued instructions, and turned the wheel over. The dairyman drove it effort-lessly, said "whoa" only once and immediately laughed at himself, and happily observed that it all went "just like it said in the book." After a while, he added, "I think I got 'er now. Let's go back."

When they got to the garage, the farmer asked, "You fill 'er with gas if I buy 'er?"

Already the salesman, Sheller said, "For you, I will."

"I'll drive 'er up to the pump. You fill 'er up, and we'll go in and settle up."

In the office that had been Sheller's for a little more than a day, the farmer reached under his milk-stiff overalls "and produced a wallet from somewhere in his several layers of pants." He paid for the car with a mixture of folding money and gold pieces, then drove it off into the winter dusk that Sheller rightly saw as the dawn of his career.

That transaction in the Yakima Valley echoed ones that were taking place in the Hudson River Valley, in the Sacramento Valley, the Valley of the Tennessee, in towns like Sunnyside, in towns like Des Moines, in towns that weren't anything like other towns: New York, Chicago, New Orleans.

At just about the time Roscoe Sheller was joyfully showing his wife the money from his first sale, the company he represented had made, in December 1915, its millionth Model T.

That Sheller's customer was a farmer was representative, too: 64 percent of those Model Ts had been sold to a rural market. Henry Ford had won over the motorcar's most stubborn enemy. Just a few years earlier, Woodrow Wilson, then president of Princeton University, said automobiles "are a picture of the arrogance of wealth, with all its independence and carelessness," and that "nothing has spread socialistic feeling more."

This sounds pretty high-strung, but those brass-bound juggernauts did foment a good deal of rural anger during their forays from the city, particularly when they killed a chicken or hurt a cow or, occasionally, a person. "I'm a Southerner and know how to shoot," Wilson said. "Would you blame me if I did so under such circumstances?" Some farmers did go that far at first, and others laid snares in the roads, hoping to break a spring or perhaps an axle.

Such occasional violence notwithstanding, the farmer's hatred of automobiles in particular and machinery in general was far from innate. Farmers had been using steam engines to saw wood as early as 1807, and it was not on the streets of Detroit but on a country road that Henry Ford first saw the self-propelled steam traction engine majestically crawling toward its day's work. Gasoline also reached the farm before the automobile did. Stationary internal combustion engines, some putting out as much as sixteen horsepower, were grinding grain and shredding corn in American fields from the 1870s on.

In any event, Henry Ford quenched whatever

hostility remained by making his car cheap enough for any modestly successful farmer to buy—"Even You Can Afford a Ford," said his billboards—and insisting that he had developed the Model T largely to lessen the toil of farming life.

The car did. The owner could, for instance, jack up his Model T and belt one of the driving wheels to a buzz saw, or use it to lift a hog from the scalding tub or corn into a silo. And when the car wasn't running a thresher, it could take the farmer and his family out beyond the boundaries of their everyday lives. It was these excursions, and their consequences, that made the Model T the single most important automobile ever, and possibly the most significant force in twentieth-century America.

The Model T is no longer any sort of force in our lives, but it refuses to look placid or quaint, to acquire that gloss of appeal that time puts on so many ugly things. The high, unlovely body and pugnacious snout still flaunt the boxy antique's power to change a world.

It was the first car for millions of Americans, and every one of those new owners found it was about as demanding as their first baby. We who live in a world where an automobile might require some trifling maintenance every twenty thousand miles or so can scarcely imagine how much tending a car needed a century ago. The wealthy then didn't hire chauffeurs merely to decorate their homes with another servant, but because keeping a motorcar in running condition was a full-time job.

The Model T was simple enough to allow an amateur to learn fairly quickly how to care for it, but the owner had a great deal to do.

Take the matter of lubrication. The manual for 1909—the car's first full year of manufacture—featured a page captioned, "Where to Oil the Model T." Everywhere, and all the time, it must have seemed to the oiler. Going aft from the radiator, you began with, "Hub, Grease every 500 miles." Nestling against the hub was the "Spindle Belt. Oil every hundred miles." A few inches away the "Steering Ball Socket" also wanted to be oiled every one hundred miles, while a little further inward from it, under the hood, the commutator had to have oil every two hundred miles, but would accept Vaseline instead. Then came the unforgiving "Fan Hub, Grease Cup": "Every fifty miles."

So it proceeded to the "Rear Spring Hanger" and its neighbor the "Hub Brake Cam"—200 miles each. The list ended with the general suggestion that "a drop or two of oil should occasionally be applied to all small connections and joints throughout the car."

One chore needed doing every morning: "Lubricate Engine and Transmission by daily

Replenishments through breather tube. Oil level in crank case should be carried slightly above lower pet cock."

That was how you checked your oil: Crawl beneath the engine and twist open the higher of two little valves. If oil drips out the car has too much, and needs draining off. Now to the lower valve. If it bleeds oil, all is well. If it doesn't, add more oil, but not, of course, enough to submerge the upper valve.

So, too, with the gasoline. There was no fuel gauge, and when the supply needed checking the owner lifted up the front seat cushion to reveal the elongated drum of the gas tank. The Ford Company published a cross section of the tank with the number of gallons on one side and the number of inches they occupied in the tank on the other. The drawing came with a chummy directive: "Here's a little diagram that will tell you easily and accurately exactly how much gasoline is in the tank of your touring car. How many times can you remember, when it would have come in handy to have known just how many gallons you had. A little care in marking on a stick the figures on the accompanying table will provide a means of always knowing your exact supply." You dipped the stick in the tank, and checked how many inches came up damp. Ford owners didn't have to make their own gauges for long, though: Every kind of automobile advertiser began producing the rulers, stamping them with the appropriate self-celebrations, and supplied them free for decades.

That was not all with the fuel. "Always strain through a chamois skin to prevent water and other foreign matter from getting in the carburetor." The carburetor: The Model T had no fuel pump to feed it, because the under-seat gas tank was set high enough for gravity to do the job, just as it had been on the Quadricycle. This worked fairly well, except on steep hills, when as the car nosed upward the gas sloshed toward the back of the tank, away from the port that fed the engine, and the carburetor ran dry. Ford owners learned to compensate by backing up steep grades.

They had to learn a great deal more about the car's foibles, and in time there were so many Model Ts on the road that this knowledge became a national shared wisdom, some of it pure superstition (good idea to drop a ball of camphor in the tank every now and again), but much of it crucial.

The dangers of starting the car took only a few years to become universally known. You always held the crank in the hollow of your hand and *never* put your thumb around it, because if the engine kicked back, the crank could break your arm. Before this wisdom was fully disseminated, there was a regular plague of bandaged right wrists across the country.

Even without imperiling an arm, starting the Model T was a chancy business. The motor pioneer Bellamy Partridge was able to give a vivid description years after he'd last done it. "Tickle the carburetor, hold the choke wire [a thin metal loop that poked out from the radiator] at exactly the right spot—a hair's breadth either way would spoil the combustion. Draw a long breath and hold it—this was supposed to protect you in the case of backfire. Then give a sudden yank on the starting crank. This had to be done just so. It wasn't a push—it was rather a flip or a flirt. You had to take the engine by surprise, make a quick delivery, and then step back out of reach. Cranking was something that had to be learned by long practice, for it was a fine art like a sinker or a knuckle ball. Some people never could learn it."

E. B. White took the same wily approach to starting his Model T: After giving the crank "two or three nonchalant upward lifts" and "whistling as though thinking about something else," he "would saunter back to the driver's cabin, turn the ignition on, return to the crank, and this time, catching it on a downstroke, give it a quick spin."

Other menaces still lay in ambush once the engine was firing. "Often, if the emergency brake hadn't been pulled all the way back, the car advanced on you . . . and you would hold it back by leaning your weight against it. I can still feel my old Ford nuzzling me at the curb, as though looking for an apple in my pocket."

In their cautious, devious courting of their car's approval, both men clearly felt it a sentient being that required psychological as well as mechanical attention. Most other Ford owners did, too, and, with the possible exception of warships and warplanes, no machine has ever been more personalized.

The proliferating Model T got christened early in its life. Lizzie had been a generic horse's name for earlier generations (as Rover was a dog's), and the car inherited it. But that turned out to be, as it were, the surname. Chris Sinsabaugh, a newspaperman who began his career reporting on the bicycle industry and moved over, along with much of the industry itself, to automobiles about the time Ford started making them, wrote that although "many wondered how the T got its famous nickname," he had never been able to find out. "One story [I] heard was that once upon a time a Ford dealer in San Antonio, who had been complaining about ill-fitting doors, wrote the factory that if the bodies were shipped without doors, a can-opener might be included in the tool kit and each dealer could cut his own doors and make them fit. Hence 'Tin Lizzie.'"

Never mind the strenuously touted vanadium steel; that "tin" would stick to the Model T for the rest of its long life.

A frugal housewife saved her empty tin cans, and one day on impulse sent them to the Ford Motor Company. A week later she got a letter from Ford saying they had repaired her car and were returning it along with seven leftover cans.

People told that joke to one another for two generations. They swapped hundreds and hundreds of others like it, too, and the surest indicator of how quickly and firmly the Model T battened itself onto the American psyche is the immense literature of jokes it produced. This was an actual literature, in that it flourished in scores of books, ranging from dime pamphlets to substantial hardcovers: *Funabout Fords*; *Ford Jokes and Stories*; *Original Ford Joke Book: If It Hurts You to Laugh Don't Buy One*; *A Book of Ford Jokes*; *More Funabout Fords. . . .*

The automobile joke is as old as the automobile. Bellamy Partridge remembered that the Duryea brothers played a part in its genesis when, a year after their triumph in the snows of Chicago, they made a poor showing at a race in Narragansett, Rhode Island. As their car repeatedly stalled, the exasperated spectators began to call out, "Get a horse!"

In 1950, the radio comedian Henry Morgan, asked to choose the most popular jokes of the last fifty years, believed "Get a horse!" was "the one that lasted longest, was told the most, and made the greatest impact on mankind." Morgan said that "the phrase made every man a comedian." He added that "it wasn't hard to remember."

In the spring of 1936 Dr. Ralph Hutchinson, president of Washington and Jefferson College in Pennsylvania, invited the seventy-four-year-old Henry Ford to visit the campus. As they were smoothly heading there in a Lincoln limousine, President Hutchinson said, "I happened to notice an old Model T Ford of the vintage of about 1915." It had long since shed its fenders, and two college students were straining at the crank to get it going. They knew it would start eventually, and so did the ruin of a car. It was just teasing them. President Hutchinson pointed to the roadside scene, and Henry Ford rolled down the window, leaned out, and yelled in the highest good humor, "Get a horse!"

Still, the majority of all the automobile jokes ever conceived bounced along with the Model T.

Few commodities age as quickly as humor, and not many Ford jokes would strike anyone as funny today. But they are eloquent of the feelings of the Model T owner: a mixture of self-mockery and pride. Many centered on how inexpensive the car was, and its relative smallness. Ring Lardner amalgamated a bushel of these into a surprisingly tiresome story he wrote in 1915 for the second volume of *Funny Stories About the Ford*. Phil, in a letter to his friend Dave, recounts buying his Model T "for $150.00 dollars and the car was . . .

in good repares. The man was going to move out of town and I suppose he didn't want to stick it in his sutecase for the fear that he would get some grease on his other shirt. . . . It was supper time when I got her home but Nell says to hell with supper and I would half to take her out for a ride and while we was out we happened to think all of a sudden that we didn't have no garridge to keep a car in it and we couldn't leave it out on the st. all night for the fear that some stew [drunk] might trip over it and sew us for dammidges and Nell says she would sleep on the lunge in the living room and I could take the car in with me." He brings the Model T up to bed, gives it a bath in the sink, and loses it down the drain. And so forth.

After tin and size, the jokes light on the Model T's loose-knit joints:

Q: Why is a Ford like a millionaire baby?
A: Because it gets a new rattle every day.

An owner explains that his car doesn't need a speedometer because "it's easy to gauge your speed. When you go ten miles an hour, your lamps rattle; when you get up to twenty miles an hour, the fenders rattle; at twenty-five miles the windshield begins to rattle; and when you go faster than that your bones rattle."

And then there was the car's cheapness. A Ford dealer comes up with the promotional idea of giving a new Model T to the first person who manages to assemble four dimes with the mintmarks F, O, R, and D. Not long after he publicizes the contest, a man comes in and hands him the dimes.

"You've done it!" the dealer says. "Look around the showroom and take your pick." After twenty minutes the man returns.

"Well?"

"If it's all the same to you, could I have my forty cents back?"

The folklorist B. A. Botkin thought the jokes largely a defensive measure on the Ford owner's part: Make fun of yourself first, and you defuse anyone else who might be planning to. A great many of the jokes, though, turn the car's supposed weaknesses into strengths, as with the one about the two brothers, George and Fred, who each inherit two thousand dollars. George spends the entire legacy on a fine, big six-cylinder limousine. Fred buys a Model T for five hundred dollars.

Driving home, George is surprised to be passed by Fred, who is there waiting when he arrives.

Nettled, George asks "what caused that terrible rattling noise" he heard as Fred's car passed him.

"Oh," Fred replies, "that was the fifteen hundred dollars in my pocket."

If the jokes ever stung the occasional Model T owner, they were only a source of pleasure to the Model T's maker. Henry Ford so obviously relished them that some of his colleagues thought he was underwriting the joke books. He wasn't, but he always made a show of buying them and passing them about. Ford saw every joke as an advertisement, free as the air and living sometimes for years. Their swarming ubiquity was one of the reasons he decided, in 1917, to cease advertising altogether.

He may even have invented a Model T joke, though he said it was a true story. He was out on a trip testing one of his cars on the Upper Peninsula when he rounded a bend and came upon a man standing beside a new Model T scowling helplessly at its engine. Ford pulled and stepped on all the things necessary to bring his car to a halt, walked over, and asked what the trouble was. The frustrated owner had no idea. Ford asked for his toolbox, and in a few minutes had the car ticking over and ready to go anywhere.

The owner took two dollars from his pocket and offered them to Ford, who declined. When the man persevered, Ford thanked him, but said he had all the money he needed.

The man laughed. "The hell you do! You drive a Ford."

But when it came time to tell Woodrow Wilson—who had bought a Model T in 1914 and was now president of the United States—a joke, Ford chose one that made a different point about the car. A farmer drafting his will stipulated that he must be buried in his Model T. When his lawyer asked why, he said, "Because I ain't been in a hole yet it couldn't get me out of."

That was always tacit in the jokes. The Model T might flap and rattle and get lost in your bathtub, but it did its job: It kept on going.

Bellamy Partridge told of anxiously nursing his Packard through a mudhole near his home, and then went on to recount a story that has the architecture of a Ford joke, but isn't one: "That mud hole, by the way, was destined to become famous. So many cars were bogged down there that Andy Brackett used to keep a team of horses close at hand most of the time to tow out the unfortunates. For a large car he charged three dollars. A medium-sized car he would pull out for two. He made a special price for a Ford, though this concession was academic, since Fords rarely were stuck there."

The car's dependability was the only luxury it offered. When it first appeared, the Ford copywriters asserted, "No car under $2000 offers more, and no car over $2000 offers more except in trimmings."

This was pushing things some. Today, for instance, few people would consider a heater "trimming," but the Model T didn't have one. Such lacks, however, could be rectified by the products of hundreds of companies that rose and prospered solely through making accessories for the Model T. In the case of the heater you could buy a tin shield that got clamped to the exhaust manifold and diverted some of the heat it generated through the floorboards. "Not a bad fix," one owner remembered. "It would warm the car up to about the temperature of a barn."

The accessories—eventually there were five thousand of them—ranged from "Top Prop Nut to replace nuts lost because of vibration . . . well made of steel, finely enameled black, 3c" to embellishments that transformed the car: "Make a Full-Fledged Speedster of your Ford. . . . Here is a real nifty, classy, up to the minute Speedster body that would do credit to any car. We have correctly named it the Cyclone because it glides so easily, noiselessly and swiftly through the air on any Model T Ford chassis." The Cyclone body cost $68.75 in lead priming paint, $78.75 in glossy red, yellow, or black. There were speed-ometers and valve grinders, and a host of mechanical starters, all of dubious utility, any number of brackets and clamps and ball joints to reduce rattling, and a spidery assemblage of levers that "permits manipulating the throttle with foot," which E. B. White thought "madness" because "the Model T, just as she stood, had a choice of three foot pedals to push, and there were plenty of moments when both feet were occupied in the routine performance of duty and when the only way to speed up the engine was the hand throttle."

One aftermarket product that lasted, however, was the "Hind-View Auto-Reflector," which went on sale in August 1911, just three months after Ray Harroun had mounted the first rearview mirror on the bright yellow Marmon Wasp he drove to victory in the Indianapolis 500.

For the unusual Model T owner who preferred the appearance of the car to its innards, Hinkley Motors stood ready to replace the works—engine, transmission, and all: the transmission for $132, the engine for $184. "All this at only a little more than the cost of a major overhaul, and without chassis alterations of any kind. Not even a hole to drill! And a Ford which, after the installation, is stronger than ever before."

Just as the owner was expected to install his own heater or starter or better headlights if he wanted them, so was it up to him to maintain his car. A midwesterner named Albert Stephenson, who had a succession of Ts in the 1920s—"like so many others, I drove only second- or third-hand models"—remembered that "the whole car was simple, accessible, and tolerant. . . . On a cold morning a quick jerk or two at the choke rod on the dash would cure a harsh and persistent coughing spell. In the evening you could tighten the bands, look at the timer, or clean the plugs. A weekend would do nicely to reline the bands or grind the valves and clean the carbon or maybe tighten the rods. A four-day vacation was plenty to overhaul the engine or the rear end. If any of these jobs was a bit beyond your experience, you had merely to ask your neighbor, who not only knew but would come over and help." The ramifications of this were far-reaching and frequently unexpected. In the Second World War, for example, German tanks were often superior to their American counterparts. But this advantage was canceled by how quickly a disabled Sherman could get itself repaired and back into action. The Germans were baffled and dismayed to find that among his other accomplishments, Henry Ford had created a whole generation of mechanics.

But the Model T's most profound impact was succinctly expressed in the *Ford Times*, a company magazine born just a few months before the car in 1908. Originally a house organ "published solely to afford a means for the interchange of ideas among all dealers and employees of the Ford Motor Company," who were frequently and forcefully enjoined to contribute articles, it was full of selling tips and pictures that could be imported into ads ("No. 106—two column cut of Coupe for newspaper advertising") and such insider news as employee bowling scores. Before long, though, it had grown into a richly produced monthly aimed not only at dealers but also at Ford owners and potential buyers. Within a decade of its founding it had a circulation of nine hundred thousand, and its popularity reflects the vigor of the product it promoted.

In 1915 *Ford Times* declared, "Best of all," the Model T "has remodeled the social life of the country."

In a decade, the Model T broke the age-old isolation of the farm. The recipients of this new freedom appreciated their benefactor, trusted him, called him by his first name. "You know, Henry," wrote a Georgia farmwife in 1918, "your car lifted us out of the mud. It brought joy to our lives. We loved every rattle in its bones."

In 1926 an Alabaman expressed the same feelings in more high-flown terms: "We of the South affectionately acclaim you, instead of Lincoln, as the Great Liberator. Lincoln has freed his thousands, you have freed your ten thousands. The rutted roads on mountain sides and water sogged wheel tracks on lower lands have been smoothed, that the wheels of Fords may pass. The sagged barbed wire gates of barren cotton patches and blighted corn fields have been thrown open that brainblinded and soulblinded recluses might rise joyously into the world with their families in Fords."

The Model T soon became as much an urban being as a rural one. When Robert and Helen Lynd published their famous sociological study of the effects of the young century on a typical small city in the 1920s—it was Muncie, Indiana, which they called "Middletown"—they met a lifelong resident who said, "Why on earth do you have to study what's changing this country? I can tell you what's happening in just four letters: A-U-T-O!"

The machine had already taken a hold on American society that it has not relaxed yet. The Lynds found that many Muncie residents were mortgaging their houses to buy an automobile, and the trend alarmed almost everyone who wasn't a part of it. The recently established custom of the Sunday drive was a "threat against the church," while a labor organizer complained that "as long as men have enough money to buy a secondhand Ford and tires and gasoline, they'll be out on the road and paying no attention to union meetings."

The Lynds found that the automobile had been "spreading the 'vacation' habit. The custom of having each summer a respite, usually of two weeks, from getting-a-living activities, with pay unabated, is increasingly common."

A mother of nine children, reflecting on this radical new gift that combined mobility with privacy, said, "We'd rather do without clothes than give up the car. We used to go to my sister's for a visit, but by the time we got the children shoed and dressed there wasn't any money left for carfare. Now no matter how they look, we just poke 'em in the car and take 'em along."

Another mother went further: "I'll go without food before I'll see us give up the car."

The Lynds were looking at the general impact of the automobile, but when they came to make an inventory of the cars in Muncie, they found that of the 6,221 registered in 1923, 2,578 were Fords, with Chevrolet running a distant second at 590.

Years after he'd ceased to wrestle with one, John Steinbeck recalled the Model T with the same fond precision E. B. White did. Olfactory memories are sometimes the strongest, and he mentioned how his car smelled—"a lovely odor . . . of oil-soaked wood and sunbaked paint, of gasoline, of exhaust gases and ozone from the coil box"—even before saying what it meant to him: "I think I loved that car more than any I have ever had. It understood me. It had an intelligence not exactly malicious, but it did love a practical joke. It knew, for instance, exactly how long it could keep me spinning the crank and cursing it before I would start kicking its radiator in. It ran perfectly when I was in blue jeans, but let me put on my best suit and white shirt, and maybe a girl beside me, and that car invariably broke down in the greasiest possible manner."

Steinbeck went on to discuss the car's larger significance, basically agreeing with the Ford Motor Company's assessment, but expressing it in terms the *Ford Times* would be unlikely to have countenanced: "Someone should write an erudite essay on the moral, physical and esthetic effect of the Model T Ford on the American Nation. Two generations of Americans knew more about the Ford coil than the clitoris, about the planetary system of gears than the solar system of stars. With the Model T, part of the concept of private property disappeared. Pliers ceased to be privately owned and a tire pump belonged to the last man who had picked it up. Most of the babies of the period were conceived in Model T Fords and not a few were born in them. The theory of the Anglo Saxon home became so warped that it never quite recovered."

CHAPTER 12
Terrible Efficiency

The Crystal Palace; taking the work to the worker; speeding up; the twentieth century's only industrial revolution; the workers hate it.

O f course the Model T could never have made such an impression had it not been deployed in vast numbers, and at a price folks like Roscoe Sheller's dairy farmer could afford. That Ford developed a way to do this is, more than the car itself, the measure of his genius.

Several automakers were turning out a hundred cars a day during the Model T's early years, which demonstrates impressive planning and organization, but as Allan Nevins points out, there is a fundamental difference between "quantity production" and true "mass production." It was by inventing the latter that Henry Ford invented the modern age.

First, though, he needed a place to invent it in. The success of the Model N had badly strained the Piquette Avenue plant. In 1906, months before the first Model T was built, Ford bought sixty acres of land in Highland Park, a small suburb six miles north of downtown Detroit.

He hired Albert Kahn to design his new factory.

The architect was still in his thirties, but he had already built a plant for Packard that impressed Ford with its advanced reinforced concrete design and broad stretches of glass. Ford wanted something bigger, and he got it: the largest building in Michigan and the largest automobile factory in the world. Four stories high and 865 feet long—equivalent to an eighty-six-story skyscraper lying on its side—its concrete corners fortified with steel supporting rods beneath a shell of decorative brick framed fifty thousand square feet of glass. That was three-quarters of the building's walls, and on fair days the workers would stand in a lake of sunlight so bright that some took to calling the place the Crystal Palace. In a few months Kahn had put up next to this prodigy a machine shop nearly as large, with an all-glass roof. The two buildings were connected by a craneway to carry materials from one to the other. Eight hundred and sixty feet long and nearly sixty high, it was itself a corridor of glass. The Highland Park factory set Kahn on his way to being the foremost industrial architect in America.

Ford operations moved from Piquette Avenue at the end of 1909, "without," the *Ford Times* pertly reported, "a brass band, a ball, a clambake, or even a speech from the mayor." The house organ had a right to its complacency. On the last day of 1909 all the new Ford cars were shipped from Piquette Avenue. On New Year's Day of

1910, most of them rolled out of Highland Park.

This extraordinarily smooth transition was largely the work of Sorensen and his immediate boss, a French Canadian named Peter Martin whom Nevins describes as "burly" and, somewhat more surprisingly, "stodgy." Martin was the plant's superintendent, although he never held that title.

Henry Ford abhorred titles. Sorensen remembered that in the spring of 1908 Ford summoned him and Martin—who was universally known as Ed—to his office. It was a brief meeting. Ford said, "You, Ed, will be plant superintendent and you, Charlie, will be assistant superintendent. Just go out there and run the place. I know you can do it. But there's one thing I want to add: work together as one. I don't ever want to hear that you can't work together. And don't worry about titles."

Martin and Sorensen received their promotions because Walter Flanders had just quit.

Flanders had blown through the company like a line squall. A Vermonter who had managed to educate himself about machine tools so effectively that by the time Ford hired him in 1906 he understood plant design perhaps better than anyone else in the country, he was everything his new boss was not: loquacious, brash, noisy (Sorensen said he had "a voice that could be heard in a drop forge plant"), domineering, and something of a libertine, at least by Henry Ford's standards. He immediately made himself so popular in the company with both the workers and the board that Sorensen thought Ford was a little scared of him: "He was aware of Flanders's ability yet feared the man might take his place. There was a streak of jealousy here."

To be sure, Flanders sounded as if he already owned the company when he stipulated what his duties would be: to hire and fire anyone he chose, and "to manage the different manufacturing departments of your companies, [and] reorganize same, on what, in my judgment, is the most economical basis of manufacture for producing commercial products at the minimal cost."

Whatever Ford might have thought of this summary, it alarmed Couzens, who wrote his boss, "I am afraid he will want the earth if he gets started on a proposition like this. The terms and salary [seventy-five hundred dollars a year] I think are all right, but he wants [needs] to be confined to the manufacturing end in the shop and have nothing to do with policy or designing or finances or sales." Couzens concluded with a request that surely reflects earlier aggravations: "Please don't leave this letter around on your desk or show it to anyone."

Flanders didn't try to fire Couzens and he didn't try to take over the company. Instead, he set about establishing principles that would drive

American manufacturing all through the new century.

He immediately began rearranging the machine tools in the factory. Previously, as in the Dodge brothers' operation, as in nearly every plant in the country, they were grouped together: here a colony of drill presses, there a dozen lathes. This made sense if a factory had to do many different jobs, but Flanders understood that the Ford works would be doing only one, and it would be done far more efficiently if the machines stood along the path the work took. That is, if a part needed to be heated between being milled and being drilled, Flanders put an oven between the milling machine and the drill.

He went on to study the stocks of materials that fed the newly rationalized sequence of machine tools and pared them down. Keep only a ten-day supply on hand, he ordered; let the suppliers carry the inventory at their expense and not the Ford Motor Company's.

Flanders also stressed the necessity of inter-changeable parts. Every axle housing and cylinder head must match every other one as closely as possible right down to the atomic level. Having to file or hammer a part to make it fit would slow production, create bottlenecks, and extinguish profits.

Henry Ford already believed this, as had generations of mechanics before him. American manufacturers had long been striving for perfect interchangeability of the elements in their product, first in firearms, then sewing machines, and most recently bicycles. But the accuracy of machine tools could not wholly be trusted until the early twentieth century, when increasing technological sophistication began to let them meet the demands of the automotive industry.

Finally, Flanders pressed for single-purpose tools. The repetitive manufacture of a single car part did not require a trained mechanic. Flanders ordered what he called "farmer tools," ones far from simple, but so easy to operate that anyone just in from the country could learn how in a couple of hours.

Henry Ford was again in agreement with his production manager, and the company would never stint in buying the newest and best machine tools.

Then, less than two years after his arrival, Flanders was gone, lured away by a fat offer from the Wayne Automobile Company and taking some valued employees with him.

Henry Ford may have felt intimidated by Flanders, but he was so angry to see him leave that his response shook the hard-minded Couzens.

"If you say the word," Ford told him, "I will have his head knocked off."

"What do you mean?"

"Oh, I have a couple of fellows who will beat him up."

"Oh, no. We will stand this without *that*."

Couzens left the office brooding. After a while he came to think what others would in the years ahead: "Mr. Ford was not one man, but two."

Ford didn't follow up on his threat, but he kept sulking about Flanders's defection. "Hereafter," he told Sorensen, "anybody who goes along with us must come up from the bottom and work right through the organization."

Despite the blow he dealt Henry Ford's amour propre, Flanders had more than justified the fifteen thousand dollars he earned during his brief tenure. Sorensen, who was never free with a compliment, wrote, "Ford, a quiet, sensitive person, got a few gray hairs at this stage, but he learned a great deal from Flanders and so did I." He went further: Flanders "headed us toward mass production."

Ford would take some time to get there, but the Highland Park factory proved itself immediately. A few months after the company had moved into its new home it was completing more than 100 cars a day, and in April alone it put out 3,728. Henry Ford had made the job easier by decreeing the year before that this magnificent new plant would be building just one car: the Model T. And so it would for the better part of twenty years. The manufacturing year closed that September with

19,000 new Model Ts on the road. The next year Ford made 34,500, and the year after that, 1911–12, 78,440.

Henry Ford sought economy in the speed of production, and wherever else he could find it. In the beginning, the plan had been to cast the crankcase, which covered the bottom of the engine and contained the oil bath in which it had to run. Casting was expensive, and the result would be too heavy.

While Ford mechanics were puzzling through this, an owner of the John R. Keim stamping mill in Buffalo came to see Ford. Rather than melt and pour and work metal, Keim's big presses took in a piece of sheet steel and punched it into shape, like a notary public's seal embossing a piece of paper. The representative brought Ford only a shiny black telephone stand the mills were then pounding out, but Ford got the idea, and sent Sorensen and Wills to Buffalo to have a look at the operation.

Sorensen was tickled by the assignment. He remembered, as a boy, visiting the Keim works. "At the time they made bicycle crank hangers and pedals. With other young bicycle enthusiasts, I used to go to the back of the plant where there was a scrap pile of rejected ball bearings. I had quite a boxful of these bearings, which I kept around our home."

When Sorensen and Wills entered the factory,

they were taken to a press busily showing its capacity to make a larger stamping than a telephone stand. The machine was doing just fine, but apparently the job required a lot of lubrication, because from beneath it, slick and black as a seal with heavy oil, "came a supervisor who had been handling the press-work. . . . The man from the pit, a tall lanky fellow, was covered with grease from head to foot. And that was my first, but not my last, sight of my fellow Dane, William H. Knudsen."

No instant friendship grew from this fortuitous reunion of countrymen. "I must correct extravagant stories told about him when he left Ford," Sorensen wrote of Knudsen forty years later. "He had nothing to do with major producing or its planning at Highland Park. Few of the basic staff seemed able to get along with him."

Here is a scent of the same alarm—and jealousy—Henry Ford must have felt about Walter Flanders. In fact, Knudsen would get along with every level of the Ford staff, and become one of the greatest car men of his century. But at the moment this oil-basted, eager stranger only wanted Wills and Sorensen to take the stampings he'd just made to Detroit and see how their boss liked them.

He didn't, much. Henry Ford felt there was something a little sleazy, a bit hasty and coarse, about stampings. Castings appealed more to the engineer in him. Galamb pushed for the stampings. When you could get away with it, bending metal was cheaper than pouring it.

Ford would not compromise on his vanadium steel, but he knew that to keep down the price of his car he would have to use the stampings. He took what comfort he could from teasing Galamb—"Hungarian stimpings," he would say, making fun of Galamb's accent, and started calling him "shit-iron Joe"—but he accepted the stampings and, in 1911, when his victory over the Selden patent suit opened the way, he bought the factory that made them.

For a while the Buffalo plant kept the flow of supplies coming to Detroit. Then, just before Labor Day in 1912, Keim factory hands, angry at what they were being paid for some piecework that had nothing to do with Ford, walked off the job on a wildcat strike.

Knudsen, now the plant's general superintendent, called Detroit with the news. "That suits me," said Ford. "If the men don't want to work, get some flat cars and move the presses and machinery to Highland Park."

A troubled Knudsen went to talk with the strikers. I know this man, he told them; he isn't kidding. Best to back off for the moment.

They jeered Knudsen, and three days later the Keim stamping machines were dispensing transmission covers in the Crystal Palace.

That was fast work, but all the work at Highland Park was fast now. Ford and Sorensen and Martin were shifting Detroit's heaviest machinery around as casually as checkers players move their pieces. Labeled with brass tags to show where they belonged (affixing these was one of the teenaged Edsel's first jobs in the factory), each new machine would shoulder aside a slightly less effective one, even if the predecessor was only a few months old. No effort, no expense, was too great if it would speed up the work by the smallest increment. "Whenever I approached Mr. Ford on the possibility of new types of machine tools, he never hesitated for a moment," said Sorensen. "'Don't wait, Charlie,' he would say. 'Let's get these things right away.' He was wonderful in that respect: he never started out being skeptical and then saying 'I told you so' when things went wrong."

The great tools themselves became increasingly specialized. For instance, in its journey from metal cube to Model T engine, a casting would be snatched by something that looked as if it might have been designed to power an ocean liner. As the machine briefly embraced the block, forty-five drills pierced the engine-to-be on every side. The machine was invaluable to the Ford shop, and worthless outside it, because the sole thing it could do was put holes in a Model T engine.

The prepared engine block would be hurried on

to its next station, but it would have to pause there. Everything moved quickly, like the second hand on a pocket watch of those days, but, as with the second hand, the motion was made up of incessant brief interruptions.

In the engine assembly room workers stood elbow to elbow at long tables, each one fitting parts kept readily at hand. The men were quick. Nevertheless, each man was working on just one engine at a time.

The engines, and all the other components of the car, came together in the chassis assembly, where groups of workers moved from car to car, fifty cars in a batch, each group with its own task, while handcarts wheeled up and down the line delivering assembled units as large as completed dashboards, steering wheels and all.

In the 1912–13 year the highly refined process yielded 181,951 cars. A finished chassis left the factory floor every forty seconds. This was quantity production at its most impressive. Still, it was at heart static. As Henry Ford put it, "The first step in [mass production] came when we began taking the work to the men instead of the men to the work."

Charles Sorensen says he invented the moving production line at the Piquette Avenue plant, in 1908: *"The idea occurred to me that assembly would be easier, simpler, and faster if we moved the chassis along, beginning at one end of the plant with a frame and adding the axles and wheels; then moving it past the stockroom, instead of moving the stockroom to it* [italics Sorensen's]."

On Sundays when the plant was quiet, Sorensen had helpers put clusters of parts along the length of the factory. They tied a rope to a car frame mounted on skids and tugged it past workers who fitted on parts. By the time it had reached the far wall, Sorensen said, they had "put together the first car, I am sure, that was ever built on an assembly line."

He had Ford, Wills, and Martin watch the demonstration. All three were skeptical. Martin didn't think it was possible to build a car on the move. Wills, according to Sorensen, said flatly that any such attempt would "ruin the company." Ford alone encouraged Sorensen to keep trying.

There could be no further progress, though, until the flow of work and materials at Highland Park had been put into rational operation. "The entire plant," Sorensen said, "had to be functioning before the Ford mass production and assembly system could be completely worked out into one great synchronized operation. . . . It was that complete synchronization which accounted for the difference between an ordinary assembly line and a mass production one."

When that happened, the nascent creative power of the new factory brought on mass production like a battle: swift, violent, and so hard to follow that even now it is not clear how the victory—and it was the great industrial victory of the twentieth century—came about. The Ford Motor Company maintains superb archives, but during the incandescent months that gave birth to the new system, nobody had time to keep track of what was happening.

The change likely started, appropriately enough, with Spider Huff's revolutionary flywheel magneto, in April 1913. On the first day of the month, the men who put it together came to work to find themselves standing not at their usual wooden tables, but in front of a long waist-high pipe-metal frame that held a row of magneto shells. The day before, each worker would have entirely assembled the magneto in front of him—sixteen bolts, sixteen of the enlivening V-shaped magnets, and so forth. This morning they were told to put on a single part, or loosely set a couple of bolts, and then push the flywheel a yard along the line to the next worker, who also would contribute only a part or two.

These twenty-nine men, working alone the week before, had been completing a magneto every twenty minutes. In company they began turning one out every thirteen minutes and ten seconds. They complained that all the bending over hurt their backs. The next morning they found the line had been raised eight inches. Some of them were faster than others. Soon a chain conveyor moved the flywheels along at a uniform speed. Within a year fifteen men were putting out 1,335 finished flywheels during their eight-hour shift. The time required to make a magneto had dropped from twenty minutes to five.

Ford wrote, "It must not be imagined, however, that all this worked out as quickly as it sounds. The speed of the moving work had to be carefully tried out; in the flywheel magneto we first had a speed of sixty inches per minute. That was too fast. Then we tried eighteen inches a minute. That was too slow. Finally we settled on forty-four inches per minute. The idea is that a man must not be hurried in his work—he must have every second necessary but not a single unnecessary second."

In fact, all this *did* work out almost as quickly as it sounds. The new system immediately flung itself at engine assembly, and once that line was up and running the time dropped from 594 minutes per engine to 226.

If Sorensen might have exaggerated his 1908 breakthrough, he now had a far more public chance to tie a rope to a chassis and winch the car past the workstations while six men attached the components. As crude as the demonstration might have been, its results were extraordinary. The Ford Motor Company was spending twelve and a half man-hours putting together a chassis. When the experimental chassis finished its 250-foot journey, it had required—taking into account all the time that went into the making of the parts it now incorporated—less than six hours to complete.

"In the chassis assembling," Ford wrote, "are forty-five separate operations or stations. The first men fasten four mud-guard brackets to the chassis frame; the motor arrives on the tenth operation and so on. . . . Some men do only one or two small operations, others do more. The man who places a part does not fasten it—the part may not be fully in place until after several operations later. The man who puts on a nut does not tighten it."

Throughout Highland Park new chutes reached down from one floor to another to let gravity do the labor of moving metal from station to station. Everything that could be hitched to a conveyor was. More and more workers found themselves standing on the same small patch of flooring during their entire shift. Ford said, "The undirected worker spends more of his time walking about for materials and tools than he does in working; he gets small pay because pedestrianism is not a highly paid line."

By December highly directed workers were taking two hours and thirty-eight minutes to build a chassis; by the next April, ninety-three minutes. Before the Model T was done, a finished automobile, chassis, body, and all, would be coming off the line, shining and ready for its buyer, every ten seconds.

Those hectic, under-recorded months at Highland Park had witnessed the beginnings of the only true industrial revolution of the twentieth century—an undiluted triumph for all who took part in it.

The only trouble was that Henry Ford's workers hated their new stationary life in the Crystal Palace, and they wouldn't stay there.

In 1914, shortly after the system of moving assembly lines was complete—or, at least fully operational: Continuous experimentation and improvement meant it would never be "complete" while Highland Park lived—a journalist named Julian Street stopped by to have a look at the factory. A New Yorker, Street was traveling across the country to write a book of impressions he called *Abroad at Home.* Few of the impressions were more vivid than those Highland Park dinned into him. "Of course there was order in that place, of course there was system—relentless system— terrible 'efficiency'—but to my mind . . . the whole room, with its interminable aisles, its whirling shafts and wheels, its forest of roof-supporting posts and flapping, flying, leather belting, its endless rows of writhing machinery, its shrieking, hammering, and clatter, its smell of oil, its autumn haze of smoke, its savage-looking foreign population—to my mind it expressed but one thing, and that thing was delirium.

"Fancy a jungle of wheels and belts and weird iron forms—of men, machinery and movement—add to it every kind of sound you can imagine: the sound of a million squirrels chirking, a million monkeys quarreling, a million lions roaring, a million pigs dying, a million elephants smashing through a forest of sheet iron, a million boys whistling on their fingers, a million others coughing with the whooping cough, a million sinners groaning as they are dragged to hell—imagine all of this happening at the very edge of Niagara Falls, with the everlasting roar of the cataract as a perpetual background, and you may acquire a vague conception of that place."

Street was free to leave this Moloch's funhouse, but the men tending all that noise and motion were not. Or at least they weren't until they got sick enough of it to stop taking Henry Ford's paycheck which, at $2.34 an hour as the minimum daily wage, was as good as or better than those being offered by his competitors.

But the work at Highland Park was different, and it told on the men who did it. Many of them felt a massive, mute condescension in the very existence of Flanders's "farmer tools," some of which, Henry Ford said, "could be attended by a child of three."

There was good reason to have such tools: "The rank and file of men come to us unskilled; they learn their jobs in a few hours or a few days. If they do not learn in that time, they will never be any use to us. These men are, many of them, foreigners, and all that is required before they are taken on is that they should be potentially able to do enough work to pay the overhead charges on the floor space they occupy."

A great many of them were the "savage-looking" foreigners that, along with everything else, alarmed Julian Street about Highland Park. By 1914, with all the assembly lines running, 70 percent of Ford's workers were foreign born: a fifth of them Polish, 16 percent Russian, smaller groups from a score of countries. Arabs were particularly valued. They'd gotten the word they were welcome at Highland Park, came with their families, and picked up the farmer tools and were glad to have them, while their wives and children ran little stores that sold coffee and pastry and sandwiches, socks and gloves and boots, to company workers during their breaks. A descendant of one wrote, "Ford Motor Company is part of our lives. Henry Ford hired all the minorities, and of course they worked so hard. . . . And I think the Arab immigrants, as hard as they worked, they were grateful for the jobs that they had."

Just as Arabs knew who was hiring, so did

American blacks. Far from being part of a newly arrived immigrant group, most of their ancestors had been in America long before William Ford came over. But they were immigrants in the northern world of heavy industry. They knew that you couldn't count on getting work at any of the plants, but that your best bets were Packard and the Ford Motor Company. If they were often assigned the heaviest jobs, like those in the foundry, these were real, paying jobs nonetheless. By 1917 the Ford Motor Company had become the industry's leading employer of African Americans, many of them on the highly paid assembly lines, and some in supervising positions with the authority—nearly unique in that place and time—to fire white workers.

So: Muslims working the lines, and African Americans, Serbs and Maltese, Mexicans, a surprising number of Japanese who had heard the Ford factory whistles ten thousand miles away. As Julian Street made his wary way past the foreigners, he would have heard scraps of Finnish slung back and forth between men who had learned the trick of talking to one another underneath the clamor of the machinery, and some high-spirited Arabic banter (until a foreman made his inevitable effort to shut down conversation on the line), the occasional French oath, and what might have been Malay speech.

But he would have heard no Yiddish at all.

• • •

However steady and spectacular the work, there were those who shared Street's view of it. A good deal of disaffection came from the workers who (and how strangely long ago it seemed now) had been with Ford when the Piquette Avenue plant was finding its legs. These men didn't like the farmer tools, and they didn't see themselves as fortunate three-year-olds. They were, many of them, skilled mechanics who could with the tilt of an ear diagnose whatever was ailing a steam engine, and fix it before the farmhands knew there'd been an interruption in the harvesting.

Now they were being asked to put three nuts on three bolts—but don't tighten them!—and then three more, and then three more, forever.

Henry Ford understood. "Repetitive labor—the doing of the same kind of thing over and over again and always in the same kind of way—is a terrifying prospect to a certain kind of mind. It is terrifying to me."

But then he goes on to say that bankers and businessmen also have jobs that are "nearly all routine," too. Here he veers off into fantasy. Bankers and businessmen rarely walked off their jobs in disgust after five days. Just when the efficiencies of the moving assembly line had proved themselves at the end of 1913, the Ford managers discovered that they were having to hire 963 workers to be assured 100 of them

340

would stay with their jobs long enough to learn them.

In *U.S.A.*, his great, jagged epic about America between the turn of the century and the Depression, John Dos Passos wrote, "Good roads had followed the narrow ruts made in the mud by the Model T. The great automotive boom was on. At Ford's production was improving all the time; less waste, more spotters, strawbosses, stool-pigeons (fifteen minutes for lunch, three minutes to go to the toilet, the . . . speedup everywhere, reachunder, adjustwasher, screwdown bolt, shove in cotterpin, reachunder, adjustwasher, screwdown bolt, reachunderadjustscrewdown reachunderadjust, until every ounce of life was sucked off into production and at night the workmen went home gray shaking husks)."

Many never returned. When, at the close of that same annus mirabilis of 1913, Henry Ford wanted to reward men who had been with him for at least three years, he had his board of directors vote them a 10 percent bonus. There were some fifteen thousand employees in the plant that winter. Six hundred forty of them had stayed long enough to qualify for the bonus.

CHAPTER 13
The Five-Dollar Day

Couzens and his conscience; "It's a good round number"; Ford bids against himself; "every worker a potential customer"; Ford at his zenith.

The authorship of the solution for stabilizing the Ford Motor Company's wavering, volatile workforce is still disputed. Sorensen, who was there, doesn't go so far as to claim it, but he is eager to make sure James Couzens gets no credit.

What happened may very well be Couzens's work, though, even if it is not an idea one would have expected from a man who, as Sorensen said, "could squeeze a penny until it hurt." But Couzens had been going through changes.

In 1913 the Ford Motor Company paid its twelve shareholders $11.2 million in dividends. Nobody could have worked harder and more grimly than Couzens to make a lot of money, but no one as intelligent as Couzens could ever have expected to become so rich in the single life span we are allotted for moneymaking. As he started into his forties, he found to his surprise that his wealth didn't sit well with him.

The men in the factory noticed no change in

Couzens. Showing an acquaintance around the plant one evening, he came upon a diligent clerk at his post long after dark. "See that gentleman over there?" he asked the visitor in the clerk's hearing. "The only man in the organization who can't get his work done in the daytime!"

When old friends from Chatham dropped by the factory for a surprise visit and said, "Hello, Jim," he greeted them with "They call me Mister Couzens here."

Beneath the cold truculence, though, things were shifting. When his daughter Marguerite read about the big dividend in the newspaper, she came to her father happily and said, "Whew, that's a lot of money we have."

"But it doesn't belong to us," Couzens replied. "It's a trust. It's a responsibility, and a tough one."

For a while his job helped: "I am never happier than when I am working at top notch, and the only reason I let down at all is to be able to work at top notch the majority of the year." Then, it didn't.

"You know," he said, "there comes a time when the fun of making money is all gone. Say what you will, every man deep in his heart just acknowledges that. . . . The battle is won; the goal is achieved; it is time for something else."

Until the nature of that something else made itself clear to him, "I seemed to have no interest in life for a while," and thinking about his money made him feel "a kind of nausea."

Henry Ford was changing, too. Late in 1913 Elbert Hubbard, writer, philosopher, promoter of the Arts and Crafts Movement, and author of the preposterously successful parable "A Message to Garcia," published an essay about Ford that lay at the opposite end of the spectrum from the Tin Lizzie jokes. Here, he said, was the carmaker as he had come to be known "in all the places where the theme is Henry Ford. You hear it in barber shops, barrooms, ad-clubs, Sunday Schools, sewing circles. . . .

> He is a man of few words—simple, plain, unaffected, democratic, direct. He uses no tobacco, no strong drink, and no strong language. Moderation is his watchword. He is temperate in all things, except in the manufacture of automobiles. . . .
>
> Into his car Ford has put the truth, integrity, simplicity, sanity and commonsense which he himself possesses. . . . Henry Ford is not a highbrow, not a theorist, not a professional reformer—he is a worker and an executive. Also he is a teacher and a learner. . . . He has the work habit, the health habit, the play habit, and the study habit.

Whatever pleasure this tribute may have given its subject disappeared when Hubbard sent him a bill for eight hundred dollars, but Hubbard had expressed the general view of Henry Ford at the time: straightforward, modest, downright as the frontier ax in the old McGuffey's Readers. And much of it is true. But just as his company's unprecedented success was working on Couzens, so, too, was it on Ford. He was drawing away from his most valuable partner. When a British Ford dealer wrote Couzens to ask how the boss was doing, he got this response: "I have not been able to visit with Mr. Ford very much . . . but I hope and believe he had a most excellent time this summer."

Ford had been chafing to assume more of Couzens's role on the business side, once saying to an acquaintance, "I own fifty-eight percent of the stock, and I can do with the company what I like, can't I?" He began to go around Couzens on business matters, overruling him in minor ways without letting him know it was going to happen, seemingly just to bait his general manager, but perhaps also to experiment with how best to assert himself.

One day Ford asked for something from the stores, and was annoyed when the employee who brought it also handed him a printed form. What's this? Ford wanted to know.

A receipt, said the employee.

Where did it come from?

Mr. Couzens.

Ah. Ford asked to be given all the copies of that particular form. He carried them out into the factory yard, threw them to the ground, poured gasoline on them, and set them afire.

Ford was overruling Couzens in more significant ways, but this time not merely to humiliate him. When Couzens approached his boss with sales strategies or a new advertising campaign, Ford would veto them. By the midteens Ford had just one sales strategy, and that was to keep lowering the price of the car. Do that, he said, and the marketing would take care of itself.

The Ford Motor Company usually announced the new prices on the first day of August and October. On October 1, 1910, the Model T dropped from $950 to $780. A year later it was $690, and a year after that, $600. So it went throughout the decade: August 1, 1913, $550; August 1, 1914, $490; August 1, 1915, $440; August 1, 1916, $360. Until, on December 2, 1924, it reached its all-time low of $290.

This complete inversion of monopoly capitalism (if you are the sole source of a universally demanded good, you should *raise* the price) baffled observers throughout the car's career.

In 1909 the company made a profit of $220.11 on each car. Once the moving assembly line was at work, the profit fell to $99.34. That was fine with Henry Ford: "Every time I reduce the charge for our car by one dollar," he said, "I get a thousand new buyers."

Ford was right. His policy was drawing more customers than any artful sales campaign could have. And the torrent of money that came with them gave Couzens and Ford one great final occasion of being in perfect accord.

Even as big an operation as the Ford Motor Company was seasonal in those days, and usually slack times came right around Christmas. Then the plant would let off workers and send them home to wait, hoping their jobs would resume in a few weeks.

So it was with Christmas 1913, when Couzens stood at his office window watching workmen shuffling homeward in the frigid early dusk from what, for all they knew, might be their final shift ever. He thought, this famously hard man, "We had been driving our men at top speed for a year and here we were turning them out to spend the Christmas holidays with no pay. The company had piled up a huge profit from the labor of these men; the stockholders were rolling in wealth, but all the workers themselves got was a bare living wage."

The thought stayed with him. "All winter I sat in my office on the second floor of the Ford building and every time I looked out the windows I saw a sea of faces looking up. These men were shivering in the cold with their coat collars turned up."

That same troubling winter Couzens was

reading a magazine "of socialist tendencies" when he came upon a passage in which the editor answered a reader's question that must have been put to him many times before: Why, "if it believed in socialism, the magazine did not practice what it preached in its own affairs." The editor replied that no one man or organization could alone deflect the flow of history—in order for there to be any real progress, change had to be universal, to somehow overtake everyone and everything at the same time. "That," said Couzens, "was an asinine answer."

Later he talked to B. C. Forbes, the leading business journalist of the day, who reported, "An idea flashed through his head. Why shouldn't the Ford Motor Company take a decided lead in paying the highest wages to its workers, thus enabling them to enjoy better living conditions?"

The next morning Couzens went to his boss and said that the company's minimum wage should be five dollars. "It's a good round number," he explained.

So it was. It was also a round number that was more than twice the average industrial worker's paycheck.

Couzens said the startled Ford was initially against it. "We pay as much as anyone pays."

His vice president—for Couzens had recently secured that title from his title-averse employer—replied with a gesture that, if accurately recalled, is impressively cinematic. Pointing out the window to the shivering job seekers below, he said, "But we're responsible for those men, because we don't pay them enough to live on. . . . We should give our people wages that permit them to save against the time we have no work for them."

Ford went to Peter Martin, who predictably found the idea ludicrous, and returned to tell Couzens, "Martin says he is ready to pay three dollars a day. That five dollars a day will cause trouble. That other firms—"

Couzens interrupted. "I know what Martin thinks. He thinks if we pay five dollars a day it will cause a general disturbance in the labor market. That we will be flooded with requests for jobs. What if it does? What if we are? We'll get the pick of the workmen and you know as well as I do that a good workman is worth five dollars a day."

"Well, I'll go back and talk with Martin."

Leave Martin alone, Couzens said. "If we talk of anything for more than forty-eight hours we never do it."

Whether he spoke with Martin or not, Ford returned with a counterproposal of $3.50.

"No," said Couzens, continuing to conduct the negotiation as if it were his company and not Ford's. "Five or nothing."

Ford raised the bid against his profit margin. "Then make it four."

"Five or nothing," Couzens persisted, and added, "A straight five-dollar wage will be the greatest advertisement any automobile concern ever had."

Ford, who had come to understand the advantages of advertising as well as anyone, once told a colleague that this final argument persuaded him.

Ford had other memories of the decision, though. He said it began on a day—also that Christmastime of 1913—when he and Edsel were walking through the factory and came upon two workers, full of fury and desperation, savagely fighting. Disgusted that his son should have seen this, Ford wondered what forces might make two of his workers turn from their tools in favor of trying to kill each other.

Soon after, he told a colleague, "There are thousands of men out there in the shop who are not living as they should. Their homes are crowded and unsanitary. . . . They fill up their homes with roomers and boarders in order to help swell the income. It's all wrong—all wrong. It's especially bad for the children. . . .

"Now, these people are not living in this manner as a matter of choice. Give them a decent income and they will live decently—will be glad to do so. What they need is the opportunity to do better, and someone to take a little personal interest in them—someone who will show that he has faith in them."

Yet Ford also insisted, once he had launched what he called "a kind of profit-sharing plan," that "there was no charity in any way involved. That was not generally understood. Many employers thought we were just making the announcement because we were prosperous and wanted advertising and they condemned us because we were upsetting standards—violating the custom of paying a man the smallest amount he would take. There is nothing to such standards and customs. They have to be wiped out. Some day they will be. Otherwise, we cannot abolish poverty. . . . We wanted to pay these wages so that business would be on a lasting foundation. We were not distributing anything—we were building for the future. A low wage business is always insecure."

In thinking this, Ford was reaching toward a conviction that may not fully have jelled in him by 1914, but that Sorensen crisply articulated years later. "Mr. Ford was saying that one ought to be one's own best customer; that unless an industry keeps wages high and prices low, it limits the number of its customers and destroys itself. Thus the wage earner is as important as a consumer as he is as a producer; and that enlarged buying power by paying high wages and selling at low prices is behind the prosperity of this country."

The innovation, Couzens and the Ford accountants figured, would cost $10 million the first year out.

On January 5, 1914, the company convened a press conference, but not much of one. Just three local newspapers were invited to James Couzens's office to hear the biggest piece of news that had ever come out of Detroit. Henry Ford stood by a window, restlessly glancing between it and the handful of reporters while Couzens explained the plan, and passed out a two-page typed press release "whose crude rhetorical flourishes," Nevins points out, "were not without justification."

It began, "The Ford Motor Company, the greatest and most successful automobile manufacturing company in the world, will, on January 12, inaugurate the greatest revolution in the matter of rewards for its workers ever known in the industrial world.

"At one stroke it will reduce the hours of labor from nine to eight, and add to every man's pay a share of the profits of the house. The smallest amount to be received by any man 22 years old and upwards will be $5.00 per day. The minimum wage is now $2.34 per day of nine hours."

"'If we are obliged,' said Mr. Ford, 'to lay off men for want of sufficient work at any season, we propose to so plan our year's work that the lay-off shall be in the harvest-time . . . not in the winter. . . . We shall make it our business to get in touch with the farmers and to induce our employees to answer calls for Harvest help.'"

(Ford backed up what he said about the virtues of farming all his life: A few years later, when the company was having a harder time than it had expected making tractors, Sorensen complained to his boss that they were losing fifty-five dollars on every one they sold. "Well, I'm glad of it," Ford said. "If we can give a farmer $55 with every tractor that's just what I want.")

Couzens got into the text with his continuing indignation about the insufficiently socialistic magazine editor: "We do not agree with those employers who declare, as did a recent writer in a magazine, in excusing himself for not practicing what he preached, that the movement toward the bettering of society must be universal. We think that one concern can start and create an example for others. And that is our chief object."

The owner had the final word in the release: "'We believe,' said Mr. Ford, 'in making 20,000 men prosperous and contented rather than follow the plan of making a few slave drivers in our establishment multi-millionaires.'"

Ford and Couzens and the other company managers knew they had taken a big step, but despite that bumptious press release, they may not quite have realized how big.

Their audience did, though. The *Detroit News* was an afternoon paper, and got the story into print that same day.

By sunrise the next morning a crowd was

standing outside the Highland Park gates in ten-degree weather—"unemployed men," wrote the *Detroit Free Press*, "and men whose jobs suddenly had grown distasteful; rough-handed, white-collared men, eager to trade bookkeepers' stools for manual labor in the gasoline Golconda where even sweepers get $5 a day." There were ten thousand of them. The shortened hours and the extra shift required hiring perhaps five thousand new hands. The company quickly posted signs that said "No hiring," but people across the country were already scraping together rail fare.

In Pittsburgh, Pennsylvania, the news reached the unhappy home of a fifteen-year-old named Frank Marquart. "My father hated his job as a common laborer in the chain mill and he hated me for not finding a steady job, and life became a living hell for me." Then came January, and his father "excitedly waving the *Pittsburgh Press* and shouting . . . 'I'm going to quit my job tomorrow and Frank and me will go to Detroit. We'll both get jobs at Ford's—why, we'll be making 10 dollars a day, think of it, 10 dollars a day!'"

Frank's mother asked how they could be sure of a job, and the father's enthusiasm changed at once to rage. "'How the hell can we ever get ahead if you always pull back like that,' he demanded, half in German and half in English."

So father and son went, like so many others right then, on a trip they couldn't afford, first to a

Detroit boardinghouse, then to a succession of streetcars that brought them finally to Highland Park.

"There were thousands of job seekers jam-packed in front of the gates. It was a bitterly cold morning and I had no overcoat, only a red sweater under a thin jacket." The temperature still stood below ten degrees, and the crowd kept building. "Suddenly a shout went up—a shout that became a roaring chant: 'Open the employment office, open the employment office!'"

A man—who must have wished at that moment he had almost any other job in the company—shouted through a megaphone, "We are not hiring any more today; there's no use sticking around; we're not hiring today."

The crowd pushed forward. "You sonsabitches, keeping us here all this time and then telling us you ain't hiring, you bastards!"

Frank, teeth chattering, told his father he thought they should leave, "and he shouted at me in German that he didn't bring me to Detroit so I could loaf like a bum." Voices started calling, "Crash the goddam gates!"

The man with the megaphone yelled something about fire hoses. "Someone near us shouted, 'Aw, that's bullshit, they wouldn't dare do a thing like that.' He had hardly finished the sentence when the water came, the icy water that froze as soon as it landed on our clothing."

The people in front drew back while those behind still pushed forward, and soon there were brief whirlpools of fistfighting as the crowd fragmented into discouraged individuals who'd had enough for one day.

Frank said his father had been lucky: "The water did not soak through his overcoat as it soaked through my jacket and sweater. By the time we were able to board a Woodward Avenue streetcar I was shivering from head to foot."

On the streetcar, his father told him that Henry Ford was a Jew "and that what we suffered that morning was the result of 'a dirty Jew trick.'"

Frank said that Ford didn't sound like a Jewish name, and his father told him not to be stupid: "Don't you know that Jews change their names for business reasons!"

That melee embarrassed the company, but it would have given bleak satisfaction to some who had been as surprised by Ford's announcement as had all the would-be employees. Sorensen was one of the first to hear the complaints. "Alvan Macauley, president of the Packard Motor Car Company, got me on the telephone that night at my home. 'What are you fellows trying to do?' he demanded. 'We got the news about your $5 day while we were having a board meeting. It was so astonishing that we broke up the meeting. We all felt "What is the use; we can't compete with an organization like the Ford Motor Company."'"

Sorensen remembered his emollient reply as, "Of course, Mr. Macauley, you don't have to follow our example unless you want to. Perhaps you have an advantage over us if you don't pay as much wages as we do."

"That would be fine," Macauley snapped, as people always do when they think something is not remotely fine. "But how are we going to avoid paying these wages once you start paying them here in Detroit?"

A good question. *The* question. And the answer was that of course Packard would have to match Ford's wages, and in time such wholly unrelated businesses as Nabisco and Armour meatpacking and Kellogg's would, too, and the entire economic climate of America would change.

The *Wall Street Journal* wrote that "to inject ten millions into a company's factory, and to double the minimum wage, without regard to length of service, is to apply Biblical or spiritual principles in the field where they do not belong. . . . Henry Ford . . . has in his social endeavor committed blunders, if not crimes. They may return to plague him and the industry he represents, as well as organized society." The *New York Times* agreed, calling the five-dollar day "distinctly Utopian and dead against all experience." The president of Pittsburgh Plate Glass foresaw "the ruin of all business in this country," but took some solace in his certainty that "Ford himself will surely find that he cannot afford to pay $5 a day."

He could, as it turned out. The turmoil at the gates of Highland Park subsided after the company made clear it would be hiring only those who had lived in Detroit for at least six months, and the complaints in the press dried up, and all that remained was a continuing tide of goodwill that flowed in from everywhere. Thomas Edison cabled the *New York World*, "Some time ago Mr. Ford reduced the price of his wonderful touring car to the extent of fifty dollars. The user of the car received the entire benefit. Now he has practically reduced it another fifty dollars, but this time the men who make them get the benefit. Mr. Ford's machinery is specialized and highly efficient. This is what permits these results. This is open to all in nearly every line of business. Let the public throw bouquets at the inventors, and in time we will all be happy."

Ford's employees were already happy. Within two weeks of the announcement Detroit's marriage license clerk had issued fifty licenses to Ford workers. A factory hand named Woljeck Manijklisjiski told a reporter, "My boy don't sell no more papers. My girl don't work in the house of another and see her mother but once in the week no more. Again we are a family." A machine shop subforeman said, "The big worry that leads a lot of fellows to the suicide route, and a lot more to the booze route, is just a lot of little worries added together mostly, and that's exactly what the big boost in pay is going to do away with in the Ford Plant."

Rabbi Leo Franklin of Detroit's Temple Beth-El said, "This is a big advance toward the day when the workingman and the employer shall cease to be sworn enemies, and will be friends and brothers."

Rabbi Franklin went on to point out that "if the workingman is to get the maximum raise, he must in return give the best of which he is capable." Ford's workingmen seemed to agree. One said, "Mr. Ford pay me two-fifty, he get 250 pieces. Mr. Ford now pay me five dollars a day, he get 500 pieces. I pay him back."

The radical John Reed, no pushover where the interests of powerful capitalists were concerned, agreed (in a way) with the *Wall Street Journal*, when he wrote, "This new Ford plan is turning into something dangerously like a real experiment in democracy, and from it may spring a real menace to capitalism." In Ford, Reed saw "that most dangerous of revolutionists—a man who translates platitudes into action."

In his book *The Public Image of Henry Ford*, which sounds as if it might be some sort of sociological study, but is in fact a lively, engaging, and thorough biography of the man as seen through the eyes of an increasingly fascinated nation, David L. Lewis quotes the French intellectual Father R. L. Bruckberger speaking in 1959: "How I wish I could find words to impress the reader with the importance of the decision of the five-dollar day! Let me speak plainly; I consider that what Henry Ford accomplished [in] 1914 contributed far more to the emancipation of workers than the October Revolution of 1917. . . . He took the worker out of the class of the 'wage-earning proletariat' to which . . . Marx had relegated him and . . . made every worker a potential customer."

No man drilling engine blocks in Macauley's factory would ever be able to buy a Packard out of his earnings. But now the prudent Ford worker could in time purchase a Ford. The business historian and management sage Peter Drucker wrote in 1974, "Ford's action transformed American industrial society. It established the American workingman as fundamentally middle-class."

That was the destination toward which all those assembly lines had been moving, the final logic of mass production: mass consumption; the middle class; the modern age.

A newspaper reporter named Garet Garrett was in the composing room of the *New York Times* when the boss, Adolph Ochs, came in with his "arms held a little out, as if he were bearing a load on his chest, and his eyes were wide and staring. . . .

When he spoke it was hardly above a whisper, saying: 'He's crazy, isn't he? Don't you think he's gone crazy?' "

Garrett knew what he was talking about; everyone in the room knew what he was talking about. The reporter spoke right up, saying, "It might be well to have a look. I'll go out and see."

The next morning he was being shaved by a Detroit hotel barber who told him, "Our Mr. Ford has gone crazy. Did you know?"

Garrett spent the next two days with Henry Ford. "He made it seem quite simple. He said: if a sweeper's heart is in his job he can save us five dollars a day by picking up small tools instead of throwing them out."

The reporter became friendly with Ford, and also with Samuel Crowther, who had helped (to say the least) Ford write his autobiography. Of this collaboration, Garrett remembered, "They wrote several books together, with Ford speaking in the first person as *I* or *we,* and the ideas were entirely his own, but as he conceived them they were wordless revelations or sudden flashes of insight. It was Crowther's part to clothe them with reason and argument and house them in the proper premises."

It was Garrett and not Crowther, though, who reported what Ford said when the newsman asked him how he got his ideas. "There was something like a saucer on the desk in front of him. He flipped it upside down and kept tapping the bottom with his fingers as he said: 'You know atmospheric pressure is hitting there at fifteen pounds per square inch. You can't see it and you can't feel it. Yet you know it is happening. It's that way with ideas. The air is full of them. They are knocking you on the head. You don't have to think about it too much. . . . You can go about your business thinking and talking of other things, and suddenly the idea you want will come through. It was there all the time."

Garrett saw it happen once. Ford started talking about money to him and Cameron: how it was essentially meaningless (Ford used the term "holy water"), yet of course necessary as a sign. "The bankers had so bitched it up, with their speculations and manipulations, that now nobody could understand it. If only—"

This went on for a solid hour, until William Cameron, Ford's spokesman, put a stop to it to by saying lunch was ready. As they went toward the dining room, he murmured to Garrett, "Do you wonder how so much chaff can come out of what you know to be a really fine mill?"

At lunch Ford started all over, on the same topic but from a slightly different beginning. "Then suddenly his tall body stiffened: the expression of his face, which had been very lively, changed to that [of] a sleepwalker, and he said to no one in particular—to himself, really: 'A-h-h! I'm not thinking about that at all.'"

An idea had come to him, and without saying another word he stood up from the table and left the dining room.

"That happens often," Cameron told Garrett. "We may not see him again for a week."

Ford behaved the same way in his Highland Park office. It had been built on the scale of the rest of the factory, but he didn't like spending time in it any more than he had in his humbler offices, and he didn't like meetings at all. Sometimes in the middle—or at the beginning—of one, he'd spring up as if he had to go to the bathroom, or mumble that he'd forgotten to check on something, always giving the impression he'd be right back. He never came back.

The office, although often silent with its railroad-station vacancies of empty air, was nonetheless just what one would expect of the world's foremost automotive executive—the dark wood walls with the austere authority of cut stone, the several glossy desktops, the heavy, richly leathered furniture. It might have been made for the director of the Cunard Line or the Mellon Bank, save for a scale model of the car that had paid for the reverent space and that kept all the heroic clockwork beyond the windows turning its unceasing revolutions.

But, if you will, imagine a meeting in this rarely visited place sometime in the spring of 1914. The five-dollar day has made its sensational impact, and, with the exception of the financial press and the heads of competing auto companies, has been nationally accepted as a near-saintly act, one that in a single stroke has wiped away the bitter legacy of all the battles—many of them literal battles, with guns and blood—between worker and owner during the last half century.

Why the meeting? Maybe just to catch a collective breath and assess all that has happened so quickly since the assembly lines started moving. Whatever the cause, Henry Ford won't stay at it long. James Couzens will be there. There is a cooling between the two men, but both have promoted the five-dollar day, and it has more than fulfilled their hopes for it. Sorensen will surely be in the room, big and still and handsome (the manager of Ford's British operations refers to him as "Adonis"), incubating behind his flat blue glare envy about this and that, but enormously capable. He will be with Ford longer than anybody but Clara.

There is a chance that Edsel Ford might be there. He'd started by attending Detroit public schools and then, after the success of the Model N, went to the excellent Detroit University School, which prepared him for college. His father didn't want him to go to college. Now he is helping keep inventory, fastening those brass tags to the machine tools. He had looked forward to college, but he is fascinated by the automobile business, and is getting a grasp of it that impresses the once skeptical superiors to whom he's been assigned. Next June he will drive a Model T across the country, he and his fellow driver sharing all the work, Edsel as competent at tightening the bands and grinding the valves as any Ford company mechanic. He and his father have few serious differences.

Joe Galamb? Again, maybe he's there, accepting with practiced good humor Ford's teasing about his "Hungarian stimpings." Wills is certainly in the room. Recently married and pleased with the way the work is going, he's nonetheless thinking that any other company meeting on a similar occasion (although actually there have been no similar occasions in the history of American industry) would have offered champagne, or at least a few swallows of wine.

Drinks won't be served. But perhaps Ford, glancing out the window as he had while Couzens read the initial announcement of the five-dollar day, will look back into the room and speak to his small audience. He can't talk to large groups, but he is good with ones of four or five.

Slim, gray-eyed (or blue or green; no two interviewers could agree on his eye color), gray-suited, he might say what he did during an initial test of the Model T: "I think we've got something here." Sometimes these days he mocks Couzens, but perhaps he doesn't now. Perhaps he says that he and Couzens have done this between them (even though that will irritate Sorensen), and that it has worked out pretty damn well.

And perhaps Couzens will briefly offer his once-a-year, break-the-Erie-ice smile.

I hope something like this happened, that there was a moment of summation when everyone understood what they had accomplished, and how they'd done it together, and made something honorable and new.

Because next year Couzens will be gone, and Ford's jealousies and the jocose anger that inspired those pranks, that made him publicly set fire to Couzens's receipts, will grow more destructive, and although he is soon to be the richest and most famous man in America, things will never be so good for him again.

All seemed well, and better than well, for quite a while. Right after the five-dollar-day announcement Couzens took his family out West for a vacation, leaving Ford alone to sop up the praise. One Michigan newspaper ran as a headline, "God Bless Henry Ford and the Ford Motor Company," while the *New York World* called him "an inspired millionaire." He had been acclaimed for his racing successes and more for the Selden suit. Yet when

Julian Street, preparing for his visit to the plant, wanted to check Ford's age, "I took up my *Who's Who in America* one evening with a view to finding out. But all I did find out was that his name is not contained therein. . . . (There is a Henry Ford in my *Who's Who*, but he is a professor at Princeton and writes for the *Atlantic Monthly.*)"

His car had carried his name everywhere, and people thought, as Elbert Hubbard suggested, that he probably shared its virtues: simplicity, honesty, no meretricious frills. But Ford remained the name of an automobile rather than of a man. That changed in a day. For the first time, Henry Ford was more famous than his car.

Long before his partnership with Malcomson he'd chafed under the obligation of answering to people, and this resistance hardened in the heat of public admiration. So, too, did a conviction he expressed in 1922. "None of our men are 'experts.' We have unfortunately found it necessary to get rid of a man as soon as he thinks himself an expert—because no one ever considers himself an expert if he really knows his job. . . . The moment one gets into an 'expert' state of mind a great number of things become impossible."

This was a way of saying that Henry Ford knew as much as anybody about anything. "Success had given him . . . a feeling that was almost infallible," wrote Nevins, and went on to quote a company executive who half believed it. Ford had given him an absurd order. "It's a fool thing, an impossible thing, but he has accomplished so many impossible things that I have learned to defer judgment and await the outcome. Take the Ford engine, for example; according to all the laws of mechanics the damned thing ought not to run, but it does."

Ford said, "I refuse to recognize there are impossibilities."

One of the first effects of the five-dollar day that Henry Ford had not anticipated was being driven out of his home.

After the long succession of rentals, and with the Model T about to swarm the roads, Clara and Henry Ford had built a house on Edison Avenue. The street's name probably weighed in Ford's choice of the location, but it was a pleasant, leafy, prosperous neighborhood. The couple put up a good-looking brick Italianate house that, while solidly at the high end of "comfortable," was far from opulent.

A Steinway grand replaced the player piano from Bagley Avenue days, along with a Victrola, which cost an impressive two hundred dollars (forty five-dollar days). Clara worked happily in her best garden yet and tried to persuade her husband that she could not crank a Model T, even though he insisted it was easy. Clara stood firm, and her husband gave in and bought her, for three times the price of a Model T, a Detroit Electric, a plush little rolling parlor that carried her through the neighborhood in a whirring hush.

The three Fords liked their new home, but Edison Avenue was a public street, and once the five-dollar-day meteor struck the city, they were never alone. At dawn, at dusk, men stood on the lawn and in Clara's garden, hoping personally to ask Henry Ford for a job.

The couple discussed moving to Grosse Pointe, but Detroit's aristocracy were building their homes there, and Henry wanted nothing to do with them. He had bought hundreds of acres around Dearborn—he was always buying land—and he and Clara decided they would be happiest here among old friends.

They were not, however, going to live like those old friends. Ford had approached Frank Lloyd Wright in 1909 to commission a house, but Wright was distracted by one of his marital imbroglios, and recommended the Chicago firm of Van Holst and Fyte. Ford asked for a house that would cost $250,000. By the time it got under way the project had become so extravagant that he fired the architects and shut down work in February 1914.

Clara found another Van—W. H. Van Tine, a Pittsburgh builder and architect—who went right to work and quickly ran the cost of the house up to $1 million. Possibly because Van Tine was Clara's choice, Ford stood still for this.

He remembered his grandfather Patrick talking about the street he had lived on in County Cork. It led to the fairgrounds, and journeys along it were sweetened by birdsong. Patrick taught Henry the birdcalls.

The street was called Fair Lane, and that was the name the Fords gave to their new home. There was plenty of birdsong, for Henry had peppered his holdings with hundreds of birdhouses, and a "bird hotel" with seventy-six electrically heated compartments, an edifice that required a full-time employee to keep it properly cleaned and stocked with suet. But the house itself does not suggest the convivial sunniness of a country fair. Built of Indiana limestone, it contained fifty-six rooms, and dark walnut paneling and darker carved oak and three-foot-thick walls ensured that many of them were gloomy. Clara had some of the paneling painted in lighter hues, but that didn't really help, and she and Henry spent as much time as they could on the sunporch. "The Fords never seemed quite at home at Fair Lane," Sorensen said. "It used to give me the creeps to go there."

The Fords evidently enjoyed the outside of the house more than the inside. There Henry could keep an eye on his birds (the naturalist John Burroughs, whom he had befriended, said he saw more birds at Fair Lane than anywhere else in the country), and Clara could oversee, with real horticultural knowledge, the five pungent acres of her roses, where twenty gardeners tended ten thousand plants.

Of the whole project, Ford was most interested in the power plant. Its two big turbines, driven by water from the Rouge River, turned twin generators that fed Fair Lane with 110 kilowatts of direct current. Thomas Edison came to Detroit in October 1914 to dedicate the powerhouse, which stood four stories high, and cost $244,000, just $6,000 less than the original estimate for the house itself. The machinery is still there, and it is one of the estate's most attractive features.

Yet perhaps Fair Lane is more emblematic of Henry Ford at this time, or a prophecy of what he would become. The walls are oppressive and suggest battlements; the house scowls and looks in on itself.

CHAPTER 14
Simple Purposes

Telling workers how to live; ugly enough to be a minister; war; Ford on the American soldier: "Lazy, crazy, or just out of a job"; Couzens quits; "GREAT WAR TO END CHRISTMAS DAY: FORD TO STOP IT"; from "peace angel to Vulcan."

An early stirring of Fair Lane's owner's messianism might be seen in his company's Sociological Department.

Ford company workers discovered that achieving their five-dollar day required more than a half year's residence in Detroit. Henry Ford was worried the sudden wealth would send its recipients into drink, gambling, domestic violence, and every other sort of dissipation. To qualify for his doubled salary, the worker had to be thrifty and continent. He had to keep his home neat and his children healthy, and, if he were below the age of twenty-two, to be married.

The job of ensuring such behavior went to John Lee, another executive who had come to the Ford Motor Company with the Keim mills. He was in charge of what today goes under the pallid name of "human resources," and he was one of the very few of Ford's high lieutenants who was universally liked.

Lee put out a booklet called *Helpful Hints and Advice to Employees*, which opened by declaring a "sole and simple" purpose that was far from simple. It was "to better the financial and moral standing of each employee and those of his household; to instill men with courage and a desire for health, happiness, and prosperity. To give father and mother sufficient for present and future; to provide for families in sickness, in health and in old age and to take away fear and worry. To make a well rounded life and not a mere struggle for existence to men and their families, and to implant in the heart of every individual the wholesome desire to Help the Other Fellow, whenever he comes across your path, to the extent of your ability."

This irreproachable aim was advanced by investigators who brought their questionnaires to the home of every Ford employee (although not Sorensen's, who from the start thought the endeavor a time-wasting distraction). The agents weren't mere busybodies. They'd been trained to offer useful advice on hygiene and on how to manage household finances. Behind them stood the Ford legal department, whose lawyers would help, free, with everything from buying a house to becoming an American citizen. Should an employee get sick or be injured, the company maintained a full-time staff of ten doctors and a hundred nurses.

The agents, initially recruited from among Ford's white-collar workers, soon grew to a force two hundred strong. Its members had to assess some thirteen thousand people, and do it quickly. Naturally they met resistance, from newly arrived Russians, for instance, whose memories of the czar's secret police were all too fresh, and from the occasional descendant of an original settler whose family had been in Detroit for generations and who didn't care to have some company hireling tell him how to live like a decent American.

For the most part, though, the interviewees took the intrusion into their lives philosophically. A few nosy questions that opened the door to the highest-paying job in the industry were easier to bear than being doused with fire hoses in the dead of a Detroit winter and having no job at all.

William Knudsen, who by now was busy sowing branch assembly plants across the nation, opposed the plan as strongly as did Sorensen, but for different reasons. He told his biographer that "as he saw it, the men were entitled to the money and, having earned it, it was theirs to spend without answering the snooping questions of investigators."

Knudsen was greatly amused to learn about a boardinghouse close to the factory on Manchester

Avenue where eleven young Ford workmen lived. None of them was married, but whenever an agent stopped by, the man he was visiting would borrow the generous-spirited landlady and present her as his wife. Fortunately, said Knudsen, the social workers never called on all eleven at the same time.

One stipulation of the new mandate was that a Ford worker needed permission from a Ford executive if he wanted to get his own automobile. Knudsen was in Lee's office when an employee came in and said, "Mr. Lee, I would like to buy a car."

"Got any money?"

"I have seven hundred dollars."

"Do you have a family?"

"Yes, a wife and four children."

"Is the furniture paid for?"

"Yes."

"Have you any insurance?"

"Yes."

"All right, you can buy a car."

"Thanks, Mr. Lee." On his way out the door the man turned and said, "Oh, by the way, Mr. Lee, my wife is going to have another baby. I'm going to buy a Buick."

The occasional worker was openly defiant. When asked if he had any savings, one man told the investigator that he had invested his earnings "in houses and lots." When the skeptical agent pressed him for details, the man explained he'd meant "whorehouses and lots of whiskey."

On the other hand, there was Joe, who had come from a peasant life in Russia with his wife and six children.

F. W. Andrews, one of the Ford investigators (they were later to be given the less provocative title of "advisors"), told his story. "Life was an uphill struggle for Joe since landing in America," Andrews wrote. But he was willing to work, and work hard, digging sewers and farming, making his way to Detroit where "for five long months he tramped in the 'Army of the Unemployed'— always handicapped by his meager knowledge of the English language, and unable to find anything to do." Joe's wife "worked with the washtub and the scrubbing brush when such work could be found."

Joe landed a job at Ford, and that's when Andrews entered his life, to find him living in "an old, tumbled down, one and a half story frame house." Joe and his family were in "one half of the attic consisting of three rooms, which were so low that a person of medium height could not stand erect—a filthy, foul-smelling home." It contained "two dirty beds . . . a ragged filthy rug, a rickety table, and two bottomless chairs (the children standing up at the table to eat)." The family owed money to their landlord, to the butcher, to the grocer. The eldest daughter had gone to a charity hospital the week before. Andrews said the remainder of the family "were half clad, pale, and hungry looking."

Andrews at once got the pay office to issue Joe's wages daily instead of every two weeks. He secured a fifty-dollar loan, and such was the Sociological Department's seriousness of purpose then that Andrews, not Joe, borrowed the money. Andrews paid the butcher and the landlord, rented a cottage, and filled it with cheap but sound new furniture, new clothes, and, he said, "a liberal supply of soap."

Then the messianic moment. Andrews "had their dirty, old, junk furniture loaded on a dray and under cover of night moved them to their new home. This load of rubbish was heaped on a pile in the backyard, and a torch was applied and it went up in smoke.

"There upon the ashes of what had been their earthly possessions, this Russian peasant and his wife, with tears streaming down their faces, expressed their gratitude to Henry Ford, the FORD MOTOR COMPANY, and all those who had been instrumental in bringing about this marvelous change in their lives."

Were those tears only of gratitude as Joe watched this strange pyre of his family's old life?

Today the Sociological Department might seem the essence of suffocating paternalism, and many felt it so even at the time. Certainly no other big industrial operation had anything like it. But with its medical and legal services, and the English language school it ran for the company's thousands of immigrant workers, the department appears to have done more good than harm. In 1914 the average Ford worker had $207.10 in savings. For those who stuck with the company during the next five years, the average had risen to $2,171.14.

The reformer Ida Tarbell went to Highland Park planning to expose the oppressive Ford system. Instead she wrote, "I don't care what you call it—philanthropy, paternalism, autocracy—the results which are being obtained are worth all you can set against them, and the errors in the plan will provoke their own remedies."

The Sociological Department also brought into Henry Ford's life a man who turned out to be his keenest observer.

Samuel Marquis, three years younger than Ford, was born in Ohio in 1866. The descendant of several generations of Episcopal divines, he liked to tell his friends, "They say that when I was born, my aunt looked at me and said to my mother, 'This is the homeliest baby I ever saw,' to which my mother replied, 'All right, then, he shall be the minister.'"

And so he was, but not before twice being expelled from his ecclesiastical studies at Allegheny College in Pennsylvania during spells of severe buffeting by religious doubts. He overcame them, got a bachelor of divinity degree in 1893, married the next year, and had four children. He was sanguine, sturdy, direct, energetic, and full of Progressive-era zeal that made him believe he should use his faith to improve social conditions. In the spring of 1906 he was made dean of St. Paul's Cathedral in Detroit.

He applied himself so strenuously to his new job that by 1915 he had become one of the city's most popular preachers, but had also driven himself to the verge of collapse. His doctor ordered him to take a year off and recuperate, but Marquis said, "A change in work would be more beneficial to me than being idle," and he volunteered to help John Lee at the Ford Sociological Department. Lee was glad to get him, and Henry Ford was, too, because Marquis and the carmaker had become friends.

Marquis and his wife had called on Ford shortly after he moved to Edison Avenue. They were seeking, as so many Ford visitors did, money. Ford usually hated this, and was good at putting them off.

When Julian Street, having run the gauntlet of the factory, managed to get an interview with its owner, he concluded the meeting by asking, "Mr. Ford, I should think that when a man is very rich he might hardly know, sometimes, whether people are really his friends or whether they are cultivating him because of his money. Isn't that so?"

Mr. Ford's dry grin spread across his face. He replied with a question:

"When people come after *you* because they want to get something out of you, don't you get their number?"

"I think I do," I answered.

"Well, so do I," said Mr. Ford.

Marquis wanted to get something out of Ford for his church, but he proved a most engaging and direct supplicant. A writer for the *Detroit Journal* said, "His activities are perpetual, save as he sleeps. He is in deadly earnest, he hits from the shoulder," yet there was "no clerical contagion of gloom for him." He liked to tell a funny story as much as he liked to hear one. What Marquis said about John Lee could equally have served as a description of Samuel Marquis: "He is a man of ideas and ideals. He has a keen sense of justice and a sympathy with men in trouble that leads to an understanding of their problems. He has an unbounded faith in man, particularly with the 'down and out,' without which no man can do constructive work. Under his guidance the department put a soul into the company."

Marquis's beliefs and qualities appealed to Ford,

who soon was calling him Mark (Mark, like everyone but Mrs. Ford and Edsel, called Henry "Mr. Ford"). It didn't hurt the friendship that Clara took to the couple, too, and was a strong supporter of the Episcopal Church.

If Henry Ford had any religion at all, it was likely Episcopal, although he once said that he was born an Episcopalian but hadn't worked at it since. As his fame continued to grow he was often cited in pulpits as a Christian exemplar. A Methodist magazine said that he prayed daily for guidance, and the *Christian Herald* wrote that he kept the Scriptures in every room of his house for swift and easy reference. After this, a reporter asked him if he attended church regularly. Ford said, "No, the last time I went somebody stole my car."

For years he believed, or said he believed, in reincarnation. Back in 1901 the McKinley assassination had shocked Ford and Oliver Barthel into having a metaphysical discussion. Barthel gave Ford a book that he said had deeply influenced him. Written by Orlando Smith, a Mississippi cotton planter and Confederate officer with a strong spiritual bent who went on to become a newspaper owner, it was called *A Short View of Great Questions* (the student will be pleasantly surprised to find that it really *is* short) and argued for reincarnation and the trans-migration of souls.

One can see why the philosophy might appeal to Ford. He hated any waste of energy, and what could be a greater waste of it than accumulating knowledge and experience over an entire lifetime only for it all to be extinguished at the end, leaving blank-minded babies having to start over again? Ford provided a compact rationale for his belief: "When the automobile was new and one of them came down the road, a chicken would run straight for home—and usually be killed. But today when a car comes along, a chicken will run for the nearest side of the road. That chicken has been hit in the ass in a previous life."

Ford was also strongly influenced by what one of his biographers rather shockingly calls "the simplicities" of Ralph Waldo Emerson. Ford had Emerson's dictum "cut your own wood and it warms you twice" hewn into one of Fair Lane's oak rafters. In his copy of Emerson's essays he put a mark next to "We love characters in proportion as they are impulsive and spontaneous" and wrote "good" beside "only in our easy, simple, spontaneous action are we strong."

Marquis said that Ford "is not an orthodox believer according to the standards of any church that I happen to know. His religious ideas, as he stated them, are somewhat vague. But there is in him something bigger than his ideas, something of a practical nature that is far better than his theories."

The minister was to learn a great deal more about Ford during their years together, but first and last he puzzled over the difficulty of actually visualizing the man. We can share his frustration today, for in any collection of Henry Ford photographs the subject looks different in every one.

"A still picture of Henry Ford is impossible," Marquis wrote, "for the simple reason that there is something in him that is never still. . . . In his presence no one is entirely at his ease. . . . You come to feel certain of but one thing, and this is that with any work he has to do the unexpected is bound to happen. . . ."

The outward man reveals what is within. The ever-changing expression of his face, the constant play upon it of lights and shadows reflecting his rapidly changing thoughts and moods are the subject of remark on the part of those who see Mr. Ford daily.

Photographers complain that he is "hard to get." There are snapshots of him a-plenty. Each looks as he looks at times. But no one of them reveals him as he is. No satisfactory photograph of him, so far as I know, has ever been taken.

. . . In spite of a long and fairly intimate acquaintance with him, I have not one mental picture . . . of which I can say "This is as he is, or as I know him." There are in him lights so high and shadows so deep that I cannot get the whole of him in proper focus at the same time.

(Burnet Hershey, a reporter who met Ford a few months later, was harsher about this duality: "There is a fascinating little illusory trick which may be played with one of Ford's portrait-photographs. If one side of Ford's face is covered, a benign, gently humorous expression dominates. When the other side is covered, the look is transformed into one of deadly, malevolent calculation. This ambiguous effect is created by Ford's hollow, heavy eyes, the pale eyes one would associate with a visionary or a killer.")

Samuel Marquis's study of Ford's lights and shadows began with a course as intense as it was unwelcome when he was dragooned into an extraordinary project. Henry Ford was going over to Europe to put a stop to the First World War.

The war would make Ford for the first time feel the claws of a hostile press. But its earliest and most damaging cost to him was James Couzens.

Relations between the two men had kept eroding. When the outset of the conflict ignited bank runs across the country, Ford told Couzens he wanted to withdraw his money from the Highland State Bank, a subsidiary of the Ford

Motor Company that Couzens had founded in 1909 and of which he was president. Couzens told Ford his money was safe there, and he should leave it be. Ford said he would. Then, without notifying Couzens, he ordered it transferred. Couzens sent him a telegram on August 5:

IN THESE STRENUOUS TIMES MEN INVARIABLY SHOW THE KIND OF STUFF THEY ARE MADE OF. WE ARE MAKING ARRANGEMENTS TO TRANSFER YOUR MONEY TO THE DIME BANK. JAMES COUZENS

The insolence of the message led no further because three days later Couzens's elder son, Homer, driving alongside a lake, overturned the Model T his parents had given him a few months earlier for his fourteenth birthday. The car trapped the boy beneath the surface, and he drowned.

Couzens started out with his family on a motor trip, but soon realized this wouldn't help any of them. As always, he needed hard work, and he went back to his office and worked as hard as he ever had in his life.

Henry Ford kept piercing this shield against grief. War was another kind of waste to Ford, and a particularly bad one. He said—and it made headlines because of who he had become—"To my mind, the word 'murderer' should be embroidered in red letters across the breast of every soldier." The only people who benefited from war were "the militarists and the money lenders."

Couzens was no militarist. He had given five thousand dollars to a "League to Enforce Peace." But he was a Canadian, his countrymen were fighting to hold the Western Front, and Ford's talk about murderers grated on him. When, in the spring of 1915, a U-boat sank the British liner *Lusitania*, killing 1,200 people, 128 of them American, Ford said that the dead (his celebrator Elbert Hubbard among them) had only themselves to blame. They'd been warned. Later he told *Metropolitan* magazine, "I think nations are silly and flags are silly too." Then, in a nod to his own nation's fighting men, he added, "In this country most soldiers are lazy, crazy, or just out of a job."

That October, Charles Brownell, who managed publicity for Ford, made a routine stop at Couzens's office to show him the proofs of the next issue of the *Ford Times*. Couzens leafed through them perfunctorily until he came to an article, signed by his boss, once again denouncing any American effort to prepare for war.

"You can't publish this."

Brownell told him that Mr. Ford had approved it.

Couzens didn't care. "This is the company paper. He cannot use the *Ford Times* for his personal views. I will go and talk to Mr. Ford tomorrow."

The brief discussion started out amicably with some chat about a vacation in California that Ford was planning with Edison. Then Couzens said he'd postponed publication of the company paper because of the antiwar article. Ford "just went off the handle," according to Couzens. "I was shocked, aghast."

"You cannot stop anything here!"

"Well then, I will quit."

Ford, his fury immediately dissipated, told Couzens to think it over.

"No. I have decided."

"All right, if you have decided."

The rest of the talk was quiet, both men perhaps remembering the summer night, now more than a decade gone, when Ford had said the two of them were together against "those fellows."

Couzens went back to his office, wrote out a letter of resignation, and left, briefly displaying a flash of anger to a colleague: "I decided that I had enough of his God damned persecution."

Couzens did not go to another car company, and he never gave the coal business a backward glance. He became mayor of Detroit, and then a Republican senator from Illinois for fourteen years, losing his seat in 1936 only because the hidden flow of liberalism deep in the stony chasms of his spirit put him on the side of FDR's New Deal.

Ford said he was glad to have Couzens gone. Sorensen didn't believe it. "One morning in 1915, Mr. Ford came to my office. 'Mr. Couzens has quit,' he told me. 'I've just left him. Charlie, he was one of the hardest men I ever had to work with, but I wish I had one just like him to take his place.'

"He never got that wish."

Henry Ford was sincere in his feelings about the war. He told the *Detroit Free Press*, "I will do everything in my power to prevent murderous, wasteful war in America and in the whole world . . . I would teach the child at its mother's knee what a horrible, wasteful, and unavailing thing it is. In the home and in the schools of the world I would see the child taught to feel the uselessness of war; that war is a thing unnecessary; that preparations for war can only end in war."

He could do more than talk to a child. He had already changed the habits of his nation. Now he would end the war.

Garet Garrett wrote, "When men say anything is possible if you don't know any better they express a kind of contempt for history, experience and expert opinion. . . . They are bound to go on to the thought that if anything is possible, so anything may be true, with the cynical notation that what people generally believe is probably wrong. With that, they expose themselves to every cracked wind that blows."

The cracked wind came from a woman named Rosika Schwimmer, who persuaded Ford to be her partner in what Garrett called "the weirdest single episode of his life."

Schwimmer, a radical Hungarian Jew, had been traveling America speaking with astringent wit first for woman suffrage and then for peace in Europe. She shared with Henry Ford energy, a genius for self-promotion, and the confidence that if people—in this case ranging from the kaiser to Lord Kitchener—would only listen to her, she could set the burning world aright.

Such were her powers of persuasion that she made Ford believe he could, too. She was able to proselytize him first at Highland Park, and then, later, over lunch at Fair Lane with Louis Lochner, a fellow pacifist. You are a man to whom anything is possible, she told Ford. You can stop this war. As Garrett put it, she said, "In the chancelleries of Europe, on both sides, they were praying for someone to show them how. He believed it."

Clara didn't, and begged her husband not to follow Schwimmer and Lochner to New York, where the two were going to make further plans. Her husband, feeling the same call of destiny that had led him to the Model T, did go to New York, and at a lunch there on November 21, 1915, heard

Lochner say it would be a great thing to hire a ship and fill it with a cargo of persuasive pacifists who, working from neutral countries, would draw the leaders of the warring ones into "continuous mediation."

This was a discussion that could have lasted for months, but the Ford of Highland Park, who would order up a new machine tool in a minute, left the restaurant and hired a passenger ship from the Scandinavian-American line, the *Oscar II*.

Then he went to Washington to call on Woodrow Wilson. The president was not eager to see Ford, but he didn't want to appear hostile to a famous American who hoped to bring peace to the world. So the two men met, and Ford got the chance to tell the joke about the farmer who asked to be buried in his Model T, and Wilson responded with a limerick—he loved limericks—and after that the meeting went much the way the final one with Couzens had.

Wilson said his position prevented him from getting involved in this peace effort. Ford offered him the use of the *Oscar II*, a remarkable piece of effrontery given that if Wilson wished to sail to Europe he could do so aboard a battleship in company with as many destroyers and cruisers as he thought proper. Ford pushed right ahead. "If you don't act, I will."

Leaving the presidential office he said Wilson was "a small man." He went back to New York and convened a press conference for the next morning, November 24.

Oswald Garrison Villard, the pacifist owner and editor of the *New York Evening Post*, had founded the American Anti-Imperialist League after the war with Spain and was already worried that America might be drawn into the European conflict. A few hours before the press conference, he wrote, "I was summoned from the breakfast table to the telephone to hear that Henry Ford, the automobile manufacturer . . . wished me to come at once to the Biltmore Hotel as he had something of the greatest importance to tell me." Villard had never met Ford, but he was a newspaperman, and by now everything Ford did was news. He went and was introduced to Ford, who told him "the astounding news that . . . Mr. Ford had chartered the steamer *Oscar II* to bring about the end of the war by rousing the neutral nations to a joint offer of mediation. Mr. Ford at once asked me to go along and explained that he had summoned me in order to aid him in presenting the news to the press."

Villard was "almost speechless." He thought that "as a means of advertising the idea that the war should and could be stopped by reason and arbitration . . . the chartering of the ship a master stroke." But everything depended on how well the expedition had been planned, starting with the initial press conference.

"I asked if any statement had been prepared and typed to be given out. There was none. I warned him that the press would be largely hostile."

Ford said he wasn't worried about that. "Oh, I always get on very well with the boys. All you need is a slogan." Then he supplied one: "We'll get the boys out of the trenches and home by Christmas. What do you think of that?"

"I thought privately that it was crazy. When I got my breath I replied: 'Mr. Ford, there are said to be at least ten million men in the trenches. You have chartered one of the slowest steamers on the Atlantic and she is not to sail until December 4. If you succeed in stopping the war the day you arrive, which will probably be December 16, it would be physically impossible to march or transport those men home by Christmas.'"

"Oh," said Ford, "I hadn't thought of that."

He thought about it then, for a moment, and came up with a modification: "Well, we'll make it, 'we'll get the boys out of the trenches by Christmas.'"

Villard regarded him bleakly. "It would be possible, if you obtained an armistice over the holidays, to have them sitting on the tops of the trenches by Christmas."

"It disheartened me no end," wrote Villard, "for I knew it laid the enterprise open to ridicule; it was already evident to me that he had no clear conception of what it was all about, what the war conditions were, or what he was undertaking."

Once ten o'clock came around and the reporters assembled, Villard saw that Ford's "brashness in regard to the press vanished. It was evident that he dreaded this interview. He pushed me into the parlor ahead of him and there ensued a scene so extraordinary that I have no parallel in my experience."

Ford opened the conference with, "Well, boys, we've got the ship."

"What ship, Mr. Ford?"

"Why, the *Oscar II*."

"Well, what about her? What are you going to do with her?"

"We're going to stop the war."

"Stop the *war?*"

"Yes, we're going to have the boys out of the trenches by Christmas."

"My, how are you going to do that?"

"Well, we're going to Holland and all the neutral nations."

"And then what?"

To Villard's horror, the reply to this last was, "Well, Mr. Villard will tell you all the rest."

Villard said, "No, Mr. Ford, I cannot do that"— "of course I knew nothing," he wrote later—"but I can explain that the idea is to seek a delegation of important Americans to induce the neutral nations to join together to offer mediation to the nations at war."

After some more questions to Ford, and then to Schwimmer and Lochner, the reporters, said Villard, "fled to their offices to ridicule the whole proposal. The *Evening Post* was almost the only newspaper to treat the peace voyage seriously and respectfully."

The *New York Tribune* ran a straight-faced headline: "Great War to End Christmas Day: Ford to Stop It."

The *Louisville Courier Journal* was more direct in its scorn. "It is worse than ineffable folly for pestiferous busybodies in this country like Henry Ford . . . to nag the president to make an ass of himself by mediating on behalf of a peace that is impossible."

Several cartoons showed Mars reclining against the wall of a trench laughing at what the god of war thought was "the best Ford joke yet."

"Prominent People to Go with Ford," ran one headline. They didn't. They sent best wishes, and some even came to the pier. But Jane Addams of Hull House, and Ida Tarbell, and John Wanamaker, a longtime Ford supporter, Helen Keller, William Jennings Bryan, Luther Burbank, Robert LaFollette, William Dean Howells, Louis Brandeis, William Howard Taft, Rabbi Stephen Wise, even Edison begged off.

When the *Oscar II* sailed on December 5 from New York Harbor, she had aboard the lieutenant governor of North Carolina, the magazine editor

S. S. McClure, Berton Braley "The Hobo Poet" (a curious choice, in that his poems rejoiced in the war: "Out there I'm in the thick of a man's sized fight / An' it's one I'm thankful for!"), several militant vegetarians, some free-love advocates, Theodore Hostetter, a patent-office examiner who was representing the Washington Sunday School Association, a number of sincere academics, Governor Louis Hanna of North Dakota, who explained his presence by saying he owed a visit to relatives in Sweden, and more than fifty newspaper reporters.

Samuel Marquis was there, too, at Clara's urging. Initially drawn to Schwimmer, she had come to believe her an egomaniacal spendthrift and she wanted the reluctant Marquis to look after her husband.

The minister "spent most of the night before the expedition trying to prevail upon [Ford] to abandon it. It was no use. His reply to me was, 'It is right, is it not, to try to stop war?' To this I could only answer 'Yes.' 'Well,' he would go on, 'You have told me that what is right cannot fail.' And the answer to that, that right things attempted the wrong way had no assurance of success, had no effect. He was following what he calls a 'hunch,' and when he gets a 'hunch' he generally goes through with it, be it right or wrong."

A plan of sorts had evolved since the press conference. The *Oscar II* would sail to Norway, and the peace delegates would travel from Oslo through neutral Sweden, Denmark, and Holland, giving lectures all along the route.

No December Atlantic crossing is pleasant, and this one took thirteen days during which the peace delegates fell to quarreling with one another and the reporters drank (although there was a prohibitionist faction aboard, the *Oscar II* maintained a fully stocked bar where the most expensive drink cost fourteen cents). Rosika Schwimmer always carried a bag, which she claimed contained crucial documents from many heads of state, but she would neither show them nor discuss their contents. She became increasingly reclusive, but Ford made himself continually available. "I questioned his judgment at the time," said Marquis, "but not his motives." Many of the reporters began to feel that way. "I came to make fun of the whole thing," one of them said, "but my editor is going to have the surprise of his life. I tell you I believe in Henry Ford and I'm going to say so even if I lose my job for it."

The press at home was not so forbearing. The *New York World* wrote, "Henry Ford says he would give all his fortune to end the war. So would many another man. But it is something that money will not do." The *Sacramento Bee* published a drawing of the Angel of Peace vomiting over the rail of the *Oscar II*.

Some ten thousand Americans in a carnival mood had come to wave and shout as the *Oscar II* sailed. There were no welcoming crowds when it arrived in Norway, a country near enough to the fighting to feel its furnace breath.

By the time the ship docked, the temperature stood at twelve degrees below zero. Ford was down with a bad cold, and went to ground in the Grand Hotel, which, despite its name, offered drab, chilly quarters. At the steady urging of Marquis, he agreed to call it a day.

"Guess I had better go home to mother," he said to Lochner. "I told her I'd be back soon. You've got the thing started now and can get along without me."

Marquis helped smuggle him out of the dank hotel and they boarded a steamer that docked in Brooklyn on January 2. Not even Henry Ford had got home by Christmas.

There were compensations awaiting him on his return from the disappointing crusade. While he was away the one millionth Model T had come off the line and snorted forth to its destiny. And the fate of its successors would surely be buoyed by the press Ford was getting now. After the initial burst of mockery, the editorial tone of the papers had become warmer. The *New York American* echoed many of its rivals when it regretted having "caricatured, lampooned, ridiculed, and vituperated" Ford. That had been wrong: "Henry Ford Deserves Respect, Not Ridicule." "No matter if he failed, he at least TRIED. Had every citizen in the United States, including the President and his Cabinet and the members of Congress, put forth one-tenth the individual effort that Henry Ford put forth, THE BOYS WOULD HAVE BEEN OUT OF THE TRENCHES BY CHRISTMAS." G. K. Chesterton, the British novelist, journalist, and almost everything else, wrote, "Now anyone who knows anything about America knows exactly what the Peace Ship would be like. It was a national combination of imagination and ignorance, which has at least some of the breath of innocence."

Ford said of his adventure, "I wanted to see peace. I at least tried to bring it about. Most men did not even try."

The Peace Ship's more blatant hangers-on came home not long after Ford, but he kept picking up the tab for the core of his delegates until, in February 1917, America severed diplomatic ties with Germany.

When that happened, Allan Nevins remarked, "The transformation of Henry Ford from peace angel to Vulcan took less than a week." He said that "in the event of a declaration of war [I] will place our factory at the disposal of the United States government and will operate without one cent of profit."

When America entered the war two months later, Ford said he was still a pacifist, but now he was that uncommon being, "a fighting pacifist."

At first he was full of febrile ideas, all of which the newspapers embraced. The correspondents may not have had much faith in the Peace Ship, but they were wholly credulous about Ford's abilities where mass production was concerned.

He was going to build 1,000 submarines a day, each of them to carry a crew of one. The captain—if that's the right word—would bring his vessel alongside an enemy warship and destroy it with a "pill-bomb." When the U.S. Navy proved able to resist this tactic (Franklin Roosevelt, the assistant secretary of the navy, said that the carmaker, "until he saw a chance for publicity free of charge, thought a submarine was something to eat"), Ford proposed mass-producing 150,000 airplanes a year, then promised to build 1,000 two-man tanks daily. The army went for these last, and ordered 15,000 of them, although the war was over before any made it across the Atlantic.

In the end, though, Ford got some real defense work done: 39,000 Model T ambulances and cars and trucks (a year earlier the U.S. Army had fewer than 80 motor vehicles), 7,000 tractors sold at cost to a U-boat-blockaded Britain badly needing to grow food, and 75 of the fine Liberty airplane engines a day. William Knudsen, back in Detroit after setting up his branch assembly plants, drew on his increasingly distant memories of the bicycle industry to form bicycle-like tubing from vanadium steel that greatly improved the performance of the Liberties.

Knudsen soon got a more unusual assignment. The U-boats that had made Britain so eager to have those tractors were constantly threatening the sea routes that kept supplies of everything from guns to grain moving across the Atlantic. The navy wasn't interested in toy submarines and pill-bombs, but it urgently wanted a horde of cheap, quickly built two-hundred-foot anti-submarine vessels, and every shipyard on the East Coast was fully occupied.

Knudsen found out about this, got hold of the designs for the ships, and took them to Henry Ford, who said he could do this job.

Knudsen went to Washington and calmly and steadily diverted what was at first a stream of politely expressed ridicule into reluctant acknowledgment that this man knew what he was talking about. That was quite a conversion of opinion, for Knudsen was saying that real warships could be built like Model Ts, on assembly lines.

The navy, with no other plausible option, gave the Ford Motor Company the contract.

Knudsen put up a building a third of a mile long—like Highland Park, made of reinforced concrete—with three production lines, each of them capable of carrying seven ships slowly toward the building's mouth, which opened on the same Rouge River that flowed past Fair Lane.

A *Washington Post* editorial had said, "The crying need of this hour is an eagle that will scour the seas and pounce upon and destroy every submarine that dares to leave German or Belgian shores," so the vessels would be known as Eagle boats. Knudsen got his plant up in five months, and the first of the Eagles was floating in the Rouge on July 10, 1918, just eight months after the concrete of its hatchery had been poured. Then things slowed down. By Armistice Day, November 11, the company apparently had only 7 Eagles heading for the Atlantic. Knudsen says the number was 14, with 46 to follow close behind. The company had 112 on order, and completed 46.

Ford wanted the Eagles produced by his mass-production methods, and, like the Model T, you can see the results in them. Slab-sided for easier construction, they have the squarish look of a child's drawing of a boat. Ford was wise to go into carmaking rather than shipbuilding, for it is difficult to find the testimony of anyone who served aboard an Eagle who didn't detest it. The ships didn't sink, but they did almost everything else possible to make their occupants unhappy at sea. Still, a few Eagles stayed in service right through World War II.

Despite the lack of fondness the ship commanded, its very existence represented a great achievement for Knudsen. Ford came to him first on November 11 when the sirens and church bells were still heralding the armistice.

"Well, William, the war is over."

Knudsen said he knew that.

"How quickly can you get this Army stuff out of here?"

"Right away, if you say so, Mr. Ford."

"I wish you would."

"All of it?"

"All of it, whether finished or not. Pack it up in boxes and put it out in the yard."

That was that for Ford and the Great War. The skeptical Vulcan had done his part, and now he wanted all the crap he'd had to make put out in packing crates in his factory yard under the winter rain until the army came to take it off, or it rusted away.

And just as he didn't want the detritus of the war cluttering up his factories, neither did he want its profits cluttering up his soul. He had pledged to return to the government every penny he made above his plant costs.

This of course impressed the public—"the only rich man of note who . . . refused to coin money out of the blood of nations"—and as late as 1941, with an even bigger war coming on the boil, the Ford company's Cincinnati branch manager was urging his salesmen to remind people of "Ford's refusal to accept personal profit from war work."

Twenty years before that an exuberant biographer had written that Henry Ford refunded to the government the entirety of his war profits, which amounted to $29 million. This made enough of a splash to cause Andrew Mellon, secretary of the Treasury, to turn his grave ascetic's face to a letter. Mellon said that as far as the Treasury knew, Ford, rather than not keeping a single cent of his war profits, had not returned one. (Mellon's letter was not quite that harsh, but its meaning was clear.)

Ford's ever-evolving sense of publicity knew this would not be a good battle to join. He said he was eager to work with the Treasury to determine the exact amount he owed, and pay it. Ford's all-but-omniscient student David L. Lewis puts the company's war profits at a satisfyingly precise $8,151,119.31. With taxes deducted this would have shrunk to about half, and by the time it got close to Ford's own pocket he had profits of $926,780.46. No contemptible sum in 1922, but one Henry Ford was then in the position to pay as casually as he might have tipped his barber.

He never did. About this time, Samuel Marquis wrote, "The isolation of Henry Ford's mind is about as perfect as it is possible to make it." Ford was working toward that isolation now: He was beginning to move away from virtually everyone who had helped him succeed.

CHAPTER 15
The Expert

The Rouge rises; the Dodge brothers sue; "we don't seem to be able to keep the profits down"; sandbagging the shareholders; probing Ford's ignorance in court: "Did you ever hear of Benedict Arnold?"

While Ford was jettisoning his war leavings, one thing he definitely didn't want the military to make off with was the factory in which Knudsen was building the Eagle boats, "Now the famous 'B' building of the Rouge River Ford Plant," remarks Knudsen's biographer in 1947.

A few miles south of the city, where the Detroit River and the Rouge meet, Ford had as early as 1915 envisioned a factory that would do it all. That is to say, make a car from dirt and sand and wood and other basic elements dug and cut from Ford holdings. It was to be an industrial fortress, a city-state really. Knudsen's biographer notwithstanding, nobody would refer to it as the Rouge Plant any more than they would call the great natural wonder the Falls of Niagara. It would simply be the Rouge.

The plant was a titanic early exercise in what came to be known as vertical integration. Largely invented by Andrew Carnegie as he came to own not only the mills that forged his steel but the mines that supplied them, it allowed the industrialist to control every step in the creation of his product. Ore would come from Ford mines, timber from Ford forests, rubber from Ford's Brazil plantation to feed his own tire factory (one of the sorriest results of his disdain for experts: He hoped people with scant horticultural knowledge might somehow master this very demanding tree on the job). Ford steamers would bring the ore across the Great Lakes (he never quite managed to acquire the Lakes themselves) to a steel plant. Ford was feeling uneasy about the quality of his steel. How much, he asked Sorensen, would a proper steel plant cost? Thirty-five million dollars or so, Sorensen guessed. "What are you waiting for?" said Ford.

He had given his government things it needed during the war, and it had given him what he needed when it was over. To accommodate the Eagle boats, the ship channel that fronted the Rouge had been dredged by military engineers, a turning basin dug, everything necessary to feed the Rouge. Glassworks, paper mill, ore docks where the ten-story-tall, thousand-ton Hulett unloaders reached with delicate reptilian grace right down into the holds of ships to take out fifteen-ton mouthfuls of iron ore. Coke ovens. Rolling mills. Cold-drawn steel shops. Ten thousand acres cross-hatched with 100 miles of railroad track, and 120 miles of conveyors bringing supplies that always arrived waist-high in front of 100,000 workers.

Not yet, though; not with the drying up of the Eagle contracts. Despite his enormous resources, despite his "what are you waiting for?"s, Henry Ford still needed money to build the Rouge. One of the ways he came up with it was to stop paying dividends to his shareholders.

At least, that's how it seemed to John and Horace Dodge, and with reason. Ford announced in 1916 that henceforth he would be paying dividends of 5 percent monthly on the company's comically low book capitalization of $2 million. He told the brothers in August that this would allow him to put $58 million into expanding his plant. At the same time he cut the price of the Model T by sixty-six dollars. Even with Highland Park running at full capacity, the supply of cars could not meet the demand for them, and this meant, the brothers calculated, that Ford had just torn up $40 million of company profits for no reason at all.

The Dodges were no longer supplying any parts to the Ford Motor Company. Three years earlier, in 1913, they had been shopping in a downtown department store when they ran into Howard Bloomer, their friend and lawyer ever since they'd retained him to look after the seven hundred dollars they had raised to found their machine shop.

Bloomer surprised them by asking, "Why don't you brothers build your own car?"

John said they had headaches enough—let Ford and Couzens cope with the myriad difficulties of putting an automobile in the hands of a buyer.

Bloomer reminded them that their contract with Ford allowed either party to cancel it on a year's notice. What if Ford did that? "Your plant equipment is too heavy to have it all depending on one customer. You've got too big an investment not to safeguard it better than you are doing."

John, still merely amused by Bloomer's suggestion, asked the lawyer if he didn't believe in the business acumen of Andrew Carnegie, and quoted the steelmaker's apothegm: "Put all your eggs in one basket, and then *watch that basket.*"

"Yes, I believe that," Bloomer said, "if you own the basket. The basket belongs to Ford; the eggs belong to you. What is to prevent Ford from kicking over his basket and breaking your eggs?"

Bloomer went to the brothers' office the next day to press his argument, and that July the Dodges told Ford that their agreement would come to an end on July 1, 1914. Despite their initial misgivings they quickly created a popular automobile. Their car was more expensive than the Model T, and thus no competition to Ford, but they were relying on his dividends to get it firmly established. Ford had stopped paying all but the most derisory dividends to his shareholders in order to invest in his own plants. As the Dodge brothers' friend had told them, it's fine to put all your eggs in one basket as long as you have control of the basket. Ford, in this case, suddenly decided the basket was his and was going to keep all the eggs.

The Dodges told Ford: All right, if that's how you want to do things, just buy us out and you'll have a free hand. Ford said he'd already given them a fortune on their initial investment, and he wasn't interested in adding to it by buying them out.

The brothers took him to court. They got a restraining order against Ford's using company funds for the Rouge—or any plant expansion—and brought suit demanding the company pay out to the shareholders three-quarters of its cash surplus, which would come to nearly $40 million.

Ford went to the press. It had stung him on the Peace Ship, but he thought he would look good in the coming fight. He told the *Detroit News*, "And let me say right here that I do not believe that we should make such an awful profit on our cars. A reasonable profit is right, but not too much. So it has been my policy to force the price of a car down as fast as production would permit, and give the benefits to users and laborers."

In the state circuit court, he faced the Dodges' attorney, Elliott G. Stevenson. Pugnacious and capable, Stevenson knew what he had to do: make the case that the first responsibility of any company was to its stockholders. But there seemed to be no way to get there without asking Ford questions that the carmaker welcomed. The more Stevenson pressed Ford on the witness stand, the more petty and querulous the prosecutor seemed. Aside from one outburst when Ford told Stevenson, "If you sit there until you are petrified, I wouldn't buy Dodge brothers' stock," the carmaker was calm, restrained, and sounded like a benefactor of all humankind.

"Now," Stevenson challenged him, quoting the *Detroit News* interview, "I will ask you again, do you still think that those profits were 'awful profits'?"

"Well, I guess I do, yes."

"And for that reason you were not satisfied to continue to make such awful profits?"

Ford looked apologetic. "We don't seem to be able to keep the profits down."

". . . Are you *trying* to keep them down? What is the Ford Motor Company organized for except profits, will you tell me, Mr. Ford?"

"Organized to do as much good as we can, everywhere, for everybody concerned."

That shut Stevenson up for the day, but he had to return to the theme the next morning. He again asked Ford what was the "purpose" of his company.

"Give employment, and send out the car where the people can use it . . . and incidentally to make money. . . . Business is a service, not a bonanza."

"*Incidentally* make money?"

"Yes, sir."

Stevenson moved from incredulity to sarcasm: "But your controlling feature . . . is to employ a great army of men at high wages, to reduce the selling price of your car, so that a lot of people can buy it at a cheap price, and give everyone a car that wants one?"

Ford punctured the mocking summary by agreeing with it. "If you give all that," he said, "the money will fall into your hands; you can't get out of it."

Ford won the sympathy of the public, but Stevenson won his case. The court told Ford he had to drop his Rouge plans, and within ninety days pay a dividend of $19,275,385.36. Ford appealed the decision and in February 1919, a state superior court ruled that he could proceed with the Rouge, "but it is not within the powers of a corporation to shape and conduct a company's affairs for the merely incidental benefit of shareholders and for the primary purpose of benefiting others." The dividend stood.

Because Henry Ford was the main shareholder, most of the payment went right back to him. The trial had evidently made him restless, though, for on December 30, 1918, he resigned as president of the Ford Motor Company. Edsel took his place, and Henry went west with Clara on a vacation in Southern California.

On March 5, 1919, the *Los Angeles Examiner* ran this headline: "Henry Ford Organizing Huge New Company to Build a Better, Cheaper Car."

He was leaving his company because of the Dodge suit, Ford told the California reporters. The court's ruling had made it clear to him that he was not free to operate as he saw fit, and his only possible course was "to get out, design a new car." After all, "the present Ford car was designed twelve years ago." The new one would be a better automobile at about half the price.

What would become of the old company? Ford acted as if this particular question had never occurred to him. "Why, I don't know exactly what will become of that."

With the same tone of bemusement, one of Ford's lieutenants wrote, "Mr. Ford's recent announcement has caused quite a stir in this community. In fact, I do not believe any of the shareholders are at all pleased over it."

Certainly the Dodge brothers weren't. They had their lawyer, Stevenson, say, "There would be no attempt to keep either Mr. Ford or his son in the firm if they simply wished to retire, but Henry Ford is under contract to the Ford Motor Co. and he will not be allowed to leave the firm and start a competing business."

Ford might have replied that this was exactly what the Dodge brothers had done to him; or he might have said that he wasn't in competition at all since the new car would be far less expensive than the Motel T. Instead he told the press, "The present Ford Motor Company employees number about 50,000 in the actual manufacture of its cars. Our new company will have four or five times that number." All those workers would be making something entirely fresh: "None of the old car will be used in the new manufacture. . . . It will have a new motor and new fixtures." And it was "well advanced, for I have been working on it while resting in California." It might cost $250.

Edsel tried to reassure the dealers, who were at least as worried as the stockholders, that they were in no imminent danger: "We know a new car could not possibly be designed, tested out, manufactured, and marketed in quantity [in] under two or three years." Then he added the hazy but disturbing statement that "we expect to make it a competitor to the streetcar rather than the Ford."

At the same time, agents began to approach the Ford stockholders, expressing cautious interest in acquiring their Ford Motor Company shares, civilly suggesting that it might be a good time to sell.

It is a powerful testament to what Henry Ford

had accomplished that the shareholders didn't at once see that the new company was a ploy, and its soon-to-be-produced car a fantasy. But look what Henry Ford *had* done. They began to agree to sell.

Couzens did not. He had been right there when his partner figured out the Model T. He knew Henry Ford would no sooner abandon that car than he would his wife or his son. He had also watched while Ford used an identical stratagem to buy out Malcomson. Couzens stayed out of the negotiations as the bidding started at $7,500 per share and the price rose and finally settled at $12,500. Then he said he was willing to sell, but only at $13,000.

John Anderson, who had grown from the eager, timid young lawyer who wrote his father the long letter begging for five thousand dollars into a gentleman of leisure, found out what was going on through a man named Stuart Webb, who was representing undisclosed parties that wished to buy his shares. Anderson had already told Webb he would sell only if all the other shareholders wanted to. On July 3, 1919, "Mr. Webb called on the telephone and said he had a document which he thought might interest me." Anderson told him to come over. The document "proved to be an option running to Edsel Ford, giving him the privilege of buying Mr. Couzens' stock in the Ford Motor Company for $13,000 a share.

Well, I read that option over and it was certainly a distinct surprise to me, because this was the first time I had any inkling who the purchaser of the stocks was to be. Mr. Ford had denied in the press that he was interested in buying the stock. . . .

"Well," I said to Mr. Webb, "I see Mr. Couzens is getting more for his stocks than is being offered me."

Webb unhappily agreed that this was true, and that there was nothing he could to about it.

Anderson said, "I don't care, Mr. Webb. If there is anybody in that organization who is entitled to a little bit more than anybody else in case of a general sale, it seems to me it is Mayor Couzens [he was then mayor of Detroit]. It was due to his efforts that the Company became a success."

Webb, surprised and relieved, handed Anderson a sheaf of papers and asked if he might go over them and give his answer on Monday, which was July 7.

Anderson's account of where he went to think it over reflects in a most appealing way his grateful wonder at the path his life had taken since his fond, doubting father had reluctantly written the check.

"Well, the next day was the 4th of July. I . . . was all alone. The family had gone away to the seashore, and there was nobody there but the servants. I had a room up on the third floor in the corner of my house, that I call a den. It is a room surrounded by shelves, with books on them, and a table in the center."

In this unique chamber, Anderson studied the figures and came to realize that if he sold he'd be getting a good deal less than his shares' true value. Because he was the only stockholder who had not committed himself to selling, he was in a position to exact more money, but did he want to "present to Mr. Ford the picture, as it inevitably would have been presented to him, that I was holding him up?" All his old colleagues had signed the agreement; if he held back, he'd be upsetting their plans. On the other hand, had he been too generous in his initial response to Couzens's getting more for his own shares?

> All of these thoughts ran through my mind. I figured out, supposing I do refuse unless I get two or two and one-half million dollars more money, then the tax thing came,—where will that land me? It meant a difference of about $600,000 or $700,000. And I said to myself, "By Jove," as I thought over what Mr. Ford had done for me; as I thought of the house I was in, and the room, and contrasted it with my humble home in 1903 when the Company started; the advantages I had had in the

meantime, and the ability to give up the daily practice of law; the opportunities afforded to travel; all of these things I could trace directly to my association with Mr. Ford in the Ford Motor Company, and I said to myself:

"John Anderson, are you going to be an ingrate, or are you going to be a man?"

And I decided that I would try not to be an ingrate.

On Monday Anderson told Webb yes, and then the deal moved so quickly that the newspapers reported it completed four days later, on July 11. Anderson got $12.5 million, having already received dividends of nearly $5 million. Couzens received $30 million. The estate of John Gray, who had gone to his grave still full of doubts about the wisdom of investing in motorcars, took in $26 million.

Henry Ford, who so distrusted Wall Street and all the haughty financial bastions of the East, had to swallow his pride to ask for a $75 million credit to cover his buyout. He did so grimly, but when everything was settled, he found he had climbed to a summit nobody had achieved before. John D. Rockefeller never owned much more than a third of Standard Oil, and Rockefeller himself had been surprised to learn how little America's foremost financier had been worth when J. P. Morgan died in 1913. But by the end of 1919 Henry Ford held the largest company ever in the hands of one person. His operation was worth half a billion dollars, and he owned it as completely as he did his piano and his birdhouses.

The $250 wonder car started its phantom engine and silently backed away to park itself forever alongside the one-man submarines and their pill-bombs.

Nineteen nineteen, that year of triumph and consolidation, also turned out to be one of the most painful of Henry Ford's life, and one that would change it.

Samuel Marquis wrote that Ford "seems to shirk encounters in which it will be necessary for him to say unpleasant things. In other words, he hates a quarrel but he loves a good fight. He is of Irish descent. He keeps his eye on his opponent—many eyes on him in fact—and is master in the art of waiting. This is one of the reasons I think he enjoys lawsuits, of which he has had his share: they are usually so long drawn out. There are so many courts of appeal, and the more the merrier."

He found little merriment in his tangle with the *Chicago Tribune*. In a rare moment of partisan heat, Nevins writes that "it grew out of an editorial that even in the history of the *Tribune* stands forth as peculiarly silly and obnoxious."

The trouble went back to 1916 when, with

Pancho Villa and his men active along the Mexican border, President Wilson summoned the National Guard. The *Tribune*, at this time in its career full of martial ardor, had its correspondents get in touch with big corporations to see whether they planned to support their employees who went after Villa. The *Tribune*'s man in Detroit somehow got the Ford company's treasurer, Frank Klingensmith, on the phone. Without consulting his boss or anyone at all, Klingensmith said that any Ford worker who went would lose his job. He later denied this in court, and indeed it wasn't true: Eighty-nine Ford employees served along the border, and they all got back their old jobs or better ones. The answer was good enough for the *Tribune*, which ran an editorial under the heading "Ford Is an Anarchist." It said, "If Ford allows this rule of his shop to stand, he will reveal himself not merely as an ignorant idealist, but as an anarchistic enemy of the nation which protects him in his wealth."

Ford might have let this pass unchallenged, but his lawyer, Alfred Lucking, urged him to take the *Tribune* to court. Ford didn't need much urging; as Marquis observed, he enjoyed speaking from the pulpit of the witness chair. He cavalierly told Lucking, "Well, you'd better start suit against them for libel."

Lucking did, demanding $1 million in damages. He began with a bad misstep. Had he simply sued over the terms "anarchist" and "anarchistic," words that had long been recognized as libelous by courts, he would likely have won a swift and early victory. But he chose to cite the entire editorial, and thus the word "ignorant." Marquis wrote that "there are hundreds of men figuring prominently in the business world of no greater erudition than [Ford], but on matters with which they are not familiar they have the gift of silence and a correspondingly low visibility."

Ford by now was eager to speak on any topic. He said he had brought the suit largely because he wanted "to educate people." He didn't know how little he knew, but he was about to find out.

As the suit gathered momentum, it attracted more and more attention. Ford's attorneys didn't want it tried in Chicago on *Tribune* ground, and the *Tribune* didn't want it in Detroit. Both sides finally agreed on Mount Clemens, a quiet little resort town—it had sulfur springs—twenty miles northeast of Detroit. There Ford set up his own news bureau to make sure his side of the story reached the smaller towns where he felt his strongest support lay.

The trial began on May 12 before a jury of eleven farmers and a road builder. One of the jurors told the court that although he owned a Model T, "that would not prejudice me against Mr. Ford."

Ford was up against his old adversary Elliott Stevenson, only this time Stevenson would not be questioning him on the one subject Ford knew more about than anyone on earth. Three years earlier Ford had told a *Chicago Tribune* reporter, "I don't know much about history, and I wouldn't give a nickel for all the history in the world. It means nothing to me. History is more or less bunk. It's tradition. We want to live in the present and the only history that is worth a tinker's damn is the history we make today. That's the trouble with the world. We're living in books and history and tradition. We want to get away from that and take care of today. We've done too much looking back. What we want to do, and do it quick, is to make just history right now. The men who are responsible for the present war in Europe knew all about history. Yet they brought on the worst war in the world's history."

Ford's lawyers discovered that Stevenson would try to ratify their client's ignorance by questioning him about American history and they hastily put together a history lesson for him. It didn't go well. E. G. Pipp, a newspaperman helping Ford, remembered that Lucking might begin with,

> "Now don't forget this; remember the evacuation of Florida. . . ."
>
> But Ford would be out of his seat, looking out of the window.
>
> "Say, that airplane is flying pretty low, isn't it?" he would ask.

Again Lucking would steer him to the chair, but Ford would hop to the window with: "Look at that bird there; pretty little fellow isn't he? Somebody's feeding it, or it wouldn't come back so often."

While these tutorials ran their barren course, the trial commenced with a great deal of testimony about the meaning of "anarchy" and evocations of the violence along the Mexican border to demonstrate the peril the nation had been in when Ford was urging pacifism. Some honest-to-God Texas Rangers had been imported to tell about gunfights with Villa's men.

Despite the presence of such exotic beings walking out in the streets of Mount Clemens, Ford was the main event. He took the stand on July 14. This was the beginning of the trial's third month, and the newspaper correspondents had developed a heartfelt slogan: "Out of Mount Clemens by Christmas." But they were all engaged and alert when Ford took the stand.

Stevenson approached him. There were to be no questions about the morality of doing shareholders out of their profits.

"You call yourself an educator? Now I shall inquire whether you were a well-informed man, competent to educate people."

Stevenson brought up Ford's already well-known comment about history.

"Did you say that?"

"I did not say that it was bunk. It was bunk to me but I did not say—"

Stevenson quickly put in, "It was bunk to you?"

"It was not much to me."

"What do you mean by that?"

"Well, I haven't much use for it. I didn't need it very bad."

Stevenson wanted to attach the bunk remark more firmly to Ford. He'd been trying to buffalo his witness with elaborate words, and now he asked a high-flown question. "What do you mean? Do you think we can provide for the future and care wisely with reference to the future in matters like preparation for defense, or anything of that sort, without knowing the history of what has happened in the past?"

The answer didn't go the way the lawyer hoped.

Ford spoke of the conflict he had tried to stop: "When we got into the war, the past didn't amount to much for us."

"Will you answer the question, Mr. Ford, please?"

"I thought I was answering it as well as I could. History usually didn't last a week."

"What do you mean, 'History didn't last a week'?"

"In the present war . . . airships and things we used were out of date in a week."

"What has that to do with history?" Stevenson asked in disgust. Although his was probably the best legal mind in the trial, Stevenson had missed Ford's point. Naturally the man who had been changing history with machines answered the lawyer in mechanical terms, but the obsolete airships stood as an emblem of a century of certainties and customs that had withered even as the war pursued its annihilating course. History, Ford was saying, is both malleable and perishable, and its lessons vital to one era can become platitudes and archaisms, mere chatter, in, as he put it, a week.

Stevenson pressed on with the *Tribune*'s labeling Ford an "ignorant idealist."

Ford said, "Well, I admit I'm ignorant about some things. I don't know anything about art."

Stevenson wanted to know if Ford was "ignorant of the fundamental principles of this government."

"I suppose it's the Constitution."

"What does 'fundamental principles of government' mean?"

"I don't understand."

"What is the fundamental principle of government?"

"Just you," said Ford. (Actually, given its brevity, a pretty good answer in the face of a question that was seeking a civics lecture.)

"Is that the only idea you have on it?"

Ford replied, again not absurdly, "This is a long subject."

Stevenson went on to ask if there had been any revolutions in America. Ford said, "There was, I understand."

"When?"

"In 1812."

"In 1812, the Revolution?"

"Yes."

"Any other times?"

"I don't know."

This went on for days, and it got worse. Savoring a kind of litigatory bloodlust, one of the *Tribune* lawyers told a reporter, "This lawsuit is like the tenth baby in a family. We didn't want it but now that we have it we wouldn't take a million dollars for it. It is worth that to show Ford up."

Sometimes Ford scored against his opponents. Stevenson asked him, "What was the United States originally?" Ford paused, but not because he was stumped, and then tartly replied, "Land, I guess." He was able briefly to reprise his Dodge trial testimony when Stevenson asked him to define the word "idealist." Ford said that it was "a person that can help to make other people prosperous."

Ford enjoyed few such moments. What was the Monroe Doctrine? "A big-brother act." Did he know the United States Capitol was burned in 1812? "I heard so." What is ballyhoo? "A blackguard or something of that nature." Treason? "Anything against the government." Anarchy? An answer inspired by editorial cartoons he must have seen: "Overthrowing the government and throwing bombs."

Finally, this excruciating exchange:

"Did you ever hear of Benedict Arnold?"

"I have heard the name."

"Who was he?"

"I have forgotten just who he is. He's a writer, I think."

The case went on until August 14, when the patient jury received it and rendered a verdict in ten hours. The decision held the *Tribune* guilty of libel. Ford was awarded damages of six cents (one reporter wanted to know how he planned to spend it).

A correspondent for the *Literary Digest* during the trial saw Ford in a characteristic pose. "He is sitting in a chair that is tilted back against the wall. His thin knee is clasped in his long hands; good-natured patience dwells upon his face. . . . When a question is asked him he rubs his hand across his long jaw, a rural gesture; he speculatively moistens his lips, lowering his eyes when he wants to think, leaning forward when something interests him. Henry Ford sitting in court with crossed legs, suggests the country store philosopher."

This sagacious disinterest was a pose, and one it

must have been very difficult for Ford to maintain. The man who loved practical jokes but never wanted to be the object of them was now, he knew, the butt of a national joke. The *New York Times* said, "Mr. Ford has been submitted to a severe examination of his intellectual qualities. He has not received a passing degree." The *New York Tribune* found him "deliciously naive and omniscient and preposterous." The *Post* said simply, "This man is a joke."

John Reed, who had become disillusioned with Ford because of what he saw as the pernicious meddling of the Sociological Department, came back to his side during the trial, taking pity on the "slight boyish figure with thin long sure hands incessantly moving . . . the fine skin of his thin face browned by the sun; the mouth and nose of a simpleminded saint."

The *Ohio State Journal*, acknowledging the carmaker's humiliating performance, allowed that "we sort of like old Henry Ford, anyway." Editorials in small-town newspapers said that their readers didn't give a damn about the War of 1812.

Ford took no comfort in patronizing kindness. The generous instincts that had led to the five-dollar day and the Peace Ship began to warp and tarnish under the acid-drip of his memories of those days on the stand. They had cured him forever of seeking the witness chair as a speaker's podium. The ordeal fortified his growing insularity and irrigated many unexamined prejudices, while seeming to have taught him no lessons at all.

That isn't quite just. The trial did spur him to earn his private degree in history, just as he'd earned his engineering degree, all by himself, putting what he'd learned on display in a great museum. But whatever good might emerge from the suit was distant. Its ills were immediate.

It made him angry, and convinced him that he had no true allies.

We don't have much to thank Lucking for. Had he not persuaded Ford to sue the *Tribune*, and then bungled the case from the outset, the impulse that launched the ill-planned Peace Ship might have evolved throughout the 1920s into something more sophisticated and effective that benefited the entire country. Ford had the means and the energy to affect things at that level.

Nevins says "the scars which the *Tribune* suit left upon Henry Ford were thus a public misfortune." By "public misfortune" Nevins means a national one. The trial had stifled Ford's altruistic instincts, and left him open to frittering away much of his time and fortune on vagrant enthusiasms that were as random and powerful as they were short-lived.

CHAPTER 16
The International Jew

The problems of civilization traced to their source; the *Dearborn Independent*; Liebold; "LET'S HAVE SOME SENSATIONALISM"; "Jewish Degradation of American Baseball"; two U.S. presidents ask Ford to stop his campaign; he carries it on for ninety-one issues of the *Independent*; Ford apologizes, saying he had no idea what was in his newspaper.

In 1917 the *New York Herald* asked a reporter to go out to Detroit and put ten questions to Henry Ford. This sounds like a compact and relatively easy assignment, but it wasn't. The reporter, William C. Richards, knew that Ford combined the trying qualities of being a publicity-seeking extrovert and making himself impossible to get near. Richards managed it, though, and asked his ten questions.

"It was the first time I had talked to him and what I remember most was his candor in saying he did not know the answers to four of the questions and would not try to guess." He answered four others at once, and "the ninth he dismissed as a trick one—which it was—and over the last he paused, as if rolling around in his mouth a medicine of tart bite, and could not make up his mind whether to swallow or spit it out. . . .

"Lastly, Mr. Ford," Richards began confidently, but then immediately lost his nerve—laying, he said, the "onus" of the question "squarely" on his editor. "The *Herald* wishes to know how you feel to be the world's first billionaire."

Ford wasn't quite that yet, but as Richards put it, "The green was an easy chip shot away." As the carmaker took in the question, "he squirmed in his chair and twisted a leg over one arm of it, and then his eyes lost their equanimity and he exploded with an earthy vulgarism. I remember writing to the editor, 'In answer to Question Ten Mr. Ford said, "Oh, shit!" Your problem is what to do with it.' "

The problem of what to do with the billion, however, was all Ford's, and he wasn't finding it easy to solve.

The war he'd failed to shut down would be over in a year. The Model Ts would keep coming, a long, unvarying black stream that Sorensen was beginning to get sick of looking at. Black, because after 1915 that was the only hue offered. This was not, as folklore durably holds, because black paint dried more quickly, but simply another step in the endless effort to speed and simplify production. Ford quoted the famous phrase about the customer being able to have any

429

color as long as it was black in his autobiography, but he didn't originate it. Like the Ford jokes, it came from everywhere.

The "Oh, shit!" was a cry of frustration. He was getting bored. He saw the decade ahead, saw it being populated with millions and millions of new Model Ts, and couldn't see beyond that. He had perfected the Model T, and you can't further perfect perfection. The fierce, brief blaze of the five-dollar day had guttered in the wartime prosperity. Ford was paying a six-dollar day now, and its inauguration had made no impact whatever. He could see, too, that the steady pressure of war had brought his production methods to many plants sooner than ever would have happened in time of peace. He'd always shared his industrial techniques, never tried to stymie rivals with patent suits, but now there were a good many freshly equipped establishments that might be competitors.

That wasn't what made him restless, though. He missed the high calling of the Selden suit, the Peace Ship, and jousting with the Dodge brothers. Surely he missed the days when Americans were adopting into their families a car, *his* car, more quickly and wholeheartedly than they had embraced any other invention ever. Even having bought out his stockholders couldn't assuage his desire to act on the largest possible stage. He'd thought the libel suit might give him a taste of that. Instead it was a searing disappointment, but not a chastening one.

After that first interview, Richards, who came to know Ford quite well, wrote "what stuck in my memory in the intervening years was not so much the expletive as his frank admission of ignorance, the fact he had no answers for four questions and would not talk—at least at the moment—of things he knew nothing about. . . . The hour would come when he would tackle the toughest without awe or misgiving and often without knowledge. He would pass judgment quickly on world controversies, needing no more than a single sentence for the panacea."

And so he came to find an answer to the most pressing problem in the world, the canker that fomented wars and kept them going, with all their blighting of constructive labor, the hidden catalyst that drew men from their lathes and plows and put them at one another's throats. Ford's answer was as simple and complex and efficient as his Model T. It was the Jews.

Why? In his scrupulous study *Henry Ford and the Jews*, the historian Neil Baldwin takes it back to what he calls "McGuffeyland." The readers included the maneuverings of Shakespeare's Shylock, but millions of other American children read them and didn't come away thinking themselves in the grip of a worldwide Jewish conspiracy.

Although there were few Jewish workers in Highland Park, the younger Ford never spoke of his animus against them as a people. Still, there was a general feeling in the Midwest of his youth that the distant forces controlling the all-powerful abstraction known as Wall Street included Jewish bankers and stock manipulators whose "orientalism"—a word of the time that often referred to Jews rather than Asians—was hostile to the stalwart values of farm and church.

Then there was Ford's growing anger about the "parasites" who did no work themselves but lived off the labors of others through returns on investments. Though none of the parasites he'd had to buy out to gain full control of his company was Jewish, at some point he began to see the Jews as a race of moneylenders who shunned honest labor. He once offered a thousand dollars to anyone who could show him a Jewish farmer.

If they could profit from the sweat of others, so could they from the blood of others. Rosika Schwimmer said that even before the Peace Ship sailed Henry Ford, after speaking to her "briskly and logically" about his pacifism, abruptly came out with, "I know who caused the war—the German-Jewish bankers! I have the evidence here"—he patted his breast pocket—"Facts! The German-Jewish bankers caused the war. I can't give out the facts now, because I haven't got them all yet, but I'll have them soon." Schwimmer said that Ford's tone had abruptly lost its intelligent vigor of seconds earlier: Now he was speaking with "that lack of conviction with which a schoolboy would recite something about the supreme happiness of being good and virtuous."

In 1918 Ford got a platform on which to display his goodness and virtue. He bought a feeble local weekly called the *Dearborn Independent*, and hired E. G. Pipp—the highly competent, liberal-minded veteran newspaperman who would witness the futile tutorial efforts at Mount Clemens—as editor, and Fred L. Black, a salesman who understood printing costs, as business manager. They were promised complete editorial independence save for a feature to be called "Mr. Ford's Own Page." That would be under the control of the general manager, Ernest Liebold.

Liebold did any number of things for Ford.

When Julian Street went seeking the carmaker, he came first to the Highland Park plant, "so full of people, all of them working for Ford, that a thousand or two would make no difference in the look of things. And among all these people there was just one man I really wanted to see, and just one man I really wanted not to see. I wanted to see Henry Ford, and I wanted not to see a man named Liebold, because, they say, if you see Liebold first you never do see Ford. That is what Liebold is there for. He is the man whose business in life is to know where Ford *isn't*."

Liebold had been keeping track of where Ford wasn't since 1911. Henry Ford, who knew exactly how much every part in his Model T cost to manufacture, who would happily buy a hundred-thousand-dollar machine to save a few pennies a day, who had used his command of prices to battle all his rivals until he had none, was surprisingly casual about his own money. One day Clara, going through a suit of his before sending it out to be cleaned, felt something in a trouser pocket. She reached in and withdrew a creased and battered but perfectly live check for seventy-five thousand dollars.

Clara, who was still thrifty enough regularly to darn her husband's socks, was appalled. She asked Couzens to find her husband someone to handle his business mail, and he said he thought Liebold would do a good job of it.

Born in Detroit in 1884, Liebold trained in business there and was working at a savings bank when his obvious capability caught Couzens's eye. Ford's lieutenant brought him aboard a newly founded bank, and when Ford himself wanted to save an ailing private bank in Dearborn, he gave the job to Liebold. He did so well that Ford put his money in what had become the Dearborn State Bank, and soon had such confidence in Liebold that he let him handle his personal finances. Holding power of attorney for Henry and Clara, Liebold managed every Ford family business that didn't directly involve carmaking. He was never officially employed by the Ford Motor Company, but he had greater access to Ford, and more influence over him, than almost anyone who was.

Liebold was so trusted that he apparently wrote his own salary checks. Nearly as competent as Couzens, he served Ford as business manager, executive secretary, and when a hospital needed building in Dearborn, he saw that it got built. When Ford bought a dilapidated railroad Liebold helped get the line in shape and sold it for a $9 million profit. Naturally Ford gave him a role in the *Dearborn Independent.*

It was impossible to find anyone who could question Liebold's integrity. It was equally impossible to find anyone who liked him. That suited Liebold. "I make it a rule not to have any friends in the company," he told Fred Black. "You must be in a position where you don't give a God-damn what happens to anybody."

That suited Henry Ford: "Well, when you hire a watchdog, you don't hire him to like everybody who comes to the gate."

Liebold was proud of his German heritage, which to him encompassed an implacable anti-Semitism.

The first issue of the *Dearborn Independent* under Ford's ownership and Pipp's direction came out on May 11, 1919. The best that can be said is that it was harmless. Between gray halftones, columns of text warned against monopoly, recounted agricultural developments, picked up various stories from other papers, and voiced the faded Populist enthusiasms of twenty years earlier. The *Detroit Times* remarked that it was "the best periodical ever turned out by a tractor plant." Another Detroit paper—almost certainly the only midwestern daily ever to swipe at a rival by invoking Samuel Taylor Coleridge—said the *Independent* was "tranquil as a Peace Ship upon a painted ocean."

"Mr. Ford's Own Page," smoothed and expanded from whatever he might have said by William Cameron, was an anthology of pithless epigrams: "Opportunity will not overlook you because you wear overalls."

Despite the interest aroused by Ford's participation, the circulation reached only 56,000 during the first year he owned it, and cost him $284,000 in losses. The next spring the readership dropped to 26,000.

Pipp thought the remedy might be a fiction contest. Joseph J. O'Neill, who had come from the *New York World* to help with the press office at Mount Clemens, did not. In a fourteen-page memo that reads as if it were designed to be heard through a gale, he wrote, "PUSSY FOOTING and being afraid to hurt people will keep us where we are. . . . ONE SINGLE SERIES may make us known to millions. A succession of series of FEARLESS, TRUTHFUL, INTERESTING, PLAIN-SPOKEN articles, if properly handled . . . will make a lasting reputation . . . LET'S HAVE SOME SENSATIONALISM."

He was right about establishing a lasting reputation. From that day to this it has cost the Ford Motor Company untold millions of dollars, and cast a shadow over its founder that has yet to entirely lift. O'Neill hadn't suggested any particular subject for the *Independent*'s sensational series. Pipp said the topic was Liebold's doing. Shortly after it had been chosen he wrote, "The door to the Ford mind was always open to anything Liebold wanted to shove in it, and during that time Mr. Ford developed a dislike for Jews . . . I am sure that if Mr. Ford were put on the witness stand he could not tell to save his life just when he started against the Jews. I am sure that Liebold could tell." Fred Black agreed: Ford's secretary "did have a fertile field to work on, but if I were to put the number one blame on anyone, I would put it on Liebold."

Pipp saw what was coming, and he quit the *Independent* in April, a month before the journal began presenting what he called Ford's "gospel of bitterness and poison-gas race-hatred."

That began on May 22, 1920, when "the Ford International Weekly (5¢ an issue $1.00 per year) *The Dearborn Independent*" ran its front-page headline: "The International Jew: The World's Problem."

The story began, "The Jew is again being singled out for critical attention throughout the world. His emergence in the financial, political and social spheres has been so complete and spectacular since the war, that his place, power and purpose in the world are being given a real scrutiny, much of it unfriendly. . . .

"The single description which will include a larger percentage of Jews than members of any other race is this: he is in business. It may be only gathering rags and selling them, but he is in business. From the sale of old clothes to the control of international trade and finance, the Jew is supremely gifted for business." And so on. And on, and on, and on for ninety-one issues. "Does a Jewish Power Control the World Press?" (Yes); "Does a Definite Jewish World Program Exist?" (Yes); "Are the Jews a Nation?" (Who knows? So many have come into America uncounted that they may already be close to taking over the country.)

Liebold found a useful ally in his campaign when he got his hands on a copy of *The Protocols of the Learned Elders of Zion*, recently translated into English. This invention of the czarist secret police had emerged in the first years of the century. It is usually called a forgery but, as the late Christopher Hitchens furiously strove to establish, a "forgery" means that there exists an authentic original that has surreptitiously been copied. The *Protocols* are a hoax or, if that word might suggest mere prankishness, a fraud. They purport to record the seven highest leaders of the Jewish faith plotting world domination through usury and the corruption of gentile traditions and morals.

Liebold seized on the *Protocols* to help fight back every assault of the hydra-headed Jewish campaign to destroy America: "Jewish Supremacy in the Motion Picture"; "Jewish Degradation of American Baseball"; "How Jews in the U.S. Conceal their Strength." The *Independent* continued also to run innocuous stories in every issue. That of August 6, 1921, includes in its cover lines, "Teaching the Deaf to Hear With Their Eyes," and, "Many By-Products from Sweet-Potatoes," but the dominant one is "Jewish Jazz—Moron Music—Becomes our National Music."

Cameron was writing much of this. Gifted, loyal to his boss, alcoholic all his adult life, he got the *Independent*'s editorship after Pipp left in disgust. Ordered by Liebold and Ford to go dig up all the facts about the Jewish conspiracy, he turned in a report that said he'd instead discovered "what a wonderful race they were, and how little he had known of their history, and what a magnificent history it was." That, at least, is what he said to interviewers years later. He did not stress to them his long-held belief that the British had descended from the only true lost tribe of Israel.

In any event he was Ford's man, and he did Ford's work.

Of course American Jews were surprised to be told by somebody almost all of them admired that they were responsible for pornography, short skirts, urbanization at the expense of the farm, increased public drunkenness, exorbitant rents, salacious Broadway shows, lewd nightclubs, and, for that matter, nightclubs. (In her 1981 biography of Ford, Carol Gelderman makes the shrewd suggestion that he may have been lashing out at the Jews as a scapegoat; that some sunken part of him feared the Model T had done more to bring the moral disintegration he deplored than had any conclave of "International Jews.") The financier Bernard Baruch was above the provocations of the *Dearborn Independent*. When reporters asked him about the accusations that he was the "proconsul of Judah in America," and a "Jew of Super-Power," he replied, grinning, "Now, boys, you wouldn't expect me to deny them, would you?"

Not many of the campaign's victims could laugh it off so easily. When the Jewish press complained, Liebold answered, telling the editors that they should shut up and keep on reading the articles so that they could "get a new light on the Jewish situation," because "all fair-minded Jews must help rid the world of the peril that threatens."

Rabbi Leo Franklin, head of Beth El, Detroit's leading reform temple, who had spoken so warmly in favor of the five-dollar day and begged its recipients to make themselves worthy of their benefactor, wrote in his diary, "Such venom could only come from a Jew-hater of the lowest type, and here it is appearing in a newspaper owned and controlled by one whom the Jews had counted as among their friends."

Franklin took this as more than an assault on his people. He had been Ford's neighbor on Edison Avenue, and his close friend. So close, that Ford sent him a new Model T every year. When one arrived a little later that spring, Franklin told the chauffeur to take it back: He couldn't accept it. Ford was surprised and shaken, and called right away. "What's wrong, Dr. Franklin? Has something come between us?"

Apparently Ford believed with Liebold that any responsible Jew would be grateful to have the venality and ruthlessness of most of his people pointed out to him, so he could help correct them. Franklin said what was wrong a few days later in a local paper: "Few thinking men have ever given any credence to the charges offered against the Jews. But his publications have besmirched the name of the Jews in the eyes of the great majority, and especially in the small towns of the country, where Ford's word was taken as gospel. He has also fed the flames of anti-Semitism throughout the world."

American Jews never launched a formal boycott against Ford products. About as close as they came was when Connecticut congregations mounted a parade in Hartford to honor Chaim Weizmann and Albert Einstein. Four hundred cars were to take part, but "positively no Ford machines permitted in line." Albert Kahn took a calm, almost philosophical view, at least twenty years later when he said Ford "is a strange man. He seems to feel always that he is being guided by someone outside himself." Kahn was pragmatic enough not to sever his architectural ties with his most important client once the attacks were under way. But he never again met with Ford personally.

Nor did the *Independent*'s campaign sit well with many gentiles. William Howard Taft, William Cardinal O'Connor, and Woodrow Wilson urged Ford to drop this "vicious propaganda."

As he usually did with his new business ventures, Ford made Clara and Edsel part of the *Dearborn Independent*: she was vice president; he, secretary treasurer. When "The International Jew" began its long run, they resigned.

Ford's dealers couldn't resign, but they did protest. It wasn't just the reputation of the newspaper that was suffocating their business; it was their having to sell a subscription to it along with every Model T. This played particularly poorly in the big towns, where many dealers simply tore a few pages out of the phone book, copied the addresses, bought subscriptions themselves, and every so often sent a check off to Detroit to cover the payments of their unwitting subscribers.

But the *Independent*, though its circulation grew to over six hundred thousand, was not a great success in the small towns, either. When an agent in Virginia, Minnesota, asked for the articles to stop because his landlord was threatening to evict him, Liebold helpfully suggested he buy his own building where he would be immune from such pressures. Other agents were more blunt: A New York dealer wrote that everything would be better if Ford put his money into improving his car instead of hawking his newspaper. Ford's curt answer to all such protests was, "If they want our product, they'll buy it."

Then, in January 1922, while Liebold was gathering evidence that Abraham Lincoln had been assassinated by "Jewish internationalists" angered at the president's wartime adoption of greenback dollars, Ford came into Cameron's office and said, "I want you to cut out the Jewish articles."

Pipp, who had started his own newspaper, and often vented his disillusionment with Ford in its pages, wrote, "There was amazement. Some who were supposed to be on the inside of things hopped around like hens with their heads cut off."

The reasons for the abrupt cessation are still unclear. Ford at the time was toying with the idea of running for the presidency, and that may have something to do with it, although Pipp believed that Gaston Plaintiff, Ford's main New York dealer and a man he trusted, had persuaded him that the series was destroying sales. Ford himself, at his most maddeningly capricious, told Cameron that he was planning to develop a new "money standard"—which is to say a new economic system—and naturally he needed Jewish help. Cameron thought of the ninety-one straight issues of the *Independent* Ford had devoted to Jewish scurrility. "They won't do it," he said. Ford was blithe: "Oh, yes, they will. We can work with them."

He didn't try to for very long. In April 1924 the *Independent* began warning the nation about "Jewish Exploitation of Farmer Organizations."

Aaron Sapiro, a well-known Chicago attorney, had spent years drafting contracts that would coordinate and strengthen the scattered efforts of southern cotton planters and West Coast fruit growers. Now he was working to recruit dissatisfied midwestern wheat farmers into a marketing cooperative. "A Band of Jews is on the Back of the American Farmer," said the *Independent*. They were "bankers, lawyers, money-lenders, advertising agencies, fruit-packers, produce-buyers, experts," and at the head of them all was Aaron Sapiro.

Ford had picked on the wrong Jew. Sapiro could be obstinate and impulsive, and not always wise in his choice of lieutenants, but he was smart and tough, and he was a fighter. He sued Henry Ford for $1 million.

By now Ford had long outgrown his relish for disseminating his views from the witness stand and he went to great lengths to avoid being subpoenaed. Meanwhile, Cameron stood in the breach.

For the better part of a week Sapiro's incredulous lawyer listened to the editor blandly but unshakably asserting that Henry Ford had no idea what ran in his own newspaper. Never mind the copious assurances by Liebold and Cameron in promotional campaigns that "the *Dearborn Independent* is Henry Ford's own paper and he authorizes every statement occurring therein," and that "we never step out on any unusual programs without first getting his guidance"—Ford had never read a line.

Not even on "Mr. Ford's Own Page"?

No.

Had he ever mentioned Mr. Sapiro to Mr. Cameron?

No. The staff had an absolutely free hand. Henry Ford had never heard of Aaron Sapiro before he brought his lawsuit. Cameron had never spoken with Ford about "any article" on "any Jew."

The Sunday evening before Ford was to appear in court he was heading back to Fair Lane along Michigan Avenue when a Studebaker sideswiped his coupe and sent it down a fifteen-foot embankment and into a tree. The facts of the accident remain clouded to this day—it's not even clear whether Ford was alone in his car—and the papers made much of it: "Ford Injured by Assassins: Hurled Over River Bank in Car." He wasn't badly hurt, but he was banged up enough to keep off the stand for the next few days, while the case dissolved amid accusations of jury tampering and the judge declared a mistrial.

This gave Ford the room to settle with Sapiro out of court, which he eagerly did.

He went further. To Cameron's astonishment, and Edsel's, he issued a sweeping apology not only to Sapiro, which was part of the settlement, but to the Jewish people in general. He worked on it with two associates of his, and two distinguished Jewish public figures, the former congressman Nathan D. Perlman and Louis P. Marshall, head of the American Jewish Committee. Marshall turned over the initial draft certain that much wrangling was to follow. "If I had his money," he wrote a colleague, "I would not make such a humiliating statement."

Ford didn't change a word.

He began by saying that he had "given consideration to the series of articles concerning Jews . . ." but ". . . in the multitude of my activities it has been impossible for me to devote personal attention to their management or to keep informed as to their contents." So he entrusted the reports to "men whom I placed in charge of them and upon whom I relied implicitly.

"To my great regret I have learned that Jews generally, and particularly those of this country not only resent these publications as promoting anti-Semitism, but regard me as their enemy. Trusted friends . . . have assured me in all sincerity that [the articles justify] the righteous indignation entertained by Jews everywhere toward me because of the mental anguish occasioned by the unprovoked reflections made upon them.

"This has led me to direct my personal attention to the subject, in order to ascertain the exact nature of these articles. As a result of this survey I confess I am deeply mortified." Ford says he was horrified to learn that his newspaper was suggesting Jews were trying to control "the capital and industries of the world," and dismayed to discover the presence of the "exploded fictions" of the *Protocols.*

"Had I appreciated even the general nature, to say nothing of the details, of these utterances I would have forbidden their circulation without a moment's hesitation . . . I deem it my duty as an honorable man to make amends for the wrong done to the Jews as fellow-men and brothers, by asking their forgiveness for the harm that I have unintentionally committed . . . and by giving them the unqualified assurance that henceforth they may look to me for friendship and good will."

There was a sparkle of mockery in the celebratory ballad issued by the Broadway hitsmith and producer Billy Rose:

> I was sad and I was blue
> But now I'm just as good as you
> Since Hen-ry Ford a-pol-o-gized to me
> I've thrown a-way my lit-tle Chev-ro-let
> And bought my-self a Ford Cou-pe . . .

And the *New York Herald Tribune* wasn't buying a word of it: "Nobody but Mr. Ford could be ignorant of a major policy of his own news-paper. Nobody but Mr. Ford could be unaware of the national and international repercussions of this policy of anti-Semitism." But in general the Jewish public seems to have been remarkably tolerant of the about-face. The *Jewish Daily Forward* said that Ford's "frank and courageous repudiation of the attacks on Jewry will have a tremendous effect in undoing the harm that has been done." Louis B. Mayer wrote from Hollywood that he was "thrilled" by the "stand which you have courageously taken in reference to the Jewish people."

Ford paid the $160,000 court costs, and shut down the *Dearborn Independent*, ending Liebold's career as de facto editor, but keeping him on his staff.

He could not, however, shut down *The International Jew*, a book drawn from the interminable series. It has kept bobbing to the surface in the publishing cloacae of the world's capitals ever since. By 1933 it had run through twenty-nine editions in Germany alone. Henry Ford is the only American mentioned in *Mein Kampf*: Although the Jews were "increasingly the controlling master" of American labor, wrote Adolf Hitler, "one great man, Ford, to their exasperation still holds out independently."

In the decades to come the Ford Motor Company would work with steady patience and intelligence to undo this part of the reputation their founder had bequeathed it.

Possibly Ford would have been more interested in the content of his apology had the Sapiro trial and his recantation taken place in any year other than 1927, when he was worrying about matters he found more urgent than angry customers deserting him for Chevrolet, or even further humiliations on the witness stand.

CHAPTER 17
The End of the Line

Edsel; his powerless power in the company; Evangeline Dahlinger and her houses and horses; the "executive scrap heap"; how to join it: suggest changing the Model T; sales dwindle; Edsel fights; the last Model T; what the car had done.

H enry, I don't envy you a damn thing except that boy of yours."

This was John Dodge talking with Henry Ford on November 1, 1916, at Edsel Ford's wedding. The remark rings with bluff bonhomie, but it may also have been truly felt. Everybody who ever met him seems to have liked Edsel Ford.

He was shorter than his father, and darker, but the greater differences between them were not physical ones. Edsel shrank from personal publicity. During all his years as president of the Ford Motor Company he seems never once to have spoken at a business-related press conference. When Ford publicists wanted to take his picture at an event, he would usually wave them off with, "See if you can't get father to do that. He likes that sort of thing. I don't." The *Philadelphia Inquirer* once groused that the single longest statement

Edsel ever made to the press was "See father."

He shared his father's fascination with the automobile, which he had loved from his earliest memory (and of course he had earlier memories of automobiles than almost any American of his generation), but he took a wider view of what one should be. When Henry Ford sought beauty in a car, he looked to the machinery beneath the skin. Edsel thought the skin mattered, too.

He'd driven his scarlet Model A runabout when he was ten. When the Model T was a year old and he sixteen, he had the company build him a sports version. Despite his implacable feelings on the matter, Couzens allowed it to be sold for two hundred dollars beneath cost. The result was by far the handsomest Model T of its year: a two-seater lower to the ground than any other Ford, with the steering shaft canted closer to the horizontal. It was dashing enough to earn Edsel's father's approval.

The boy had already made himself so popular around the factory that the workers never resented carrying out his projects. Edsel was modest, alert, and cheerful. Decades later none of that had changed. His secretary, A. J. Lepine, wrote that he "had a keen mentality . . . and bright, observing, intelligent eyes. . . . He had a sense of humor, quick laugh, and a bright smile. He also had a very good memory . . . and he was even-tempered and well-controlled. . . . He never said anything sarcastic or resentful about people. He expressed his disapproval with silence. . . . He never used profanity. Well, hardly ever. He might come out occasionally with some apt expression . . . but he didn't use cheap language."

Edsel married Eleanor Lowthian Clay, whom he had met at dancing school. She was the niece of H. L. Hudson, founder of Detroit's leading department store and, according to one newspaper account, "the wealthiest merchant in the city."

Both Fords were fortunate in their marriages. Eleanor was every bit as loyal to Edsel as Clara was to his father (though Edsel never felt it necessary to invent an honorific to bestow upon her), and just as important, they enjoyed the same things, and each other.

But in that closeness lay seeds of the troubles that would grow between father and son. When Clara and Henry built Fair Lane, they put in a bowling alley, a swimming pool, a golf course, and other amenities they believed would keep their only son on hand. They expected him and his bride to move in once the Hawaiian honeymoon was over, but instead the newlyweds built a house in Grosse Pointe, the nest of gentry that alarmed and disgusted Henry.

Edsel was following the almost inevitable course of second-generation wealth. He wanted to be near the friends he'd made in the school his father sent him to, and thus became part of a society that tended to smoke, and, worse (but just slightly) from Henry's point of view, drink. Edsel drank and apparently smoked with them, although Sorensen says he never saw Henry's son with a cigarette in his hand. Clara seems to have been more alarmed by the smoking, but then she had held firm against Henry on her favorite beer, Rolling Rock, which the man who managed the Ford farms made sure was always close to hand however far Clara traveled from the Pennsylvania brewery that made it.

"For all their ambition for Edsel to make a name for himself," wrote Sorensen, "Father and Mother Ford never wanted their son to grow up. They wanted to keep him close to themselves and to guide his every thought." His move to Grosse Pointe among what the Fords saw as his louche friends opened a rift between the generations that would never quite close.

The Fords lived well, but were nothing like the racketing, feckless moneyed young whose doings fascinated novelists and moviemakers as the 1920s began. Sorensen, who was quick to celebrate his own tireless dedication to his Ford duties, nonetheless said, "Edsel worked hard and was always on the job early."

That job was at first secretary-treasurer of the Ford Motor Company, which Couzens vacated when he quit in 1915. Edsel took it over, and walked a steep road for the rest of his life. Once the Dodge brothers began their suit, his father wouldn't attend board meetings, and Edsel was introduced to those always barbed gatherings at their most tumultuous.

Greater tumult was on the way. When the nation entered the war, Sorensen immediately drew up draft deferment papers for Edsel, with Henry Ford's grateful support. Edsel would have nothing to do with them. He told Marquis, "There is one job in this war I do not want and will not take, and that is the job of a rich man's son." Both Marquis and Sorensen argued hard against his stand. Edsel was no figurehead: He was running the business side of the company, and he had shown himself to be thorough, organized, sensible, and productive. If he wasn't privileged to receive his father's occasional thunderclap of intuitive genius, neither would he sneak out of a meeting at the first pinch of boredom and spend the rest of the day watching a sparrow take a bath.

Edsel gave in. He took the deferment and stayed with the company throughout the war. "And it was a martyrdom," wrote Marquis, "as we knew who saw him day after day going steadily about his work, facing the great problems, and shouldering the enormous responsibilities in changing over from a peace basis to a one hundred per cent war basis one of the largest industries in the country." E. G. Pipp said, "It took more courage for Edsel

Ford not to put on a uniform than it would have to put one on."

Not surprisingly, Theodore Roosevelt disagreed. The one man in America who, with the possible exception of Flo Ziegfeld, was as thirsty for public attention as Henry Ford had begun fussing years before about the carmaker getting more of it than he deserved. Roosevelt kept up a mutter of general complaint—"Henry, like Barnum, has been a great advertiser"—until the war and Edsel's deferment gave him something to sink his formidable teeth into: "The expenditures on behalf of pacifism by Mr. Ford in connection with the Peace Ship . . . [were] as thoroughly demoralizing to the conscience of the American people as anything that has ever taken place. The failure of Mr. Ford's son to go into the army at this time, and the approval by the father of the son's refusal, represent exactly what might be expected from the moral disintegration inevitably produced by such pacifist propaganda. Mr. Ford's son is the son of a man of enormous wealth. If he went to war he would leave his wife and child"—Eleanor had in September given birth to her and Edsel's first son, Henry Ford II—"immeasurably distant from all chance of even the slightest financial strain or trouble, and his absence would not in the slightest degree affect the efficiency of the business with which he is connected."

Part of the animus in this statement must come

from the fact that Roosevelt's youngest son, Quentin, had recently been killed flying a pursuit plane on the Western Front, but part probably comes from TR's desire to keep Henry Ford out of the Senate. Despite their disagreements over the Peace Ship, President Wilson asked him to run in 1918, and in response Ford was conducting one of the most lackadaisical political campaigns in American history. During its entire course, he did not give a single speech.

The Democratic candidate's near-invisibility failed to keep the campaign from becoming vicious, and much of its spleen was directed at Edsel. "Why not send the indispensable Edsel to the Senate?" asked the papers. One editor wrote that on the day Quentin Roosevelt was shot from the French skies, Edsel and his wife were giving a party for some of their rich friends beneath the more hospitable ones above a Detroit country club. Ford's opponents said, "He kept *his* boy out of the trenches by Christmas."

This would have been hard on anybody, and it was very hard on Edsel Ford, who was far from thick-skinned. Despite the draft-dodger taunts and his father's inert campaign, Henry Ford came close to winning. Twenty-two hundred more votes and he would have beaten his Republican opponent and, very possibly, have put America in the League of Nations (one more Democratic vote in the nearly split Senate and the matter would have been up to Wilson's vice president to decide).

While this defeat gave Henry Ford yet another resentment to chew on, the Dodge trial arrived— Edsel spent as much time on the stand as his father, and impressed both sides with his unshowy grasp of company management—and then came the buyout, and the libel trial.

During the chimera of the $250 car, Edsel became president of the company, and held the position for the rest of his life. It proved different from the presidency of any other company, as the founder was not only the new president's father, but he never handed over the wheel.

Sorensen wrote that "Henry Ford's idea of harmony was constant turmoil." He early began pitting his lieutenants against one another, giving them overlapping authority to see which turned out to be tougher in defending what he thought was his own territory. Throughout, Ford would innocently warn one against the other as if he were a well-meaning neighbor who had overheard something at a party.

Edsel hated turmoil. He knew that an operation the size of the one his father owned guaranteed as much of it as any human enterprise required. Don't throw your most spirited managers against one another like fighting cocks, he believed: Get the best you can out of them by fostering cooperation.

This approach held no appeal to Henry Ford, and he was worried that it showed a streak of softness in his son. For years he said, "Edsel needs to be tougher." The way to toughen him was to harry and contradict and poke at him until he screamed. But Edsel wouldn't scream. The only complaint anyone ever seems to have had against him was that he should have been stronger in defying Henry Ford.

That wasn't in his nature. He always deferred to his father, not because of any kind of filial cowardice, but through a deep respect for what his father had accomplished. Cut off again and again, often in the most humiliating way, in the midst of initially approved projects that would have advanced the company, Edsel would only say, albeit sometimes on the verge of tears, Father invented this. He's the boss.

Even before Henry Ford began to harass his son, he turned against his managers. This was at the dawn of the 1920s. The Model T had done every-thing it was going to do, save continue to pour wealth on its creator. Ford became increasingly jealous of the men who had helped him invent the car. One of the half dozen most famous people in the world seems to have felt he was receiving insufficient recognition.

In the early years, back when he had the gift that Edsel would inherit for making friends, Ford had been happy to share credit with his colleagues.

Wills did as much as Ford did to create the *999*, the *Ford Times* said in 1908, and three years later the magazine ran a photograph with the caption: "Mr. Henry Ford and Mr. C. H. Wills, the two men who developed the Ford car."

With the advent of the five-dollar day there would be only one man. The change took place quickly. Sorensen wrote, "After the name Henry Ford became a household word, men in the Ford Motor Company who might temporarily get more publicity than he did aroused his jealousy, and one by one they were purged."

Marquis saw what was happening, and how the wise Ford employee responded to it. Praise—any praise at all—belonged to the boss alone. "Every time anyone handed John R. Lee a bouquet for his bigness of heart he tossed it over to Henry, and when there was no one around explained what it was all about. And Henry kept the flowers."

About the same time Edsel started his tenure as president, his father began to discard even the flower-bearers.

Around 1920 "a judge of national repute" told Marquis, "I have a great admiration for Henry Ford, but there is one thing that I can't understand, and that is the inability to keep his executives and old-time friends about him." Marquis said it was not a matter of inability but disability. "He can't help it. He is built that way."

Couzens was one of the first to go—over a

legitimate disagreement, it is true, but Ford could have kept him if he'd tried.

If Ford and Couzens had never enjoyed much more than an allegiance of shared goals, Ford and Wills were at first close friends. Just as Wills's boyhood type case had supplied the Ford emblem, so had his mechanical vision helped supply the Model T itself. Wills grew tired of having one responsibility after another taken away from him, but his departure may have reflected something more than Henry Ford's increasing impatience with anyone who wasn't Henry Ford.

During his time at the company, Childe Harold Wills had gained the reputation of being what the era called a ladies' man. When word began to go around that he was leaving, a young engineer named Harold Hicks, who had gotten a job working directly for Henry Ford, impudently asked the boss if women had anything to do with Wills's departure. "Women!" Ford was amused. "Why Hicks, women won't do you any harm. You can screw any woman on earth excepting only one thing—never let your wife find out."

Henry Ford didn't say many things like this, and the statement may have been an ebullient half declaration of something that was going on in his life then. Perhaps it was another symptom of the same restlessness that had started him hounding his executives out of their jobs, although such impulses have shown up in men far more tranquil than Ford.

Womanizer or not, Wills had no trouble gathering attractive females about him in his work, and he didn't take long to notice Evangeline Côté.

She was a French Canadian who joined the company at sixteen to support her family after her father fell ill. Smart, energetic, spirited, and ambitious, she entered the stenographic department in 1909 and by 1912 was running it.

As soon as Wills became aware of her, he made Côté his private secretary. During the incandescent years of inventing the assembly line that followed, Ford and Wills were often together and Ford got to know her. Before long she became his special assistant.

Save for her admiration for Henry Ford, which was genuine and which would last for three decades, Evangeline Côté was the opposite of Clara Ford. No fussing around a flower garden for her: She was as athletic as her boss, and as confident, too. She became the tristate women's harness racing champion, and then the first woman in Michigan to get a pilot's license, whereupon she acquired a Curtiss flying boat.

She did not accomplish all this on a stenographer's salary.

Henry Ford seems to have taken to her immediately. Most men did; she was short—just over five feet tall—with a jaunty athlete's body and an insolent, merry, confiding smile.

She was eight years younger than a man named Ray Dahlinger, whom Ford had come to like and trust. Dahlinger had been a thirteen-dollar-a-week floorwalker in a Detroit department store when he met John Anderson's partner Horace Rackham shopping there with his wife. Dahlinger saw his chance, and was persuasive enough to talk the shareholder into finding him a job at the young company. He moved from the assembly line to just off it, taking the finished cars through brief, sputtering tests to determine they were ready for shipment. Ford often liked to pick a brand-new car at random and see how it did, and he noticed Dahlinger, took a shine to him, and sometimes chose him as his personal driver. When the Peace Ship sailed, Dahlinger served as both bodyguard and monitor over the considerable amount of cash his boss had brought to cover expenses. Back in America, Dahlinger did not return to the factory, but took up an amorphous role at Fair Lane: chauffeur, landscape consultant, handyman, and, later, overseer of all Ford's farms, and a test driver. (He was the cause of much frustration to Ford engineers in this last role, as after each run he would provide—and not enlarge upon—only one of two diagnoses: "Damn good"; or "No damn good.")

Henry Ford evidently saw a way to remove

Evangeline Côté from any licentious ploy Wills might be planning by getting her to marry Ray Dahlinger. He pressed the suggestion on them both, and they took him up on it in February 1918.

The couple immediately went on Ford's personal payroll and moved into his wedding gift, a big, modern farmhouse in Dearborn, where he would spend hours talking things over with them. The farmhouse was followed by a summer home on Lake Huron with a seaplane-docking ramp and, of course, the Curtiss. Then, a three-hundred-acre tract with three hundred head of cattle to occupy it and, a year after that, a Tudor manor house a mile up the Rouge from Fair Lane: nine fireplaces, eight bathrooms, a refrigerated fur-storage vault, a half-mile racetrack for Mrs. Dahlinger's horses, a six-car garage, and a show barn that Ford told his architect Edward Cutler, who contributed much to Greenfield Village, should be fitted out as an apartment for Mr. Dahlinger to live in.

Dahlinger couldn't have been happy about this last: A letter to his wife survives in which he wrote, "You said about twin beds. I think they're made only for sick people, not people that love each other . . . I wish our room would have *one* bed just for *you* and *me*. Is that alright to say that?"

On April 9, 1923, Evangeline Dahlinger gave birth to a son in the Henry Ford Hospital. Henry Ford arrived there immediately, looked the baby over, and quickly hired Nurse Lynch, the head of the maternity ward, to go to the Dahlingers' home and take care of the baby, which was to be named John. She stayed with the family for twenty-four years.

A month later Ford sent John a present somewhat beyond his comprehension, a Shetland pony, and the infant's parents the turned-wood cradle his mother had rocked him in sixty years earlier.

Ford never made the least effort to hide his liking for Mrs. Dahlinger, and she would be near him for the rest of his life. The impertinent Hicks and many others believed the child was his. Ford spent a good deal of time with the boy—it was John whom he told he had invented the modern age—but the evidence is circum-stantial nonetheless, especially in Henry Ford's case. Here was a man perfectly capable of developing a benign interest in a couple of his workers and rewarding them in the most openhanded ways.

Still, there is no other passage in his life quite like this one. John Côté Dahlinger believed he was Ford's son and in 1978 published an aggrieved memoir making the claim.

Certainly John Dahlinger received treatment the equal of what the bastard son of any royal Henry ever enjoyed. The just-postnatal Shetland pony was followed by a miniature but fully motorized roadster, and a scale model working tractor that couldn't have cost much less than a real one. When John was seven he got a Ford Model T race car that had been dashingly modified to run the Indianapolis 500 and, still warm from the contest, further modified to let the pedals reach its young owner's feet so the boy could drive the car around his mother's horse track.

John was imported to Fair Lane as a playmate for Clara and Henry's grandchildren, who at first accepted his presence as children will, but later began to wonder about it, and, as they grew, to draw away from him. Dahlinger, who called his putative father by his last name, wrote, "Ford didn't have a hell of a lot of tenderness, but I got the feeling he liked having me around, and that was sometimes enough to give me a nice feeling of security."

Some of the stories Dahlinger tells in his memoir are clearly quarried directly from Nevins, but now and again there is one that rings absolutely true to his own experience. "Ford had a thing about jew's-harps. He thought they were wonderful." This is the lyre-shaped musical instrument, slightly more exalted than a kazoo, that you play by putting its two metal arms between your teeth, thus making your mouth the resonator, and plucking its single metal tongue. "He always had a couple in his pocket and more in the car. If I didn't have mine with me, he would give me another. And he was always handing them out to little kids around the Village."

When Dahlinger was eight, he came upon Ford "sitting on a stump, his back to me, looking out over the Rouge River and playing a jew's-harp as if he had an audience of thousands.

"He didn't know I was behind him, and I guess he thought he was alone. When he had finished, all you could hear were the sounds of birds, and he took a little bow. Not exactly a bow; he nodded his head to the birds."

John Dahlinger writes that Ford was always pressing him to take over some large sector of the business. But he makes much of his own independent streak. He demanded to go east to attend the Deerfield Academy in Massachusetts, where he received letters from his mother like this one, about the upholstery of a car he wanted shipped to him from Detroit.

Here is the paint sample, also the leather—you see I haven't seen the blue leather 'til late last night, and then waited 'til this a.m. for sunlight—this is the Zephyr Blue—We would have to go outside for the other blue and it would take too long now.

But in the meantime I can get busy and get other samples. . . . It seems that US Royal Cords *[tires]* can not be bought from Ford Motor Company—Mr. Edsel's orders, but Harold is going to find out today if we can't take a set of Firestones and trade with some US dealer and pay whatever is necessary if you much prefer Royals—better let me know about that. Mom.

John Dahlinger eventually ended up running not, say, the Ford marketing department, but a Detroit nightclub.

His mother and father became ever closer to Henry Ford, Ray handling the landscaping of Greenfield Village as well as the farms, Evangeline doing any number of jobs, from furnishing the rooms in Greenfield to lecturing in them dressed in period costume.

She was a real force in the creation of the Village. When Henry Ford was vacationing down South, she wrote Frank Campsall—the secretary who had far too late replaced Ernest Liebold in Ford's regard—knowing that the final recipient of the letter would be Henry Ford, "The trees are moving into the village fast and furious and it's starting to look real nice. There are five maples at the Edison house now and you know it looks like they had been there always. You know there's something real homey looking about that old place, sort of a mellow and lived-in look. The McGuffey house is being set up O.K. and it is starting to take on a look of having always been in just that setting—with that very severe and substantial old Lincoln Court-house, it seems as though you just naturally expect to see a log cabin in the offing. You know what we mean, Lincoln, log cabins, books, education, McGuffey—don't they seem kind of all to belong together? Took some pictures, thought the boss might enjoy looking at them."

Once, during the two decades that reporters were asking Ford about anything from pancake recipes to the British parliamentary system, one of them wanted to know what he felt about why men often embarked on extramarital affairs in middle life. Ford said it was in effect a twenty-four-hour virus: They are "simply trying to hold onto their youth. I say to the woman whose husband is in this situation: Treat it like the measles! It's a disease that strikes a lot of people. That's all it is, at the most. Help your husband through it. Stand by. Don't let it hurt you. Don't let it break up your home."

Clara didn't. She came to rely on both Ray and Evangeline, and toward the end of her life formed a friendship with the latter.

She insisted on having Ray on the estate as long as she lived. When she died in 1950, it was the third generation of Fords who had him abruptly locked out of his office. Evangeline ended her days in a nursing home. When her son visited her and asked for confirmation that Henry Ford had been his father, she would say, "I don't want to talk about it."

Clara Ford didn't miss much. It is absurd to suppose she didn't have feelings about her husband's thirty-year friendship with Evangeline Dahlinger. Whatever those feelings might have been, some of them were impressively spacious. On the last night of her husband's life, Clara Ford summoned Evangeline Dahlinger through a storm so that she, too, could be at Henry Ford's side when he died.

While Mrs. Dahlinger tended her trotting horses and her seaplane, Frank Klingensmith, to whom Ford had entrusted much of Edsel's education around the plant, joined Wills on what Samuel Marquis was beginning to call "the executive scrap heap." Norval Hawkins, a sales manager who had come to the company in 1907, went, and so did the Sociological Department head whom Marquis so admired, John Lee. "The Ford executive," Marquis wrote, "has added to those two certainties in life—death and taxes—a third, that is discharge."

LeRoy Pelletier, Ford's first great advertising man, had lit on the company briefly in 1907 and left behind him a slogan that was famous for decades. The next year it went up in lights on the Temple Theatre in downtown Detroit, blazing out the message: "Watch the Fords Go By." In 1922, people who worked for the company were trading the mordant catchphrase, "Watch the Ford executives go by."

In one case it is possible that Ford acquired a company for the main purpose of firing its owners. Henry Leland and his son Wilfred had founded the Lincoln Motor Company in 1917. Both father and son stayed true to the exacting standards that had made the elder Leland the most respected machinist of his day, and they were building a car of the highest mechanical quality. They and it got caught in the brief but sharp depression of 1921, and Henry Ford paid $8 million for the company. Helping an old friend out of a tight spot, people said approvingly. But Ford didn't see Henry Leland as an old friend; he saw him as the somber martinet who had driven him away from his second company. He assured the Lelands that they would be left alone to run their business as they saw fit, and then turned Sorensen loose on them. In months, the Lelands had left their company.

Whatever his father's reason for the purchase, it greatly pleased Edsel. "Father made the most popular car in the world," he told his friends. "I would like to make the best car in the world." He maintained the engineering standards while putting designers to work on the car's somewhat dowdy body—Henry Leland, like Henry Ford, cared little for outward appearances—and by the end of the decade was selling a luxury car that many believed edged out the Cadillac and even the mighty Duesenberg. A decade later Edsel created, in the Lincoln Continental, what Frank Lloyd Wright declared the single most beautiful automobile ever built.

One day in March 1921 William Knudsen wrote to Edsel. The next morning Henry Ford was in Knudsen's office: "What's the matter, William? Edsel tells me he has a letter from you, saying you are resigning."

"Yes, Mr. Ford."

"What's the matter, William?" Ford asked again in his most guileless manner.

Knudsen wouldn't quite tell him. "Well, Mr. Ford, I've thought it over very carefully, and I've made up my mind to quit."

Knudsen did, however, tell his friend and colleague William Smith, who had been with him when he first showed Ford the stampings from the Keim Mills. Smith, like Knudsen, had come to the Ford Motor Company when it bought Keim, and Henry had sent him over to ask Knudsen to stay.

Knudsen said to him, "My job with Mr. Ford, since 1918, was being production manager. Is that right?"

Smith nodded.

"All right. Well . . . starting a few months ago, there have been quite a few times when I have found that my shop instructions on production matters were countermanded or ignored. I did not like it when I found it out and I still don't like it. I found out who was countermanding them and who was nullifying them. It was Mr. Ford. I asked him about it. He just smiled, and didn't say much."

Knudsen said he couldn't work for someone who didn't have confidence in him, and that the lack of confidence had been shown in a particularly unpleasant way: "If I'm doing something wrong, he ought to tell me about it and not go out in the shop and tell other people."

It was Ford's company, Knudsen went on, and he realized that "he has every right to run it as he sees fit. Mr. Ford and I have never had any serious arguments, any serious differences in opinion about how things should be run in the shop. We are not going to have any now. To keep from this, I am going to quit."

Smith said he understood, and would tell the boss only that he couldn't change Knudsen's mind.

At least one Ford manager seems to have been as fortunate in his marriage as the Fords were in theirs. When Knudsen told his wife he'd just thrown away a sixty-five-thousand-dollar-a-year job she laughed, hugged him, gave him a kiss, and said, "That's good. Now we can have some sort of peace around our place."

Knudsen was capable and Knudsen was popular, traits for which Henry Ford had dwindling patience. The man who had built his career by running a friendly shop, by being so congenial that people would give up their weekends to cut gears and turn crankshafts for him, now complained that "some organizations use up so much energy and time maintaining a feeling of harmony that they have no force left to work for the object for which the organization was created. . . . I pity the poor fellow who is so soft and flabby that he must always have 'an atmosphere of good feeling' around him before he can do his work. . . . Not only are they business failures; they are character failures also. . . . People have too great a fondness for working with the people they like."

Knudsen, however, had been dealing with something more volatile than an agreeable working atmosphere. At about the time he was clearing out the leavings of war production at the Rouge, he approached his boss.

"Mr. Ford, this war has changed our whole industrial setup."

"How do you mean?"

"I mean, we've learned to do a lot of different things with different materials. I think we are going to have to make a whole lot of everything because the people are going to want a whole lot of everything. . . . With the war ended we've got a lot of equipment, a lot of buildings, a lot of blast furnaces. We've got to use them."

"What have you in mind, William?" Ford never called Knudsen Bill, and Knudsen certainly never called him Henry.

"Well, Mr. Ford, the day is coming, and you know it, when maybe 80 or 90 per cent of all the motor cars sold in this country will be in the low-price field."

"What is it you have in mind, particularly?"

"The Model T."

Knudsen showed a surprised Ford some drawings he'd had made at the Rouge plant, and explained them. "I think we ought to start in and refine our product. We can do it in three ways. We can make the same car we have been making for less money; we can make a better car for more money; or we can make a better car for the same money."

Knudsen would have been justified in a satisfied little pause before he concluded, "*This* one we can make for the same money."

Ford kept studying the drawings. "This car has a gear shift," he said finally.

"Yes."

"What color?"

"The customer would be given the choice."

"Is it heavier than the Model T?"

"A little, not much, and the lines are different, too."

"So I see." Of course he did. "How long will it take you to get into production with this new model?"

"A few months, maybe six."

"How long will it take you to get into production on the Model T?"

"Sixty days."

"There's your answer."

Did Knudsen know this conversation had ended his career at Ford? Likely he did; he understood cars, and he understood Henry Ford, as far as that was possible. He knew both that the Model T had to evolve, and that its creator would be remorseless toward any apostate who suggested significant changes.

Knudsen would have heard what happened two years before he joined the company, when the founder returned with his family from visiting his overseas plants in 1912. On his first day back at work, Henry Ford discovered that Wills and some of his other lieutenants had prepared a home-coming surprise for him.

The Model T was already five years old, and they'd been working on an improved design. They were pleased with the results, and were so sure their boss would be that they parked the prototype in front of his office for him to discover. The car was less boxy than its parent, lower and more than a foot longer, altogether a better-looking machine.

It caught Ford's eye, and he went over and walked around it, hands in pockets. The new model had four doors. On his third or fourth circuit Ford paused before one of them and, according to a company accountant named George Brown who was watching from a safe distance, "He takes his hands out, gets hold of the door, and bang! He ripped the door right off! God! How the man done it, I didn't know! He jumped in there, and bang goes another door. Bang goes the windshield. He jumps over the back seat and starts pounding on the top. He rips the top with the heel of his shoe." At no point did Ford say anything, and of course by the time he was through working on the top he didn't have to.

Wills was eventually shunted into purchasing, and Joseph Galamb took his place in engineering and design. He, too, ventured into the fraught territory of changing the car. In 1914 Ford was driving fast along a country road when the rear wheels left the ground and the car threw its inventor into a ditch.

Galamb laid the blame on a radius rod, and set about designing a stronger one. Ford wouldn't consider it. "He was practically killed with the old rod," Galamb said years later, "but he still didn't want it changed."

Ford had told Galamb, "Your job is going to be to watch it so that nobody will make a change on that car." He said he was worried about production costs, and he did pay close attention to them. But, as his response to Wills's improvements suggests, there was more to it than that. The Model T represented the culmination of his life's work, and he had come to see it not only as a mechanical force but as a moral one. It was exactly as much automobile as people needed, and no more. One fundamentalist Dunkard sect forbade its members to drive Buicks, but approved of the Model T because it was not "haughty and sinful."

Garet Garrett wrote that Ford "was always sensitive to the slur that Model T was not a finely made car. In early Ford practice there was no fetish of precision. That is why the Model T was noisy and rattled; that was why it also possessed the animal qualities of the mountain ass, such as hardihood, extraordinary powers of endurance, phlegmatic courage and a kind of cheerfulness when not too much abused."

Here again, as so many who owned one have suggested, the car has the spirit of a living thing. Ford himself said that for all their endless uniformity every Model T drove a little differently.

David L. Cohn, who ran a New Orleans department store before becoming a popular historian, enlarged on this in 1944: "It was discovered, when earnest men compared notes, that no two Model Ts were temperamentally alike; they reacted to different stimuli and drew their strength from different sources. Consequently no man could pass on to his brother the secret of his own success because success was a combination in constantly varying proportions, of prayer, prestidigitation, and intuition. Only the vulgar would expect such mystical elements could be reduced to a mathematical formula, and the owners of the Model T, scorning such attempts, were content to move about the world each with his secret locked in his breast."

If this sounds as though the author finds in the Model T a little ribbon of mysticism passing through the case-hardened heart of the Machine Age, Henry Ford might have agreed with him. He always saw his car as an idea as well as a machine, and attempting to tamper with its design may have come to represent to him a sort of spiritual insolence.

He could hector and goad those in his company who did, and eventually fire them. But he couldn't fire the president—only hector and goad him more and more. Edsel took it, year after year, and did not make life easier for himself by steadily pushing to improve the Model T. He believed that all the constantly renewed production equipment, all those house-high machines his father would replace the minute something better came along to keep the plant the most modern in the world, were beginning to be in the service of producing an antique.

He was always respectful to his father, never publicly contradicted him on anything. When a delegation of Ford dealers visited Detroit to urge that a modern ignition system replace the once-revolutionary magneto, a Ford executive named William Klann brought the request to Henry.

"You can do that over my dead body," Ford said. "That magneto stays on as long as I'm alive."

Afterward, Klann spoke to Edsel. "Didn't you think your dad made a mistake?"

"Yes," said Edsel, "he did; but he's the boss, Bill."

Still, Edsel stood his ground, glum and fatalistic and always deferring to his father, but unbending in the certainty that sometimes flashed tiny defiance from his wrists: His cufflinks bore in Latin the legend, "All Things Change."

He had few allies. Sorensen boasts in his autobiography about his valiant support of Edsel in the face of his father, but nobody in the shop at the time noticed this fealty. Before one of the daily luncheons where Ford talked things over with his managers, Edsel got Sorensen and Martin to say that they'd back him in his proposal that the company consider hydraulic brakes for its cars.

Edsel made his pitch. When he was finished, his father stood up and said, "Edsel, you shut up!" He looked around the table. Martin and Sorensen returned the glance in bland silence.

Later, when Edsel was promoting a six-cylinder engine, Ford said, "We have no intention of introducing a six. We made sixes twenty years ago [for the costly Model K]. The Ford car is a tried and proved product that . . . has met all the conditions of transportation the world over. . . . We do not intend to make a six, an eight, or anything else outside our regular production. It is true that we have experiments with such cars, as we have experiments with many things. They keep our engineers busy—prevent them from tinkering too much with the Ford car."

He showed his distaste for the six in a more vivid way. Lawrence Sheldrick, who followed Galamb in his engineering post, had worked with Edsel to develop a six-cylinder engine. Edsel thought he'd gotten his father's permission to build a prototype. It was finished and about to be tested when Ford called the engineer. "Sheldrick, I've got a new scrap conveyor that I'm very proud of. It goes right to the cupola at the top of the plant. I'd like you to come and take a look at it. I am very proud of it."

When Sheldrick arrived on the high platform he was surprised to find Edsel there with his father. Henry signaled, and the conveyor started crawling upward. The very first thing it was bearing toward the scrap heap below was Edsel's six. As the engine dropped into oblivion, Henry said, "Now don't you try anything like that again. Don't you ever, do you hear?"

Ford had been adding to the executive scrap heap, too. As the Rouge grew, the plant's gravitational pull became greater than that of Highland Park. Not only was the Rouge bigger—

bigger than any industrial plant on earth—but things were going to be done differently there. Sorensen was in charge.

"Let's get rid of the Model T sons of bitches," he said.

One of them, Samuel Marquis, had been trying to establish the services of his Sociological Department in the new factory. Sorensen had consistently blocked him. Ford assured Marquis that nothing had changed: Don't worry about Charlie. Charlie was in control, though, and he told Ford that Marquis was getting in the way of production.

The mutual discontent, Sorensen wrote, "all came to a head one day in [1921] when Mr. Ford asked me to come up to his office. . . . When I arrived I found Dean Marquis there. I had no more than entered when he sailed into me for 'interfering' with him and his staff. It was a surprising accusation, but that did not take me back half so much as the vigor of his language. I had always treated clergymen with deference. Many times in my life I have been called an s.o.b., but never before or after was I called one by a supposed man of God—in fact, that day I heard from Dean Marquis some words I'd never heard before."

Unlikely, but Sorensen's horror at being exposed to such language was allayed when Ford backed him instead of the minister.

Marquis was amazed and infuriated, and then, for a long time, bitter. He felt a friend had betrayed both him and a great mission. A few days later he quit—the only high Ford employee to do so, Clara remarked: All the rest were forced out or fired.

Marquis thought he'd been forced out, and he went off to write a book about it. His wife tried to dissuade him—think of the thirty-five thousand dollars a year Mr. Ford used to pay you, she said. She did get her husband to cut out some of his harshest passages, but *Henry Ford: An Interpretation* is stingingly frank, yet judicious. It is also fair-minded, very well written, and touching. More than just a record of grievances, the book is an elegy to a cause and a friendship with a man that Marquis believed was visibly being consumed by his worst impulses.

Ford's "puzzling mixture of opposing natures," Marquis wrote, "are generally accompanied by outward changes in physical appearance. To-day he stands erect, lithe, agile, full of life. . . . Out of his eyes there looks the soul of a genius, a dreamer, an idealist,—a soul that is affable, kindly, and generous to a fault. But tomorrow he may be the opposite. He will have the appearance of a man shrunken by long illness. The shoulders droop, and there is a forward slant to the body when he walks as when a man is moving forward on his toes. His face is deeply lined, and . . . the affable, gentle manner has disappeared. There is a light in the eye that reveals a fire burning within altogether unlike that which burned there yesterday."

Marquis says Ford's executives would recognize this storm warning and do what they could to prepare for the gale that followed. "Old policies are swept away. New policies are set up. Departments are turned inside out and upside down, or altogether done away with. . . . Desks are removed on one or two occasions with an ax. The men who worked at them return to find them gone, and possibly their jobs gone also. Men are discharged without warning, and no reason is given them in response to their inquiry."

Marquis was realist enough to know that business sometimes had to be hard. "A major operation may be necessary to save the life of an industry, but just because there must be a major operation is no reason why you should engage the services of a butcher and not a surgeon."

With his leaving, though, there would be more butchers than surgeons in the Ford Motor Company. The Sociological Department withered, and then disappeared.

Marquis ends his short book with two hopeful chapters devoted to what he believes will be the coming beneficent reign of Edsel. "I credit him with an intellectual breadth and balance, with a sympathy and tolerance of mind, an understanding heart, a less ruthless manner of putting down his foot, than I credit to the father. The son is a composite in whom is to be found much of the father's ability, broad humanitarian impulses, together with certain elements of strength inherited from his mother . . . I can see no reason to fear that the House of Ford will suffer at the hands of the son."

What the House of Ford got instead was Harry Bennett.

Here is how Harry Bennett described the departure of Samuel Marquis.

> Under Dean Marquis the Sociology Department had a staff of investigators who visited every employee. . . . They asked the wives how much money their husbands saved, how much they brought home, whether they drank, whether they had any domestic difficulties. If a workman had kept out of his pay a few dollars for a crap game or a glass of beer, he was in trouble. . . .
>
> I felt the whole setup was a stupid waste of time and money for the company and petty tyranny over the employees . . . I criticized the whole thing to Mr. Ford, and he said, "Well go ahead and stop it." So in 1921 I ended the Sociology setup as it existed, and Dean Marquis left the company.

Who was this man who could saunter into Henry Ford's office and get him to shut down a department? One of the strangest figures in American industrial history, given the eminence he achieved at the Ford Motor Company.

Bennett wrote that "during the thirty years I worked for Henry Ford I became his most intimate companion, closer to him even than his only son." Sorensen made the same claim—"We had a business relationship closer than even his family had with him, and in many ways I knew him better than his family"—but in terms of intimacy, Bennett had Sorensen beat.

His career is in ways a preposterous, grimy fairy tale. Harry Bennett was born in Ann Arbor in 1892. His father, a sign painter, was killed in a brawl when Harry was two. He joined the navy as soon as he was old enough, and liked the life, even though moving coal on a cruiser in 1915 was about the hardest job one could find in the postmedieval world. He took up boxing and excelled at it. Although he stood five seven and weighed 145 pounds, he was physically fearless. All his life he would take on anybody of any size at the least provocation and with a ferocity that usually prevailed.

When his tour of duty ended in 1916, he planned to reenlist, but wanted to have a little fun ashore first. He got as far ashore as the Customs House in Battery Park in lower Manhattan, and there managed to ignite a spontaneous fistfight with a customs official. "I gave a good account of myself—" Bennett said, "until a big cop got me by the back of the collar." Whereupon Arthur Brisbane, the most famous journalist of his day, walked over and asked the policeman, "What's going on?"

"Oh, I've got a tough one here," he said. And on the basis of this, and apparently nothing else other than that Bennett turned out to have been born in Michigan, Brisbane decided to take him to Henry Ford, who was visiting New York.

Bennett wrote, "When Brisbane and I arrived at 1710 Broadway, Ford sales headquarters in New York, he at once introduced me to Mr. Ford. Mr. Ford was already in his fifties, he had sharp, gray eyes and heavy eyebrows, and was of medium height and a spare build. He was alert and almost nervously quick. As I was to learn later, he was a grasshopper in his capacity for locomotion, and got in and out of a car with a jackknife motion that made men years younger seem awkward."

Bennett added, "I wasn't very impressed."

Not impressed by being rescued from a potentially bad situation by one famous American and hurried uptown into the presence of a more famous one? Nope, said Bennett—it's just the way I am.

Still, he got interested when Ford asked, "Can you shoot?"

"Sure I can."

Ford said, "The men who are building the Rouge are a pretty tough lot." Bennett wasn't alarmed to learn this. Ford said, later, that he wanted the sailor to be his "eyes and ears." Bennett said that all he wanted was to go back to sea. Ford persisted, and Bennett made a concession. "Well, I won't work for the company, but I'll work for you."

And so he did, to the dismay of almost everyone else in the company.

The Rouge was, as its owner said, a pretty rough place, but not too rough for Harry Bennett. In his first few minutes there he "turned to a giant Polish foreman I saw" and said, "Where can I find Mr. Knudsen?"

"Why do you want to see him?"

"That's my business," Bennett replied, and "without another word the big Pole clipped me on the jaw and knocked me down."

The foreman stooped and helped Bennett to his feet. "The next time you're asked a question," he said, "don't get so cocky."

" 'Thanks,' I said. Then I pushed his chin up with my left and swung with my right. Only his jaw didn't come down, as I had expected, and I hit him on the neck. The blow not only laid him out, but left him speechless as well. He went around the Rouge whispering for weeks."

The incident, which could have been taken whole from a Popeye cartoon, concisely prefigures

Bennett's tenure at the Ford Motor Company. Bennett became the head of the Ford "Service Department," a grotesque successor to the old Sociological Department. It, too, was interested in the workers, but only to make sure they didn't loaf, or steal, or communicate with one another. Most important, they must not whisper a word about organizing, although Ford's battles against the United Automobile Workers union, which would be ferociously and disastrously led by Bennett, lay over the rim of the next decade.

After hiring Bennett, Ford lived in a thickening atmosphere of apprehension. He was worried that he or members of his family would be kidnapped, and he trusted Bennett to shield him. Bennett fertilized Ford's imagination with illusory plots, but he also made friends with gang leaders, whom he offered food concessions at the Rouge in return for protection. Henry Ford came to believe him an indispensable protector.

Bennett must have possessed considerable charm along with his belligerence. It shows in *We Never Called Him Henry*, an autobiography he published in 1951. It is "as told to Paul Marcus," but it carries a persuasive sense of its subject speaking. Bennett tells engaging stories, casually throwing in the occasional detail that rings absolutely true. Who could doubt this description of Liebold? "A short bull neck and close-cropped hair; for some reason, his coat collar always stood out about three inches from the back of his neck." The book's tone is affable, even avuncular, and yet every now and then there comes through a note of what most of his colleagues saw in Bennett: "Edsel, who had a mild voice and quiet manners, was built like his father—slender and long-legged. He was a nervous man; when he got angry, he threw up. He was just a scared boy as long as I knew him." Which was up to his death. Sometimes, although not in his autobiography, Bennett would refer to Edsel as "the weakling."

It is Edsel's tragedy—and Henry's, too—that the father believed this. The United Auto Workers organizer Walter Reuther, long after he had been victorious in the labor wars, but still a man not likely cavalierly to praise a car magnate, said, "I believe fully and completely that Edsel Ford was a decent human being and a man who hated with every drop of blood what was going on there at the plant. I know he knew it because he talked about it. I told him what was going on, but I didn't have to because he already knew. He hated it, but he was completely without power to do anything about it. He was helpless. His soul bled. . . . He was a decent man and he cared. I felt sorry for him. I still do."

What Edsel and Reuther saw happening was an increasing corrosion of working conditions. Reuther, who began his career at Ford on the shop floor in Highland Park sitting at a bench handling small parts, was shifted to the Rouge and ordered to do the same job on his feet. "You can't work with those fine tolerances standing up," he said. "You need to be firmly planted. But that wasn't the big difference. Those two places were different as day and night. Highland Park was civilized, but the Rouge was a jungle. The humanitarianism that Henry Ford had shown so dramatically in his early days just didn't exist anymore. Sorensen and Peter Martin were in charge of production and that's all they cared about. I didn't think they were sociologically aware that the harshness and speedups for which they were responsible, combined with the terror and brutality for which they weren't, actually interfered with production. The Rouge was a jungle because of one man, Harry Bennett. His gangsters ran that company. He was a mean man, a neurotic man, a man with a gangster mentality. It was absolutely fantastic that a man like that could reach the position he did with a great company like Ford."

The Ford Motor Company never paid Bennett for his work. Liebold occasionally doled out his salary, which Bennett later complained was "peanuts," and Henry Ford would augment it with things like houses and yachts. For it was Ford who was setting the tenor at the Rouge. Bennett never directly defied him any more than Sorensen did.

After a while the head of the Service Department

had three thousand men under him, all of them hard, many of them criminals. Henry Ford liked that. He thought it picturesque when Bennett would brandish a handgun, and enjoyed firing .32 pistols with him in the target range in Bennett's Rouge office. He suggested that Bennett build not a house but a "castle"—ramparts, towers—in his Detroit suburb. There should be secret passageways, too, Ford said, and both men enjoyed this adolescent's paradise. Bennett raised lions there, and would take them for walks in the Rouge. Once, as a practical joke his boss must surely have enjoyed, he smuggled one into the back of a departing friend's car. (The animal ended up dead in a Detroit police station. Bennett explained that "it had hanged itself.")

Ford also liked Bennett's willingness to take a swing at anyone. Bennett said Ford's attitude could be summed up as, "Harry, let's you and him have a fight."

Bennett claimed he once pulled off his coat to fight Ford's son. Edsel declined. Not John R. Davis, a sales manager and supporter of Edsel's. Henry Ford managed to provoke a row between Davis and Bennett, but as soon as his security chief threw the first punch, Ford hurried out of the room. This put a damper on the scrap: Antagonists though they were, Davis and Bennett both believed that while Ford loved stirring up a fight, he never wanted to see the blood.

Ford encouraged Bennett's high-strung savagery, and was complicit in how his paladin got rid of Frank Kulick.

We last saw Kulick in Ford No. 1 falling behind in the 1909 New York–Seattle race after a local had given him bad directions. Kulick couldn't get lost on an oval track, though, and for years he proved nearly unbeatable. Ford hired him as a racing driver about 1904, the year his twenty-horsepower car shut down a ninety-horsepower Fiat and a sixty-horsepower Renault. In 1907 a rear wheel disintegrated and put his car through a fence. "The old man wouldn't let me have a differential," Kulick said of Ford, "and the strain was such it broke the wheels." The driver's kneecap was shattered, his leg broken in two places, and he seemed to have internal injuries.

Ford may have been stingy with his equipment, but it's a good thing he was there to see the race, for his swift, intuitive sense of action found a solution. While spectators were muttering around the bleeding Kulick in worried futility, Ford borrowed a saw from somebody, sheared off the top of a touring car parked nearby, laid a plank across it, and in this improvised ambulance got Kulick to a hospital. The driver was in a brace for two years and limped for the rest of his life. But he was racing again by 1910, winning more often than not. Until 1927, when Henry Ford fired him.

Kulick went to his boss as soon as he got the

word. Of course Mr. Ford knew nothing about it. Clearly distressed, he told Kulick to go to Mr. Sorensen, who would put him back to work at once. Sorensen handed the driver off to Harry Bennett, who needed him to fix a car that was misbehaving. Kulick found that the camshaft had been badly ground. He turned a new one and got it installed in the car despite a puzzling swarm of small obstructions from Bennett's men. Then he asked Bennett to come check it.

The engine was running beautifully. Too noisy, Bennett said. Kulick didn't understand. Bennett told him to lie on the dashboard and put his ear next to the hood to listen to the engine from the outside, and "we'll take it for a ride."

Kulick took his place. Bennett put his foot down hard, bounced out of the plant, and swung the wheel sharply enough to send Kulick rolling in the dust and grit of Miller Road. Bennett sped back inside the factory.

When Kulick picked himself up and limped back to the plant gates, Bennett's men wouldn't let him through.

Bennett wrote, "I believe Mr. Ford thought of me as a son." Bennett and Edsel had been born just a year apart, and the former showed all the combative spirit that Ford tried to implant in the latter. "Harry gets things done in a hurry," he told people. Bennett never made it into the executive dining room, but Ford liked bringing him to board meetings. After a few minutes of cowed remarks from the directors, Ford would jump up and say, "Come on, Harry, let's get the hell out of here. We'll probably only change what they do anyway."

The historian Julie Fenster, who believes that the influence of Couzens on Ford's career is decisive, remarked that "I think the white-collar strongman was replaced by the blue-collar strongman." Bennett might also have proved satisfactory to Ford in other ways. Couzens was tough enough, but he never spared Ford from his promiscuous acerbity. Bennett was just as tough on everyone *but* Ford. So was Sorensen, although he had technical abilities that may have made Ford jealous. Bennett could offer all that enticing brutality free of enviable talents.

Ford spent as much time as he could with Bennett, had lengthy conversations with him every evening, gave him more and more troops to police the Rouge until, by the early 1930s, people around the plant were asking one another: Who invented the Gestapo first? Henry or Adolf?

A worker named Al Bardelli, who came to the Rouge as a teenager in the 1920s, said of Bennett's men, "They were all rotten, no-good sons of bitches. You couldn't go to take a crap without one of the bastards following you into the rest room. Take too long and you were out of a job."

Drive a Buick, and you were out of a job, too. Knudsen's old story about the worker who got the Sociological Department's permission to buy a car and then announced he was getting a Buick lost its point as a joke. If a worker showed up in a Rouge parking lot in an Essex or a Hudson or anything but a Model T, he'd be told he was late. When he protested that he was on time, he was fired.

Those other cars were beginning to look pretty good, as Edsel well understood. He kept pressing his father in perhaps the sole area in which Henry didn't want his son to display some spirit: Change the car; the car must change.

And it did, some. Henry Ford had ordered that no Model T could be built that made an earlier one obsolete, but as the Ts flowed out of Highland Park and the Rouge in the millions they went through a slow evolution both in their scant decorations and their mechanisms. Leather upholstery gave way to leatherette after 1912, the same year a smart little Torpedo Roadster died after its twenty-four-month life. A water pump on the first twenty-five hundred models was deemed too expensive, and abandoned for the "thermo-syphon" cooling system, which took advantage of the fact that heated water rises, and thus left the matter in the hands of Newton and God. Sheet steel replaced wooden bodies, and the car lost its sole gleam of panache in 1916 when a painted steel radiator replaced the brass one. A year later, the fenders grew a gentle crown to smooth their original squared-off geometry, and in 1919 the car finally could have an electric starter.

Ford, a believer in suffrage and women's rights in general, had long campaigned for them to drive the Model T. Very early in his company's life he ran ads showing female drivers rolling joyfully through the countryside in the billowing road costumes of the day. But although many women did master it, that often vicious starting crank spared neither sex.

As the 1920s went on, Edsel pressed for the Model T to get lower, handsomer, more convenient. He won small victories, and the car of the mid-1920s was different from its predecessors: It was softer, rounder, how the 1908 prototype might have looked had it been reshaped by a gentle fall of snow. This car had wire wheels and lighter connecting rods, but in every significant way it was the same machine.

Alfred Sloan had come a long way from Newark and his Hyatt roller bearings. He had done well with them—so well that he got worried. The bulk of his business rested on massive orders from a few car companies, Ford among them. If they decided to start making their own bearings, Hyatt would be done for.

So Sloan sold it, and in 1923 Pierre du Pont made him president of General Motors. The new president's largest decision was also his first: "to determine whether we would operate under a centralized or decentralized form of administration. Decentralization was analogous to free enterprise. Centralization, to regimentation. [Here he would have been thinking of the most centralized of all great companies.] We decided on free enterprise. . . .

"We would set up each of our various operations as an integral unit, complete as to itself. We would place in charge of each unit an executive responsible, and solely responsible, for his complete activity."

While Sloan was building this managerial structure a friend came to him and said he had met a big fellow who seemed to have a lot on the ball. Would Sloan speak with him?

"As soon as I saw him I remembered him. 'You are Knudsen, of course! I had some business with you at Ford's some time ago.' "

They talked. Sloan explained he had developed "a General Staff similar in name and purpose to what exists in the army" to coordinate the efforts of his managers. He had no particular job to offer Knudsen at the moment, but he'd like him to join the staff and see whether he might help.

Knudsen said that was fine with him.

"How much shall we pay you, Mr. Knudsen?"

"Anything you like. I am not here to set a figure. I seek an opportunity."

"It was not long after that," wrote Sloan, "that he was made general manager and chief executive of the Chevrolet Motor Division, in complete charge of that entire business." Soon enough Knudsen was again earning what Ford had been paying him.

Sloan once remarked that the Ford organization was "run like a northern lumber camp." If so, for a while in the 1920s that seemed a fine arrangement. Between 1921 and 1926 Ford built more than half the trucks and automobiles sold in America. Production peaked in 1923, with 1,866,307 Model Ts, and on Halloween two years later the plant turned out 9,109 in a single day.

In 1924 the ten millionth Model T came off the line and was driven from New York to San Francisco along the Lincoln Highway, a road that was both unimagined and unimaginable the year the car was born. After the trip it posed for a photograph beside the original Quadricycle of 1896. In the picture, Henry Ford stands—dressed in the neat gray suit—to the left of his first car, his head slightly inclined toward it. In between the two automobiles is Edsel, solemn and composed, his hands clasped before him with a gravity that somehow gives the celebratory photograph a funereal air. Both cars look like relics to us now, but even in 1924 many people thought that the Model T was following the

Quadricycle into antiquity. Edsel was one of them.

Two years later the industry journal *Motor* wrote that Ford's tremendous sales figures were at once real and illusory. "Ford ate up his primary market with amazing rapidity, but it was not until last year that he reached 'the point of diminishing returns.' In the biggest year the industry as a whole ever had, his domestic sales actually fell off slightly."

In 1921 Americans had a choice of just three touring cars selling for under a thousand dollars, two of them Fords. Five years later they could choose among twenty-seven models made by ten different companies—and "if the roadsters and coupes are counted there are under $1,000 today 41 models."

In 1925 the Ford Motor Company sold 200,000 fewer cars than it had the year before. That was still 1,675,000 automobiles, but during the past two years Knudsen's sales of Chevrolets had risen from 280,000 to 470,000.

Henry Ford fought back, as he always had, by cutting prices—finally to $290. The Chevrolet cost $525 with its roomy body, longer wheelbase, and stick shift, and Knudsen built 520,000 of them. As the Dodge brothers had put it when they started to build their own car, "Think how many Ford buyers would like to own a real automobile by paying only a little more." Chevrolet stood second to Ford in car sales during 1925.

That same year, Ford revived colors—phoenix brown, gunmetal blue, highland green, and fawn gray—and nickeled the T's radiator. "Yes," said a New York dealer, "you can paint up a barn but it will still be a barn and not a parlor."

Henry Ford's heart was not in any of the changes. His car jolted through the mid-1920s with an oil lamp still casting its sallow glow on the license plate. He was experimenting with a new engine, an X-eight, with four cylinders pointing up, four down. It ran, but not well, as road dirt constantly fouled the four lower plugs. Perhaps Ford was pursuing this bizarre configuration because he felt that only something truly radical was worthy to replace his car; or perhaps he was doing the same thing he told the reporter he did with his engineers: keep them busy experimenting so they wouldn't have time to be "tinkering" with the Model T.

Months passed and sales fell, while Chevrolet's grew by a third and Knudsen's plant expanded to produce a million cars. The Ford Motor Company was fighting not only the competition but itself. As secondhand Model Ts came on the market, they cut into the sales of the not-so-different new ones. And anybody who found a good secondhand Buick for the price of a new Ford was likely to choose it instead. For a while the Ford company was making only two dollars in profit on every car it sold.

The public mood of sardonic fondness for the car began to curdle. The Keith-Albee Vaudeville circuit was said to have imposed a ban on Ford jokes—they were stale—and the ones going around had lost their undertone of affection:

Q: Why is a Ford like a bathtub?
A: Because you don't want to be seen in one.

Before expiring completely, the Ford joke devolved into a final form that the humor magazine *Judge* called "Lizzie Labels," or, when the editors were in a loftier mood, "Ford epigrams." These were slogans painted on the sides of Model Ts by teenagers and college students who had bought their cars fourth- or fifth-hand for about the price of a steak dinner.

"Henry makes 'em faster 'n you can wreck 'em"; "Ford runabout—runabout a mile and stop"; "Lincoln's poor relation."

Most of the labels had shifted from referring to the qualities of the car to advertising what might go on inside it: "Shy girls walk home"; "Capacity 5 gals"; "Peaches, here's your can"; "I'm a wanderer of the waistlands"; "I take 'em young and treat 'em rough"; "Mayflower—many a Puritan has come across in it"; and "Chicken, here's your coupe." ("Chicken" being the forgotten World War I–era slang term for an attractive young woman that lasted into fairly recent times in its truncated form of "chick.")

Henry Ford refused to notice the change of tone in the raillery. He held fast to the idea that an automobile was basic transportation. Alfred Sloan understood that it had grown up to become an object of desire as well. An engineer speaking of the difference between the cars in the T's natal year of 1908 and those of 1926 wrote, "It is like comparing a sleek greyhound with a mid-Victorian pug dog. . . . Our cars should be made fashionable and given style appeal, because it is our most important asset. No one cares about engines; their satisfactory functioning is taken for granted. In fact, we turn in a car with a perfectly good engine and buy a new car because the new one appeals to our style sense, our desires and our developing needs. The automobile is not merely a machine. . . . Cars produce a form of emotional thrill."

The Ford company tried to put some emotional thrill into its aging star by resuming advertising in a campaign that featured paintings of russet-haired young women gathering boughs in an autumn bower while a Model T waits nearby ready to "take you there and back in comfort, trouble-free. Off and away in this obedient, ever-ready car, women may 'recharge the batteries' of tired bodies, newly inspired for the day's work."

Henry Ford had second thoughts about the campaign. "I think we'll have good times if we don't do too much advertising. A good thing will sell itself. . . . You've just got to let people know where to get it, that's all."

This graveyard whistling did no good. The Ford executives did no good. Sorensen and Martin were for killing the Model T, but wouldn't say so, because they'd seen what happened to the people who did.

The man who finally spoke up to Henry Ford was named Ernest Kanzler. Business heroism is of course on a different scale from military heroism. Nevertheless, Kanzler must be accounted an uncommonly brave man. He knew just what he was doing and what it would cost him.

He was a close friend of Edsel's, and his brother-in-law. Trained as a lawyer, he impressed Henry Ford, who put him in charge of production at Highland Park, where he quickly cut inventory costs by $40 million. When Knudsen left, Kanzler became second vice president of Ford, and it was under his and Edsel's guidance that production reached the plateau of 2 million cars a year, which the company would not again approach until 1955.

Everything Henry Ford should have seen as a success grated on him. He was jealous of Kanzler's friendship with his son, and possibly jealous of his son, too. Once he grumbled that "both Edsel and Kanzler should have been bankers," a profession less honorable in Ford's view than the pickpocket's. Kanzler, he said, "was getting too big for his britches."

In January of 1926 Kanzler put in Ford's hand a letter of unusual frankness. "I write certain things I find it difficult to say to you. It is one of the handicaps of the power of your personality which you perhaps least of all realize, but most people when with you hesitate to say what they think."

What Kanzler thought, what they all thought, was, "We have not gone ahead in the last few years, have barely held our own, whereas competition has made great strides. You have always said you either go forward or go backwards, you can't stand still. . . .

"The best evidence that conditions are not right is the fact that with most of the bigger men in the organization there is a growing uneasiness because . . . they feel our position weakening and our grip slipping. We are no longer sure when we plan increased facilities that they will be used. The buoyant spirit of confident expansion is lacking. And we know we have been defeated and licked in England. And we are being caught up [with] in the United States. With every additional car our competitors sell they get stronger and we get weaker."

Ford never replied to Kanzler, and he was gone in six months. Edsel wanted him back, and his wife pleaded with her father-in-law with tears on her cheeks. Henry Ford was adamant. But the letter had done its work.

Ford blamed his slipping sales on dealer laziness. In June he cut 41 percent of his San Francisco branch and fired twenty-five employees in Seattle. But despite such flailings, he seems to have made up his mind by the end of 1926. Galamb thought Edsel was too reticent ever to confront his father about the car, but Sorensen wrote that "Edsel had quite an argument with Henry Ford lasting a long time, but he finally forced his father to give up the Model T. That was Edsel's victory."

Right before Christmas Henry Ford pledged that "the Ford car will be made in the same way." Then, with 1927 less than a week old, he said that the company would experience a "little let-down"—that is, make fewer cars—"which will give us an opportunity for closer inspection that will be in every way desirable." This might have sounded vague, but the press and the public fastened on his next sentence: "We are not contemplating any extraordinary changes in models, although, of course, the whole industry is in a state of development."

On May 25 every paper in the country carried the news that the Ford Motor Company would be replacing the Model T.

The next morning, engine block number

15,000,000, wearing a bright coat of paint to distinguish it from its fellows, started its way along the line at the Rouge. As with the move to Highland Park years before, there were no noisy ceremonies, no band, no mayoral remarks. The engine was complete by ten o'clock, when the company's eight longest-lasting employees— Wandersee and Kulick, Martin and Sorensen among them—each helped stamp the serial number onto the block. All of them were the Model T sons of bitches Sorensen had wanted to get rid of, and all of them save him would soon be gone.

Then the engine went to Highland Park, where Henry and Edsel were waiting. The car's progress is well filmed. We see the engine lowered onto the chassis, and Edsel and Henry walk along beside it while the body, "The Fifteen Millionth Ford" painted in silver on its sides, drops down over the car's vitals.

Henry and Edsel walk through the factory not quite side by side. Henry is a few paces ahead, bent forward stiffly as if moving against a wind. Edsel is behind, walking like a modern person, someone who has grown up in the century that his father invented for him and all the rest of us. Both look as if they are strangers called together on some distressing errand—to identify a corpse, or explain themselves to the Internal Revenue Service.

Edsel gets behind the wheel of the Fifteen Millionth and Henry climbs in beside him. They drive a few hundred yards and then stop to pick up Sorensen and Martin. Sorensen lounges in the right rear seat, his grim, handsome face expressionless, or perhaps slightly vexed by this intrusion into his working day. Martin seems to have much more trouble than an engineer should buttoning his overcoat, and briefly jumps out of the car to adjust it. Then Edsel leads a parade of other cars beneath a sky that even ninety-year-old black-and-white newsreel film shows is leaking desultory rain. At one point, while Martin and Sorensen are settling themselves, Henry Ford, in the background, puts his right hand to his forehead and draws it slowly down over his face in a gesture that might be a kind of tic, but that any 1927 movie audience would identify as grief.

Some newspapers reported the car's passing with a brief flurry of warmed-over Model T jokes. But most sensed the end of an extraordinary epoch, and saw the Model T off with warmth and respect. Arthur Brisbane, who had blessed the Ford Motor Company with Harry Bennett, was appalled. He at once bought a new Model T sedan and Model T truck, and wired Ford that he should keep production going in one of his plants, manufacturing five hundred thousand Model Ts a year. Other admirers of the car found this unlikely, and took steps to compensate. An elderly woman in Montclair, New Jersey, bought seven Model Ts in order to make sure that the car would outlive her. A Toledo resident bought six, but found the supply insufficient: The sixth quit on him in 1967.

Despite the Ohio man's having had to say good-bye to his friend forty years after it was built, the Model T will be with us forever.

It had drawn, from its spindly rear axle, as a spider casts its web, thousands and then tens of thousands of miles of new roads that gentler, prettier cars could navigate. It had given birth to a national culture that Americans were already taking for granted at the time of its death.

When, in *The Great Gatsby*, the twenty-nine-year-old Nick Carraway, driving home from dinner at Daisy and Tom Buchanan's Long Island mansion in 1922, notices that "already it was deep summer on roadhouse roofs and in front of wayside garages, where new red gas pumps sat out in pools of light," he is looking at perfectly familiar things that had not existed when he was a boy.

The departing Model T left us the landscape we know today—gas stations, suburbs, parkways, hot-dog stands shaped like hot dogs, motels, and much that goes with all that: vacations and spending money, for instance. The Model T lived a long time for an automobile, but a short one in which to transform a nation.

The novelist and critic James Agee took a lengthy and rapturous inventory of the still-fresh automotive world a few years later, certain his readers would understand what he was saying, and so do we eighty years later:

The automobile you know as well as you know the slouch of the accustomed body at the wheel. . . . You know the sweat and the steady throes of the motor and the copious and thoughtless silence and the almost lack of hunger and the spreaded swell and swim of the hard highway toward and beneath and gone and the parted roadside swimming past. . . . Oh yes, you know this road; and you know this roadside. You know the roadside as well as you know the formulas of talk at the gas station, the welcome taste of a Bar B-Q sandwich in mid-afternoon, the early start in the cold bright lonesome air. . . . God and the conjunction of confused bloods, history and the bullying of this tough continent to heel did something to the American people— worked up in their blood a species of restiveness unlike that any race before has ever known. . . . The American in turn and in due time got into the automobile and found it good.

Henry Ford understood that people liked to move around, and he had showed them how to do it in a new way, with a machine whose dowdy looks belied its revolutionary soul. There had never been anything like the Model T before, and there will never be again, because what it did could happen only once in a civilization.

"The Model T was a pioneer," its creator said. "It had stamina and power. It was the car that ran before there were good roads to run on. It broke down the barriers of distance in rural sections, brought people in those sections closer together, and placed education in the reach of everyone." If this last might seem a non sequitur, it reflected Ford's most closely held convictions, and given the machine's socializing power, and its capacity to generate wealth, the statement is hard to gainsay.

Everyone who owned a Model T, or even just rode in one, had a supply of stories about the car. One of these might serve as a good epitaph for the vexing, indefatigable machine. On a black May night in 1917 a man named Howard A. Doyle, a driver with the American Field Service bringing in wounded French soldiers on the Western Front, was flogging his Model T ambulance across the glutinous moonscape of Verdun. "We got within a mile of the fort," Doyle wrote, "when we struck a big abrupt hole filled with mud and water, and dropped. I thought we would come out in China.

My Frenchman thought that the car had broken the axle, but I gave it a little more gas and put her into low and she walked right out. Up half a mile, we smashed into another huge hole, and went right down to the chassis that time. Personally I thought it was hopeless even to try to get out. But still I thought I would give her a try. So I again started the motor and shoved her into first, and to my extreme surprise I went up out of this hole and climbed up the side of it like a cat, and kept agoing."

Epilogue

The Model A; "The Rouge is no fun anymore"; buying every steam engine; "Maybe I
pushed the boy too hard"; the reluctant
armorer of Democracy; to bed by candlelight.

Number 15,000,000 wasn't the last Model T.
Henry Ford made 458,781 more before he
finally turned off the tap.

Nineteen twenty-seven was not, of course, the
final year of the Ford Motor Company. "I'm sixty-
three and facing the hardest task of my life," its
owner said, as he set to work on the T's successor.

The whole country watched. Automobile sales
fell everywhere during a boom time while
Americans waited to see what Ford would do
next. Henry Ford symbolically swept away all he
had done before when he decided that the new car
would be called the Model A. When in August
Edsel announced that it would be available late in
the year the public was, to say the least, interested.
Only Lindbergh's transatlantic flight drew more
attention in 1927. Crowds gathered everywhere
for the car's unveiling. In Manhattan, said the
reporter for the *New York World*, "the excitement
could hardly have been greater had Pah-Wah, the
sacred white elephant of Burma, elected to sit for
seven days on the flagpole of the Woolworth

Building." The *New York Sun* wrote that "it was just exactly as if Mr. Mellon had thrown open the doors of the Sub-Treasury and invited folks to help him count the gold reserve."

The Model A didn't come quickly, because it couldn't, even with the full pressure of the Rouge behind it. Forty thousand machine tools, perfect for building a Model T, useless for any other task, had to be scrapped. Given how thriftily close together they stood, every difficulty magnified itself.

The metallic cries of the big machines' uprooting echoed all across the country. Thirty assembly plants in America and a dozen around the world suffered the same brutal rebirth.

In a way, the new car was worth the wait. The Model A was a fine automobile. Just as the Model T still looks ugly today, so does the A still look handsome. People immediately started calling it "the baby Lincoln." It had the stick shift and gauges of its competitors, and its hurried gestation had brought out flashes of the young Henry Ford. At one point that summer he jumped behind the wheel of a prototype and banged away across a stony field. "Rides too hard," he said at the end of his spin. "Put on hydraulic shock absorbers." Hydraulic shocks were unknown on modestly priced cars, and this flash of Ford intuition gave his engineers many long nights and lost him millions in potential profits.

Within two weeks of its debut the Ford company had received four hundred thousand orders.

A *Detroit Times* cartoon showed Henry Ford driving off smiling in a sleek new car while "Lizzie," her radiator sadly steaming, stands abandoned around a bend in the road behind him.

There were songs, of course, and one of them became quite a hit:

> . . . They used to park her in a lot,
> For that they charged two bits,
> But now they charge you nothing,
> And you park her at the Ritz.
> She once had rattles in her wheel,
> But now she's full of "sex appeal . . ."
> She's like all the other vamps,
> Pretty shape and lovely lamps,
> HENRY'S MADE A LADY OUT OF
>   LIZZIE!

The Model A bore out Edsel's abilities. It offered good looks and impressive mechanical sophistication for almost the same price as its predecessor. But it couldn't change the world. Another car had already done that.

By the end of the year the Ford Motor Company had turned out eight hundred thousand Model As. But Knudsen sold more than a million Chevrolets.

In 1933 Henry Ford said, "The Rouge is no fun anymore." It hadn't been for years. Sorensen wrote that "after Ford started Greenfield Village and the Museum at Dearborn, he seldom came to the Rouge plant. . . . In his later years he actually put more hard work into the museum than he did into the Ford Motor Company."

His communications with an English Ford agent named Herbert Morton reflect the way he went about it. Britain was the cradle of the Industrial Revolution and Ford asked Morton whether it would be possible to put together a complete collection of steam engines from the very first ones, the huge, slow seventeenth-century Newcomens that had gasped water out of mines. Morton said he thought he could do this: Steam engines lived long lives and Britain wasn't so voracious as America in devouring the artifacts of its recent past. But, Morton said, "the cost . . . would be enormous." Ford thought that over. "Well, I'll tell you—I'll spend ten million dollars." He got his steam engines.

From the start people condescended to his museum and village. His early biographer Keith Sward, diligent and hostile, set a tone that lasted: "The favorite of those who have made the grand tour at Dearborn is Ford's vest-pocket village. The miniature community is running over with nearly every outward souvenir of the years of Henry

Ford's youth. Plain gravel roads wind through the village. Gas street lamps stand at every corner. The only mode of transportation is provided by several horse-drawn hacks. An imitation New England chapel graces the far end of an immaculately tended village common. An original Cape Cod windmill stands on the premises—said to be the oldest relic of its kind in existence. Ford doted on its mechanism. He had the shaft remounted on ball bearings. Moored at the dock in an artificial lagoon lies an old stern-wheeler, long since retired from service on the Suwanee. The proudest specimens of the village are an ancient apothecary shop and an original old-time country store. Both are internally complete, with all the fixings. In quaint little shops, scattered here and there, hoary handicraft workers ply their trades full time. These artisans include a glass blower, a village blacksmith, a cobbler making shoes by hand and a wizened photographer at work in a tintype studio."

In fact Henry Ford was doing more than building a mountain of butter churns. "History is being rewritten every year from a new point of view," he said, "so how can anybody claim to know the truth about history?" He chose, as he always did when he was at his best, history's tangible leavings. Ford could see any mechanism with an intimate understanding that verged on the uncanny. He could look at a dozen identical carburetors spread out on a workbench and point to the one that wasn't working properly. He could handle a valve or a rifle breech and know "what the man who made them was thinking, what he was going at." In this sort of understanding, he found that "there's a beauty in machinery, too. A machine that has been run fifteen years tells its own story."

He meant it. "I have not spent twenty-five years making these collections simply to bring a homesick tear to sentimental eyes. It's serious, not sentimental."

But of course sentimentality will put its not entirely spurious gloss on every useful object. Often in the Ford Museum I have heard a sixtyish man like me, transfixed by a Chevy Bel Air or a Mercury Comet, cry from his heart, "God, I loved that car."

This happened on a more exalted level when Ford first showed Edison his reconstruction of his Menlo Park laboratory in 1929. Edison said, "You got it ninety-nine per cent right."

What's the one percent? Ford wanted to know.

"The floor's too clean." Edison grinned, then wept, and said he could sit right down and start working with his old tools.

Later that day, at a banquet celebrating the fiftieth anniversary of the electric light bulb, Will Rogers pointed to Ford and said without a trace of his occasional folksiness, "It will take a hundred years to tell whether you have helped us or hurt us. But you certainly didn't leave us where you found us."

The museum shows us that journey as the man who made it saw the way he had come. No bankers, no law offices in Greenfield Village, but amid the pretty plantings and tall old trees we see the history of industrial America asleep in machines that still look every bit as potent as they did when they were wide awake, flinging electricity and messages and motor carriages out across the land.

It is the most interesting museum I know. In support of this possibly silly-sounding statement, I offer my wife, a publishing executive who has never given ten seconds' thought to the planetary transmission.

Some years ago, when I was at *American Heritage*, a magazine devoted to our history, I told Carol that we were going to Dearborn in December. She wasn't pleased. "Why the hell can't you work for a travel magazine? We could be in St. Bart's! But, no, we're going to Detroit for Christmas."

We took a room in a hotel at Henry Ford's museum and explored it. At the end of three gray, icy, fascinating days, Carol said, "Let's stay for just one more day."

The institution that is now called the Henry Ford didn't leave us where it found us, either.

• • •

Henry Ford's absorption in his museum did not prevent him from sending Sorensen and Bennett against his son. "Who is this man, Bennett," Clara once burst out, "who has so much control over my husband and is ruining my son's health?"

Edsel had endured, with a dogged, somber courage, all his father's taunts and torments. Well might they have made him sick. If so, they manifested themselves in stomach cancer. Surgeons removed half of the stomach, and then the Ford cow proved its malevolence. Even though Henry had said, "The cow must go," as long as it was hanging around, its milk was not to be tinkered with: No pasteurization was permitted on any Ford farm. Those farms supplied the Ford offices, and the raw milk seems to have added to Edsel's afflictions an all-but-untreatable undulant fever.

His father thought Edsel's friends and late hours were to blame, and wanted his chiropractor to heal his son.

Edsel died on May 26, 1943. He was forty-nine years old.

"Maybe I pushed the boy too hard," was about all Ford said, but Edsel's death dealt him a blow from which he never recovered. He had little to say about reincarnation. Instead, he built in Greenfield Village a replica of the brick garage on Edison Avenue where father and son had once worked amicably together forty years earlier.

With Edsel's death, Henry Ford announced he was resuming his duties of running the Ford Motor Company. For months, he had thought World War II was a hoax gotten up by munitions makers to sell field guns and newspapermen to sell stories.

Sorensen knew better, and took on the tremendous project of building, at Willow Run, a small creek outside of Ypsilanti, a plant that would make heavy bombers. When magazines began hailing Sorensen as Master of the Rouge and the wizard of Willow Run, Ford saw the stories, and that was the end of Sorensen. "My last days with him were rather formal. The day before I left for Florida I went over to Dearborn to say goodbye to the staff there. On my way out I ran into Mr. Ford. I told him I was leaving in the morning and not coming back. He made no response except to say, 'I guess there's something in life besides work.' He followed me to my car. We shook hands, and I was off. I never saw him again."

Charles Sorensen left the Ford Motor Company in the midst of an achievement he saw as larger than having been one of the Model T's creators. He called the Willow Run plant "the biggest challenge of my life." He had proposed to build B-24 Liberator bombers on an assembly line exactly as the Model T had been made, even though a single one of the Liberator's four engines was far more complex than a Model T.

In early January of 1941 Sorensen flew to San Diego to visit Consolidated Aircraft, which had designed the Liberator, and discovered that the company was having trouble turning out one bomber a day. This was hardly surprising; the plane was new, and it contained 1.2 million parts. Nevertheless, the government wanted thousands of them. As Sorensen looked over the half-finished planes, his mind went back to "when we were making Model N Fords at the Piquette Avenue plant. That was before Walter Flanders rearranged our machines and eight years before we achieved the orderly sequence of the assembly line and mass production. The nearer a B-24 came to its final assembly the fewer principles of mass production there were as we at Ford had developed and applied over the years. Here was a custom-made plane, put together as a tailor would cut and fit a suit of clothes."

As always, Sorensen expressed himself bluntly, and of course the air force response was "How would you do it?" Sorensen realized, "I had to put up or shut up."

He put up, the next morning. He'd gone back to his room in the Coronado Hotel thinking, "To compare a Ford . . . with a four-engine Liberator was like matching a garage with a skyscraper, but despite the great differences I knew the fundamentals applied to high-volume production of both, the same as they would to an electric egg beater or a wristwatch."

He was back in the slapped-together room with the blackboard and Wills and Henry Ford in his mother's rocking chair. No Wills or Ford this time, but Sorensen remembered his boss saying, "Unless you can see a thing, you cannot simplify it. And unless you can simplify it, it's a good sign you can't make it."

Sorensen spent the night with the Consolidated production figures, breaking operations down into ever-smaller segments. "And instead of one bomber a day by the prevailing method I saw the possibility of one B-24 an hour by mass production assembly lines."

He sketched out on a piece of Coronado stationery a bomber plant "a mile long and a quarter mile wide, the largest single industrial building ever." In 1956 he wrote, "I still have that sketch, signed by Edsel Ford . . . and I still get a kick out of it."

Edsel had agreed to a $200 million project without knowing whether the government would back him. The air force did balk a bit, but soon signed on. Willow Run put its first bomber in the air nineteen months later. The unprecedented operation had a troubled beginning, and during the first months some journalists and plant workers—there were fifty thousand of the latter—

started referring to the factory as Will-It Run? But in a couple of years Willow Run was turning out 650 heavy bombers a month, and by war's end had built 8,600 of what remains America's most copiously produced warplane.

The immense factory early became seen as a symbol of America's industrial muscle, and in September of 1942 Sorensen got word that President and Mrs. Roosevelt planned on paying it a visit.

This would be FDR's first view of an airplane plant, and Sorensen put on a great show for him. He had made sure Willow Run was wide enough to drive a car its entire length, past a panorama that began with sheets of aluminum being offloaded from freight cars and ended with the finished planes shuddering on runways while aircrew who had been awaiting each one (thirteen hundred beds were provided for them) tested the virgin engines.

Sorensen said the afternoon would have been perfect, save for the presence of the owner. When the president arrived, he suggested Henry Ford sit in the backseat of the waiting Lincoln between him and Mrs. Roosevelt. Ford did, Edsel perched on a jump seat facing the First Lady, and Sorensen on one in front of FDR.

Roosevelt, fascinated and in full coruscation, at once impressed the staunchly Republican

Sorensen with both his charm—he immediately started calling his guide "Charlie"—and his shrewd, swift understanding of what he was being shown. So did his wife, who often asked the driver to stop so she could find out what a particular group of workers was up to. The visit had been scheduled to last for about thirty minutes; it took an hour and a quarter.

Sorensen was not a man easily discomfited, but as his guests rolled past welders and stamping machines, he became increasingly aware that his boss (whom he had already infuriated by referring to FDR as "the boss") was touring his $200 million holding in fuming silence. "Sitting between the Roosevelts, who were good-sized people, he was almost hidden. He could not enter into the spirit of the event. When Edsel and I tried to look at him he would glare at us furiously."

Henry Ford detested FDR. At this time in his life he even sometimes suspected the president was plotting, in concert with General Motors, to take his company away from him. He had fought the New Deal—if there was to be paternalism for workers, *he* was going to dispense it—and here was the New Deal's author shining and chuckling and calling one of Ford's own hirelings "Charlie," while Edsel (who had always liked FDR and had sent him a Model A, requesting in return a "signed photograph") chatted with the First Lady. "No one," said Sorensen, "could resent others receiving attention as Henry Ford could. When he was around, the spotlight was for him." As the workers cheered their president, Ford scowled and pouted and said not a word during the entire journey.

Roosevelt acted throughout as if he hadn't noticed his seatmate's mood (fat chance), and once they were back in the sunlight with the big airplanes starting their engines around them, the president put all his irresistible cordiality into making his farewells.

Sorensen said, "It was one of the worst days, up to that time, that I ever spent with Henry Ford."

There wouldn't be too many others. He resigned in March 1944, with, as he had every right to point out, "Willow Run ahead of schedule."

Henry Ford hated not only Franklin Roosevelt, but the entire war. Having gone from believing it a hoax, he moved to thinking all the combatants equally at fault. He softened some on this when the Luftwaffe bombed his British factories, but he still forbade the Ford company from making Rolls Royce engines for British warplanes, even though Edsel had already promised to.

At the last press conference he ever gave, on his seventy-ninth birthday in the summer of 1942, he said the war had been "precipitated by greed, lust for power, and financial gain; it won't end until some sense of sanity has returned to those who believe in armed might for selfish gain."

This was the old Peace Ship impresario talking. The Ford plants were entirely given over to war production then, but he would have stopped them if he could—indeed, would have taken all the tools of war from their users' hands. He had lost any chance of that, however, thirty years earlier when he first set his production lines moving.

Henry Ford's life is spiky with ironies. In a small way by developing the Cadillac and in a far larger one by driving William Knudsen to another shop, he can claim responsibility along with Alfred Sloan for the success of General Motors. His unceasing demands for a more capable son while he relied on Harry Bennett make for a much sadder irony. His yearning for a one-room-schoolhouse America tenanted by small farmers while using all his unique powers to annihilate such a possibility is an irony that echoes throughout our history.

But it is the irony that flickered about his final years that had the greatest consequences. He disliked every war, but particularly the one on offer after he moved into his eighties.

By the time that war was over, America had sent it 300,000 airplanes, 12 million rifles, 90,000 tanks, nearly that number of landing craft, 147 aircraft carriers (Germany was never able to launch even one), and close to 1,000 other warships. In his fine recent history *The Storm of War*, Andrew Roberts writes, "Grossly to over-simplify the contributions made by the three leading members of the Grand Alliance in the Second World War, if Britain had provided the time and Russia the blood necessary to defeat the Axis, it was America that produced the weapons."

It was Henry Ford who produced the weapons. That was never his goal, of course, but without the industrial techniques he developed in 1913, America couldn't have done it. Over the years those techniques would surely have come about—time brings all her children to life sooner or later—but would they have been here when Hitler started battering down the dikes of civilization?

Under Harry Bennett the company got into such a ramshackle state that the United States govern-ment may have come close to ratifying Henry Ford's fears by taking over the plant. Instead, they sent for his grandson Henry Ford II, who was training for Pacific duty in the navy, and wanted to stay there.

The service said—with more urgency than it had about his father—that he was needed in Detroit. He came, this twenty-four-year-old man who was generally considered to be a good-humored playboy, and found that Bennett had made the Rouge a dangerous place.

Once, years later, after he had rebuilt the tottering company, he got drunk with John Bugas, a sometime FBI man who had been hired into the Ford fold by Bennett and, once there, hated it. He had sided with the young Henry.

Bugas started talking about what it had been like then, in the days when both of them felt they had to carry revolvers into their offices. Harry Bennett was that scary.

"Henry," Bugas said. "Why did you bother? You didn't have to do it. Why didn't you just go out and play?"

Henry II answered the question for the only time anyone knows about. "My grandfather killed my father in my mind. I know he died of cancer, but it was because of what my grandfather did to him."

In the end, Bennett went without any gunplay, and Henry II became head of the company. That wasn't an easy transition. Henry Ford wanted to keep full control. Clara the Believer sided with Eleanor the daughter-in-law: Give it over to your grandson. Henry Ford gave his grandson the control he had never yielded to Edsel. Possibly they made the unprecedented threat of selling their Ford Motor Company stock. Whatever pressure they applied, it finally proved sufficient.

John McIntyre, a Scottish immigrant, for twenty-five years had charge of Henry Ford's particular pride, the powerhouse at Fair Lane. McIntyre was with his boss often, and saw him change. "After Edsel died, I met Mr. Ford on the path going up to the kitchen, and I wasn't six inches from him; he walked right past me and looked down at the cement. He didn't even see me. It just seemed to me that his mind was on the boy, and he was gone. When the boy left, it just seemed to take something out of him."

Afterward, strokes made Henry Ford more remote. Around Thanksgiving in 1946, while McIntyre was at work on the grounds, Clara Ford came by taking her husband for a walk. "I was fixing the two radiators for the swimming pool. . . . He didn't even know me. He just looked at me and never even smiled. Mrs. Ford asked me what was the matter, and I told her two of the radiators wouldn't shut off and I said, 'I have to change the valves, Mrs. Ford.'

"She said, 'I suppose these things have to be done.'

"Mr. Ford never spoke, never said a word."

Half a year later, on April 7, 1947, McIntyre, coping with a spring storm, checked to make sure the powerhouse could handle it. "On that Tuesday night we had a couple of motors from the Rouge plant, and I saw when I went down that they wouldn't take the load. They were smoking pretty bad, and I thought . . . I would go up and warn the butler, Mr. Thompson, that if anything should go wrong . . . they would be in darkness that night.

He went in and saw Mr. Ford and Mr. Ford rose from the living room and he came into the hallway and shook hands with me."

"Hello there, Scottie," he said. "Are you having trouble?"

McIntyre thought him "more like himself that night than I had seen him in eighteen months."

"Well, I just came up to warn Mr. Thompson here that I was afraid we weren't going to hold the lights for you tonight. I thought maybe if you or Mrs. Ford woke up in the middle of the night and found the lights were out, it would be nice for me to come and tell you ahead of time."

"That's all right, Scottie." Ford smiled and tapped him on the shoulder. "I know you will all stick by me; you've always done it for years. I never worry about these things. You fellows are pretty good." He nodded to Thompson and then said, about the motors, "Don't pay attention to them. Just leave them alone, and they will be all right."

"That was ten minutes to nine," McIntyre remembered. "My motors blew up at 9:25, but they were already in bed by that time."

The rain was falling hard, the Rouge high, the power plant useless. Henry Ford wanted a glass of milk, drank it, and went to sleep. He woke in a couple of hours complaining that his throat was dry. Clara spoke with him and then went and woke up the maid, Rosa Buhler, and told her, "I think

Mr. Ford is very sick." With the telephones out and the roads awash, Buhler and the chauffeur did very well summoning a doctor, but he didn't get there in time, and even had he been able to could likely have done nothing but record "cerebral hemorrhage."

The next day there would be telegrams from Harry Truman and Winston Churchill and Josef Stalin, and the day after that a hundred thousand people filing past a bier in Greenfield Village. But right then there were only Clara and Henry Ford in the tall, shadowy room. She held him and asked him to speak to her, while around their bed the candles and oil lamps that had survived the remaking of a world stood calmly doing their old duty, just as were the two hundred thousand registered Model Ts still traveling the roads of the Republic.

A NOTE ON SOURCES, AND ACKNOWLEDGMENTS

In his introduction to a badly needed 2007 reissue of Samuel Marquis's *Henry Ford: An Interpretation* (Ford had seen to it that most copies of the original 1923 edition disappeared), the historian David L. Lewis wrote that by 1976 he'd already published more than a million words about the man. Many of these had appeared in his excellent *The Public Image of Henry Ford*, which came out that year. He went on: "I probably know more about Ford's life and work than any other writer. But I cannot say that I have completely sorted him out, nor am I sure that I shall ever fully understand him." Making Marquis again available in 2007, Lewis added, "Thirty-one years and millions of words later, I feel the same."

In his own ninety-year-old book, Marquis says pretty much the same thing, and so, too, do a surprising number of people—it might even be safe to say all of them—who worked with Henry Ford.

Such statements about the man's inscrutability were not meant to be cautionary, but they struck me that way when I began the research that led to this book. So did the remark of a friend who, when I told him my subject, said, "Isn't that story about as well known as the Nativity?"

Sure: the Man Who Put the Nation on Wheels, the Man Who Said History Is Bunk, the Anti-Semite, the Greatest of All Twentieth-Century Industrialists. The man who has already been the subject of scores of books.

But he got his hooks into me almost the same way he did his earliest colleagues, when I first went through his museum in Dearborn years ago. The place is personal in a way that I find hard to describe, but I left it feeling drawn to its creator as if I'd met him, even as if I bore him some vague obligation.

When I got to know him better, I liked him more, and less: The slim gray spirit suddenly blazing with the possibilities of the whole twentieth century and drawing disciples to his heat, the friend of all humankind, the friend of nobody, the most famous living American going from being a great man to a rather awful one within what seems the span of a single year.

The story fascinated me, and this book is a story: not an attempt to turn new ground (the ground has long been turned by more capable historians than I), nor a technological history where, again, students (like David Hounshell) have advanced far more than I ever will. But early I began to sense the emotional ties between Henry Ford and the Model T. Each incarnated the flaws and virtues of the other so closely that I can't think of a parallel in all our industrial history. As far as I know, nobody has written exactly that story, and I hope this effort may find a space open on the large shelf.

From the start, I came across things I hadn't known—for instance, that Ford gambled his late-blooming career on building and campaigning race cars in which none of his backers had the least interest. I remembered only the sketchiest details of the Selden suit; I don't believe I could have said a thing about James Couzens.

Henry Ford was, in his way, as busy a man as his friend Thomas Edison, and had as widespread interests. Although my story ends early, with the demise of the Model T, it is incomplete even in its own truncated terms. There is nothing here about the aviation career that produced the durable Ford Tri-Motor, or about its inventor's efforts to decentralize his industry so that smaller factories, set down in farm country, would produce Model T parts for some of the year, and still allow their workers to plant and harvest their own food. Nor is there anything about Ford's lifelong dietary and agricultural obsessions that sometimes had his guests sitting down in dread to a dinner that would begin with soybean canapés and pass on through soybean bread, soybean soup, soybean croquettes garnished with soybeans, soybean ice cream, soybean pie, and soybean coffee.

I see that I have not once mentioned the other

name the Tin Lizzie universally bore, which was "flivver." (Nobody knows where it came from, although *The Oxford English Dictionary* unhelpfully explains that it can also mean "a destroyer of 750 tons or less." For some reason, the word has always grated on me.)

All these omissions and a thousand more are covered in the myriad books, very many of them of exceptional quality, that have followed in the path the Model T and its maker cut.

The three stout piers that support so much Ford research are the volumes that make up the history by Allan Nevins and Frank Ernest Hill. Published between 1954 and 1963, they trace the company's fortunes from Henry Ford's beginnings until the early 1960s (they missed the Mustang only by months).

These books run to nineteen hundred pages, and although their production was strongly backed by the Ford Motor Company, they are admirably frank and thorough, and they draw on the talents of many fine people. William Greenleaf, for instance, who was largely responsible for the chapter on the Selden suit, later wrote the classic 1961 history of it, *Monopoly on Wheels*, which has just been reissued by Wayne State University Press—and a good thing, too, as far as I'm concerned: Over the years the first edition has been so avidly sought that it is hard to find even in libraries, and the cheapest copy I could locate for sale before Wayne State came to my rescue was going for $895.

The Ford company also conducted extensive interviews—over three hundred of them—with people who had been there at the dawn, everyone from floor-sweepers to Liebold. A good many of the quotations in this book represent memories at least four decades old; still, those who are remembering what was said had really been there to hear.

The company's hundredth anniversary in 2003 inspired several histories, among them Douglas Brinkley's *Wheels for the World*, which is lively and comprehensive and engaging. Nearly two decades earlier, in 1986, the historian Robert Lacey surprisingly deviated from recording British royalty to write about what might be seen as its American counterpart, and produced *Ford: The Men and the Machine*: It's racy, highly readable, and solid.

Many good books focus only on Henry Ford, and not his company's later life. Steven Watts's *The People's Tycoon* is the most recent and diligent, divided into chapters that address various facets of this endlessly faceted man: "Entrepreneur," "Folk Hero," "Victorian," "Positive Thinker," and so forth. Anne Jardim, in *The First Henry Ford*, wrote a study that is shrewd, canny, and well worth finding. But it was published in 1970, still the high noon of Freudian psychology in America, and the narrative occasionally stops for a bolus of Freudian speculation presented as solid medical diagnosis, which makes those passages—but only those—feel as much a relic as the planetary transmission.

There are innumerable accounts by Model T drivers, all carrying the wistful sense of fond annoyance with which one recalls a loyal but difficult friend. Roscoe Sheller's memoir *Me and the Model T* vividly follows its author from enthusiast to dealer; a fine little book called *The Ford Dealer Story*, published by the company on its fiftieth anniversary, contains several particularly good tributes and diatribes.

The memory—actually, the immediate experience—of driving the car lives on in several websites that crackle with intimidating exactitude. Take this exchange, which cropped up on a site called "The Ford Barn." The questioner has bought a Model T ("with a bill of sale but no title") and although the "engine #3373006 places this component as 1919," how can he determine the year of the frame and body?

A Florida enthusiast helps him out: "Motor # is Sept 1919, does it have a starter and generator? Electric start began in 1919. If original to a Sept 1919 chassis, look for wishbone bolted below the axle. And the running board brackets should be forged with tapered like ends. Those brackets were changed to pressed steel U shape in 1920."

Make sure the gas tank is round (an oval one wasn't coming until the next year) and see that "the drive shaft end that mounts to the rear axle should have exposed bolt shafts." Then the car will be a pure-blood 1919 through and through.

The Model T keeps a-going.

As is the case with anyone who has written a book outside of solitary confinement, I have received more friendly support on this one than I can possibly acknowledge.

Among those to whom I owe particular gratitude are: my friend Ellen Feldman, who interrupted her own writing to read mine and offer valuable advice and equally valuable enthusiasm; Colin Harrison, my editor, who amiably saved me from a constellation of solecisms in the initial manuscript, and wholly salvaged the ending; the copy editor (every writer's invisible but indispensable ally), Sean Devlin; André Bernard, who assured me from the start that people really would tolerate yet one more book about Henry Ford; my history-teacher son, William, another early and helpful reader; my daughter, Rebecca, who never once interfered with the work (and who made clear there would be hell to pay if I mentioned her older brother and not her); my agent, Emma Sweeney, who was initially a bit dubious about the topic, but who encouraged me throughout; my former boss (and nobody ever had a better one) Tim

Forbes, whom I believe was the first person to speak with me seriously and knowledgeably about what Ford accomplished; and finally to the John Simon Guggenheim Memorial Foundation, which immensely heartened me by discerning enough virtue in this project generously to offer me the means to complete it.

And my wife, Carol, who has seen me through this, and worse.

BIBLIOGRAPHY

Agee, James. "The American Roadside." *Fortune*, September 1934.

Alvarado, Rudolph, and Sonya Alvarado. *Drawing Conclusions on Henry Ford*. University of Michigan Press, 2001.

Automobile Manufacturers Association, Inc. *Automobiles of America*. Wayne State University Press, 1962.

Bak, Richard. *Henry and Edsel: The Creation of the Ford Empire*. Wiley, 2003.

Baldwin, Neil. *Henry Ford and the Jews: The Mass Production of Hate*. Public Affairs, 2001.

Barnard, Harry. *Independent Man: The Life of Senator James Couzens*. Wayne State University Press, 2002.

Beasley, Norman. *Knudsen, A Biography*. McGraw-Hill, 1947.

Bennett, Harry. *We Never Called Him Henry*. Fawcett, 1951.

Botkin, B. A. "Automobile Humor: From the Horseless Carriage to the Compact Car." *Journal of Popular Culture*, Spring 1968.

Bridenstine, James A. *Edsel and Eleanor Ford House*. No date, no publisher (but it's worth your while: a lovely house and a handsome book).

Brinkley, Douglas. *Wheels For the World: Henry Ford, His Company, and a Century of Progress, 1903–2003*. Viking, 2003.

Bryan, Ford R. *Clara: Mrs. Henry Ford*. Ford Books, 2001.

———. *Friends Families and Forays: Scenes from the Life and Times of Henry Ford*. Ford Books, 2002.

———. *Henry's Attic: Some Fascinating Gifts to His Museum*. Wayne State University Press, 2006.

———. *Henry's Lieutenants*. Wayne State University Press, 1993.

Burlingame, Roger. *Henry Ford: A Great Life in Brief*. Knopf, 1955.

Cabadas, Joseph P. *River Rouge: Ford's Industrial Colossus*. MBI Publishing, 2004.

Casey, Robert. *The Model T: A Centennial History*. Johns Hopkins University Press, 2008.

Chandler, Alfred D., Jr., ed. *Giant Enterprise: Ford, General Motors and the Automobile Industry, Sources and Readings*. Harcourt, Brace & World, 1964.

Clymer, Floyd. *Henry's Wonderful Model T, 1908–1927*. McGraw-Hill, 1955.

———. *Treasury of Early American Automobiles, 1877–1925*. Bonanza, 1950.

Cohn, David L. *Combustion on Wheels: An Informal History of the Automobile Age*. Houghton Mifflin, 1944.

Collier, Peter, and David Horowitz. *The Fords: An American Epic*. Summit Books, 1987.

Collins, Tom. *The Legendary Model T: The Ultimate History of America's First Great Automobile*. Krause Publications, 2007.

Dahlinger, John Côté. *The Secret Life of Henry Ford*. Bobbs-Merrill, 1978.

Dos Passos, John. *U.S.A.* Library of America, 1996.

Edmonds, J. P. *Development of the Automobile and Gasoline Engine in Michigan*. Franklin DeKleine Company, no date.

"1895 Chicago to Evanston Race: The Greatest Race in American History." *Horseless Age Magazine*, 1895.

Fahnestock, Murray. *The Model T Ford Owner*. Lincoln Publishing Company, 1999.

Ferguson, Eugene S. *Engineering and the Mind's Eye*. MIT Press, 1992.

Flink, James J. *America Adopts the Automobile, 1895–1910*. MIT Press, 1970.

———. *The Automobile Age*. MIT Press, 1988.

Ford, Henry. *Edison as I Know Him*. American Thought and Action, 1966.

———. *My Life and Work*. Doubleday, 1922.

———. *The International Jew: The World's Foremost Problem*. CPA Book Publisher, 1995.

"Ford at 100." *Autoweek*. June 16, 2003.

"Ford a Winner in the Munsey Reliability Run." *Ford Times*, October 15, 1909.

Ford Division, Ford Motor Company. *The Ford Dealer Story*. 1953.

Friends of France: The Field Service of the American Ambulance Described by Its Members. Houghton Mifflin, 1916.

Garrett, Garet. *The Wild Wheel: The World that Henry Ford Built*. Pantheon, 1952.

Gelderman, Carol. *Henry Ford, the Wayward Capitalist*. St. Martin's Press, 1981.

Genat, Robert. *The American Car Dealership*. MBI Publishing, 1999.

Gerber, John. *O Marvelous Model T! A Diary of a Great Model T Expedition in 1928 From Pittsburgh to the West Coast and Back*. Maecenas Press, 1991.

Grandin, Greg. *Fordlandia: The Rise and Fall of Henry Ford's Forgotten Jungle City*. Metropolitan Books, 2009.

Greenleaf, William. *Monopoly on Wheels: Henry Ford and the Selden Automobile Patent*. Wayne State University Press, 2011.

Gunther, John. *Inside U.S.A.* Harper, 1947.

Halberstam, David. *The Reckoning*. Morrow, 1986.

Havighurst, Walter. "Primer From a Green World." *American Heritage*, August 1957.

Henry Ford Museum Staff. *Greenfield Village and the Henry Ford Museum*. Crown Publishers, 1978.

Herndon, Booton. *Ford: An Unconventional*

Biography of the Men and Their Times. Weybright and Talley, 1969.

Hershey, Burnet. *The Odyssey of Henry Ford and the Great Peace Ship.* Taplinger, 1967.

Hooker, Clarence. *Life in the Shadows of the Crystal Palace, 1910–1927.* Bowling Green State University Popular Press, 1997.

Hounshell, David A. *From the American System to Mass Production, 1800–1932.* Johns Hopkins University Press, 1984.

Hughes, Jonathan. *The Vital Few: The Entrepreneur and American Economic Progress.* Oxford University Press, 1986.

Hyde, Charles K. *The Dodge Brothers: The Men, the Motor Cars, and Their Legacy.* Wayne State University Press, 2005.

Jardim, Anne. *The First Henry Ford: A Study in Personality and Business Leadership.* MIT Press, 1970.

Jensen, Oliver, and Joseph J. Thorndike, Jr. *Ford at Fifty, 1903–1953.* Simon & Schuster, 1953.

Karp, Walter. "Greenfield Village." *American Heritage*, December 1980.

Keats, John. *The Insolent Chariots.* Lippincott, 1958.

Kimes, Beverley Rae. *The Cars That Henry Ford Built: A 75th Anniversary Tribute to America's Most Remembered Automobiles.* Princeton Publishing, Inc., 1978.

————. "Henry's Model T." *Automobile Quarterly*, vol. X, no. 4, 1972.

————. "Young Henry Ford." *Automobile Quarterly*, vol. X, no. 2, 1972.

Kraft, Barbara S. *The Peace Ship: Henry Ford's Pacifist Adventure in the First World War.* Macmillan, 1978.

Lacey, Robert. *Ford: The Men and the Machine.* Little, Brown, 1986.

Latham, Caroline, and David Agresta. *Dodge Dynasty: The Car and the Family that Rocked Detroit.* Harcourt Brace Jovanovich, 1989.

Leonard, Jonathan Norton. *The Tragedy of Henry Ford.* Putnam, 1932.

Levine, Leo. *Ford: The Dust and the Glory—A Racing History.* Macmillan, 1968.

Lewis, David L. *100 Years of Ford: A Centennial Celebration of the Ford Motor Company.* Publications International, Ltd., 2003.

————. *The Public Image of Henry Ford: An American Folk Hero and His Company.* Wayne State University Press, 1976.

Lewis, Eugene W. *Motor Memories: A Saga of Whirling Gears.* Alved Publishers, 1947.

MacManus, Theodore F., and Norman Beasley. *Men, Money and Motors: The Drama of the Automobile.* Harper, 1929.

Marquis, Samuel S. *Henry Ford: An Interpretation.* Wayne State University Press, 2007.

Maxim, Hiram Percy. *Horseless Carriage Days.* Harper, 1937.

May, George S. *A Most Unique Machine: The Michigan Origins of the American Automobile Industry.* William B. Erdmans, 1975.

McGuffey, William Holmes. *McGuffey's Fifth Eclectic Reader.* Van Nostrand Reinhold, no date.

McShane, Clay. *Down the Asphalt Path: The Automobile and the American City.* Columbia University Press, 1994.

Merz, Charles. . . . *And Then Came Ford.* Doubleday, Doran & Company, 1929.

Meyer, Stephen III. *The Five Dollar Day: Labor Management and Social Control in the Ford Motor Company, 1908–1921.* State University of New York Press, 1981.

Miller, Ray, and Bruce McCalley. *The Model T Ford: From Here to Obscurity: An Illustrated History of the Model T Ford, 1909–1927.* Sierra Printers, 1971.

Morison, Elting E. *Men, Machines and Modern Times.* MIT Press, 1966.

Musselman, M. M. *Get a Horse! The Story of the Automobile in America.* Lippincott, 1950.

Nevins, Allan, and Frank Ernest Hill. *Ford: The Times, the Man, the Company.* Charles Scribner's Sons, 1954.

———. *Ford: Expansion and Challenge, 1915–1933.* Charles Scribner's Sons, 1957.

————. *Ford: Decline and Rebirth, 1933–1962.* Charles Scribner's Sons, 1963.

Newton, James. *Uncommon Friends: Life With Thomas Edison, Henry Ford, Harvey Firestone, Alexis Carrel & Charles Lindbergh.* Harcourt Brace Jovanovich, 1987.

Olson, Sidney. *Young Henry Ford: A Picture History of the First Forty Years.* Wayne State University Press, 1963.

Partridge, Bellamy. *Excuse My Dust.* McGraw-Hill, 1943.

————. *Fill 'er Up! The Story of Fifty Years of Motoring.* McGraw-Hill, 1952.

Pipp, Edwin Gustave. *The Real Henry Ford.* Pipp's Weekly, 1922.

Post, Dan R. *Model T Ford in Speed and Sport.* Post-Era Books, 1974.

Presto Publishing Company. *Funny Stories About the Ford: Uncanny Stories About a Canny Car, Vol. II.* 1915.

Quaife, Milo M. *The Life of John Wendell Anderson.* Privately printed, Detroit, 1950.

Rae, John B. *The American Automobile: A Brief History.* University of Chicago Press, 1965.

Rae, John B., ed. *Henry Ford.* Prentice-Hall, 1969.

Richards, William C. *The Last Billionaire: Henry Ford.* Charles Scribner's Sons, 1948.

Roberts, Andrew. *The Storm of War: A New History of the Second World War.* Harper, 2011.

Ruddiman, Margaret Ford. "Memories of My Brother Henry Ford." *Michigan History*, September 1953.

Saal, Thomas F., and Bernard J. Golias. *Famous But Forgotten: The Story of the Automotive Pioneer and Industrialist Alexander Winton.* Golias Publishing, 1997.

Scharff, Virginia. *Taking the Wheel: Women and the Coming of the Motor Age.* Free Press, 1991.

Sheller, Roscoe. *Me and the Model T.* Binford & Mort Publishing, 1965.

Simonds, William Adams. *Henry Ford and Greenfield Village.* Frederick A. Stokes Company, 1938.

Sinsabaugh, Charles. *Who, Me? Forty Years of Automobile History.* Arnold Powers, Inc., 1940.

Sloan, Alfred P., Jr. *Adventures of a White-Collar Man.* Doubleday, 1941.

Smith, Orlando J. *A Short View of Great Questions.* Brandur Company, 1899.

Sophir, Jack, Jr. *Get a Horse!* Wayne County Press, 1989.

Sorensen, Charles E. *My Forty Years with Ford.* Norton, 1956.

Steinbeck, John. *Cannery Row.* Viking, 1945.

Stephenson, Albert B. "Secrets of the Model T." *American Heritage*, July 1989.

Stern, Philip Van Doren. *Tin Lizzie: The Story of*

the Fabulous Model T Ford. Simon & Schuster, 1955.

Street, Julian. *Abroad at Home.* Century Company, 1914.

Sward, Keith. *The Legend of Henry Ford.* Rinehart, 1948.

Villard, Oswald Garrison. *Fighting Years: Memoirs of a Liberal Editor.* Harcourt, Brace, 1939.

Volti, Rudi. "Why Internal Combustion?" *American Heritage of Invention and Technology*, Fall 1990.

Wamsley, James S. *American Ingenuity: Henry Ford Museum and Greenfield Village.* Abrams, 1985.

Watts, Steven. *The People's Tycoon: Henry Ford and the American Century.* Knopf, 2005.

Wik, Reynolds M. *Henry Ford and Grass-roots America.* University of Michigan Press, 1973.

Wood, John Cunningham, and Michael C. Wood, eds. *Henry Ford: Critical Evaluations in Business and Management.* Routledge, 2003.

ABOUT THE AUTHOR

Richard Snow was born in New York City in 1947, graduated with a BA from Columbia College in 1970, and worked at *American Heritage* magazine for nearly four decades, serving as editor in chief for seventeen years. He is the author of several books, among them two novels and a volume of poetry. Snow has been a consultant for historical motion pictures—among them *Glory*—and has written for documentaries, including the Burns brothers' *The Civil War* and Ric Burns's award-winning PBS film *Coney Island*. His most recent book is *A Measureless Peril: America in the Fight for the Atlantic, the Longest Battle of World War II.*

Center Point Large Print
600 Brooks Road / PO Box 1
Thorndike ME 04986-0001 USA

(207) 568-3717

US & Canada:
1 800 929-9108
www.centerpointlargeprint.com

LEO GRAY
AND THE
LUNAR ECLIPSE

Published by Greenleaf Book Group Press
Austin, Texas
www.gbgpress.com

Distributed by Greenleaf Book Group

For ordering information or special discounts for bulk purchases, please contact Greenleaf Book Group at PO Box 91869, Austin, TX 78709, 512.891.6100.

Design and composition by Greenleaf Book Group and K.J. Kruk
Cover design by K.J. Kruk
Illustrations by K.J. Kruk

Publisher's Cataloging-in-Publication data is available.

Print ISBN: 978-1-62634-584-3

eBook ISBN: 978-1-62634-585-0

Part of the Tree Neutral® program, which offsets the number of trees consumed in the production and printing of this book by taking proactive steps, such as planting trees in direct proportion to the number of trees used: www.treeneutral.com

TreeNeutral

Printed in the United States of America on acid-free paper

19 20 21 22 23   10 9 8 7 6 5 4 3 2 1

First Edition

To the one who put up with all of my loafing to write this,

To my little moon,

And to all the children, young and old, who gaze up at the stars in awe,

This book is for you.

LEO GRAY

AND THE

LUNAR ECLIPSE

K. J. KRUK

GREENLEAF
BOOK GROUP PRESS

CONTENTS

A mariner sailed across the sea,

Singing a simple melody:

Time has no ending,

And always will be,

For you and me,

Ticking . . .

And ticking . . .

In

T

I

M

E

.

.

.

(Hiccup!)

T he Grays were not your "typical" family in the year 2113. In fact, some would go so far as to say that the Grays were "z-typical." While most families in the small suburb of Riverdale enjoyed the luxury of robotically maintained homes, self-flying cars, and ozone-protective clothing, Mr. Gray believed his family didn't need to dabble in the likes of such modern things; why, all that high-tech stuff—one would presume—gave poor Mr. Gray a great deal of anxiety.

The family owned a local clock-fixing shop, Minutes & Widgets, a few blocks down the street from where they lived on Sylvan Avenue. Minutes & Widgets was the last place on Earth where one could find or fix ticking antiques, and undoubtedly so, sales were dwindling. These days, all anyone seemed to "ogle" and "boggle" over were trendy holographic timepieces and flashy optical-reflectional screens. It was only the occasional collector looking for a rare pocket watch or Swatch that made the Grays a decent enough penny to keep the small store running.

Mr. Gray himself was a rather ponderous-looking fellow (to say the very least). He was round like an eggplant with large out-struck ears and a good-sized gap between his two front teeth. Mrs. Gray, on the other hand, was shaped more like an onion . . . or pumpkin, as some would insist. She half-willingly entertained a head full of frizzy blonde curls, a tiny round nose, and eyebrows plucked too thinly.

Together Mr. and Mrs. Gray had two children, one ten, and the other two years past three. The younger, Lily, was the mirror image of her mother, and had recently acquired the rather pestilent habits of sneaking off with her brother's things and asking questions about *everything*. The elder, Leo, (whom our story is about) was luckily a notch more discerning. He looked more like his father, however, fortunately, lacked most of his more "prominent" features. Leo, instead, was shaped lean like an asparagus, with possibly too much messy auburn hair, a freckle-spotted nose, and eyes the color of Mercury. His favorite hobby (when he wasn't reading books on science, physics, and astronomy) was bicycling.

Though as far as the Grays being z-typical was concerned, Lily was much too little to notice a thing; but Leo, unfortunately, was perfectly old enough to be horribly embarrassed by his parents' non-modernity. It was, after all, *their* fault he was considered strange at his school, Saint Margaret's Academy. No one else's parents that he knew of used a dishwasher, vacuum, or sewing machine. None of them lived in a wooden-paneled home, trimmed their grass with a lawnmower, or drove a yellow Beetle from the 1960s, either.

This, of course, made Leo extremely grateful to wear a uniform instead of just anything. He could hardly imagine what sorts of taunting he would have been subject to showing up to public school in blue jeans and cotton tees from 2013! Unquestionably, in Leo's mind, there were no other parents in the entire *universe* more embarrassing.

"Cheetos or Doritos? *That* is the question," said Mrs. Gray undecidedly while peering at the family's ridiculously fat and smushed-faced Persian cat for an answer that dull Friday evening.

As predicted, Misses Kisses was in *no mood* to respond to such stupid questioning. She instead strutted to her litter box in the corner of the black-and-white-tiled kitchen to mind her own "business."

"Cheetos it is, then!" tittered Mrs. Gray. She stood on her tippy-toes and pulled out the crinkly plastic bag from the cupboard, when just then, a brush of hot air filled the kitchen from the breezeway as Mr. Gray walked in.

"Any word on the election?" he inquired sternly. He tossed his bowler hat clumsily across the kitchen table as the garage door slammed behind him, scaring the cat straight out of her box.

"No, no news yet, I'm afraid . . . ," sighed Mrs. Gray. She greeted her husband with a wet, sloppy smooch and proceeded to make her way into the living room. "Just the same-ol' same-ol' on the *Daily Grief*—talk of another tree burglary down on 7th Street—who knows what street they'll hit next!" she gossiped. "At least *you and I* are fortunate enough to still boast a live and living shrub without means of atrocious pork-q-wire or laser-tape!

"And *oh*," she thought to test, trying to sound inconspicuous, "more to-do about that new city inside *the moon* . . ."

Mrs. Gray waited pensively for a response, but all that came from her husband was a "humph" and an unimpressed scowl. Talk of the moon was always a touchy subject with Mr. Gray, but regardless, there was something pressing on Mrs. Gray's mind that had to be dealt with tonight—other than the meowing that beckoned from beside the pea-green recliner.

"One too many micey-wicey, have we?" chortled Mrs. Gray. She sat down heavily and picked up the overweight lump of fur, who immediately began batting her fluffy orange tail at the bag of Cheetos while kneading her claws deep into the fabric of the armrest. *Who did he think he was anyway? A cheetah wearing SUNGLASSES?* Misses Kisses hissed.

Meanwhile, in the kitchen, Mr. Gray was in search of a

piece of pie. He was dreaming of a piece of apple, key lime, or maybe even banana cream—all of which sounded extremely tasty as Mr. Gray was reasonably famished from a very long and *boring* day at work:

No customers . . .

No sales . . .

No anything!

Just the sound of ticking clocks, aging . . .

He very quickly replied to Mrs. Gray's gossip, "Association dues starting at *twenty-million zozobucks A YEAR* for a lunar studio? Ha!" He snorted piggishly. "I'm sure one day we'll see *that* kind of moola fixing watches."

He returned his thoughts to which topping sounded yummier: chocolate chips or crumbled walnuts?

If only he could find that pie . . .

Mrs. Gray stared numbly at the television set as her husband rattled on inside the fridge. She still wasn't sure how she wanted to ask the question she wanted to ask, *without* actually asking it. She was almost certain his answer would be a "NO," or maybe more conceivably a "NO, ABSOLUTELY NOT!" But there was no more putting it off. So she began by suggesting, lightly, "I suppose we'd better start selling *newer* things, then, if we'd like to find our son a nest *up there* before the big—" She stopped, deciding it better to go a less direct route, and started over. "You know Miss Witz?"

Mr. Gray frowned at the name. "Yeah? What about *her*? Has she and everyone else around here found some magical avocados to get to the moon? . . . Bah!" He puffed irritably, still scrummaging through the leftover tuna casserole and cans of Coke in search of something sweet. "You know what I said about talking to that—*lady*. I still think we should have sent Leo to the public school . . . at least there the teaching-bots wouldn't be so . . . so *rooty-snooty!*"

"Expecting compliments from a robot during parent-teacher conferences, *dear*, isn't any *less* snooty," said Mrs. Gray, licking her orange-crusted fingers, still pondering the question that needed to be asked. "They're not programmed to be as cordial as you or me . . ."

"Well, that's still no excuse," Mr. Gray continued to grump, having finally spotted a promising-looking Tupperware container in the far back of the fridge. "It was a nice tie—*and even if robots don't fancy polka dots, I* don't particularly care for some bundle-of-wire-and-steel giving *me* advice about my son's education!"

However, as Mr. Gray removed the silvery foil, he regrettably realized with the aroma of week-old fish that his favorite dish was missing. "And speaking of things I *DON'T* like," he thundered and sulked all at the same time, "is NOT being able to find any pie!"

"If I recall *correctly*," said Mrs. Gray, "a certain *someone* was supposed to pick us up a can of whipped cream earlier from the store. Whoever heard of any person eating pie *without* whipped cream?"

Mr. Gray stood flummoxed at the thought: he didn't remember seeing anything about "whipped cream" on the pick-up list. Then again, he didn't actually remember seeing any pick-up list at all! He dug into his pockets, as if to prove his wife incorrect, only to discover a crinkled-up piece of paper with the word "CREAM" smeared underneath a pile of sticky yellow goo.

"Er—um—right," he mumbled sheepishly, tossing the mistaken handkerchief into the trash before his wife could take notice of it. "As you were saying—Miss Witz, was it?"

"Yes, *well*," Mrs. Gray finally began, "like her or *not*— *she* said that—the government will be having a contest for *free-entry!*"

"A 'contest'?" Mr. Gray choked a little, nearly toppling over the carton of extra-percent-fat milk as he poured himself a bowl of frosted flakes. "What sort of *contest*? One to see how many poor people think they actually have a chance at winning their way up to the moon? . . . HA! What a load of gobbledygook!"

"Not *exactly* . . . ," said Mrs. Gray, dawdling with the question. "It's something, well, Miss Witz thought *Leo* would be good for." She couldn't possibly tell Mr. Gray the whole thing was, in all actuality, her very *own* idea—at least not now anyhow. He was already being difficult enough without any pie!

However, at the sound of his wife's suggestion, the carton of milk came crashing onto the counter. "*Our* Leo?" Mr.

Gray thunderously scoffed, hurtling himself into the living room with his bowl of frosted flakes splashing alongside. "Participating in a contest for *the government*? For WHAT?"

"Oh—*you know* how he is with all that *sciencey* stuff," Mrs. Gray started to fret as Mr. Gray sank uncomfortably into the custard-yellow couch. "Why, Miss Witz thought he might just have a chance at winning, as it's a *science* contest—a very *prestigious* science contest, at that! Even the lunar president is said to make an appearance!"

But spotting her husband's forehead beaming redder than a cherry, Mrs. Gray realized that she needed to be much more persuasive (and much more clever) if she was going to get Mr. Gray to agree to their son partaking in a government competition. And so she pressed on more tactfully. "I suppose they're looking for the next junior Einstein—*or some such thing* . . . for that accelerated school of theirs: The Lunar Academy! I mean, wouldn't it be nice if Leo won and he could at least get his ticket up there, to Luna City, before—well—you know what they've been saying about the big—"

But with that, Mr. Gray rose swiftly to his feet, wildly waving his beefy pointer finger in front of the television as an ad for condos (inside the moon) shot across the screen. "You see that man there on the TV, Darrell Dilluck?" he barked bitterly. "Don't let his suave hair, pearly-white teeth, and cool-looking space clothes make you think life would be any better for our son *up there*! And the big—well, *I* don't even want to say it—but you know as well as I do that it's all a bunch of horse-talk!

It's all because of that *President Soenso*—trying to force everyone on this planet into giving away their hard-earned pennies so he can build his little dream city!"

"*Pennies?*" Mrs. Gray chimed in innocently.

"Oh, you know what I mean—pennies, zozobucks—same thing! Either way, up there is not here; and it's certainly *not* where our ancestors imagined us to be. Yes, of course, it's nice and new and filled with fantastically fantastic things—but mind you, Lucy, unless the-big-you-know-what actually happens, Luna City is *no place* anyone in *my* family will be going," Mr. Gray said furiously.

Just then, a small murmuring came from down the hall in response to all the loud conversing.

"*Mommy*," a pigtail-headed five-year-old said with a whine and a pout, entering the living room dressed in bright pink bunny pajamas with her battered and stitched teddy, Mr. Winky. "I *can't* catch any *sleepy-pies!*"

"Oh, Lily-lumps-and-bumps," babied Mrs. Gray, shooting her husband a dirty look, "what are *you* doing up? Mommy here will try to keep *Daddy* more quiet. Now run along and get back to catching your sleepy-pies and cakes. Try to catch Mommy one of those yummy cinnamon pastries for the morning, would you? And *ooh!*—maybe a nice warm cappuccino, too!

"Oh, and don't go waking up your brother," she continued with an unfortunately telling smile. "Leo has a very *big* day tomorrow!"

However, Mrs. Gray didn't catch her slip of words.

"A '*big*' day?" questioned Mr. Gray as Lily waddled back to bed. If there was anything that Mr. Gray hated more than the government, it was secrets.

"Oh!—*you know*," faltered Mrs. Gray. Her mind raced to think of something to say; however, as she sat there, trapped between Mr. Gray's demanding glare and Misses Kisses's tail swatting past the ad for lunar condos, she simply couldn't help but want her son to get his ticket *up there*—especially with all the talk of the big—why, she couldn't bear to think of it!

And it was with that thought that a very dishonest, yet somewhat practical idea fluttered into Mrs. Gray's head: Mr. Gray didn't *need* to know about Leo entering any sort of government competition; in fact, if Leo won, she could simply tell him that she, herself, had acquired the ticket at a lotto or street fair. He'd never have to know that Leo had ever participated in a government competition to begin with!

Yes, of course . . . Mrs. Gray smiled cleverly to herself: It was the perfect idea! And so she lied: "Leo has a—oh, um—" She thought for a second, tapping on her tooth.

"A *tooth* appointment?" suggested Mr. Gray.

"A TOOTH appointment!" sang Mrs. Gray with revelation. "Yes, yes! He has one of *those* tomorrow morning."

"As I was saying," Mr. Gray continued to grump, poking around at the remote, "there will be *no* government competitions for anyone in *this* family—especially contests to go to that ridiculous school inside *the moon!*"

However, as Mr. Gray removed the back of the remote,

he soon found the batteries (much like his piece of pie) were conveniently missing.

"Life . . . tranquility . . . stress-free economy—*that's* the motto of Luna City," rang Darrell Dilluck's voice smoothly over the television set, as Mr. Gray got up to bop the receiver, and Mrs. Gray sat there, daydreaming about how envious Marge Houagan and Sally Watzernaim from down the street would be to find out *her* son would soon be on his way to the moon.

Little did Mr. Gray know that a contest entry for Leo had already been arranged.

T he next morning, after Mr. Gray left for work, Miss Witz arrived in her flying blue van-jet with a large cardboard box.

"Has he left yet?" she asked Mrs. Gray, standing in the front entrance alongside an intimidating set of garden gnomes and a tropical pink flamingo.

Rumors of what to expect inside the Grays' family home had long been circulating Riverdale's streets: painful beds filled with sharp protruding springs; dangerous lamps powered by cords flowing with electricity, and the terror of preserved food dating back to 2013! Some rumors even went so far as to say that the Grays still used *toilet paper* to clean their cheeks. This was all a very "frightening" idea to say the least—especially for a robot.

Miss Witz was a tall, one-wheeled, silver teaching-bot with ink-blue hair, bronze-plated lips, and fingertips that un-swiveled into useful things like a pocketknife, flashlight, Phillips-head screwdriver, and a light-shield umbrella. Miss Witz was extraordinarily intelligent for a robot, designed to learn to imitate an array of human emotions, wants, and needs. And as Leo's science teacher at Saint Margaret's Academy, getting him to win the competition for free-entry under *her* training seemed like the perfect opportunity to leverage a pay raise—or at least a properly functioning floating desk chair.

Mrs. Gray welcomed Miss Witz with a fat, hospitable smile. "Ah, Miss Witz! Yes, do come in. Leo's just finishing his Fruity-Loopys!"

Miss Witz selected her best mechanical grin and followed Mrs. Gray timidly through the home. The rooms were unlike anything she had ever seen before. The walls were covered with a weird textured floral paper (which was very different from the computer-touch-walls she was accustomed to); the furniture was massive and oddly accompanied by dainty lace doilies (even more bizarre than the modern-day hover-de-cor); long, shaded fixtures stood with light beaming out of them; and in the corner of the living room, next to the china cabinet filled with little glass cat figurines, stood a thick black box, which Miss Witz recalled from her pre-installed history manual was a television!

"Lovely s-s-set-up you have here," stuttered Miss Witz, glitching as she tried to decide whether or not outlets brimming with electricity would cause one to panic. *They certainly couldn't be as safe as the current wireless electric magnetic field system!*

"We do our best to keep up with the Joneses," chirped Mrs. Gray, leading the way into the kitchen.

Leo, who had been attempting to finish his cereal without being seen by his favorite teacher, jumped at the sight of Miss Witz. She was early—*too early*; he was still dressed in his polar bear pajamas!

"I have two last pieces to add before it's finished!" he announced skittishly, disappearing into his room to change and get his things. Leo could only hope his mother *and* Lily wouldn't embarrass him while he got himself ready. Lily, however, was anxiously waiting to interrogate the new guest.

"*WOW,*" she gasped with a mouth full of Cheerios. "You 'ook just 'ike my POOFIE!"

"Your *what?*" Miss Witz asked, setting the box on the table (and privately hoping that Lily's final word hadn't been about anything brown and foul smelling!).

"*This* . . . ," continued Lily eagerly, reaching behind her chair, "is—my—POOFIE!"

Miss Witz's eyes widened at the sight of the plastic

mini-human with ratted-up hair and duct-taped clothes; the creature looked *nothing* like her! Well, that is, everything minus the Sharpie blue hair, to her calculations.

"Don't be shy, have a seat," instructed Mrs. Gray, taking the whistling teakettle off the stove. This was yet another contraption Miss Witz had never seen before. She made a mental note it was to be avoided—it sounded monstrous! But the dressings around the room were stranger still: the walls were stacked with black-and-white family photos (though very strangely, most of them were of a terribly fat and misshapen-faced cat); a horrifying swirling thingy hung from the ceiling collecting mobs of dust; and at precisely forty-five after, a little man in jade suspenders emerged from a miniature house on the wall and began bopping the head of a cooing bird.

"Sugar?" offered Mrs. Gray, returning to the table with some lemon and hot tea.

"NO!" shouted Miss Witz. "I mean," she added, once realizing her host had not been trying to short-circuit her, "I *can't* drink."

Back inside his bedroom, Leo took out two plastic cylindrical pieces from an old shoebox that he kept under his bed for things that needed safekeeping. Even Leo didn't fully understand why anyone would use *a box* to store shoes if shoes weren't box-shaped? Common sense had certainly advanced a lot since *those* days! Shoes were now sold in perfectly fitting, fully recycled biodegradable bags—to not waste trees. In the year 2113, you were considered very well-off if you had more than one tree in your yard. The Joneses down the street boasted twelve tall cypresses in comparison to the Gray's one and only precious shrub, Spruce.

Leo finally returned to the kitchen with his things, having changed into his school uniform composed of slim gray solar pants, a white ozone-compressive top, and a maroon thermal vest sporting Saint Margaret's electronic crest.

"Here are the last parts!" he announced eagerly, passing them to Miss Witz to fit inside the box.

"But aren't you going to wear your nice *Sunday* clothes?" his mother inquired, looking rather unimpressed with his choice of attire.

Leo cringed.

"I *would* . . . ," he said thoughtfully, "but it's *Saturday*—and um . . . everything else is . . . *dirty?*"

Leo had hoped the conversation would end there, but it didn't.

"Oh, fuddy-duddies!" Mrs. Gray snapped, throwing her hands over her hips. "I ironed a clean outfit for you yesterday, especially for today. Now go on, recheck your closet!"

And as Leo returned to his room he found a freshly pressed pair of slacks, a white-collared cotton shirt, and an olive-shaded sweater-vest hung neatly in his closet—how *hadn't* he noticed them there before? Leo moaned!

"This looks ridiculous," he said under his breath, pulling the scratchy wool sweater over his head and examining the dated ensemble in his bedroom mirror. He couldn't possibly

imagine being seen dressed *this way* in front of Miss Witz—
let alone, the entire competition! But Leo knew better than to
start a debate. So he reluctantly clipped on the small bow tie,
gave his hair a good shake, and made his way back into the
kitchen, feeling as much pride as a featherless goose.

"*There*," Mrs. Gray squealed as Leo reentered the room,
blushing. "Now don't you look *charming!*"

"Charming," however, was the very last way Leo wanted
to appear.

"Alright then, if that's it," prompted Miss Witz while trying to hold back her systemic urge to laugh at Leo's vintage
wear, "we really should get going now if we want to check in
before nine-thirty to be earl—"

But just then, Lily began to shrill like a baby pterodac-
tyl. "BUT *I* WANTED TO LOOK AT THE SPACE-
THINGY!" she demanded feverishly, popping her Poofie's
head off in a tantrum.

Leo, who couldn't wait for *the second* when he and Miss
Witz would be out the front door, tried calming his younger
sister as he urged her, "You can look at it *later*, Lily."

But as if things weren't already prolonging Leo and Miss
Witz from getting to the competition, Misses Kisses squeezed
her fat self through the rear pet door with a small white mouse
dangling between her lips. The mouse, however lucky or clever
it was, wiggled its way out of Misses Kisses's teeth and dashed
straight up the kitchen table.

"AHH! THERE'S *A RAT*!" Mrs. Gray shrieked at the top

of her lungs, stumbling over her chair to get to the pantry in search of a killing weapon. "GOOD HEAVENS, THERE'S *A RAT*!"

Misses Kisses tried her best to get up onto the table after it, but there was nothing her chubby little paws could do. Lily instead began whacking her now-headless doll at it, while Leo couldn't help but imagine that he and the mouse were having the *exact* kind of day: chaotic!

Miss Witz, all the while, sat completely unfazed by the sight of the small rodent. She instead found the "freeze" button on her holographic wrist-panel; and at the push of it, pointed in the mouse's direction as it leaped toward Mrs. Gray's chair, the mouse froze in thin air.

Lily's mouth dropped in amazement.

"*SHE* DID IT!" she called out, pointing to the robot.

"Thank *HEAVENS*," cried Mrs. Gray, reemerging from the pantry with her favorite yellow broom. "I can't *stand* rats. Can you imagine if the nasty little thing had made it to the pastries?"

"It's not *dead*, is it?" Leo asked Miss Witz, hoping the mouse was alright.

"Not at all," Miss Witz assured him. "It's just reverse gravity molecules freezing him in place. It only lasts a few minutes, but that's more than enough to stop the little guy and get him outside . . ."

"I'll take him," Leo offered. But before his fingers had reached the mouse, the broom came hurtling across the kitchen table.

"Don't touch it!" Mrs. Gray yelped.

Leo looked at his mother with mortified eyes.

"You know . . . ," she went on, attempting to compose herself as she removed the broom from the tip of Leo's nose, "rats are, uh, said to carry DISEASES!"

"She's right," agreed Miss Witz. "Leptospirosis . . . Rat-Bite Fever . . . THE PLAGUE! *Just to name a few.* But don't worry, I'll get him down from there. The only infections I'm prone to come from weirdos obsessed with computers!"

Mrs. Gray smiled acceptingly and hurried to escort everyone to the door. "Right, then," she started stressfully, as Miss Witz let the mouse into the garden. "Remember, Leo, *win-win-win!* . . . Oh, and don't forget—"

"Don't worry," said Miss Witz; "I'll have him home before four. Wish us luck!"

And with that, Miss Witz and Leo hopped inside the van-jet and started off toward the first-ever National Junior Science Competition for free-entry to Luna City.

"So . . . ," Miss Witz began as they turned off Sylvan Avenue, "are you getting nervous yet?"

"A little," Leo admitted. He was currently preoccupied admiring the number of high-tech seat controls and the floor-to-ceiling see-through encasement of Miss Witz's self-flying van. He had never been inside a flying car before and liked it very much—it definitely beat riding around in his dad's rickety old Beetle!

"Well, don't worry," said Miss Witz. "You're going to do great."

But it wasn't the competition Leo was worried about. Leo knew it wasn't likely, but he couldn't help feeling concerned about what might happen if his dad found out he had gone to a government competition. And as they reached the laser-lit highway, swarming with car-jets buzzing above and below their heads, Miss Witz better-guessed at Leo's train of thought.

"You haven't forgotten the reason *why* you're going, have you?" she asked, as the van-jet hovered into a robotic-ticketing lane that propelled them down a long hydro-tunnel filled with underwater condos and curious fish. "Government contest or not, it's *still* a ticket to Luna City."

Miss Witz did have a point. Ever since Leo could remember, he had dreamed about going to the new city inside the moon. He had read all about it while it was under construction. He knew everything about the oxygen chambers, which hosted all the air needed for life. He knew all about the self-sustained gardens, which genetically grew every single plant, fruit, and vegetable you could think of. And, of course, he knew all about the anti-gravity gyms. The opportunity to go there, let alone *live* there, would simply be incredible.

"You're right," said Leo finally, "it *is* Luna City."

As the underwater tunnel reached its end, their view was soon replaced with a thousand spiraling skyscrapers billowing with holographic real-D ads. The streets were packed with a million busy people and robots whirling by in flying taxi-jets and hover-spheres. And as Leo rolled down his window, he was instantly greeted with the mouth-watering aroma of spicy ketchups and relishes steaming off the floating hot dog stands.

"It's really something out there, isn't it?" said Leo, taking in the pleasantly smoggy air.

"I *know*," groaned Miss Witz, peering out with contempt into the multilayered traffic. "Crowded, as always—welcome to the Big Apple!" But as Miss Witz turned to Leo, she realized what he had meant. "You don't get out here often, do you?" she asked curiously.

"Not *exactly* . . . ," Leo admitted, staring out the window at a man jogging past them in hovering track shoes with matching hover-booties for his robotic beagle. "To be honest, it's my first time!"

Miss Witz could hardly believe that Leo had never been to the center of New York City before, but before she could say anything more, she was distracted by a fiery-red Ferrari-jet that had pulled up to the floating stop-signal beside them. Miss Witz tried not to stare, but the man's pearly-white teeth and suave dark hair seemed to be causing another glitch!

"Wait, isn't that—" Leo thought aloud as he noticed what looked like the Channel 4,000,014 announcer inside the flying red sports car.

"I think it *IS*!" whispered a very giddy Miss Witz, who was suddenly draped over the control board. "It must be a *sign*, seeing a CELEBRITY this morning!"

Leo, however, couldn't help but worry otherwise.

"You don't think Darrell Dilluck's going to be *announcing* at the competition today, do you?" Leo asked.

A perplexed brow replaced Miss Witz's starstruck look. "I don't *think* so," she said thoughtfully. "I mean, they didn't say anything about it being broadcast on the visi. Anyway, Studio 4,000,014 is just a few blocks from here. That's likely where he's headed."

Leo allowed Miss Witz's assumptions to comfort him, but as the hovering stoplight changed to a neon green and Mr. Dilluck's Ferrari-jet zoomed off with a puff of hot-pink steam, the sudden sensation of a butterfly—or, more reasonably, a moth—fluttered within Leo's stomach.

"Well, this is it!" Miss Witz announced at last, pulling up to a large white tent in the center of the city.

Leo looked out at the lot—it was overflowing! Car-jets were triple-, even quadruple-stacked; a ground spot would be ideal if they didn't want to pay to keep the van-jet hovering!

"Anything decent yet?" Miss Witz asked, looking around for a spot to direct the auto-park.

"Not *really*," Leo replied, astonished.

"Ah-ha! There's one!" Miss Witz shouted a second later. Though right before they reached it, a flying beat-up moped hovered in and stole their spot.

"Blasted!" Miss Witz burst out as the van-jet auto-backed around.

But before Leo could look for another empty spot, they were soaring through the air: first upward, then back, then making a few rounds of horribly jolty loops—and Leo, who was remembering the first and only time he had taken the bus-jet to Saint Margaret's, was imagining that he was about to lose his breakfast in a similar way—until, to his greatest relief, they had parked!

"Now let's get you to that competition!" said Miss Witz, as Leo sat there, collecting his spinning head.

Though as Miss Witz turned off the engine, something peculiar brought her to a stop. She went to check the stereo— it was off—but whatever was that strange humming noise?

Miss Witz looked to Leo, who shrugged. It was such an odd sound, whatever it was. It reminded him of a motor dying, or a—

"Wait. Is that . . . ?" he muttered to himself wildly.

No—it couldn't be . . . *Could it?*

But as Leo turned around, the culprit became crystal clear.

"*MISSES KISSES?*" he stammered, staring incredulously at his fat orange cat, who was purring like an electric hair trimmer in the backseat. "What are *YOU* doing here?"

"She must have snuck in through the back when I was loading up your entry box," said Miss Witz. "But check-in finishes in just half an hour from now—we don't have time to return her and make it back before lunch-hour traffic starts."

"Then can't we just leave her in the van-jet until the competition's over?" Leo suggested as raindrops prompted the van-jet's auto-ventilation-wipers to turn on.

"I'd get a nasty ticket from the robo-patrol, for sure," said Miss Witz. "And I doubt they'd let us bring an actual *cat* into the competition . . . I don't know, Leo," she said at last, "but I think I'm going to have to take her back."

"'Take her *back*?'" Leo repeated, following Miss Witz out of the van-jet and around to the trunk. "But if we take her back, we'll miss check-in!"

"I know," said Miss Witz sadly. She passed Leo the box. "That's why you're going to have to do the first part without me."

Leo's eyes widened with disbelief.

"What do you mean, 'do the first part without you'? But what if I forget how to set the base-plate up, or I—"

"Don't *worry*, you're going to do great! Just make sure you don't let the boiler pieces get stuck like you did last time, or you'll blow the whole tent up!"

"Right," Leo muttered while Miss Witz hopped back inside the van-jet and started out of the lot.

His day had gone from worse to impossible, all thanks to a stupid orange cat.

"What's next," he said to himself gloomily, as raindrops

plummeted onto his head, "*lightning?*" And nearly just as soon as he said it, a yellow flash cracked across the sky, and the thunder came rolling in behind it. Whether he liked it or not, he was going to be completely on his own for the first half of the competition.

At the very same moment, at Minutes & Widgets, Mr. Gray was industriously mending a broken timepiece of sorts when he was interrupted by a knock on the store's front door.

"Top of the morning to ya, Larry," said a man in a brown short-and-shirt electro-suit. He handed Mr. Gray an illuminated techni-pad to sign, and Mr. Gray took it with gusto; he *loved* getting packages!

"Same to you, Douglas," he replied with a wide, enthusiastic grin. "Is it a *big* package today?"

"I believe so," answered the man. "It's quite heavy with a large 'FRAGILE' sticker on it."

"Oh, goodie!" sang Mr. Gray, watching anxiously as a rectangularly squat quadrupedal robot with forklift arms carried the package toward him. "That should be the one!"

Mr. Gray hurried the box inside the shop and dug hastily through the drawers in search of the box cutter. He had been expecting this delivery for months and could hardly contain his excitement to open it up.

"C'mon, where are you? *Sneaky little devil!*" he murmured, rummaging around without any luck. "Alright then—scissors it is!"

And as he finished cutting through the muck of invi-sa-tape, he could hardly believe what he saw inside.

"By George!" he wailed rapturously. "What a BEAUTY!"

There he was, in the year 2113, the proud father of an old, yet new, 1972 color TV. There was not a man in the world more happy.

All that was missing now was an outlet to start it up!

And so while Mr. Gray went to look for the adapter to plug in his baby television, and Miss Witz was off bringing the naughty Misses Kisses back home, Leo stood outside in the rain, waiting patiently to be let into the competition.

"What do you mean my name's '*not* on the list'?" he asked the security guard for what had to have been the hundredth time. "It's very simple: first name, capital L. E. O., Leo. Last name, capital G. R. A. Y., Gray."

"I'm sorry, kid, but without yer teacher here to sign for ye, I can't let ye in. Yer a MINOR, capital M . . . I . . . N . . . O . . . ARRRGH!" said the security guard mockingly like a pirate. His neck was so wide Leo imagined that the guy could probably swallow him whole if he wanted. And the top of his head was also very bald and shiny, which complemented his overinflated arms (which were causing Leo to unwittingly reminisce about Thanksgiving Day turkeys).

"I *promise* she'll be here for the second round," Leo pleaded. "She just left to drop something off . . . but it's really, *really* important that I'm in there for the first round!"

"*Right* . . . ," said the guard, pulling out an electro-cig from behind his fat, droopy ear. "And what was it that she had to 'drop off'?"

Leo looked at the guard impatiently as he replied, "A cat."

"A *CAT*?" the guard burst out, blowing a thick, repelling puff of vapor straight in Leo's face. "Boy, yer one funny show, kid. First a bow tie . . . now a *CAT*? Ye really crack me up!"

"No, I'm being completely honest!" said Leo desperately. "Miss Witz is her name—please, just look—one last time!"

"Alright, alright," the guard allowed. This time, he seemed to scroll through the list more attentively. But after a good minute of searching, he said, "Nope! No Bitz here."

"Not *Bits*," said Leo, realizing he had already been in line for twenty whole minutes. "It's *Witz*—capital W. I. T. Z."

"*Ahh*, I see," said the guard. "We have one . . . two . . . three . . . four . . . FIFTEEN Witzes on the list. Do ye happen to have a first name, kid?"

But Leo couldn't take in what he was hearing. He had never heard Miss Witz being called anything other than Miss Witz! So how could *he* know what her first name was? But with fifteen other Witzes on the list, he figured one of them had to be a common name, so he guessed: "Sarah . . . Sarah Witz? Is *that* name on the list?"

"Nice try, kid, but she checked in with her protégé an hour ago."

Just then, a familiar voice spoke behind Leo: "Don't worry, I'll account for him. The name's D. I.—"

"Oh, I-I-I know the name, sir!" said the guard in an apologetic stammer. "Mr. Dilluck, sir—b-b-by all means, go on ahead! Sorry for messing with th-th-the kid!"

Leo couldn't believe his fortune—and *misfortune*—all at the same time. He had finally gotten into the competition, but with Darrell Dilluck showing up, it had to mean that the competition was going to be—

"LIVE from Times Square, we're at the first-ever National Junior Science Competition for free-entry to Luna City," Dilluck announced lively, clapping an arm on Leo's shoulder as a series of miniature film-drones fluttered all around them. "That's right, one of these lucky kids here today will have the chance to win it ALL: life, tranquility, and stress-free economy at the Lunar Academy. So don't mind-swipe that clicker-app, and we'll be right back, LIVE, after these delightfully long messages!"

Leo hurried out of the way as Mr. Dilluck's film-drones zoomed in on the massive crowd gathered behind him. He was at least relieved to know there was no way his dad could be watching the competition from the shop—all he had there were clocks!

Students and teachers from every state were lined up, testing their entry parts and practicing launch durability; model space shuttles were flying in every which way alongside metallic floating replicas of the moon's ringed loading-dock. And as Leo passed through the rows of contestants, in search of his booth, he began to feel as though he had very little chance of winning: all the entries were meticulously designed compared to his cheaply built model space-shuttle.

"Guess I missed the memo on it needing to look *realistic!*" Leo said to himself while finding his chair: lucky number thirteen.

"It's not FAIR!" a boy cried from the floor beside him, gathering up bits and pieces of a broken rocket. "I KNEW I should have brought a spare!"

Leo hurried to help the boy pick up the mess.

At least I'm not the only one not having a great day, Leo thought as a high-pitched screech filled the air and a woman's voice sounded through the tent: "Attention, attention! Boys, girls, teachers, parents, and friends, the competition is about to commence! We'll begin with booths one through ten in precisely five minutes, so please finish your trials and testing promptly."

Trials and testing? Leo hadn't even had a chance to attach his shuttle to his rocket, let alone *test* it! He hoped the first twelve booths would take long enough to allow him to get all his pieces together. But as Leo reached inside his box, eager to start assembling his rocket, he jumped as something warm brushed across the back of his hand. He looked down, and as he did, Leo instantly understood why Misses Kisses had snuck herself a ride in the van-jet: the very same mouse she had dragged into the kitchen was fast asleep in the bottom of the box.

"*That* explains things . . . ," said Leo under his breath. But his muttering was interrupted by a voice that was all too familiar: Gavin Jones—the stuck-up creation of the Mayoress of Riverdale.

"Well, well, well . . . if it isn't Leo—the *Strange!*" the blond-haired boy snickered, adjusting his techni-shirt to light up "WEIRDO" across its electro-panel display. "Happen to have some *toiley paper* to wipe a crying nose?"

Leo started putting together his shuttle, trying to ignore Gavin; but it was proving rather difficult.

"To be correct," said Leo, adjusting his tie, "noses *don't* cry."

Gavin looked at Leo bitterly and snapped, "You're funny . . . *NOT!* I'm sure I'll see you out riding your *bikey* tonight, crying over ME having won the ticket to Luna City!"

"Funny your parents don't just buy your way in," said Leo, attaching a stabilizing fin.

"They won't need to since I'm gonna win today, you dork-head," replied Gavin. "Nice *tie,* by the way—I didn't know they were allowing *clowns* into the competition." Gavin laughed evilly, tripping the slightest bit over his high-top hover-kicks as he walked away. Leo privately smiled over the occasion, though he knew better than to think *that* way and continued putting together his shuttle.

What did Gavin have against him anyway? Leo wondered. It's not as though he had ever done anything bad to him. It really was, in Leo's mind, the strangest thing—but whatever the reason, it didn't matter. Leo knew there was no way Gavin would be winning; he could hardly pass math class, let alone science!

And so Leo attached the final tail fin to his rocket, imagining Gavin's: painted pink without any feasible way to launch into space. And with that thought, Leo suddenly felt much, much better about his chances of winning the competition.

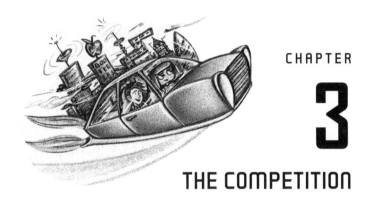

C ontestant ten's turn was on. He was a short, semi-over-
fed kid with gelled-over yellow hair and laser spectacles
as thick as an encyclopedia. His name tag read "Greg
R," and he seemed terror-stricken as his name was announced.
Even Leo felt sorry for him as he stood there stuttering every
other word.

"Th-th-this here is my m-m-model, the MR13-9005. It's
made out of a-a-aluminum and alloy, and it's sh-sh-shaped like
a b-b-beaver to blast more e-e-effectively through the s-s-sky.

It's p-p-painted to reflect its-s-s name: L-L-LOG-EATER. In f-f-full scale, it sh-sh-should take just f-f-five minutes to r-r-reach atmosphere, if calculations a-a-are correct."

The crowd began to laugh as a large visi-screen lit up behind the podium, highlighting Greg R's entry; both the shuttle and the rocket really were just as Greg R described: one was painted like a log, and the other, a beaver!

"Very well then, let's start the launch," prompted an older woman with black-and-white-striped hair wrapped into a spiral bun. She wore a crystalline suit of a light blue color beneath a long white lab coat and tall, leather-strapped boots. Her electronic name tag read: Principal Yin.

"Remember, you'll only have one try to liftoff," she said sternly. "If your shuttle prematurely detaches from your rocket— *or if your rocket explodes*—you'll be ineligible to compete in the following round. When you're ready, you may begin."

Contestant ten propped his "beaver" in place and took the ignition switch shakily in his hands. He squeezed his eyes tightly behind his thick laser-specs as the drone-o-camera zoomed invasively in on him, prompting more snickering from the crowd.

The countdown began:

Three . . .

Two . . .

One . . .

Then the rocket took to the air. The crowd "*oohed*" and

"*aahed*" as the beaver flew higher and higher; but then, without warning, a loud, terrible hiss filled the tent.

Greg R's rocket had completely diffused!

Principal Yin did not look pleased by the unsuccessful launch. She wrote an "X" in her notes and proceeded to the next contestant. And at the sight of its intricate symmetry, Leo at once felt as though his entry was a total joke—*this* contestant's rocket seemed without a flaw!

Contestant eleven began her introduction: "My name is Mai Chi, and this is my shuttle entry, *Euphoria*," she said boastfully. "My design is based on a prototype for a *luxury* airjet, rather than your typical shuttle. The ride technology is *resemblant* of an ultra-first-class seat, though it's far more advanced. Instead of being restricted to sitting backward, its riders can sit comfortably in any direction, as the seats rotate in or out of gravity."

Principal Yin gave the girl an accepting nod and repeated what she had said to the contestants before her.

The countdown began:

Three . . .

Two . . .

One . . .

But nothing happened.

The girl's face lit with panic as she stood there, fiddling with the ignition switch. But then, her rocket blasted off, so fast that it flew straight past the replicated moon base and out through the top of the tent—only to later burst into a firework. But if looks were deceiving, Leo could only hope that the next rocket would do even worse, as he realized it was Gavin's.

Though of all things surprising, Gavin's entry managed to look even *better* than the previous contestant's; in fact, it looked *too* nice. It was a long, metallic shuttle with an electronic 'G' symbol flashing in the middle of it. But however great the shuttle may have appeared, it soon became apparent that Gavin didn't have the slightest clue about what he was doing with it—first laying it sideways, then propping it upside-down, then pointing it straight toward the crowd!

Gavin's teacher, a short, sticklike bot with bright orange hair, a copper-colored core, and an extra set of arms and legs, hurried over to help Gavin adjust everything into place. And as he did, Leo at once found himself becoming even more discouraged that someone with Gavin's IQ had gotten into the competition. He still couldn't put the two together: *Gavin, at a science competition? How is it possible, if he always gets the worst grades in our year, especially in science?* Leo wondered.

Principal Yin prompted Gavin to begin.

"This here is *THE GAVINVENGER*, designed by ME, Gavin Jones the Third," said Gavin pompously. "But before I AMAZE you with my state-of-the-art rocketry, I'd first like to thank my parents over there, Gavinold and Bethany Jones, Mayoress of Riverdale, for their support. If it wasn't for them, I wouldn't have been able to afford to bu-*build* such a nice rocket.

"It's composed of two parts," Gavin went on, looking over for some sort of direction from his teacher. "The top and the, uh—bottom! Both parts come apart when it launches. It looks really cool, especially when it does the separating-thingy at the top. So sit back, relax, and prepare to be GAVINIZED!"

Gavin stepped aside and waited, as if by magic, for his rocket to launch. His teacher frantically nudged him, reminding him to hit the ignition switch, and as Gavin did, a stunning stream of hot blue fire jetted out from its engine. The rocket went up smoothly and then, midway, its shuttle separated without a hitch, connecting to the replica moon base, just as Gavin had described.

Leo rubbed his eyes with disbelief. *How did Gavin do it?* Leo was certain there had to be a catch, but he didn't have time to think of it now—he was up next!

Meanwhile, at Minutes & Widgets, Mr. Gray had finally found his portable outlet, along with the perfect spot to display his "baby" television: on the counter, next to the cash register, alongside a rack of vintage newspapers and an old vending machine.

Mrs. McGregor, a neighbor from down the street, stopped in for her weekly "peek."

"*Hel-lo*, Mr. Gray," she called out whimsically, ogling the ticking antiques hung around the shop's walls. She was dressed in her favorite purple puffy outfit (a knee-length electro-dress with one-too-many shade-shifting violas) with matching short-heeled springy shoes and an ostrich feather stuck out of her fascinator hat—a work of "art," as always.

"Anything *new* this week?" she inquired, wandering nosily around the shop.

"No, nothing '*new*' this week," answered Mr. Gray, fiddling away with the antenna. He typically tried not to pay much attention to the "old bat." He wouldn't mind Mrs. McGregor's weekly visits so much if she actually stopped in to *buy* something for a change. For eleven years she'd been popping in with no purchases whatsoever, and Mr. Gray was certain it was people like her, with her quirky modern outfits, that kept his usual customers away—even if her visits did last only a few minutes.

Mrs. McGregor, however, was quick to notice Mr. Gray's new television. "Then what's that *thing-a-ma-do* you're messing with there?" she demanded.

Mr. Gray had been hoping she wouldn't notice. "What? This ol' box?" he mumbled evasively. "It's um—my new TV; nothing important or interesting to *you* . . . bought it on auction a few weeks ago . . . and *no*, it's *not* for sale."

Mrs. McGregor gave Mr. Gray a sour look and continued to stare much more intently at the television after *that*. She reached her hand out ever-so-lightly to touch it when Mr. Gray spotted her and shouted, "Oh-no-you-*DON'T*! No fingerprinting is allowed on *THIS* baby television—with or without little pink gloves!"

"Uh! They're *purple,* Mr. Gray!" Mrs. McGregor gasped

with offense. "I suggest you see Dr. Boughstein to get your vision checked—'*little pink gloves*'? *HUMPH!* But none the matter, does it light up?"

"Well, I was just in the process of fitting in the antenna," replied Mr. Gray with a grunt. And as he clicked it in, the screen lit to static.

"*My word*," said Mrs. McGregor in amazement.

"And that's not *all!*" said Mr. Gray, proudly flipping through the fuzz in search of a steady channel. But right when he landed on an ad for car-jets, the store's door chime went off. A man in a long vintage trench coat with a tall top hat was entering the shop.

Mr. Gray dropped the remote—and with good reason; it was the first customer of the year!

"Welcome to Minutes & Widgets! Best widgets for your minutes!" he called out full of zest, slightly tripping over the heel of Mrs. McGregor's outstretched springy-heeled shoe as he hurried over to greet the customer.

Mr. Gray could hardly wait to attack the man with his well-rehearsed sales pitch (which he practiced every morning without fail while shaving his stubble). And judging from the man's fine tailoring and good taste in silken hats, he clearly had to have some sort of money.

"What can I help you find today, good sir?" Mr. Gray asked, watching the man in the top hat glance over his antiquated ticking collection.

"I was actually looking for a Double-Hunter pocket

watch—any vintage whatsoever," answered the man from behind the collar of his coat. "That is, of course, if you have any?"

The sound of zozobucks rattled through Mr. Gray's out-struck ears. He escorted the man toward the rear shelf display, his fingers wiggling with excitement. He had only one Double-Hunter pocket watch, and its price tag was more than three years' worth of their family's typical income.

"*If I have any?*" Mr. Gray chuckled, as nervous salesmen tend to do. He could already see himself and the Mrs. sipping drinks with little umbrellas from the deck of that cruise ship she'd been wanting to go on so badly.

But before Mr. Gray could conjure a sip, Mrs. McGregor found it pertinent to interrupt.

"Oh, oh! Mr. Gray! Mr. Gray!" she chirped excitedly. "Looky here! It's your boy, Leof! His face has been flattened on your new TEA-LEAF!"

The old bat! Mr. Gray mentally snapped. Couldn't she get herself *out* of his shop? Whatever was she blundering about *tea-leafs* for?

"As I was *saying*," Mr. Gray continued, shaking his head apologetically to the customer.

But a second later, Mrs. McGregor was at it again. "Really! Looky here, Mr. Gray! *MY!*—What a *fascinating* contraption this is!"

Mr. Gray tried to keep his temper under his belt as Mrs. McGregor carried on with her squawking. *Couldn't she see he had a customer?* He excused himself briefly to see what all the commotion was about.

"What is it that you *want?*" he snapped at her through gritted teeth.

Mrs. McGregor looked at him curiously. "Why, *your boy,*" she replied, pointing at the television, "Leof, he's right here on your new tea-leaf!"

Only as Mr. Gray walked around the counter, he frustratedly found nothing but a silly ad for Luna Puffs playing.

"Good grief, Mrs. McGregor!" he bellowed. "Can't you keep your hallucinations *out* of my shop? And it's called a *TV*—not a *tea-leaf*—and there's absolutely no reason why my son would be on it. Now, if you don't mind getting back to *your own* business, I have a very important customer to take care of."

But Mrs. McGregor was now looking at Mr. Gray very strangely. "Why, *you're* one to talk of hallucinations, Mr. Gray," she retorted, full of indignation. "There isn't a single other person here except the two of us!"

Mr. Gray's stomach sank to his feet—*the man couldn't have left the store without the door chime going off . . .*

But as Mr. Gray turned from the counter, there was no man in sight.

"It—can't—be—" he stammered, running to the rear shelf display where the rare pocket watch was—but it was gone!

"B-b-but *how?*" he cried out, panicked.

"There he is again," Mrs. McGregor rang in. "Your boy, Leof! He's right here, on your new TEPEE!"

And it was at that moment when the memory of something terribly unnerving from the night before ran through Mr. Gray's mind like a freight train on ice; he remembered Lucy talking about Leo and some stupid science competition; he had told her no—it wasn't even a proper question! Leo had never even mentioned the event before . . . But as Mr. Gray turned toward the television, he nearly fainted from the sight. This time, it was not an ad for Luna Puffs or car-jets playing. Instead, it was the face of his very own son.

"*See,* what did I tell you?" said Mrs. McGregor, smug and clearly unaware of everything that had just happened in the store. "Your boy's a CELEBRITY! And ever so fashionable with that vintage *bovine*!"

Mr. Gray's face reddened like a chili pepper as Leo's flashed across the screen. Mrs. McGregor hadn't been making the whole thing up; Leo was at a government competition, without his permission—and his store had just been robbed because of Leo's little publicity stunt. The only thing Mr. Gray wanted now was for Mrs. McGregor to do one thing. And so he suggested she do so with one low, frightening blow: "GET OOOOOUT!"

Unaware of his dad watching, Leo's turn was on. He placed his rocket on the launch pad and glanced back at the entrance; Miss Witz still wasn't there, and from the looks of it, she wasn't going to get there in time to see his launch, either. He would have just one chance—just one chance to launch his space shuttle properly. But *that* thought didn't go over easily in Leo's head.

"I can do this," Leo said to himself; but the Can't-do-ums sniggered back: "*You?* You're not going to win—you're going to *LOSE*, you big idiot!"

"No, it will be okay," Leo tried harder, as the Can't-do-ums hissed: "Are you *NUTS?* You're gonna make a FOOL out of yourself in front of everyone on LIVE VISI!"

"Actually, I *won't* make a fool of myself," Leo tried again. "There won't be any problems."

"*No problems?* Your ENTIRE rocket's a problem! And so is that ugly bow tie. Gavin really was right—you do look like a CIRCUS FREAK!"

"Alright," said Leo to himself finally. "Just calm down— *breathe!*—stop thinking you're going to lose, and WIN! Beat Gavin Jones if anything else—"

"Contestant number *thirteen?*" called Principal Yin, kicking the Cant-do-ums out of his head.

"Oh, uh—right! Sorry," said Leo. "Er—um . . . my name's Leo, Leo Gray. I'm from Riverdale, New York . . . and this is my shuttle entry, the RX-10. It's designed ultra-aerodynamically with an extra-lightweight external tank, solar paneling, and two hydro-powered rocket boosters on its end. Its max speed should reach 10,000 miles per second once full scale . . . and the cabin's expandable upon orbit. I like to call her Rexy, for short."

Leo's rocket was slim like an arrow with an all-white shuttle base and two cylindrical turbo boosters. It was, if anything, the most simplistic form of a model space shuttle anyone had yet seen at the competition; very basic in every sense—minus, of course, its clever engineering.

Leo took one last look at Rexy and stepped back, waiting as the countdown began:

Three . . .

Two . . .

One . . .

Leo's mind went blank as "one" rang through his ears for what seemed to be an eternity; he hit the ignition switch, squinted his eyes, and waited for his rocket to blow up in an imaginary disaster. But then, to Leo's surprise, the crowd was cheering. And as he looked up, Leo saw his rocket, perfectly separated, and his shuttle floating effortlessly around the moon's simulated atmosphere. Leo went completely speechless—Rexy was a success!

Leo could feel his heart leaping in his chest as he returned to his chair, more thrilled—and more relieved—than he had ever been before. Nothing had diffused or gotten stuck; nothing had fallen apart; and best of all, nothing had blown up! All he had to do now was wait for the remaining five-hundred-and-some contestants to finish their launches and hope to get a high enough score in the following round. But as Leo began setting up his replica of the moon's ringed loading dock, he spotted a familiar head of blue hair bobbing through the crowd.

"Leo!" Miss Witz called out to him, "I saw everything! You did GREAT! . . . *See?* What did I tell you?"

"Really?" Leo asked, surprised. "But I didn't see you come in."

"You wouldn't have," said Miss Witz. She took a chair next to him. "I had just pulled into the parking lot when your face showed up over the external visi. Your launch was *INCREDIBLE!*"

Leo couldn't have been more relieved that Miss Witz had actually gotten to see his launch; but as the final round started, he began to feel less and less hopeful about his chances of winning as he watched the judges ask the first twelve contestants question upon question about their floating loading docks; until, at last, it was Leo's turn.

Leo felt his stomach twisting into knots as the judges approached his booth. They stared for a long moment at his loading dock, a very simplistic display of self-shifting metallic glass that resembled the moon's current singular-ringed-connecting-pad, then left, heading to the next contestant without asking him a single question.

Leo looked at Miss Witz worriedly. "Did you see *that?*" he whispered with suspense. "They didn't even ask me anything!"

"That's not necessarily *bad,*" replied Miss Witz sensibly. "We'll just have to wait until they display the final scores to find out. But hey," she added, pointing to a nearby booth, "isn't that the Joneses' kid?"

"Yeah," Leo huffed at the sight of a bunch of contestants gathered around Gavin's "cool-looking" loading dock, "that's Gavin."

"Wait here a sec," said Miss Witz, getting up. But before Leo could ask where she was headed, she arrived at Gavin's booth.

"What does Miss Witz want to talk to *Gavin* for?" Leo wondered aloud. He imagined she, like everyone else, was wanting to check out his "cool" loading dock; or maybe she was going to talk to Gavin's teacher, Mr. Screwzy . . . And as Miss Witz stayed at Gavin's booth a second longer, Leo realized his assumptions were correct: she was talking to Mr. Screwzy. Leo had never met a more bizarre teaching-bot at Saint Margaret's Academy; not only did he perpetually glitch when he spoke, Leo could have sworn he had seen him pick a kid's nose once and put it in a test tube while at his locker.

The speakers buzzed back on, only this time to announce that the judging for the final round was complete and that the winning numbers would soon be displayed over the visi.

The room filled with anxious chatter and Leo locked his eyes on the screen.

Then, at last, the scores lit.

Leo's eyes raced to the top of the list; he very quickly found his number, number Thirteen, right under number Twelve; and ahead of number Twelve . . . was no other number.

"Who's contestant *Twelve?*" Leo wondered.

But it can't be—he desperately thought, trying to conceal the disbelief emerging across his cheeks as he retraced the scores—*Did I really lose to . . . Gavin?*

"And so we'd like to announce our winner!" said Principal Yin brightly from the podium. "As you can see, contestant Twelve has collected the highest combined points in each of the two rounds, resulting in a perfect score! Contestant Thirteen came in second, missing by only two short points, along with contestant Two-hundred-and-thirty-four coming in third. Will our winner please come up and claim their prize?"

A shrill came from the audience as Mr. and Mrs. Jones realized their son had won. They trampled down the bleachers, pushing past people in their way to get to the stage. Gavin, however, didn't seem to notice that his number had been called at all, being far too busy soaking in the compliments other constants were giving him about his loading dock—that is, until he was alerted by his mother's shouting:

"Gavin! GAVIN JONES! Get up here! YOU WON!"

"Won what?" asked Gavin dumbly. Then he realized it: "I DID IT! I WON! I'M GOING TO LUNA CITY!"

Principal Yin, notably vexed from having her floating mic-piece taken from her by Mrs. Jones, reclaimed it and gestured the Joneses toward a towering crystal trophy for drone-o-photos.

"So we have our winner," Principal Yin continued. "All of you showed a superb display of effort and engineering. And we'd like to thank each of you again for trying, but, as you know, simply trying doesn't cut it—and it certainly doesn't cut it at the Lunar Academy. Our institution has been built on perfection, and perfection is what we've found in contestant Twelve!"

"Gavin? *Perfect*? Yeah right," Leo laughed to himself. "They have *no idea* who they're letting into that city!"

But Leo still couldn't understand how Gavin had managed a perfect score to begin with.

I should have known the second I saw him here that the competition was going to be bogus!

And with that thought, Leo began putting away his things, eager to get going home. But just then, a nasally voice echoed through the tent: "Excuse me! Excuse me! I'm Gavin's teacher!"

"Oh, yes! Of course!" said Principal Yin, motioning the crowd to part for the teaching-bot as he crawled onto the podium. "Please come up and collect your trophy!"

"Actually, I have something to say first," said Mr. Screwzy, taking the floating mic-piece from Principal Yin. "Something I'm . . . *not* . . . very proud of . . ."

Mr. and Mrs. Jones exchanged shocked looks as Mr. Screwzy straightened himself up and declared, "Gavin Jones is NOT your winner!"

Mrs. Jones jumped to her feet. "*Don't you say that, Screwzy!*" she vehemently hissed. "*Gavin* is the winner! *Remember,* that's *his* ticket."

The bot shook his head defiantly and shouted, "No, no it's

NOT, Bethany! You're LYING! This whole thing is a FRAUD! Mr. and Mrs. Jones PAID me to build Gavin's rocket!"

The crowd gasped with disbelief. An even more shocked Mrs. Jones collapsed over her husband's lap. Leo, however, had never found himself listening to anything more attentively!

"And I didn't even build it," Mr. Screwzy continued to confess: "I bought it off eBegs!"

The audience roared with disapproval. Principal Yin motioned the Joneses off the stage with disgust. And Miss Witz hurried to get Leo. "Leo! Come on!" she shouted, rattling his shoulders. "You're the runner-up! Or, actually, Leo, you're the *winner*! YOU WON!" Leo had been so focused on Gavin's cheating that he hadn't yet stopped to think of himself. But Miss Witz was right: With Gavin having been disqualified, that made Leo the rightful winner—he had done it! He had won the competition!

"But how did you get Mr. Screwzy to *confess*?" Leo asked as they made their way through the mob. "I mean, how did you know Gavin's rocket was fake?"

"Oh, *that*?" Miss Witz laughed wittily. "That was easy. The guy's been asking about my hard-drive ever since I started working at Saint Margaret's—*horrifying*, I know! So I promised I'd let him peek at it if he'd fess up.

"Either way, I knew Gavin's rocket wasn't his from the moment I laid my scan-o-vision on it. His parents tried to pay his way into my classroom last year, and I didn't give in after seeing his poor test results. I knew the second I saw him here that something was amiss!"

Leo was beyond ecstatic. He simply couldn't have done it without Miss Witz.

Principal Yin announced the disqualification. "Well, then, it appears as though we've had some adjustments . . . The rightful winner of this competition is contestant number Thirteen!"

Leo took his spot on the podium as a large, round-bellied man hurried up beside him, munching sloppily on a bag of pretzels.

"You're *late*," Principal Yin snapped at him, looking unnerved.

"Pretzel?" he offered merrily, seeming unaware that he had completely missed judging the competition.

"Our *winner*," Principal Yin hissed, gesturing toward Leo.

The man, well-known as Dr. Row, looked quite confused about where the time had gone off to as he brushed the crumbs from his copper-colored whiskers and said, "Congratulations, young man! Outstanding win, *if I may*."

Principal Yin looked at the doctor's bag of pretzels, repulsed, as she passed Leo a sealed envelope. "Yes, and inside here is your ticket. It has all the instructions on when and how you'll get to Luna City; your first stop being Space Camp! I look forward to seeing you again then."

Leo took the envelope gladly as a final judge approached him; he was wearing a dark, official-looking cape and had long onyx hair and a face that reminded Leo somewhat of an upset cobra. His name tag read: Senator Mallock.

"A lucky win," said the senator sternly, staring back at Leo with a penetrating verdant gaze. "Pity the president couldn't be here to see it—he had a more *important* conference to attend. But I'll be sure to inform him of your . . . *talents*."

The senator extended his hand to Leo; however, as Leo took it, he shivered: Mallock's skin was like ice. Leo glanced down at the senator's long pallid fingers, and for a moment, he thought he saw his veins glitter.

The senator grasped Leo's hand harder, then released it, pulling it back behind the cover of his long black cape. No, clearly Leo hadn't seen anything "glitter" in the senator's veins; it must have been the flashing lights of Darrell Dilluck's film crew, which were suddenly swarmed all around him, propping the announcer on a floating step to start their interview.

"So that's it, everyone!" Dilluck announced sprightly. "This lucky boy will soon be on his way to the moon!"

4

THE WORST
DINNER EVER

T hat evening, at the dining table, Mr. Gray sat unusually quiet while Lily smeared green peas across her Poofie's face and Leo mashed away at his potato with his fork. Mrs. Gray hummed giddily while cutting into her pork chop. She shot an excited look at Leo, who was going to act surprised when she brought out the ticket—going along with the idea that she had won it at a bingo game.

Mr. Gray threw a large forkful of broccoli into his mouth and chewed it like a pensive goat. He hadn't touched the

oni, which lay in the middle of the table, steaming with
.... e crispies on top of it. And no one else dared to touch it
until Mr. Gray took the first serving.

Leo could feel his stomach start to churn once his mother
finally got to the subject. He still didn't think it was the *best*
idea to go along with her story on how she had "acquired"
the ticket; he knew full well how his father reacted to talk of
Luna City, but furthermore, he knew how his father reacted
to lying.

"Before anyone gets started on those *yummy golden noodles*," Mrs. Gray sang cheerfully, winking at Leo, "I have a very
special announcement to make!"

Mr. Gray swallowed his bite; he was waiting to hear Mrs.
Gray say it first.

"Today, while I was at *bingo*, you're never gonna believe
it . . . but I won this ticket." She pulled out Leo's passport to
the moon. "A LUNA CITY TICKET!"

Mr. Gray didn't flinch. "You're right," he said gruffly. "I
don't believe it."

"Oh, no, I really won," said Mrs. Gray, trying to convince
her husband of the now-truth inside her head. "You should
have *SEEN* all the ladies' faces at bingo. They were so jealous
when they found out *my son* would soon be on his way to
THE MOON!"

Mr. Gray turned to face Leo.

Leo gulped.

"Well, Leo," he said, his eyebrows crinkling like poisonous

caterpillars toward the bridge of his nose, "do *you* have any-thing to say about that ticket?"

Leo did, but he wasn't sure he was ready to say it.

"Nothing at the moment," he answered.

"Nothing at *all?*" Mr. Gray asked, his fingers tapping like weighted drumsticks over the dining table.

"No, sir—nothing at all."

"Well, then," Mr. Gray huffed, adjusting the napkin at the collar of his shirt, "do you have anything to say about a certain *science* competition?"

Mrs. Gray's bouncing stopped—*he knew!*

"Well, I had wanted to tell y—" Leo rushed to explain, but Mrs. Gray interrupted him. "Larry, now, it really wasn't *Leo's* idea," she insisted. And further trying to keep the blame off herself said, "It was that Miss Witz!"

"I'm not sure I care *whose* idea it was," said Mr. Gray, look-ing unconvinced at his wife's begging eyes. After thirteen years of marriage, he knew by now when Mrs. Gray wanted something, she'd go to any length to get it—including a walk around the good ol' bluff!

"I thought I had made it very clear to you, Lucy, that Leo was to have NOTHING to do with that government com-petition! And as for you, Leo," Mr. Gray continued to bark, his fork now completely bent in two, "I don't think you need to continue classes at Saint Margaret's, since this was all that robotic teacher's idea!"

Mr. Gray looked at his wife as if waiting for a truthful

answer, but Mrs. Gray sat with sealed lips. Why, she couldn't possibly tell him it was all her idea *now*—not after seeing how angry he'd become!

"So, I'm going to Luna City then?" Leo interjected. Though he was perfectly aware of the absurdity of his question, he could only hope what his father meant by saying he didn't need to continue school at Saint Margaret's was that at the end of summer break, he'd be on his way to the Lunar Academy.

But what Mr. Gray had in mind was far, far away from Leo going to the moon.

"What I mean is that you're *BANNED* from seeing Miss Witz or going back to that overpriced private school ever again," he said thunderously. "I had an interview with Principal Whitwad this afternoon, and you're officially enrolled at the Bronx Middle School. You begin September fourteenth."

"BUT DAD!" Leo gasped with stress. "I *can't* go there! The teaching-bots are HORRENDOUS. They don't know anything about ANYTHING! They don't even get proper updates! And everyone will poke—"

"What's this I hear?" said Mr. Gray, holding out a mocking ear: "Now *I'm* supposed to care what *you* think? HA! Clearly you didn't care what *I* thought about you entering a government competition behind my back. Thinking you could win your way up to the moon? Bah!" he grunted bitterly, turning to his wife. "You might as well tear that ticket up, Lucy—no, better yet, sell it! If it wasn't for this little lunar-stunt of yours, Minutes & Widgets wouldn't be half-empty!"

"'*Empty*'?" Mrs. Gray repeated in disbelief.

"Empty? . . . ROBBED!" Mr. Gray shouted, his face morphing into the color of a blueberry. "All thanks to Leo's little TV shenanigans!"

Lily's eyes glistened at the sound of a new word. "What's a chin-nanny, mommy?" she asked curiously.

"*Not now, Lily!*" Mrs. Gray snapped, shooing her away with her napkin. She was now certain she could forget about calling Marge and Sally from across the street to brag about Leo's winnings. "But I don't understand," she said finally. "How could the store have gotten robbed if *you* were in it?"

"Well, I guess you can say Mrs. McGregor is partly to blame," answered Mr. Gray. "But all the same, I was setting up that TV I had bought off eBegs a few weeks ago when *she* barged in . . . and a few moments later a customer shows up. Right when I was in the middle of showing him our finest pocket watch, Mrs. McGregor pointed out my son's face on the television. By the time I had returned to close the sale, the man was gone; and so was half our life savings!"

"But what about the Zozocops?" Leo asked, trying to help. "I mean, can't they find the thief? Won't they keep looking for him and try to catch him to get everything back?"

"The *ZOZOCOPS*?" Mr. Gray haughtily shrieked. "You think the *ZOZOCOPS* would take time out of their day to see to the robbery of a little antique store? Ha! Certainly not. Not when there are much more 'important' tree burglaries going on in the rich man's yard. The Zozocops don't even patrol our street anymore—not since the Joneses moved down those few blocks. Now I'm the one left to worry over Spruce!"

"Come now, dear," said Mrs. Gray, trying to lighten her husband's temper, "Misses Kisses does a fine job watching over little Sprucy for us."

"Regardless," said Mr. Gray, "until school starts, Leo, you're going to need to get yourself a job to chip in for the loss your stunt's caused the store. Public school doesn't start nearly as soon as Saint Margaret's, so you'll have two extra weeks to make up for the lost income. I've already spoken with Mr. Dawgspat down the street, and he said he'd be more than happy to give you a job helping him out on tree patrol until then."

Leo couldn't take in what he was hearing: tree patrol? With Mr. Dawgspat? He was already distraught from being banished to public school, but to spend the rest of the summer working the most dangerous job in town? That had gone too far. Even Mrs. Gray agreed.

"But Larry!" she gasped with concern filling her pale pink cheeks. "Don't you think that's a little harsh? I mean, cripes! He's just a kid! . . . And don't you think if we were to *sell* the ticket, *that* would make up for the money lost at the store?"

"I'm sure it would," said Mr. Gray, "but until then, Leo

needs to learn a lesson. And there's no better way to do so than by sweating it out on tree patrol."

And so that night, after everyone had finished their meal, Leo lay tucked underneath his star-covered sheets, staring longingly at the dark ring wrapped around the moon. He was never going to make it *up there*—he was now certain of that. He would instead be stuck guarding trees and shrubs alongside the unimaginable stench from Mr. Dawgspat all summer long. He would be working the most dangerous job in town, and he wasn't even a teenager! With all the tree burglaries going on left and right, Leo had completely stopped worrying about showing up at public school in century-old clothes: He was certain the job with Mr. Dawgspat would leave him unconscious, missing, or more plausibly, dead.

The sun rose quickly the next day, and the events from the night before twirled around in Leo's mind like a dream gone horribly wrong.

"You know, Leo," said Mrs. Gray while flipping strips of Spam over the stove, "it's not always easy being a parent. You don't always have the right answers—including your father and me—but try not to worry about everything that happened last night. We'll find another way to get you up there!"

Leo doubted that would happen. *Hadn't she been there last night? Didn't she see how angry his father had become?* With or without any money, Leo knew there was no way his dad would agree to let him go to Luna City.

Mrs. Gray looked at Leo's untouched plate. "You don't *really* think your father's always disliked the moon, do you?" she asked meaningfully.

"It's not like he was very excited about it last night," said Leo with a sigh.

"I guess then there are some things you ought to learn about your father," said Mrs. Gray, looking at the clock. "But it's getting late. You should hurry to finish your plate—Mr. Dawgspat will be expecting you."

"I'm not really hungry . . ." Leo replied, staring at the grease-covered meat.

Mrs. Gray took out a pop-tart from the cupboard. "Here, take this," she insisted. And Leo headed, unwillingly, off to Mr. Dawgspat's.

The air was cool and crisp that morning as Leo made his way down Sylvan on his Huffy red radio bike. It used to be his dad's dad's before it was his, but they had refurbished it to make it run and look like new. Unlike his clothes, Leo didn't really care about what the other kids thought about him riding it (given it was the funnest thing he had to ride). Leo had always dreamed about having an air-board or hover-skates, like everyone else, but his dad would never allow such "high-tech" and "dangerous" things.

Leo remembered the one time he had tried a pair of hover-skates, after briefly becoming friends with the new kid in town, Aabher Pawar, the previous summer. Aabher had just received a new air-board for his birthday when he had given

Leo his old hover-skates to try out. It was the most fun Leo had ever had, but back in school when Aabher learned from Gavin that Leo was considered the "strange" kid, he was quickly asked to return them.

Mr. Dawgspat's house was the very last on the street; it was a tall, modern two-story with a dark electronic glass frame and a large satellite dish stuck out of a dome-shaped roof. On the front porch was a holographic Irish flag, adjacent to a half-filled kiddy pool that consumed Mr. Dawgspat's untrimmed front yard. The kiddy-pool, however, was not for children, but rather, for Mr. Dawgspat's two Great Danes, which rightfully kept passersby on the other side of the street. But what frightened the neighbors more than Mr. Dawgspat or his dogs was Mr. Dawgspat's wife. Leo shuddered just to think of her. She was a tall, gangly lady with long black hair and a plump mole on the edge of her chin (which had properly earned her the nickname "witch" among the neighborhood's kids).

Each morning last year, while Leo was making his way to school, Mrs. Dawgspat would stand on her front porch and wave him down for one of her "deathly" cookies. Rumor had it that Gino Gambino, a boy in Leo's grade, had received his famous limp after accepting one of them. Needless to say, when Mrs. Dawgspat had stopped coming outside (ever since Leo's tenth birthday), he was greatly relieved not to see her again—though he put his bets on it that she'd be out later this year to try her luck on Lily.

Leo finally reached the Dawgspats' front porch, yet after

only a slight creak of the first step, he was greeted by the blood-curdling howls of the two Great Danes, barking ferociously at the front door's screen window.

Leo reached for the crow-shaped doorbell and scurried himself a safe distance back from the pointed yellow fangs of the canine beasts. His heart pounded as he stood there, hoping the "witch" wouldn't be home to offer him any sort of life-threatening treats. And then he became aware of someone coming down the main stairs—however, it sounded far less like a person and much more like an elephant.

The dogs' barking lowered to a whimper as a towering shadow consumed the front entrance.

A black eye peeped through the shutters.

"*Humph*—been expectin' you!" a deep voice grunted.

Leo took another cautious step back.

"G-g-great!" he stammered, trying to keep his knees from buckling.

Leo could already smell something awful escaping from underneath the door; a man that size was sure hard-pressed to fit underneath a shower—especially a modern automatic robo-wash! This made Leo come to think that maybe *that* was the reason the Dawgspats had such an unusually tall back fence. Though if it wasn't for concealing a massive outdoor shower, Leo couldn't help but imagine it was where Mr. and Mrs. Dawgspat hid the stacks of bones from all the leftover children!

The door finally opened, but just a sliver.

"Wanna come in for a bite ta eat?" Mr. Dawgspat asked.

"No!" Leo shouted, his voice trembling midway as he nearly toppled down the stairs. "I mean, I've—uh—already eaten, sir."

"Suit yourself," said Mr. Dawgspat, letting the door slam in Leo's face. Leo released a stressful sigh as he stood there, listening to the renewed clamoring throughout the Dawgspats' home. Then, after a good moment of booms and bangs, the door reopened—only this time fully.

Leo had never stood very close to Mr. Dawgspat, and now that he was, Leo instantly understood the magnitude of his height: he was at least seven feet tall (or so Leo presumed), with a wide, porous nose, deep pitted cheeks, and a wiry red beard (that appeared to have some leftover biscuit in it. That is, assuming it was biscuit, and not actually a piece of Gino Gambino's leg!). He wore a thick, studded, heat-resistant, leather techni-jacket and large, muddy biker boots, with matching leather cutout gloves. Alongside him was an old russet sack filled with bundles of electronic barbwire, robotic shovels, and an array of high-tech tools. And it was then that Leo noticed something he had never noticed about Mr. Dawgspat before: There was something undeniably curious about his right eye.

At first, Leo couldn't think what it was, but then he realized: *It's robotic!*

"Here's ya list," said Mr. Dawgspat. He handed Leo a crinkled-up piece of electro-paper, along with a whiff of month-old lemons and stinky socks.

Though as Leo looked back up, he jumped as he discovered Mr. Dawgspat's right eye was staring back at him! Leo at once adjusted his glare toward the paper; it was a bunch of street addresses and last names with weird little tree symbols next to them: the Pearlywacks, Lintrums, Longruns, Timberponds, Pawars, Gateses, and Joneses. They all lived on Luxury Lane; the neighborhood just beyond Leo's.

Leo folded the note into his pocket and hurried toward his bike.

"Hold on there just one second!" Mr. Dawgspat barked after him.

Leo froze.

"Ya won't be needin' that ol' thing!"

Leo looked at him skeptically as he asked, "But don't we have a long way to go before we reach any of the houses?" The last thing Leo wanted was to get stuck carrying Mr. Dawgspat's filthy bag of shovels all the way to Luxury Lane.

"O' course we do," said Mr. Dawgspat, opening the side shed to reveal a flying go-kart with turbo engines and a back-wagon scattered with twigs and leaves. "That's what this here is for!"

Leo hadn't even *thought* about tree patrol allowing him to fly around in Mr. Dawgspat's cool ride! It was a metallic violet-black with silver pipes and flames detailed on its sides. And at the thought of getting to ride around in it, Leo was much more excited about the day ahead tree patrolling.

"But where should I put my bike?" Leo asked, suddenly eager to ditch it.

"Er—uh, you can just leave it over there, on the porch," said Mr. Dawgspat. "Muffin an' Princess will be sure to watch over it for ya. Don't think anybody will try ta steal yer bike next ta them! . . . Then again, not sure why anyone would wanna steal it ta begin with? It's kinda old, don't ya think?"

Mr. Dawgspat was probably right, but Leo didn't want to risk it. He ran his bike over to the porch, despite the ferocious yaps of Muffin and Princess, and hopped on the seat next to Mr. Dawgspat.

"So, um . . . if you don't mind me asking, Mr. Dawgspat," said Leo. "What *exactly* will we be doing, tree patrolling?"

"Ah, nervous, are ya?" said Mr. Dawgspat with a dark, satisfied grin. "Should be! Risky business we'll be doin' out there today, but well worth it once the pay comes—plus the advantages of free security!

"We'll be gettin' dirty though," he went on, glancing at Leo's t-shirt, jean shorts, and scrubby Converse sneakers. "Good thing you wore some ugly clothes!"

"Oh—right," Leo replied, uneasy. He had worn his favorite outfit (outside of his uniform), just in case he didn't live to see another day.

"But not ta worry," said Mr. Dawgspat, revving up the engines, "no one around here messes with me—ain't passed me a snatch yet!"

And before Leo had the chance to ask anything more, his penny-colored hair was being tossed back with the speed of the passing wind. Within seconds (which otherwise would have taken Leo at least fifteen minutes on his bike) they arrived at the first house on Luxury Lane. It was a tall Victorian electro-stone, with six perfectly lined up evergreens and a deck of electronic rosebushes trimming the front drive. Leo at once found himself wishing the ride had been longer, because as soon as it stopped, he was greeted with an unwanted reminder of rotten lemons and stinky socks.

"Oh-key-doke then, which will it be?" Mr. Dawgspat asked, rummaging through the satchel of wire and tools.

Leo took out the list. He read the numbers on the house and then looked at the piece of electronic paper, finding the Pearlywacks' name.

555 LUXURY LANE PEARLYWACKS 🌲🌲🌲

"Um, three large trees?" he replied, still not sure what the symbols meant.

"What color?" Mr. Dawgspat asked.

"Pink, Mr. Dawgspat," Leo answered.

"OKAY, OKAY! That's about enough of *THAT*! It's Gudrun to you now—I know, I know! S'posed ta be a lady's name . . . named after me own mother, Gudrun Harryhide Dawgspat. Guess somehow she thought I'd be a girl and couldn't think of a better name ta name me. *Anyhoo*, it's what I'd prefer ya call me, since we're gonna be a team an' all.

"So three large pink ones, eh?" he said, scratching at his

unkempt beard. "We'll need a snitchtork, a halfscrew, and a good amount of pork-q-wire; we'll be wrapping us up some deciduous Evergreens! I'll let you be in charge of pass'n me the wire and keep'n an eye out for any of those there snatchers—gotta make sure it's nice an' even though—ya *don't* wanna know what happens when it gets tangled up!"

Leo was relieved: the job sounded easy enough, though he still wasn't sure he felt entirely safe from the snatchers, or Mr. Dawgspat's lack of deodorant. He remembered hearing about people on the news, standing by a tree one second, only to turn around and find it missing the next. Whoever it was that was doing the snatching sure knew what they were up to! This news, however, didn't make Leo feel any more comfortable knowing that the last spot where it had happened would be the homes they'd be patrolling.

THE DISAPPEARING TREES

After finishing the first house, the next few passed along quite quickly as Mr. Dawgspat—or Gudrun, rather—wrapped up trees, and Leo sat as snatcher lookout and pork-q-wire detangling assistant. But as they reached the end of the day, Leo regrettably realized that their final home would be the Joneses. Leo had hoped Gavin wouldn't be home (so as not to notice him tree patrolling), but he soon realized it was inevitable.

Leo hurried himself behind one of the tall cypresses as the Joneses' flying Hummer-jet pulled up their stately drive.

Aabher, who was across the street toying around on his hover-skates, fell over as Gavin yelled at him to come admire his latest weekly gift: a brand-new air-board.

Leo's eyes ached as he peered through the gaps of the leaves, making out the board's perfectly lacquered metallic-red trim. Gavin, of course, always had the latest of everything despite any real need, which one could easily gather from the stacks of air-boards collecting dust in the Joneses' garage. And this board would prove no exception as Gavin already appeared to be losing interest in it the second Aabher pointed toward something else: Leo's hiding position behind the tall cypress.

"Hey, *LEE-WAD*!" Gavin shouted from across the yard, hopping on his board and hovering up beside Leo, shrunken behind the tree. "Nice *JOB*! Thought you would have been halfway to the moon by now?"

Gudrun, of course, had picked the perfect moment to visit the park nearby in search of a shrub to relieve himself.

"At least I didn't need to *cheat* my way up there," said Leo coolly, as he rather un-coolly unsnarled a twig from his hair.

"If it wasn't for that stupid teaching-bot of yours, that would have been a different story," said Gavin, elbowing Aabher dumbly as if to confirm he was making a good enough jab.

"Yeah, that's right," added Aabher, wobbling unsteadily on his hover-skates. "But either way, Gavin's parents can afford to buy him another ticket, unlike *yours*." The words tore through Leo like a knife, but Leo knew better than to tighten his fists.

"And thanks to you stealing my first-place win, my parents bought me this new air-board," said Gavin snobbishly. "*The Evion 10,000.* Bet it *costed* as much as that stupid wooden house of yours!"

"Cost," Aabher thought to correct. He, too, tried to show off on his hover-skates; however, Leo couldn't fully understand why he suddenly cared so much about them if he had previously tried to give them away? He must not have been very good at air-boarding!

Though as Gavin and Aabher continued with their lack of kind words, an idea slithered through Leo's head; it was a horrible idea—possibly the worst idea he had ever had—but it was the only logical thing Leo could think of to help his family get back the money for the store.

Leo cringed as he gave the thought another go-around, but he had decided: He would tell his parents to sell his ticket to the Joneses. The Joneses clearly wanted the ticket for Gavin. Even if that meant a certain teasing from Gavin and Aabher as soon as they found out he was no longer going to Luna City, Leo knew it was what he had to do.

Gudrun finally emerged from the park, adjusting the clasps of his suspenders to his heavily sagging trousers. And at the sight of him heading their way, Gavin and Aabher took off like a pair of startled cats in the opposite direction. Every kid in town was afraid of Mr. Dawgspat, though Leo was slowly coming to realize he wasn't *that* scary after all—that is, everything minus his horrendous stench!

The rest of the summer went on like this, though much more swiftly than Leo could have ever imagined: Leo helping Gudrun, and Gavin and Aabher bugging him every second they could get about Gavin's parents having bought Leo's prized Luna City ticket for zozos less than what it was really worth. Aabher was now going too, as his mother, Dr. Pawar, was invited to join Luna City's research team. With both Aabher and Gavin being up there, Leo was almost relieved that he was no longer going; though he'd still rather be going to the Lunar Academy than having to be stuck wearing century-old clothes at public school.

It was then, officially, the last week of summer. Leo clenched onto every second of it, especially the time he spent laughing with Gudrun about Gavin and Aabher missing flip-kicks and ollie-glides over their homemade air-ramp (which only ever thrusted them a pathetic foot higher than their one-foot hover). Leo felt extremely lucky that no trees had been snatched during his time tree patrolling, and with summer reaching its end, he had nearly forgotten about the snatchers existing, too. That is, until an unusually foggy morning while Leo was making his daily trip to Gudrun's when he felt that something—though not the foggy air—was out of skew.

At first, Leo couldn't place it. Then he noticed that the old oak in Mrs. McGregor's yard wasn't there. Leo hopped off his bike to take a better look at the enormous hole in the ground, but as he did, three more trees from neighboring lawns popped straight up into the air! Leo couldn't believe what he was seeing—he was witnessing his first snatching!

Leo jumped back on his bike and raced down to Gudrun's.

"C'mon, c'mon," he said under his breath, banging on Gudrun's front door to wake him. Muffin and Princess had by now gotten used to seeing him, and instead of barking at him like ravenous wolves, they wagged their tails and whimpered with excitement.

It took an extra long moment, but Gudrun finally stumbled down the stairs with his usual amount of clamoring. "For cryin' out loud!" he yawned, rubbing the sleep out of his normal eye, dressed in a giant fleece robe, bunny slippers, and an eyepatch to conceal his missing lens. "What'd I tell ya 'bout comin' early! Remember? I still be asleepin' till eight forty-two an' a second!"

Leo didn't have time to apologize . . . or comment on Gudrun's massive rabbit feet. "It's the snatchers!" he said breathlessly. "They're here! Every tree on Sylvan's gone!"

Gudrun's good eye widened in horror. He pulled together his robe and stepped out onto the porch to find the treeless, foggy street.

"Impossible—" he stammered, starting toward the shed. "Hurry in the go-kart, Leo! We got us some catchin' ta do!" And in the next second Leo and Gudrun were flying down the street, chasing after the rows upon rows of disappearing trees.

But after what felt like hours of searching, Leo had no better clue where the snatchers were coming from. The fog had become so thick by now that Leo could hardly make out more than a few feet ahead of them. He took the robonoculars from Gudrun's satchel and began scanning the ghost-gray sky, when a second later, a streak of green flashed across the lenses.

"Did you see *THAT*?" Leo shouted over the roaring engine. "That shrub over there, on the Tillknocks' yard—it just FLEW straight into the air!"

But as Leo looked further, he couldn't find the tree again anywhere. "But I don't get it?" he said funnily while the go-kart climbed out of the fog. "It's as if it . . . disappeared into *nowhere*?"

Gudrun brought the go-kart to a rumbling hover. He took the robonoculars from Leo's grasp, looked up, then growled lowly, "Err . . . knew it!"

"Knew what?" Leo asked, trying to make out whatever it was that Gudrun had seen.

"Those there trees ain't disappearin' inta nowhere, Leo—they're headin' straight inta that DARK NIMBUS!"

"A dark *what*?" Leo wondered.

"A dark nimbus!" Gudrun repeated just as a flowerpot floated off the Tillknocks' porch and into a raincloud hanging overhead. "Ya know, that there cloud above ya head! The gray one, see it? That there's a nimbus cloud—though *not* the kind you'd be familiar with!"

Leo didn't get it—what did a "*cloud*" have to do with finding the snatchers?

"Thought they were the ones up ta it," said Gudrun darkly. "Though I never thought they'd be up ta ALL THIS!"

"But the snatchers!" Leo shouted as Gudrun backed around. "They're getting away!"

"Erg, it's too late, Leo," Gudrun replied with a heavy sigh. "They must 'ave spotted us."

"They *what*?" said Leo. "You can't know that—they have to be close by!"

"Nope, don't think so," said Gudrun, ever darker.

"Why not?" Leo asked.

"The cloud's gone."

"'The *cloud's* gone?'" Leo repeated incredulously. "What's *that* have to do with anything?"

"Oh, it's no good, Leo . . . still not sure if I should tell ya . . . but a cloud like that can only mean one thing!"

"What?" Leo urged him impatiently. But what Gudrun said next nearly threw Leo completely off his seat.

"Aliens!" Gudrun replied in a cloaked whisper.

"*ALIENS?*" Leo shouted with disbelief. "You think *aliens* are the ones doing the snatching?" What was Gudrun thinking? This was no time for jokes!—the snatchers were getting away!

"Don't just think so," Gudrun continued; "*knows* so! But not the silly green, big-headed kind you'd be used ta seein' in ya picture books; but a dark kind—a vicious kind—with the taste for human blood!"

"You mean like . . . *Lunalings?*" said Leo, trying to stretch his brain back to the story of ugly little moon men that supposedly invade Earth and take things, like people's keys, for no apparent reason. Of course, it was just some silly fairy-tale parents used to make kids keep their rooms clean; no one actually believed it . . . or at least not anyone Leo knew.

Gudrun nudged Leo sharply in the ribs. "*Shh!*" he hissed at him. "Ya can't go yellin' words like that round these parts— 'less ya wanna wind up missin' like all these here trees!"

"Yeah, but aliens don't exist," Leo decided smartly, "— especially Lunalings. I mean, they're just an old wives' tale, like Bigfoot, or the Chupacabra. I'm almost eleven, you know. I don't really believe in that kinda stuff anymore."

Gudrun looked at Leo with a crooked grin. "Ah, ya think aliens are only make-believe, do ya? Well, then, ya got another thing comin' to ya! Don't go thinkin' I got meself a robotic eye here for nothin'. Not just any ol' human could manage ta knock *me* down, let alone be up ta stealin' so many of this city's trees without nobody seein' um! And that there nimbus cloud was filled with 'em; snatchin' our precious oxygen-makers in search of, er—well, who knows what!"

"Alright," said Leo, deciding it couldn't hurt to give Gudrun's tale a second thought. "Let's say it *was* Lunalings that took your eye and are stealing all of Riverdale's trees. Tell me, then: What would they want with *your* eye and all of *our* trees?"

"Er—um, that's just the thing . . . ," answered Gudrun, "dunno."

Leo sighed. It was now obvious that Gudrun had no inten-tion of talking to him more like an adult. And by the time they returned to Gudrun's driveway, the entire neighborhood lay completely treeless.

Terribly discouraged, Leo tried to get Gudrun back on a more normal-minded subject. "So how *did* you lose that eye of yours, anyway?" Leo asked, following Gudrun out of the go-kart and around to its back-wagon to help unload the tools and sort them in the shed.

Gudrun appeared deep in thought for a long moment before he said, "It was back last September, September the thirteenth—*hate ta think we're comin' up ta a year's anniversary! Anyhoo*, back then I was still workin' with the government, Space Engineer; and me wife, Begonia, was workin' in Section Twelve, the *private* section. We was both outside on our lunch break when she was tellin' me sumthin' 'bout some strange file she had intercepted from a satellite . . . or um, UFO! Sumthin' 'bout an eclipse! Then the next thing we knew, alarms were going off and we was runnin' for our lives—that's when I saw 'em!"

"Saw who?" Leo asked.

"The Lunalings!" answered Gudrun, more serious than ever. "Nasty little creatures with crescent-shaped foreheads, mouths full of razor-sharp teeth, and lizardy see-through skin. Looked a bit like a rotted gray peach, if ya ask me! And then I guess I was runnin' so fast that I hadn't noticed me Begonia had fallen behind. By the time I had turned 'round, she had vanished; and all that was left was a dark cloud, just like the one we saw here today, hovering above me head—they had snatched her!"

Leo looked at Gudrun with an unconvinced brow as he asked, "And what about your eye? How'd they get that?"

Gudrun himself looked confused as he tried to explain. "Well, it wasn't 'til half a year later when I woke up from me coma with a terrible pain comin' from deep within me skull, that I learned it, too, had disappeared. Luckily the doctors had already gotten Ol' Glassy's socket here in while I was still asleepin'—*can't stand getin' pricked by no robo-needles!* But I don't remember how they got it from me, them Lunalings, that is . . . I can only imagine it was sumthin' horrifyin'!"

"So what did the doctors say happened?" Leo asked.

"Well, that's just the trouble of it," replied Gudrun. "When I asked the doctor lady what had happened, she told me I had been in a car-jet accident; and I almost believed her, too— until she started talkin' all funny. At first, she tried tellin' me that I had never worked with the government . . . that I wasn't ever a space engineer . . . that I was, of all things, a mail manager! Can you believe *that*? I done got me a college education ta oversee empty-headed bots sortin' through people's mail? It didn't make sense . . .

"And then, ta make me even more angry, she tried tellin' me me dear Begonia had died in the accident. They had even gone so far as ta have a proper funeral for her, all the paperwork drawn up from the crash, and me boss's name at the post office; everything you could think of! But sumthin' wasn't clickin'. I had no other scars like you'd expect ta see from a car-jet accident . . . and I don't remember workin' at no stupid post office. All I know is that I know who I was and I know what I saw!"

"So what did you do then?" Leo asked, helping Gudrun untangle a mess of pork-q-wire.

"Well, luckily, I had heard over the news 'bout these here trees disappearin', just the same as me dear Begonia had, when I decided I'd do whatever it'd take ta find her. I got meself a job out here tree patrolling, as dangerous as it may be since I had a hunch those darn gizzards were the ones doin' the snatchin'! Luckily, we got ta see that there nimbus cloud today, so now I knows it was them for sure!"

Leo couldn't wrap his head around it: Gudrun had to be joking, but he sounded so serious. And the date Mrs. Dawgspat "disappeared," September thirteenth, was Leo's birthday! That would explain why he hadn't seen her since, especially during all his time spent tree patrolling. But it simply couldn't be true. Aliens don't exist; everybody knows that, and besides, there was no reason for a doctor not to tell Gudrun the truth . . .

It was a nice try, but Leo wasn't going to buy it that quickly.

"So . . . ," said Leo, deciding to let Gudrun run off on him with his wild story, "what do we do now?"

"Nothin' left to do, I s'pose," said Gudrun, sorting the last of the tools into the shed. "At least not for you, anyhow. I'll be on the lookout once we get some new trees in, but by then, I'm sure you'll have your nose stuck somewhere in a unibook! So I guess I best be getin' ya your check . . ."

Leo had imagined he would have been much more excited about having the last few days of summer off from tree patrol; but instead, he nearly wished he could continue working with Mr. Dawgspat, especially now to see if there was any ounce of truth behind his crazy tale.

Gudrun rummaged through his techni-jacket in search of Leo's payment.

"Argh, that's right," he grunted, pulling out a miraculous amount of lint from his pockets, and, of all things unexpected, a small white mouse, "Forgot ta order me one of them money-drones from the bank! Is it okay if I get it to ya later?"

Leo didn't mind. His family had what they needed now, thanks to the Joneses having bought his prized ticket.

"Sure," said Leo, who was more intrigued with Gudrun's pet than anything else. "So, where'd you get the rat?"

"Argh, he's not a *rat!*" Gudrun barked protectively. "This here is a mouse. And his name's Archimedes, if yer so polite ta ask."

"Sorry," Leo muttered.

"None the matter, he was Begonia's pet."

"But what's he doing in your coat?"

"Oh, I uh, take him with me everywhere now that she's gone," explained Gudrun. "Lil' brute gone run off on me a few weeks ago when I was takin' out Muffin an' Princess—nearly put me back inta me coma, too! Luckily, he showed up after I put out some of Begonia's famous cookies onta the porch—er, well, me own attempt at makin' 'em . . . *still not sure why they turned out so gooey . . . Anyhoo*, I think sumthin' tried ta eat the little fella, thus the wee bandage on his leg."

Leo recognized the mouse at once: It was the same mouse Misses Kisses had been chasing in the kitchen and that had so cleverly snuck inside his rocket box at the competition.

"Well, thanks, Gudrun," said Leo finally, petting the side of the mouse's fluffy white belly. "If you find the snatchers, or um, 'Lunalings,' before school starts, you know where to find me."

"Sure do," Gudrun hollered after him. And Leo hopped on his bike and headed back home down Sylvan Avenue.

The next few days were possibly the longest days of summer that Leo had ever experienced. The entire family was at home, with Mrs. Gray prepping Lily on reading and numbers for kindergarten, and Mr. Gray arguing all day over the phone about prices with various security companies, having finally decided to order some semi-high-tech surveillance-cameras for Minutes & Widgets. Everyone, including Misses Kisses, left Leo to himself, which probably wasn't the *best* idea, given Leo seemed to spend every second of the day imagining rotten banana peels being tossed across his new school's cafeteria at his archaic clothing—he hadn't exactly been "killed" by tree patrolling.

Then, at last, the day before public school was set to begin arrived.

"LEO!" Mrs. Gray shouted down the hall while sorting through the junk dropped off by the mail-o-drone. "YOU'VE GOT A LETTER!"

Leo let his unibook drop onto his bed and ran to the front entry, eager to see who it was from. But his excitement faded when he read the label: BRONX MIDDLE SCHOOL.

Leo, grudgingly, opened it up; and as he did, a stern-faced woman emerged on the front of the holographic card and read:

Dear Leo,

We would like to remind you that your first day at the Bronx Middle School will begin tomorrow morning at precisely 8:00 a.m. Please be sure to bring your unibook, two number 2,000 electro-pencils, and your most intelligent behavior.

Sincerely,

Principal Whitwad

P.S. The word "precisely" can be defined as definitely, strictly stated, and/or fixed. Therefore, arrivals to class past 8:00 a.m. will be awarded a special hour lecture at the end of the day on The Joys of Punctuality with Dean Chitz.

Leo tried to keep his hand from crushing the letter. Why, this year, with Gavin and Aabher going off to Luna City, school at Saint Margaret's was going to be better than ever! Even if classes had already started there, Leo had seen plenty of new kids getting accepted late all the time. He was certain they could make some sort of arrangement for him, especially with his impeccable grades and having just won the National Science Competition for free-entry to Luna City!

However, as Leo put down the holocard, he noticed another envelope addressed to him. Leo opened the second envelope much more quickly (having recognized the wobbly scrawl); and as he did, a drone-o-card fluttered out with his Grandma waving to him from a beach (alongside his Grandpa, snoring underneath a large yellow-and-white striped umbrella). His Grandma smiled and read:

Aloha Leo!
Hope this year is special and sweet,
Wish I could be there, but I'm off with your
Gramps in the tropical heat;
It's not every year that a boy turns eleven,
So here are some zozobucks to get yourself
something worth two cents and a melon!

Hugs and Kisses,

Granny and—(she nudged her husband impatiently to wake him, but he instead mumbled something which sounded like "van fan cooler" and rolled over)—*Grandpa G.*

Wait, Leo thought to himself wildly—*he couldn't have missed it . . .*

Had he?

No—there was just no way!

Was there?

Leo dashed into the kitchen, shouting across the living room: "Mom! What day is it today?"

"Check the calendar, honey! That's what it's there for!" Mrs. Gray echoed back.

Leo hurried to the calendar on the fridge, hoping it wasn't too late:

It was Wednesday . . .

September . . .

THE THIRTEENTH!

Leo couldn't *think* of how he had almost missed it! It must have been the change of schools (as he normally would have been in class on such a day); but there was no way his dad could say no to him asking to return to Saint Margaret's now—not on a day like today—not on his eleventh birthday!

6

GUDRUN'S GIFT

Unbeknownst to Leo, who had nearly missed turning eleven, Mrs. Gray already had everything in the oven. Within an hour, the entire house was filled with the aroma of freshly baked carrot cake and warm vanilla frosting. Leo, however, couldn't wait for dessert; but not for the purposes of eating it, nor for the gifts following, but rather to ask his father one last time if he could continue classes at Saint Margaret's. He was certain it would be a foolproof "Yes" on a day like today!

Dinner was composed of Leo's favorites: spaghetti with

meatballs, a side of green beans, and buttered French baguettes. It was also Mr. Gray's favorite meal, and that being so, he was extra chipper at the dining table.

"Well, Leo, today's your big day," he said proudly, twirling a sizable forkful of the long, sticky noodles. "You're no longer a little kid anymore, now that you're eleven. And I'm sure this summer out tree patrolling has taught you some much-needed responsibility."

It had, but Leo didn't know it. He had instead had so much fun working with Mr. Dawgspat that the summer hadn't been a drag at all!

"I guess I do feel a *little* more responsible," said Leo, hoping that was the response his father was looking for.

"Well, *I* feel like a piece of CAKE," demanded Lily, stuffing her headless doll's neck into a meatball.

"It's just up for Leo to say '*when*,'" prompted Mrs. Gray.

"Alright, alright," Leo allowed. He did, after all, have a very important wish to make.

Mr. Gray helped Mrs. Gray clear the table, and in a moment's time, the lights dimmed, and they returned with a triple-stacked carrot cake with eleven spindly candles on top of it. In shiny blue icing, it read:

Leo smiled, gazing at the rocket ship shooting off toward a lopsided moon.

"Mr. Winky's new *girlfriend* bumped into it this morning," grumbled Mrs. Gray, shooting Lily and her headless doll a perturbed look.

"It's perfect," Leo assured her, not imagining a cake looking any better.

The room grew quiet as everyone waited for Leo to make his wish. Leo held it in his mind, and then, with one large puff, blew out each of the eleven candles—minus one, which was semi-inhaled by Lily.

"*Soo!*" said Mrs. Gray excitedly. "What did you wish for?" She was privately hoping it was for a particular science book that she had pre-ordered to Leo's unibook and had rewrapped in silvery star paper.

Leo took another breath and said, "Well, it's just a wish . . . but I—"

"Go on!" his mother gushed impatiently.

"Okay, okay!" said Leo. "I wished I—I wished I could go back to Saint Margaret's!"

Anticipation built in Leo's fingertips as he crossed them underneath the dining table (hoping to hear an instant "Yes!"); but instead, as the seconds slipped into minutes, he found both of his parents sitting with sealed lips.

"Well, do *you* want to tell him?" Mrs. Gray whispered to her husband.

"What do you mean, 'do *I* want to tell him?'" Mr. Gray retorted, wiping his mouth evasively with his napkin.

"Tell me what?" Leo asked, suddenly worried that whatever it was that had gotten his parents so stiff, was not good news for him returning to Saint Margaret's.

"Fine, I'll say it," said Mr. Gray, settling it. "Leo, you have proven to us over the summer that you do deserve to continue classes at Saint Margaret's, if that's what you wished; but I'm afraid plans have already been arranged for you to—" However, these words were already more than Leo could bear.

"But I *can't* go to public school—the bots there are *TERRENDOUS*! They don't know anything about ANYTHING! I won't even get a proper education! And the kids there will—" But it appeared as though Leo's new age kicked in. "Forget it," he said, lowering his head. "I guess I'll just . . . get used to it . . ."

Mrs. Gray gave her husband a look of frustration. "I think, dear, it may be best if we hold off on the cake this year until *after* presents?"

"Oh, right, of course," Mr. Gray agreed.

"Mine first!" Lily shouted, jumping out of her chair and running to her room to retrieve a box wrapped with a hundred strips of sparkly unicorn tape and globs of glitter glue.

"Here!" she said, passing Leo her gift proudly. "I did ALL the wrapping myself."

Leo tried to suppress the disappointment that was still radiating inside him as he took the gift from his little sister. But as he opened it, he was surprised to find something he hadn't seen in several years: a small toy rocket ship figurine that his father had given to him back when he was only six or seven.

"I thought maybe you'd like it back before you—OH!" Lily stammered, having been alerted by a sideways wink from Mrs. Gray not to say anything more.

Leo didn't notice. He was simply glad to have found his lost rocket!

Mrs. Gray passed Leo her present next, and Leo at once guessed what it was from the weight and shape of it. "*The Entirety of Science*, by Dr. Bombardious Row . . . ," he read aloud, sliding his finger across his ultra-thin unibook, discovering its newest download. "This is perfect, Mom . . . it's just what I've been wanting." However, Leo couldn't feel as appreciative as he would have normally for such a great gift; the thought of every kid at public school teasing him for his century-old clothing was running rampant through his head.

"And no birthday's complete without a gift from Dad!" said Mr. Gray, giving Leo his present, which was wrapped in plain packaging paper from the store.

Leo expected it was going to be something "ticking and timeless" (just as it was every year). By now, Leo had enough vintage watches from birthdays past to open his own Minutes and Widgets. But as Leo tore away at the wrapping, his fingers came to a halt: a Luna Watch box was sitting underneath it.

Leo, however, quickly shook *that* idea out of his head. He knew better than to think that it was anything other than recycling; the newest watch he had ever owned was from the year 2000!

Though as Leo lifted the box's lid, his mouth fell open at the sight.

"Wait—*what*?" he stammered breathlessly, staring at the perfectly new Luna Watch perched within its box. "This—this is incredible! . . . But I—I don't get it? How did you—"

"Well, I figured you'd need it—you know, to keep time and all at your new school," said Mr. Gray, craning his neck furtively across the dining table to examine the high-tech timepiece. "But before you get all worked up about starting school tomorrow, you still have Mr. Dawgspat's gift to open."

Leo had forgotten about the payment he had been expecting from Gudrun. Maybe with the money he had earned over the summer tree patrolling his dad might allow him to buy something less dated to wear to his new school! But as Leo opened the long, slightly disheveled envelope (careful not to rip the money it contained inside) he didn't find the flashy green color of zozobucks—but rather, something else.

In it was a simple white pamphlet with a holographic seal that read:

LCSC

"LCSC?" Leo wondered aloud.

But what the inscription meant made Leo jump from his seat:

Luna . . .
City . . .
SPACE . . .
CAMP!

"It can't be!" Leo muttered, giving himself a pinch. "Gudrun's given me a ticket to Luna City?" Though just as soon as he said it, Leo was sitting back down as his father looked at him and said, "You know my thoughts on the moon, Leo . . ."

Leo nodded.

"But," he continued, "your mother and I have decided—given you had rightfully won that first ticket of yours, and you did more than make up for the loss it caused the family by selling it to the Joneses—that it should be *your* decision on which school you attend."

Leo looked at his parents in disbelief.

"You mean . . . you'll *actually* let me go to Luna City?" He turned his gaze meaningfully toward his father.

"That is, of course, unless you'd prefer to go back to Saint Margaret's?"

Leo shook his head, still in a state of shock as he shouted, "No, not at all!—I want to go to the Lunar Academy!—I want to go to Luna City!"

"Well, then, you best get a run on to Mr. Dawgspat's to thank him before it gets too late," prompted Mr. Gray. "If it wasn't for him not wanting that ticket, you might have been starting school tomorrow somewhere else!"

"Right," said Leo, bolting from the table before his parents could change their minds. "I'll be back in a bit!"

"But what about—" Mrs. Gray shouted after him, only to be cut off by the slam of the door, "the *cake*?"

Leo felt higher than the clouds, or the moon even, as he made his way down Sylvan Avenue to Gudrun's. For the first time in his life, things finally seemed to be going his way: he had gotten his favorite toy rocket back from Lily; a new science book from his mom; an actual high-tech timepiece from his dad; and, of all things unexpected, a ticket to Luna City from his neighbor, Mr. Dawgspat. And as Leo reached the Dawgspat's front lawn, he was thrilled to find that Gudrun was already out in it, busily attaching a funny looking clawlike contraption to the roof of his flying go-kart.

"Hey, Gudrun!" Leo shouted, hopping off his bike.

Gudrun, however, didn't seem his typical self. "Oh, uh, hey there, Leo," he replied gloomily.

"What's the matter?" Leo asked.

"It's the anniversary . . . one whole year now—"

"One whole year for what?"

"One whole year since I lost her," answered Gudrun, ever darker. "Thought I'd already have her back by now. Feel a bit like a failure, you know?"

"Oh," said Leo, who wasn't particularly the best at being consoling. "So um . . . what's that you're working on?"

Gudrun looked content with the change of course.

"What's *this*?" he bellowed, petting the large chunk of metal. "This here's a mechanical arm!"

"What for?" Leo wondered, looking at it weirdly.

"Ta catch me them gizzards with when they return, o' course!" said Gudrun. "This time, they can be certain I'll be ready for 'em!"

"That's—er—great," said Leo. "Well, I just wanted to stop by, to, you know, thank you—for the gift."

"So ya got the ticket then, did ya?" said Gudrun. A wide grin stretched across his face. "See, told ya the pay would be worth it!"

"But, if you don't mind me asking," said Leo, who couldn't help but imagine that Gudrun could have otherwise sold the ticket for a small fortune, "why didn't *you* want to go?"

"Arr—I was thinkin' 'bout it," replied Gudrun. "Got me a hunch there's more goin' on inside of that there moon than what the government's lettin' me or you know . . . But it'd be too risky. If they caught me snoopin' around—a guy as big as me, you know, ain't too good at snoopin'!—who knows what they'd do. Figured I've got me a better position down here ta try ta get a lead on anything suspicious!

"Not ta mention, Leo, you're a whole lot smarter than that there Garvin kid—or whatever his name is. It really got me jarred-up ta see him take away that ticket from ya like he did."

Leo couldn't help but smile. "Well, thanks, Gudrun. It means a lot, and you know, if you ever need someone to talk to about tree burglary stuff—or if you *do* catch one of those, er—'gizzards,' I'll be just a visi-chat away!"

Gudrun let out a deep laugh and a snivel all at the same time. He threw out his large burly arms to hug Leo goodbye, and at the sudden realization of what was heading his way, Leo hurried to sneak a breath, but missed; and in the next second his nostrils were engulfed with a painstakingly familiar stench.

"Oh, and uh, Leo! I almost forgot," Gudrun shouted, letting Leo plummet to his feet like a sack of potatoes as he rummaged through his jacket pocket. "I, uh, wanted ta see if you'd take Archimedes with?"

Leo looked at Gudrun strangely.

"*Uff, I know*, it might be hard gettin' the little fella through security, but I figured without any of your family up there with ya, ya might be needin' an extra bit o' company."

"Sure," said Leo, taking Archimedes gladly. "I'd be happy to."

Gudrun released another sniffle and wiped away a stray tear, giving Archimedes one last pet goodbye. "You'll be alright now," he said to him gingerly. "You'll be alright."

"And you!" said Gudrun, turning to Leo and placing a firm hand on his shoulder by means of goodbye, "you're gonna be alright, too."

"Well, thanks, again, Gudrun," said Leo, putting Archimedes into his side-bag and hopping on his bike. "I'll be sure to let you know what everything is like as soon as I get up there."

"You bet ya will!" Gudrun hollered as Leo headed back home.

That evening Leo found himself in bed three whole hours earlier than usual, more excited (and reasonably more nervous) than he had ever been to fall asleep before. Only, sleep was the last thing his brain would allow. His mind danced wildly over the day's events and projections of what life was going to be like in Luna City. It wasn't until a quarter after midnight before Leo finally caught a glimpse of a fluffy white sheep; but just as soon as he spotted it, it was being startled off by the dreadful tune of his mother's humming.

"Already?" Leo yawned into his pillow.

"Yes, UP!" Mrs. Gray snapped, digging around hastily through his closet. "You can't expect me to do all your packing for you. I'm not a fancy-dancy robo-maid!"

Leo bolted to life—he had completely forgotten about packing!

"Unibook? . . . check. Socks? . . . check. Underwear? . . ." He paused for a second, looking slightly unimpressed at his mother's excessive packing. "Triple check!"

". . . *Archimedes?*"

Fear washed over Leo as Misses Kisses' tail slipped past the door. He rushed to his nightstand, hoping the mouse was still inside, and as he pulled open the drawer, he was relieved to find Archimedes was right where he had left him: neatly tucked away inside a small toy house he had borrowed from Lily (and properly out of view from his mother!).

"All set?" Mrs. Gray asked, cramming another whitey tighty into Leo's suitcase.

"Nearly," Leo replied, slipping Archimedes into the mesh area of his book-bag.

"Oh, and I almost forgot!" said Mrs. Gray, retrieving a long floral-wrapped package from the top of Leo's dresser. "Last night you ran off without opening Mrs. McGregor's gift!"

Leo wasn't the *slightest* bit excited to open it. Mrs. McGregor was known for giving the most bizarre and embarrassing gifts of all time. Last year for his birthday he had received an extra-large violet-shaded sweater with a hundred electronic change-your-color feathers sticking out of it; and the year before that, a snowman-infested holographic scarf! Even if her gifts were from a modern high-end designer, they were far more embarrassing than Leo's twenty-first-century clothes.

But as Leo opened the box, he was receiving another pinch.

"*Soo*, what do you think?" Mrs. Gray asked eagerly, watching Leo unfold the brand-new ozone-compressive tracksuit with select-your-color electronic stripes and matching insta-fit sneakers. "I might have said a word or two to make sure she got the proper sizing . . ."

"It's great," said Leo, shaking his head with disbelief. He had always dreamed of having one just like it. "It's more than great—but can I, *wear* it?" Leo couldn't imagine that his dad would be okay with him going out in public wearing something from 2113!

"I don't see why not," said Mr. Gray from the doorway. "After all, it's not every day that a boy gets to go to the moon!"

Leo was beyond ecstatic. "Great!" he said happily. "Then there's just one more thing?"

"What's that?" his parents asked simultaneously.

"Could I—er—get some privacy, please?"

"Oh, yes! Right! Ahem—of course!" they quickly agreed, leaving Leo, at long last, to himself inside his bedroom.

Leo hurried on his new modern outfit and was thrilled to find that everything fit *and looked* better than his old school uniform did. Leo took one last look at himself in his mirror, and then back to his beloved room. He would be leaving his astronomy posters taped across the walls; his collection of antique model rockets scattered beside stacks of vintage comics; his shoebox filled with all his things that needed safekeeping from Lily, neatly arranged at its tape-marker underneath his bed for her future discovery; and, of course, (though not without minor hesitation about packing him) his stuffed teddy.

"Well, Frostbite," said Leo to his toy bear, "take care of yourself. And *try* to take care of Lily."

The polar bear stared at Leo blankly, but that was enough for Leo to know that he'd do exactly as he was told. And as Leo left his room, he found his mother waiting in the hall, with Lily draped over her shoulders like a baby possum.

"So, we're going to keep behind," she muttered softly,

holding herself back from a certain onset of tears. "Just your father is going to take you."

"Don't worry, Mom," said Leo stoically. "I'll be fine. And Dad's got you one of those new visis now, so you can see me, just as I am here now, at your side, whenever you'd like!"

Mrs. Gray gave her son a warm hug goodbye. "Then I request a call every night!"

And as the rickety old Beetle pulled away from the Grays' family's drive, Mrs. Gray, at long last, cried.

"*So . . . ,* " Leo started stressfully, breaking the semi-tense air as he and his father putzed onto the laser-lit highway, "I had been meaning to ask you—"

Mr. Gray allowed for the question with a raised brow.

"—*Relatively* speaking—if the store hadn't gotten robbed—and if I still had that ticket, the Luna City ticket— would you have even let me go? I mean, don't you hate the moon, technology, and all that stuff?"

Mr. Gray looked expectantly at his son. He wanted to tell Leo the truth, but he simply couldn't tell him about why he was now willing to let him venture so far away from home. He couldn't tell Leo the real reason why he had been so determined for him to not have anything to do with a government competition, or why his mother had been so dogmatic that Leo go to it against his will: These were things that Leo would learn in time, but that time was not yet.

"I don't *hate* the moon . . . or technology, for that matter, Leo, but certain things aren't always up to me to decide."

"What do you mean?" Leo asked.

"Back before you were born, this planet was a different place. Cars were different . . . clothes were different . . . heck, even people were different! But then, suddenly, things began to change. And all this change, I guess you can say, scared me. It scared me to think you'd one day grow up different from me."

"But I *am* different from you," said Leo, looking rather worried by his father's enormous ears. "Though, I still have your ears."

"And that's just the thing," said Mr. Gray importantly. "You'll always be a Gray, whether you're here on Earth, or up at that moon school—and don't you go forgetting that! Lunar gravity is said to do strange things to the cerebellum!—but enough of that—looks as though we're here."

Leo turned his attention out the window to find that the massive multi-modular airport came with an even larger crowd of onlookers as the yellow Beetle wheezed and puffed into the terminal.

"So then," said Mr. Gray, helping Leo gather his things from the trunk. "You're set to take off at 8:30 . . . Gate E10 . . . Oh, and try to take care of that watch I gave you, remember—"

"I know, I know," said Leo. And he recited: "'What once is new will someday be old too!' Thanks, Dad."

And as Mr. Gray hugged his son goodbye, Leo finally felt as though he understood him—though not fully—but enough to no longer be mad at him for keeping things as he did.

Leo watched the rickety old Beetle rattle away from the

terminal, then turned, facing the airport's entrance; he was, for the first time in his life, completely on his own.

Leo walked through the large automatic doorway of the terminal and into a room filled with a billion busy people and their hovering luggage. Having never been to an airport before, he was naturally taken aback by it all, especially the loud whooshing of the oval-shaped airjets landing and departing outside the domed window, and at the number of hover-bots busily buzzing about, directing people which way to go.

Not entirely sure where he was headed and without much time to try to figure it out, Leo asked a nearby robo-guard to point him in the right direction.

"Excuse me, sir—" he said to the bot, "do you happen to know which line it is for Zolta Airlines?"

The robo-guard looked highly unimpressed with Leo's obvious request as he pointed to an enormous line that started right beside him and said, "You're in it!"

After fifteen minutes of wondering what language the people in front of him were speaking, Leo, at last, reached the checkpoint.

"NEXT!" yelled a beefy man from behind the ticket-inspection podium. Leo stepped up and handed him his documents. The man scanned Leo's ticket with a funny robotic contraption around his head, and the next second, a miniature identification-bot was fluttering around Leo's eyes, shining an ultra-bright laser light in them!

Half-blind, Leo was motioned to pass and was prompted by another robo-guard into the next queue. "Bags on the robo-check," the bot instructed loudly, "then on to line two!" Meanwhile, the man behind him restarted shouting, "NEXT! NEXT! NEXT!"

Leo watched what the people ahead of him were doing to better prepare for his turn. He took one last peek at Archimedes and placed his bags on the robo-check: a conveyer-belt covered by a clear glass tube, filled with a hundred miniature poking prongs and robotic-arms flashing strange devices. Leo was then waved forward into a thin black tunnel by another bot, where he waited for instructions on what to do next. But then (without warning) the floor began to move below him and a low humming noise buzzed through his head.

The tunnel lit up a dim scarlet red, and a melodic voice said, "Commencing bomb and weapons check."

Leo's eyes widened with panic as a series of robotic arms came hurtling toward him, and as the tunnel lit green after a few invasive frisks, it said, "Hold breath for sterilization process." The tunnel then filled with a chalk-like substance, of which Leo (who hadn't been properly prepared) got an unfortunate mouthful.

"Flu and Virus Antibody," the voice went on, as Leo was moved farther down the tunnel where he was pricked by a disposable needle, had a sour fizzling tablet placed under his tongue, and then, after a few more beeps and a buzz, he was through!

Leo grabbed ahold of his freshly pricked arm and hurried to find his things, which were (stressfully) still being inspected. A rather robust security lady sat scanning Leo's bags between long sluggish sips from a hovering coffee mug. Leo could see from the corner of the waiting area that Archimedes was smack-dab in the middle of the screen.

Leo watched on anxiously as the security guard stared intently at the screen for a moment and then summoned over another guard on duty. The two began talking, glancing periodically at Leo. And then, to Leo's horror, they started to laugh.

"Now there's a good prank, Jo!" the second guard cackled, pointing at the x-ray. "A rat in a bag!"

"You're telling me," agreed the first, shaking her head unacceptably. "That's my FIFTH stuntzer this morning! And I bet he thought he had one on us—a RAT! Can you believe that? They've been on the extinction list now for what—?"

"AGES!" the second guard chuckled, hitting a large green button to let Leo's bags go through. "My wife says we ought to thank all that Antisocial Media for the overtime we've been seeing on our paychecks!"

Leo looked at the two guards in utter disbelief; they clearly hadn't even considered that Archimedes could have been a lab mouse (which were a far cry from being extinct!).

Leo didn't waste a second to reclaim his bags, eager to get out of there before either of them could think of it. He quickly pulled out his electro-ticket to double-check his gate, but as he stepped into the terminal's main hub, he soon realized just how enormous the airport was. There were a hundred multi-layered tunnels swirling around in every direction—thousands of tubular glass elevators shooting off toward their connecting gates, all crammed with more people and robots than Leo had ever seen in one place.

"Alright . . . ," said Leo stressfully, stepping out into the throng, "now I just have to get to an elevator . . ." But as Leo made his way through a hundred bumps of hurried bottoms and whacks from their floating suitcases, he soon found that getting *inside* an elevator wasn't any easier than getting *to* one. Each time its doors would open, they'd instantly fill up, and before Leo had a chance to get in, the elevator took off, leaving Leo more smushed between the crowd than he was before.

For three whole minutes, Leo stood there, watching dizzily as the doors whooshed open and then shut, and then open and then shut, causing Leo to think that he wouldn't get inside an elevator at all. Until, at last, a hover-bot caught on to his dilemma and gave him a helpful push in.

"Gate E," the elevator announced in a series of foreign languages. All the while, Leo stood there, feeling somewhat like a canned sardine.

And the second the door reopened, Leo at once shoved his way out!

Leo looked at his Luna Watch; there were just two more minutes before the waiting area would seal itself off for departure. He proceeded to reread his ticket one last time to make sure he was in the right place.

Zolta Airlines

Passenger: **LEO GRAY**   Class: **ECONOMY**
Departing from: **NEW YORK CITY, NY**
Arriving to: **JACKSONVILLE, FL**
Gate: **E10**   Seat: **B8**   Time: **8:30**

Then hurrying over to the ticketing counter, he passed his ticket to the robotic attendant and watched as the jet base lined up outside the window below, connecting to the detachable waiting area.

"Your seat, B8, will be down the middle, on the left," said the robot, scanning Leo's ticket and directing him through a security-blocker into a large, rounded waiting area with rows of body-conforming pod-chairs nestled beneath a dome of insta-tint glass.

Leo, however, couldn't care less about the particularities of the airjet, being far too worried about how to get himself buckled! But when Leo finally found his seat, his luck appeared to be missing. B8 was next to a girl who was loudly humming the melody of some annoying tune.

Leo shuffled his bag into the pod-chair's side compartment, trying to avoid drawing attention to himself; but just as he got himself seated and was having a quick check on

Archimedes, an extra-large man with an extra-large bag of Galacto Chips and a hovering Slurpee, crammed himself into the pod-chair next to him. The girl's previously distracted attention turned away from the window, straight toward Leo.

"You know, you're not supposed to have *pets* in here," she whispered to him, taking off her headphones and peering nosily into Leo's bag, "especially rats!"

"He's not a *rat*," said Leo, starting to panic.

"Oh, *right*," said the girl, looking at him weirdly, "and I'm a MIRAGE!"

Leo's face went blank.

"Calm down," the girl laughed, clearly catching on to his dilemma. "I'm not going to *rat* you out."

"Thanks," said Leo, exchanging a half-hearted grin with the girl whose hair couldn't decide if it was blonde or brown, long or short, or whether her eyes wanted to be blue or green.

"So, um, if you don't mind me asking," said Leo, hoping to get the girl off the topic of his forbidden cargo, "where is it you're headed?"

"Well, if it's any interest to you, Mr. I-look-polite-but-don't-ask-for-names, *I'm* headed to the Lunar Academy!"

Her? Going to *Luna City?* Leo hoped she wouldn't share any of his classes—or try to follow him around as if they were already best friends! She was already pretty nosy from the looks of it, but she did have a point: It was rude of him not to introduce himself.

"Oh, uh—right," Leo stammered, reaching his hand out to

shake hers, still at a loss for words at having been so corrected. "My name's Leo, Leo Gray."

A sudden bell-like noise rang through the airjet, and the pilot's voice sounded over the intercom: "Good morning, folks! Time's now two minutes to eight-thirty-and-a-second and we're getting ready for takeoff. We'll be arriving in sunny Florida in approximately ten minutes. Outside's clear skies with a bit-o-weather as we pass over Georgia; so go on ahead and buckle up!"

Leo's face turned a shade of cabbage as the announcement reached its end. And as the airjet's pod-chairs began shifting back toward the dimming ceiling, and the waiting area detached from the terminal, connecting to the jet-base below, the girl sitting next to him seemed to notice that, too.

"Well, my name's Andromeda, An-dro-*may*-da Groves. And that there in front of you is a barf bag—you know, if you're feeling *dizzy*! Just um, if you don't mind . . . ," she said, nudging her head toward the snoring man beside them, "lean toward the *other side?*"

"Sure," said Leo with embarrassment, though he hoped he wouldn't need to use it.

CHAPTER

7

A MYSTERIOUS NOTE

Thehe airjet's engines beamed to life at 8:30 on the dot. Leo held on feverishly to the armrests and tried to imagine himself sitting someplace safer—like on a swing at the park, or even safer yet, on the sofa back home. But with the floor beneath him buzzing him like an upset hornet, he was instead reminded of one of those horrible roller coaster rides at the fair.

Andromeda passed Leo her headset. "Here," she said, "try this."

Leo looked at the jell-shifting earbuds skeptically.

"Just put them on—*you'll see!*"

Leo placed the buds to his ears, which soon suctioned all around them, so perfectly that he couldn't hear a single thing other than the music and his own thoughts. It was a strange song, whatever Andromeda Groves was listening to: the sound of rain, a soft rhythmic humming, and some sort of bizarre techno drum. Leo tried to distinguish exactly what the humming noise was, but before he could, a miniature city appeared outside the airjet's window.

"Hey, thanks," said Leo, surprised by his sudden ease as he returned the headset to its owner, watching the view of the city exchange itself for a thousand sunlit clouds.

"And what about your rat?" Andromeda asked, looking into Leo's bag.

"I told you, he's not a *rat*," said Leo. "He's a mouse—and his name is Archimedes."

"So you're sneaking a *mouse* into Space Camp?" said Andromeda, looking at Leo as though he were crazy. "You do know if they find him, they'll never let him through to Luna City?"

Leo did know, but he was bringing him for a friend, and that was all the convincing he needed. Besides, it's not as though Archimedes could get into that much trouble—all he did was sleep!

"He is pretty cute, though," Andromeda allowed, petting the side of his fluffy white belly.

"I guess," said Leo. He quickly put Archimedes away and

opted for his new science download instead. He hoped *that* would prove a better encouragement for Andromeda Groves to start minding her own business, but instead, as Leo slid his unibook open, she said even louder, "DR. BOMBARDIOUS ROW! I've read *all* about him." She helped herself to swipe through the book's halo-pages. "He's said to be a genius— *obviously since he claims to know everything about every single branch of science!* So I'm guessing you're hoping to get placed in the Science Sectional?"

"'The Science Sectional?'" Leo repeated, looking at Andromeda strangely.

"You know, at the *Lunar Academy?*"

Leo's face showed a definite haze.

"Well, everyone's split into different Sectionals—or work groups within the city—after core lectures finish, based on what our talents are," Andromeda explained.

"*Work* groups?" Leo repeated with surprise.

"It's not actually '*work*,'" said Andromeda, "if you love what you're doing. That's what stress-free economy is all about. The academy will help us figure out what work we're naturally inclined to excel at, removing the need for any sort of corrupt monetary system.

"Anyway, there are Sectionals for nearly everything: mathematics, arts, sciences, and so on. And each offers opportunities to work under world-renowned experts, like Dr. Row. I figured with you having his book and all, that *that* would be the Sectional you'd want to be placed in."

"I guess I hadn't looked more into it," said Leo honestly, having never heard of any "Sectionals" before.

"Well, don't worry," said Andromeda, "we'll get to find out which Sectional we'll be placed in during orientation . . . *after* the placement exam."

"'The placement *exam*?'" repeated Leo.

"*Wow*," said Andromeda, shaking her head and starting to laugh. "I can't BELIEVE I actually thought you didn't know where you were going!"

Leo let out a short chuckle to confirm Andromeda's assumption of him joking; however, inside he felt completely chagrined: He actually *didn't* know all that much about where he was headed!

"So how did you get your ticket?" Leo finally asked.

"At a code hacking competition," answered Andromeda, indifferent. "You and I are really lucky you know—other than the small few who were allowed to buy their way in, or were specially 'gifted' tickets from the government, no one else is ever going to get to live in Luna City—I've heard it's reached capacity!"

Leo hadn't yet stopped to consider that not just anyone could go to the moon. If he had, he probably would have asked Gudrun how he had received his ticket in the first place. This left Leo to only wonder that maybe Gudrun really *hadn't* been kidding about having worked for the government—though he was clearly pulling his leg about Lunalings existing . . . or so Leo had himself happily convinced.

"And what about your family?" Leo wondered, trying to

get the silly thought of ugly little moon-men pulling out Gudrun's eye from his head. "Are they going, too?"

"No . . . ," said Andromeda, for the first time, dispirited. "My parents, they—um—died a few years back, in a boat-jetting accident. I've lived with my grandmother, in Quebec, ever since—and she's *much* too old for space travel: She's almost one hundred and seven! So it will just be me up there, along with my cousin Pavo, from Brazil. He won his ticket for his skills at playing Ping-Pong."

But before Leo could ask anything else, a slight trembling shook the floor below them. Leo's hands hurried to the armrests as the pilot's voice rattled in, "H-H-Hey there a-a-again! Just that l-l-little bit-o-w-w-weather we were e-e-expecting over G-G-Georgia! We'll be s-s-starting our d-d-descent to the Space Coast Regional Airport s-s-shortly; so go on a-a-ahead and b-b-buckle up!"

Leo watched as the clouds above him shifted to a bitter gray. *It would be a very long drop*, he thought to himself, which rightfully prompted his glance at the barf bag.

"*You can let go now,*" said Andromeda, chuckling as Leo's hand lay clammily clenched over hers on the armrest. At the sudden realization of this, Leo quickly returned it to its proper place!

The man, who had been previously snoring like a broken lawnmower beside them, had now woken up and was yawning like an ape without covering his mouth, consuming the bulk of Leo's personal airspace. Leo couldn't remember a time in his life when he was ever more annoyed by a stranger, or rather two, as Andromeda sat there, giggling away. But right when Leo was starting to think there was no way anyone could be more off-putting, the man's blubbery elbow stretched itself out an inch more and bumped straight into his bag of Galacto Chips. In an instant, the chips flew into the air and then, in a faster instant, tumbled back down, landing all over Leo's lap!

"Turbulence," the man chuckled jocosely, trying to salvage the bits and pieces from the armrest. Yes, next time Leo traveled in an airjet, he would try to see if he could get one of those nicer individual pod-chairs where he could seal himself off completely and not have to worry about nosey girls or neighbors spilling their chips!

As the airjet finally connected to the terminal below, to Leo's relief, everyone found their way off without any pushing or shoving; however, his walk down to baggage claim with Andromeda wasn't any more pleasurable than his flight in, as she made sure to tease him every step of the way about his date with "Mr. Spillingchips."

"You should have *SEEN* your FACE!" she burst out, beaming. "Honestly, if I were a doctor, my diagnosis for you would be you're claustrophobic!"

"Yeah, well, you're *not* a doctor," said Leo. "And I'm *not* claustrophobic. Anyway, how is it again that we're supposed to get to Space Camp from here?" he asked as the two shot down a spiraling elevator to a lower level to claim their bags.

"They're going to have a shuttle waiting for us," said Andromeda, scanning her pick-up ticket at an electro-claim booth, which prompted a miniature drone to find her suitcase and float it toward her. "I can't *wait* to get there! Space Camp is supposed to be just like Luna City—it was their prototype before they started construction, and its location is totally top secret!"

The two soon spotted a short silver hover-bot waiting outside of baggage claim with a holographic sign lit above his head that read:

...ANDROMEDA GROVES...LEO GRAY...GRUSWALDIOUS PINWHEEL...

"*Gruswaldious Pinwheel?*" Leo wondered aloud, as he and Andromeda placed their bags next to the robotic chauffeur and waited for whoever Gruswaldious was to show up. "Who do you think *that* is?"

"I dare to say we're about to find out," said the robot wearily, directing everyone's attention to a comfortably plump boy who was chasing after a flyaway suitcase.

"BAD BAG! BAD BAG! SIT! STAY!" the boy shouted, tackling his ill-tempered piece of luggage to the ground, causing an array of multicolored undies to burst out of it.

"You must be Gruswaldious?" the bot inquired, wincing as he pulled a pair of lime-green briefs off his rectangular face. His name tag read simply: Weathers.

"That's me!" replied the boy, hopping up to shake Leo's and

113

Andromeda's hands with a hand full of undergarments. He was dressed in a vibrant display of purple, pink, and orange, and his hair was a short, meticulously spiked snow-white blond. "But you can just call me Grus!"

"Very well then, Grus," said the bot, assisting the group with their luggage, "we're the limojet out front."

But as they made their way toward it, it soon became apparent that Grus Pinwheel had no intention of having a quiet journey as he shouted in amazement, "By jimmeny-jim-jims—this limojet's A-MAZE-ING! . . . I call dibbies on the backseat! . . . What's this? No one's objecting? . . . *CRAY-Z'S!*"

Andromeda, of course, wasted no time to ask Grus the question that Leo was wanting to know most. "So how did you get *your* ticket?"

"At a singing competition," he answered cheerfully, stretching himself out over the entirety of the backseat. "My mum and mum'mum say I have the voice of a canary. Would you like me to sing something?"

"*Um . . . ,*" said Andromeda. But before Leo had the chance to mention that he had actually been looking forward to admiring the limojet's ultra soundproof cabin, they were taking off and Grus began to sing:

> 'Tis the sky, oh, very high,
> My dearest Luna City!
> I'd once be shy, my love, my pride,
> My dearest luna moooon!

To you, I sing, oh, starlight beam,
I think you are so pretty!
'Tis thy song, so sing along,
Lunaaa, I love you!

At the end of that, everyone had to clap: Grus Pinwheel really could sing like a canary—*or at least like some sort of bird . . .*

"Where'd you learn to sing like *that*?" Leo asked, instantly impressed with Grus's vocal capabilities.

"Probably the bathtub . . . ," Grus replied, looking as though he were giving it some serious thought. "That's where I belt out most of my tunes!"

"And let me guess," said Andromeda, "your first composition was about three little ducks?"

"Actually, I think it was about three little dingos," said Grus thoughtfully. "Do you know what a dingo is? . . . It's a feral dog, from Australia—that's where I'm from!—and their pups are *SOO CUTE!*"

Leo turned his attention to the floating pink condos and seagulls gliding over the ocean as Grus carried on about baby wallabies and other "A-*DORE*-ABLE" marsupials. Then, after a few more heavenly songs sung by Grus, the limojet arrived at a large stone wall, which was guarded by a tall barbed-wire fence.

"Outside, to your right, is where you'll be staying," Weathers announced as they hovered past the gate's security.

Leo, however, didn't feel certain they were in the right

place. *Was Space Camp really a time-forgotten fort?* Even Andromeda didn't seem persuaded as she asked, "Are you *sure* this is *it*?"

"This is it," said Weathers reassuringly.

The group followed the bot out of the limojet, only this time far less swiftly than they had once gotten in it. No one appeared enticed by the crumbling stone blockading wall or the dilapidated wooden drawbridge that they needed to cross to reach the fort's entrance.

Weathers reached out and knocked on the large brass doorstopper, which caused an echo throughout the fort as though it were an empty box of tin.

"Well, while we're *waiting*," said Grus uneasily, looking highly discomforted by the infinite number of treefrogs hanging out in the moat beside them. "I could sing another *singy* if everyone would like?" But before anyone had the chance to refuse, the door was opening and a familiar face emerged.

"Finally!" shouted Principal Yin, glaring at the robot. "Weathers, how many times must I ask you to *visi-message* me when you're planning on taking the scenic route?"

"Well, I had thought—" Weathers began, but Principal Yin cut him off.

"Next time leave the thinking to *me*."

"Yes, ma'am," replied Weathers gloomily.

"For the rest of you," she went on, greeting everyone else with a chipper grin, "I hope you had a pleasant trip in. Though a bit dated—*and cumbersome to open*, this door does the trick of keeping what lies behind it secret!"

Principal Yin motioned everyone inside. And as Leo walked in, behind the "*oohs*" and "*aahs*" of Grus Pinwheel and Andromeda Groves, he instantly understood their surprise! What he had once thought would have been dark and dreary behind the fort's door was instead the most spectacular gathering of high-tech materials he had ever before seen: The halls were paved with an electro-crystal flooring; the ceiling (which looked as though it would have previously been made out of concrete) peered into the sun-filled clouds. People dressed in lab coats with techni-pads zoomed past them on high-tech skydisks alongside rooms filled with robots testing gravity-walks, organizing spacesuits, and analyzing data for shuttle preparation.

"Welcome to Space Camp!" said Principal Yin, looking pleased with everyone's astonished looks. "This is where you'll learn how to eat, sleep, and how to live life like a true Luna Citizen prior to your arrival at Luna City. That said, we have only four more days until departure, so it's in your best interest to pay close attention. But before we get started, I must warn each of you that the flooring ahead is not a typical floor—it's a Quickpath."

"A quick *b-b-bath*?" Grus stammered, looking freaked-out by the shimmery electro-floor.

"Not a *bath*," said Principal Yin, "a *path*—designed to

take you wherever it is you say you want to go in the shortest amount of time possible. Most of Luna City's halls are composed of them, so you'll need to get familiar with them quickly. Just be careful because they really will take you wherever you say you want to go!

"Ah, here, Hannah!" Principal Yin called out to a younger scientist passing by. "Would you be so kind as to give our guests a demonstration, please?"

"Certainly," the young scientist agreed, stepping onto the path. "It's really simple. You just step on, say where you want to go, and you'll be off, like this: *Quickpath, cafeteria!*" And in a matter of a second, she was zooming down the path and disappearing down the far end of it.

Everyone's mouth dropped with amazement.

"We'll be following Miss Hannah's lead to lunch in the cafeteria," said Principal Yin. "Who would like to try fir—?" But before she finished, Andromeda ran up to the path, declaring: "I'm *SO* first!—*Quickpath, cafeteria!*" And just like that, she was speeding down the hall after Miss Hannah.

Principal Yin motioned for Grus to go next. Grus, however, did not appear as eager to go.

"So, um . . . you just stand on it, like this?" he mumbled nervously, twiddling his thumbs. "And—um—say something, like Quickpath, Room 1 . . . 2 . . . 3?" But before Principal Yin could correct him, Grus Pinwheel was swung off, shouting wildly in the wrong direction.

"Don't worry," said Principal Yin to Leo, "he'll figure out where to find us!"

"Right," said Leo under his breath. He took a cautious step onto the Quickpath and said, "*Quickpath, cafeteria!*" And the next thing he knew he was zooming down the hall, flying past the auditorium and through a series of automatic doorways and spindly tunnels (all the while standing perfectly upright) until a silver tray was plopped into his hands and he was transported down the cafeteria's conveyor-belt lunch-line.

"What'll ya have?" a robotic chef grunted at him, while Leo stood there, thunderstruck at how he'd gotten there in the first place!

Leo looked bewilderedly at the assortment of silvery meal pouches situated behind the counter: Some were labeled Sorta-Turkey on Non-glutinous Rye, others Hot-Ham-Alike and Swiss, alongside various assortments of moon-shaped veggie chips, H2O pouches, and select-your-own "lunarganic" condiments.

"I'll have a *Sorta-Turkey* . . . some taro chips . . . and an H2O, please," Leo replied. The chef-bot spun his six arms into something that resembled a tornado. He then tossed three silvery meal pouches onto Leo's tray and said, "Careful not to take the Hot Seat!"

"The hot-*what?*" Leo asked, turning around; but the chef had already moved on to "*hurricane-ing*" dishes.

Leo continued to the floating table, where he saw that all

the hover-chairs at it were white, less one, which was dimly lit red. Leo decided he'd take the chef-bot's advice and opted for the last white one as Grus Pinwheel ran in behind him, shouting excitedly: "Hey, you guys! . . . You have GOT to check out Room 1.2.3! It's the bathroom, in case you were wondering— and *BOY*! THE TOILETS ARE *A-MAZE-ING*! They puff out AQUAMARINE SANITATION STEAM!"

"Now that we're *all* here," said Principal Yin, forcing Grus into the Hot Seat with a wave of her eyes, "I will demonstrate how we *eat* in Luna City. But before we get started, I suggest you each take hold of your seats."

"What for?" Grus asked, trying to tear open his meal pouch with his teeth.

"Because of gravity!" said Principal Yin. And with a click of her pointer-pen, Grus Pinwheel (along with his pouched meal) was hovering out of his chair, floating straight toward the ceiling.

"*No way,*" Andromeda gushed, her eyes sparkling with delight. "It's an anti-gravity chair!"

"Precisely," said Principal Yin, smiling as though she had invented it herself. Though her excitement was short-lived as Grus began shouting: "*SOMEBODY GET ME DOWN FROM HERE!*" And within a second, the entire table filled with laughter.

"I do have to say," Andromeda called up to him, "the ambiance is much more entertaining with you up there!"

"I don't think he's very keen on heights," said Leo, trying to hold himself back from snorting.

"Well, he's going to need to get used to it fairly quickly," said Principal Yin as Grus continued whimpering. "In just a few days' time, he's going to be a long way from the comfort of Earth's floor—that is—" She stopped for a second, fidgeting with her pen. "Provided I can get him *down* . . ."

"WEATHERS," she shouted at the bot, throwing her pen at him, "FIX this stupid thing, will you?"

"Yes, ma'am," Weathers replied, stumbling to catch it.

Weathers gave the pen a good whack, and Grus Pinwheel finally floated back to his seat.

"Why m-m-me?" Grus warbled with distress.

"Because you were 'lucky' enough to have chosen the *Hot Seat* . . . ," answered Principal Yin, her voice trailing as if she wished she had previously checked to make sure whoever sat on it wasn't acrophobic.

"Now, as you're aware," she continued, "gravity does not exist the same way in Luna City as it does here on Earth. So, to keep you from floating around—like Grus here so kindly demonstrated—you will each be needing to wear one of these . . ."

Weathers passed everyone a thin see-through belt.

Grus looked at his as though it were something utterly repugnant and asked, "What *is* it?"

"A gravity-belt," answered Principal Yin. "It's composed of

an ultra-thick magnetic-gravitational substance, designed to keep you from floating off to the top of the moon."

"So if you take it *off*—" Andromeda started to suggest.

"—You'll have the exact same experience Grus just had. But not to worry, most objects already have the substance built into them. Your chairs, tables, and beds, for example, won't be floating off at random if you're not next to them. That said, taking them off anywhere other than in your rooms or an anti-gravity gym is strictly forbidden."

"'An *anti*-gravity gym?'" worried Grus.

"You'll be seeing one of those soon enough," said Principal Yin. "But first, you must master the art of eating in lunar gravity!" With another click of her pointer-pen, everyone's meal pouches were hovering up over the table. And in a moment's time, they were unwrapped, releasing their cube-shaped sandwiches, moon-shaped chips, and floating blobs of H2O. And the Sorta-Turkey, to Leo's amazement, was actually delicious.

After everyone finished their meals, Principal Yin led the group down a long hall boasting four stately gymnasiums on either side of it. One side was clearly set in standard gravity, and the other, a lack thereof. Leo quickly noted one of the anti-gravity gyms had a pair of robots fluttering around on odd-looking octagonal disks, batting around a ball with something that resembled banana-shaped tennis racquets.

"What's that they're playing there?" Leo inquired, staring into the all-white, fully padded, cylindrical gym.

"Ah! *That's* a sport no Earthling has yet to discover!" said Principal Yin proudly. "And it's a secret well-kept in Luna City, as it's our only sport."

"'Our *only* sport?'" Andromeda repeated as though she were being cheated out of something

"How *exactly* do you play?" Leo asked with interest.

"It's really simple," said Principal Yin. "Apart from needing to learn the proper skydisking techniques, the rules are just like tennis, only the goal is to bop the other player's Hed!"

"Bop the other player's *HEAD*?" Grus shouted with fright.

"Yes, *Hed*," said Principal Yin. She pointed out a series of miniature robots that were inching away toward either end of the court from the center net. "Each team has a series of remote-controlled robots—or Hed-bots, as we call them—whose goal is to make it to the goal line on the other end of their team's court *without* getting hit by the gravityball.

"The Hitter's goal—or players on the skydisks—is to try to knock out as many of the other team's Hed-bots as they possibly can."

"And what about those players, up there?" Andromeda asked, pointing out two chairs hovering above each end of the court.

"Ah, those are our Pilots!" said Principal Yin. "They're responsible for navigating the Hed-bots with their remotes. Each Hed-bot to make it across the goal line wins their team 100 points, while each Hed-bot knocked out wins the other team 100 points.

"One of each team's three Hed-bots, however, is a bonus bot, worth an additional 500 points. It disguises itself as a regular 100-point-bot during the match and is only revealed as the bonus bot at the very end."

"Well, that seems easy enough," said Leo, who was finally figuring out how the game was played: the Pilot position was ideal for gamers, and the Hitter position for those more athletic.

"Yes, well, it's easier said than done," Principal Yin assured him. "If you float a Hed-bot before the gravityball crosses the center court line, you'll lose your team 100 points. And you'll very quickly realize just how difficult it is to make up for a lost Hed!"

The group followed Principal Yin into one of the open gymnasiums, where they were each given a double octagonal gravity-shifting propulsion disk and instructed to spread out over the soft padded floor.

"We'll begin in ground position," said Principal Yin as everyone anxiously waited for the anti-gravity to kick in. "Then, once gravity is off, you'll simply lift up and position yourself onto your skydisk . . ."

And before Leo knew it, he was lifting off the ground and floating in the air, feeling a rush like he had never before felt!

"Very good," said Principal Yin, encouraging Leo's wobbly position while his feet connected to his skydisk. "Now, once you're able, simply slide your right foot back to start. Then lean toward whichever direction you want to go: foot up to go up; foot down to go down . . . but just make sure you don't lean in too quickly or you'll—"

But it was too late. Leo had already leaned his hip too far to the right and was dashing straight out of the gymnasium!

"WOOOAAAH!" Leo shouted in a wave of fright, as the wind tugged through his ruddy hair and the hallways flashed past him in streams of light. At first, Leo had zero control over anything as the skydisk picked up more and more speed once adjusting its mode for standard gravity. But then, after what felt like an eternity of mazing around a hundred missed collisions with doorways and walls, Leo was starting to get the hang of it; skydisking wasn't *that* difficult and was certainly a lot more fun than Aabher Pawar's hover-skates!

But there was one thing that Leo hadn't quite figured out; however, he wouldn't come to realize it until it was much too late: there he was, flying rapidly down the hall, heading straight toward Senator Mallock, with no clue how to brake!

Leo panicked—swung his hips up in the hope of stopping, but instead flew even faster than before!

"WATCH OOOOUUUTTT!" Leo shouted; but within seconds the air filled with an enormously loud BOOM!

Papers flew in every which way as Leo and the senator lay smack down in the middle of the cold tile floor. Leo looked up dizzily to find the senator's expression had suddenly transformed into that of his father's without any pie!

"Senator M-Mallock!" Leo stammered, picking up the electro-papers that had fallen beside him. "I'm—I'm so sorry, sir!"

"Didn't anyone ever teach you to *watch* where you're going?" Mallock snarled, snatching the papers from Leo's grasp.

"I couldn't figure out how to stop," Leo replied, offering the senator a helping hand as soon as he got up.

The senator sneered at it and chose to straighten out the tangles from his long licorice hair. "Then I suggest you *learn*," he said icily, and he continued briskly down the hall.

Leo waited until the senator was out of sight before he dared move another inch. But as Leo lifted his skydisk, he noticed one of the senator's notes had fallen underneath it. Leo picked it up and hurried after him, eager to return it, but when Leo reached the end of the hall, he found nothing but an empty Quickpath in sight.

"Now that we've all learned how to use our skydisks *properly*," said Principal Yin, while Andromeda and Grus shuffled in behind her, giggling, "Weathers here will show you to your rooms. Luckily, since you're the last and smallest group to attend Space Camp, you will each have your own quarters for the remainder of your time here. The rest of the evening will be yours to review your Luna City Rule Books prior to your Placement Exams tomorrow morning."

"And what about the rest of the week?" Andromeda asked.

"Day Three will be your Physicals . . . Day Four, the Purification Process . . . Then, finally, on Day Five you'll view a short Launch Instructional Video prior to launching to Luna City!"

The group thanked Principal Yin and Weathers escorted them down another Quickpath to their rooms. And the second Leo was shown his, he went directly to his book-bag to check on Archimedes and get studying.

At first, Leo tried to memorize each rule perfectly, but he soon found there were a whole lot of things *not* to do in Luna City as he read:

NO LEAVING YOUR DORM ROOMS AFTER HOURS.

NO RUNNING UNLESS IN A GRAVITY GYM.

NO ENTERING AREAS MARKED RESTRICTED.

"Or *no* bumping into Senator Mallock," Leo said to himself jokingly, which reminded him of the note he had buried in his pocket.

Leo took it out, but as he looked at it a second more, he realized it was composed of strange symbols he'd never before seen.

Y⋒ᵇ Σᵇᵣᵇv̌ʒ ȯɪ ɏ⋒ᵇ ≻Zɏîȯv̇ȯⱮᵇîʒ Ⱶ>✳

"Backward z's and dotted v's?" he muttered, trying to figure out what the symbols could be.

A soft ding rang through the room's intercom and rattled the thought out of Leo's head. Dinner had arrived through a small tube on the wall, and Leo dug into the plate of faux roast beef and carrots eagerly. Before Leo knew it, he had finished, and he was just as eager to get some rest. But that, too, proved to be a problem: he couldn't find the bed! Instead, where a bed should have been, were two long metal boards hanging laterally across the wall with no sign of a mattress, pillows, or any sheets.

"This has to be the bed?" Leo said to himself strangely, analyzing the thin metal panels. But as he went to test a seat, he was lifted up by thick currents of lavender steam, tucking him into the most comfortable position he had ever been in. And before Leo had time to think of anything else, he fell fast asleep.

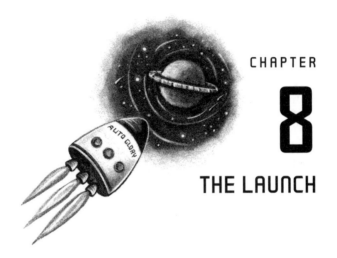

CHAPTER

8

THE LAUNCH

The next morning Leo awoke to a buzzy little noise ringing around his head.

"Good morning, Leo Gray. Your temperature is perfect, along with your blood pressure, heart rate, and spinal positioning. Your vision, however, is slightly blurred—and so is your thought pattern!"

Leo lifted his lids in search of whoever it was that was speaking to him, but when no one else appeared in the room, he quickly began to doze off. Only, the second his eyes had shut, they were once again opening as his face smacked against the frigid steel of the shut-off air-wave-bed.

"I said good *morning*, Leo Gray—not good night!" the little voice snapped.

Leo looked around the room, only this time, after he rolled over and looked up, he was greeted with the outline of a not-so-happy face on the visi in front of him.

"So the *screen's* talking?" Leo mumbled, sleepily.

"I'm a bit more than *that*," the voice replied, popping out of the screen and materializing into a semitransparent, fluttery little ball. "Though my name's Meta, and I'm afraid you can't go back to sleep. Your breakfast is scheduled for 7:00 a.m. in the cafeteria, followed by the first half of your Placement Exam starting at 8:00 a.m. in Room 14. You'll then break for lunch at 11:00 a.m. and will return no later than 12:00 p.m. to your testing room to commence the second half of the exam—which, I'll add, you're expected to complete no later than 4:00 p.m. You'll finally return here for peace and relaxation prior to your dinner arriving at 5:00 p.m. sharp."

Leo looked completely dazed.

"Was I supposed to memorize *all* that?"

"*No*," said Meta, as though this were obvious, "that's what I'm here for: I'm your M. E. T. A."

"My M. E. T—*what?*"

"Your very own Molecularly Efficient Tasking Assistant," replied Meta.

Leo, however, continued to look at it as though it were speaking gibberish.

"You *know*," Meta went on, "your schedule keeper, health monitor, alarm clock, message reader, information seeker—all easily accessible via your Meta badge!"

"A Meta badge?" Leo wondered aloud.

Meta nodded toward the nightstand. On top of it was an ultra-thin, shimmery electronic crest.

"You'll find I attach quite nicely to your uniform when I'm not waking you up over your bed's visi!"

"So to turn you on or *off*?" Leo asked tactfully.

"Simply say Meta-on or—"

"Meta-OFF!" Leo shouted. And its priggish little face finally unlit.

"That's better!" Leo said to himself smugly, turning on the air-wave-bed to catch himself a few more z's. "Now where was I?"

But just as he got himself cozy again, Meta turned back on and said, "—About to make your way to the bathroom to get ready, Leo Gray!"

"But how did you—" Leo started to say as his chin once more found itself pressed onto the bitterly cold steel.

"You don't really think they'd allow me to let you oversleep, do you?" Meta asked, astonished.

"Right," Leo grumbled. And he unwillingly got up to get ready for the day.

The bathroom, however, wasn't any easier to figure out

than the bed. That is, until Meta directed Leo to step on the right spot, and Leo was then hurtled through a mess of robotic arms scrubbing him with loofas and soaps, brushing and flossing his teeth with an ultra-hygienic sanitation laser, fixing his hair neatly to the side, and dressing him from head to toe in an insta-printed sanitation smock.

"*That's* going to need some getting used to!" Leo shouted, exiting the robotic changing contraption feeling more out of sorts than ever.

Grus was already at the cafeteria, practicing mixing globs of butter bubbles and syrup into his floating blueberry pancakes when Leo arrived. Leo opted for Kinda-Ham and It's-Alike-Eggs, as it was the closest thing to a dish his mother would always make—less the silvery pouching.

Even if it had only been just one day, it was still the longest Leo had ever spent away from home.

Andromeda arrived at the table, fuming.

"What's the matter with you?" Grus asked while trying to maneuver as many floating Sorta-Sausage pieces into his mouth as humanly possible.

"Urgh—these clothes are *DRABILIATING!*" Andromeda groaned, taking a seat and tearing apart her grapefruit. "I can't BELIEVE they're making us wear these! What are they—hundred-year-old cotton or something?"

"'*Or something,*'" Leo repeated, who was privately just realizing his current attire wasn't all that different from his twentieth century pajamas.

"Either way," she continued, "I can't *WAIT* for the launch!"

"I . . . CAN," Grus blurted, spewing bits of Sorta-Sausage from his lips while a miniature-bot fluttered down from the ceiling to suction them up. "I'm still not . . . sure . . . I like the idea of . . . ROCK-ET-ING off to . . . OUTER SPACE! . . . Do you know . . . how *FAST* . . . that thing has to . . . GO?"

The very thought made Leo quiver.

"That makes two of you, doesn't it?" said Andromeda cheekily to Leo.

"Really, Leo?" said Grus with surprise. "You're afraid of flying, too? *GEEZIDINKS*! And here I thought I was the only one!"

"I'm not '*afraid*' of flying," Leo corrected. He returned an unappreciative look to Andromeda. "I just . . . don't like the idea of *falling* . . . Anyway, I think I'm finished. I'll see you guys after the test."

"Good luck!" Andromeda and Grus called after him as Leo left the table and made his way to Testing Room 14.

Room 14 was at the end of a long, seemingly endless Quickpath with absolutely nothing in it but a single hover-chair and a stern-looking robotic proctor.

"This is where you'll take your Placement Exam," the bot said, directing Leo to his chair and flicking Meta away. "All Metas and electronic devices are automatically disabled inside the testing area, just as they'll be in your classrooms at the academy. You may begin immediately."

The proctor left, and as she did, the door of the testing room sealed itself off completely, leaving Leo surrounded by nothing but white sterile walls and an onset of troublesome nerves. Though no studying was required for the Placement Exam, Leo still didn't feel entirely ready for it. He released an uncomfortable huff and sat down, eager to get started.

But before Leo could worry any more about the exam, his chair was reclining and a thin electronic band was wrapping around his forehead.

Leo's mind raced as a deep voice chuckled and said, "No need to get worked up! It's only a think-band to monitor your thoughts."

"*To monitor my thoughts?*" Leo repeated, his eyes scanning the empty room madly.

"Often how one arrives at an answer is far more important than the answer itself," replied the voice calmly. "Are you ready to commence?"

"Er . . . ," said Leo, trying to get a better hold on himself, "yes?"

"Good," said the voice. And the room shifted to a neon black. "We'll start with the basics. I take it you're Leo?"

"Um, yes," answered Leo.

"And you're eleven years old?"

"Erm—yes."

"Have you ever cheated on a test before?"

Leo thought about this question for a much longer moment.

"I see," said the voice darkly. "Are you really finding the test difficult thus far?"

"Actually . . . no," said Leo, his nerves were finally

settling. But no sooner had he said it, when much more difficult questions started to be asked, and not just yes or no questions, but questions where Leo had to come up with his own answer and describe in great detail the reasoning for his selection.

The walls lit up, and Leo had to properly match paintings from Van Gogh to Botticelli; the entire room would turn into a real-D replica of the sky, where Leo was asked to realign the constellations and name far-off stars; there were questions in mathematics and science, along with questions in history, literature, and language arts. And Leo was certain he had answered five hundred of them before he broke for lunch. But his return to Room 14 found no pause in the number of questions that were tossed at him.

Then, after Leo's brain had been through more "who was who?" and "when was this?" and "which was what?" than he had ever imagined possible, "Would you like to be finished?" was asked, and Leo quickly shouted, "YES!"

Day Three, in contrast, required Leo to spend the entirety of the day inside a room filled with various workout machines. There were weight-lifting sets and bizarre-looking bikes, equipment that resembled treadmills and ellipticals, in addition to numerous robots surveying monitors that displayed various stats.

"Ah, Leo! This way, please," called out a hover-bot to Leo the second he arrived. The bot directed him toward a hovering bench, where Leo sat and found Grus Pinwheel, running (or attempting to run) on an anti-gravity treadmill.

"Just need to check your basic reflexes before we can get you started!" said the bot. And Leo's knee was suddenly bopped with a mallet; his tongue yanked out by a miniature drone; his ears dug into with a series of cottony swabs, and his tummy tickled until his cheeks turned a bright, embarrassed pink!

"All clear!" said the bot, directing Leo toward the bicycling machine.

"Have a seat, love," instructed another bot, patting the bike's cushion with an unsettling grin. "Now, on *three*, I need you to pedal up a twenty-percent incline . . .

"THREE!" she shouted without warning.

Leo hopped on and pedaled away speedily, relieved to have a test that he was at least somewhat familiar with. Yet not more than a few minutes in, his legs began to cramp with pain.

"H-how . . . m-much . . . t-time . . . l-left?" he asked with difficulty; it seemed as though he had been pedaling for ages!

The robot glanced at her stopwatch and said, "None! You've been done for a whole FIFTEEN minutes now—*passed the How-Much-Time-It-Takes-You-To-Complain test*—you can head on over to the treadmill, love!"

"'*The How-Much-Time-It-Takes-You-To-Complain test*'?" Leo repeated, boggled. Leo hoped the next test would be the same (as he'd be sure to complain right away!); however, this test, despite his attempts at complaining, was a true test of agility. And Leo was soon tossed through a series of jogging and sprinting exercises, first running forward, then jogging backward, all the while breathing into an oxygen tube every two minutes for bacteria sample collections. And then, after Leo had finished bouncing on a trampoline to measure gravity resistance and had done a hundred handstands to see how fast his heart could run, he was making his way to Day Four.

However unlike the rooms Leo had visited before at Space Camp, the Purification Process's room was only reachable after traveling through a long tunnel filled with a series of automatic doors. And as the final door opened, Leo was at once wishing it would shut again, as he was greeted by a group of scientists gowned in bright orange protective suits, each equipped with one too many intimidating poking devices.

"Name?" asked a scientist from behind a thick protective mask.

"Leo," Leo gulped, looking around uneasily at the hospital-esque room.

"Last?" the scientist continued.

"G-g-gray," Leo replied.

"Date of birth?"

"September . . . the, uh, thirteenth . . ." Leo double-blinked as his eyes landed on an enormous robotic spider contraption hung from the ceiling being dressed with various medical tools and scalpels.

"*Year?*" the scientist droned.

"21 . . . 02," Leo mumbled with hesitation. And he was suddenly escorted toward the area he was dreading most!

Leo stood completely still as the spider contraption was positioned over his head. He could feel his stomach lurch as he imagined what terribly painful things it would soon be doing to him. And then, its legs sprang into life! Its long metallic arms buzzed all around him, collecting epidermal samples from his arm, scanning his fingertips and eyes, and plucking a dozen hairs from the top of his head.

Then, after a few uncomfortable scrapes and pricks, Leo was moving down an automatic changing contraption, which swapped out his comfortable cotton smock for a pair of jet-black compressive pants, matching insta-fit boots, and a silver shaded thermal top with a designated spot for his Meta badge.

"You're free to go," said another scientist to Leo, escorting him to the door.

"Thanks," Leo replied gratefully. And he had never actually been more grateful to leave anywhere before.

The next morning, Meta led Leo to an all-white circular room, in which he found a cinema-like visi-screen and rows of deep cushioned hover-chairs. After everyone had taken their seats, the lights dimmed, and the Luna City Launch Etiquette video began. Then, after a half hour of do's and don'ts, and tips on how to properly buckle a space shuttle harness (which was pretty self-explanatory, as it buckled itself), everyone's eyes were flooded with light, back to attention.

"Now that everyone's awake," said Principal Yin, looking out expectantly at her suddenly sleepy crowd, "Weathers here will take you to the shuttle dock. The others and I have some closing up to do before we depart, but I look forward to seeing you each again this evening at orientation!"

The group all clapped to thank Principal Yin and followed Weathers to the shuttle dock.

"HOLE-E-CRAPPER-BAPPERS," Grus muttered at the sight of a gigantic, all-black space shuttle, "it's HUMUNGOUS!"

"It is," said Weathers, "but I'm afraid it's *not* what you'll be voyaging in."

"It's *not?*" said Andromeda, looking perplexed.

Weathers led them around to the shuttle's end, where they were instead greeted with an incredibly dinky departure capsule.

"Since you're such a small group, there's no need to bother with her much larger sister, the *Omega-10*," Weathers explained. "You'll be the first ever non-robotic passengers of the *Autoglory*! The first solely ground-operated and robotically controlled space shuttle!"

"You mean to say," said Andromeda thoughtfully, "that on top of the fact that no human's ever flown in this thing—and that it isn't even a proper-sized shuttle—that there's not going to be *a REAL PERSON* navigating it?"

"Precisely," said Weathers proudly.

"Then what would happen if there's an emergency or a—"

"Not to worry," said the bot. "Ground control hasn't had any problems with it . . . Then again . . ." He stopped for a second, appearing deep in thought. "I've always wondered what became of that cute little monkey, Zuzu?—but never mind that—off you pop!"

Andromeda gave Weathers a frustrated look as she walked up to the shuttle's steps and said, "Here goes nothing!" Grus hurried after her while Leo stood there, frozen at the entrance—this wouldn't be the first time he had a sensation of something uncomfortable fluttering in his stomach. And as he made his way through the shuttle's door, he found three tall rotating chairs with three clear helmets perfectly perched on top of them. Aligned in front of each chair was a small circular window and a dimly lit visi-screen.

Grus immediately shoved his head into his helmet, while Andromeda and Leo both took an extra moment to examine how skillfully crafted theirs were first.

"Does mine look like it's on right?" Grus asked, stressed, while attempting to twist his helmet around.

"*Yes, Grus,*" answered Andromeda. Her harness wrapped around her. "It looks great!"

"AHHH!" Grus shouted as his harness constricted around him. "IT'S SUFFOCATING ME!"

"It's not suffocating you," said Leo, "it's *supposed* to be tight."

"Well, if anything goes wrong—" Grus started to fret as Weathers' voice interrupted them.

"One minute till takeoff . . ."

The engines rumbled on.

"Don't worry Grus, everything is going to be fine," said

Andromeda. "Just imagine, in only *minutes*, we'll be in Luna City!"

"Ten seconds . . ."

"—as I was saying—" Grus continued squeamishly.

"Five seconds . . ."

"—if anything happens—"

" . . . THREE . . ."

"—it was nice knowing—"

" . . . TWO . . ."

" . . . ONE."

"—*YAAAAAAHHHHHH!!!!!*" Grus screamed at the top of his lungs as the rocket blasted through the sky, so fast, that their bodies sank into their chairs like clay.

Leo held his breath, staring nauseously at the streaks of white zooming past his window. All the while, Grus Pinwheel screamed like a baby, and Andromeda Groves woo'ed and yay'ed as though she was having the most spectacular time of her life. And then, within only a matter of seconds, the rocket slowed to a near stop.

There was silence and then . . .

"Are we dead yet?" Grus whimpered with the abrupt change of velocity.

"*No, Grus,*" said Andromeda, her body lifting against her restraints as she pointed at the window. "Look outside—It's *A-MAZE-ING!*"

Leo sat there without a word as the stone gray coldness of the moon sauntered into view. There was something so spectacular, yet so completely frightening about it, chills trickled up his spine. The moon was no longer that place he remembered from books, paintings, or television—it instead was something Leo Gray had never seen in his entire eleven years of life.

As the *Autoglory* crept ever closer toward the moon's gargantuan loading dock, small shaded windows began to emerge from within the hollowed craters of the moon's silvery crust.

"Prepare for gravity connection," Weathers announced through the intercom.

Andromeda's face lit with a very large grin; Grus frantically rechecked his safety-harness; and Leo took another deep, stressful breath as a large boom and a bang informed them that they had attached!

"*Finally!*" Andromeda shouted at the sound of the locking latch. Both Leo and Grus (despite looking slightly feverish) were equally just as glad.

A soft ding echoed through the cabin, and Leo felt his once-weightless body settle back in his seat. Andromeda was the first to take off her helmet to try to find her way out of the shuttle; but as her tawny locks floated out of it, how to get *out* of the shuttle didn't appear as obvious as it had when they had first gotten in it.

"That's funny . . . ," she said, examining the cabin's seamless walls. "Where'd the door go?"

Leo returned his gaze into the cabin. "It's obviously here

somewhere," he said reasonably. But as he looked further, he realized Andromeda was correct. "Or there *isn't* one?"

"*W-w-what* do you mean there's NO DOOR?" Grus shouted, frantic. "What if they forgot to tell them we're COMING? They wouldn't know we're HERE! And if they don't know we're HERE . . . then we'd be STUCK in here like this . . . and . . . AND END UP STARVING!"

"Is that *all* you think about—" said Andromeda, "—*food?*"

"That is what would happen," said Leo in Grus's defense. "Anyway, they have to know we're here—"

"That's correct," a deep voice said from the opposite side of where the shuttle's door had been. "You've been *expected* . . ."

Leo turned and found the expressionless face of Senator Mallock in the newly appeared doorway behind them. He was staring idly at a thin black timepiece strapped around his wrist and was wearing the same dark cape, with his wispy onyx hair dripping in his face like icicles. He didn't exactly seem "thrilled" about their arrival.

"Ten minutes late, but I guess that's typical poor behavior for ground control," he said with contempt. "When you're ready, you may follow me. Apparently, since all the academy's staff are 'far too busy' preparing for orientation this evening, you'll have the honor of having *me* taking you on a brief tour of the facility."

Everyone threw on their gravity belts straightaway, but as they exited the *Autoglory*, Grus appeared to be having some difficulties keeping up.

"Hey, you guys, WAIT!" he called out, tugging on his helmet until his face was a pale blue. "I'M STUCK!"

Andromeda put her floating suitcase to the side and stepped back into the shuttle. *"Grus,"* she groaned motherly, "you're forgetting to hit the *ejection* button!"

Grus looked completely dumbfounded at this realization, despite his guffawing, "HA! I knew *that*. I was just checking to make sure you guys didn't lose your minds—or something—from the crazy GRAVITY!"

Andromeda gave Grus an unamused look as they caught up to the senator and Leo. Grus, meanwhile, pulled out a spare hydro-pop to attempt to conceal his embarrassment; however, his treat never reached his lips.

"Hey! Where'd my—" he began to pout, until it became unfortunately clear.

"Luna City is no place for jokes—*or sweets*," said the senator sternly, tossing Grus's hydro-pop into a robotic-trash-bin beside a tall set of interlocking doors.

Grus looked more than puzzled by the loss of his pop, but his frustration soon faded as the senator reached inside his pocket and pulled out a shiny triangular key. He then held against the lock-pad, turning it a bright fluorescent blue. There was not a word from anyone as they stood in awe of the sight unraveling in front of them.

9

A THOUSAND
FLOATING CHAIRS

From the ceiling of the moon, which looked out into the stars, spiraled a giant reverse waterfall of a deep turquoise blue. Surrounding it were tall, tubular glass gravity-shafts, each nestled between thin, see-through skyways connecting the city's many circular corridors. Floating effortlessly in its center was the main amphitheater, a massive mountain-like rock, so lush with flowers and forest-like trees, no one believed it was real. It was the picture-perfect vision of nature-adapted technology.

"It's not at *all* like any of the photos," Andromeda exclaimed, her mouth agape as she ran toward the balcony's edge, admiring the people gliding past them on skydisks.

"It's even *b-b-bigger* than the LCSC," muttered Grus, looking down squeamishly at the space in which one could fall below.

Leo, however, couldn't manage more than a breathless "Wow" as he realized it: *He* was in Luna City!

"We'll begin with locating your rooms," said the senator, bringing everyone to attention as he passed them each an electro-card with their room number printed on it.

"I'm room nineteen!" said Andromeda, excited.

"And what about you, Leo?" Grus wondered. "What room are you in? . . . I'm in . . ." He stopped for a second, flipping his card around. "—ROOM EIGHTY-SEVEN!"

Leo pressed his finger to his card and discovered the exact same number on it.

"I'm—uh—" he started to say when Mallock cut him off.

"*Ladies* first?"

Leo smiled weakly as the senator instructed everyone to follow his lead down the nearest Quickpath.

"Hey—um—Leo," said Grus the second Andromeda had disappeared down the Quickpath behind Mallock, "did you— uh—want to go ahead of me?"

"That's okay, Grus," said Leo, half-courteously, half-realizing room 87 was directly behind them. "I'll uh—be right behind you."

Grus released an unconfident groan and wobbled off after the senator and Andromeda. Leo, however, had other plans than to follow straight behind; this was the perfect opportunity to claim the better half of the dorm room before Grus Pinwheel did!

Room 87 was located at the start of a Quickpath, next to a gravity-shaft and a globule-releasing drinking fountain. Inside were three equally sized air-wave-beds: two double-stacked and one single off to the side. Already perched on top of the single bed were two suitcases, and a large electronic flag was pinned across the wall that read: *CAMPEÃO MUNDIAL*!

With the room's better half spoken for, Leo decided he'd claim the bottom bunk. (He imagined the extra floor room would prove an ideal spot to keep Archimedes.) Leo quickly threw his things over it, gave his pet a quick check, and rummaged through his book-bag in search of the note he had been meaning to give back to Senator Mallock. But what lay between the three beds was possibly the most enticing part of the entire room: a large circular window that looked directly out at Earth.

Leo was drawn to it like a bug to a lamp.

"Pretty stellar view, huh?" a voice interrupted Leo's ogling from the room's shared bathroom.

"Yeah, it's really something," Leo replied. He turned around to find a boy who was about his size—if not a few inches taller—with deep olive skin, curly brown hair, and wide-rimmed laser-spectacles (which looked more like goggles than anything else). "If only I had a telescope!"

"Don't you have the new *LT 2,000,010*?" the boy asked, pointing at Leo's Luna Watch. "It's got one built right into it!"

Leo hadn't had a chance to read the entire owner's pamphlet; a watch that was also a telescope? *That* he hadn't been expecting!

"Oh, I uh, just got it a few days ago," Leo explained, noticing the boy had the exact same timepiece. "Still don't know how it works yet."

"Oh, it's *muito fácil*," said the boy. "You just swipe it to T-mode and you'll be in telescope. Then, just put your eye against the hole on the side, *e voilà*!"

Leo swiped through the different modes until he found "T" and pressed his lid against it.

"*Legal*, huh? And if you push in the hour button, it will automatically zoom in so you can make out people's faces. I heard 2114's version should have better zoom capability, so that you can actually *see* past people's sunglasses."

Leo hit the zoom and was soon staring at a herd of zebras galloping off in an African field. He only later realized, after spotting a kangaroo, that he had been instead staring at a zoo.

"Wow, that's pretty neat," said Leo, turning to shake his new roommate's hand. "I'm Leo, by the way . . . I'm assuming you're the bed with the um, flag over it?"

"That's right," said the boy, "it's for Brazil's team! I'm Pa—" But the boy was cut off by Andromeda's squealing through the doorway.

"PAVO!" she shouted, flinging her arms around her

cousin's slim neck. "It's so GOOD to see you! I can't believe we're BOTH here!"

"Oh—uh—*olá* Andromeda," the boy responded, trying to appear indifferent to the sudden burst of girly attention. "How long have you been here?"

"Only a few minutes," answered Andromeda, admiring the boys' room. "Oh, Leo! This is my cousin, Pavo, from Brazil . . ." She turned to Pavo. "I was telling Leo *all* about your Ping-Pong skills on the plane. Anyway, I've not yet met my roommate, but Senator Mallock assures me she's nice. And *whoa!*—check out this VIEW! Totally not fair—mine's of nothing—well, just some stars off in the distance . . . I guess I'm on the 'dark side.'"

Just then a large floating suitcase spun uncontrollably into the boys' room and Grus Pinwheel appeared chasing after it with an imaginary lasso. At the sight of Leo's things in the same room as his, he nearly ran straight into the bunk!

"YIPEEE!" Grus shouted, pushing his luggage over the top of it. "We're gonna be ROOMMATES, Leo! Boy, what LUCK!"

Luck, Leo thought to himself—*if only I could manage to find some!*

Andromeda got back to introducing everybody. "Grus, this is my cousin Pavo—Pavo, Grus."

Grus peeled himself off the bed and held out his hand to greet Pavo. "Get it?" Grus asked, while shaking Pavo's hand like a jackhammer. "Hand *S-S-S-S-SHAKE?*"

As the four gathered around the boys' window, taking in the terrestrial view, an irritated cough gained everyone's attention.

"*Ahem.*" Mallock entered with an arid scowl. "Now that you're all familiar with where your rooms are, you can follow me for the *rest* of the tour." He then turned an unpleasant glare toward Leo and said, "Try to stay with the group this time, Mr. Gray. Since you're not expected to know all the rules yet, I'll let that go as a warning.

"And as for you, Mr. Digbi," he continued, turning to Pavo with an equally unpleasant look, "as it appears you, too, have lost your way to the amphitheater for orientation; that will be an equal warning for you as well."

Leo and Pavo exchanged shocked looks—they had *both* received a warning? No one had told them that they needed to keep up with their groups, let alone that they would get in trouble if they didn't! And with that thought, Leo stuffed the senator's note deep inside his pocket, deciding that for now, he didn't necessarily *need* to give it back.

"First things first," Mallock began, leading Leo, Pavo, Andromeda, and Grus to a nearby gravity-shaft that shot them all the way up to the top of the moon. "You should all be made aware, that except for right now—for the purposes of me show-ing you where you're *not* allowed—none of you will ever be allowed back to the uppermost floor. Is that understood?"

Everyone nodded a yes and as the gravity-shaft opened, they found themselves surrounded by rows of clear tubular tunnels, each howling a ferocious wind at the waterfall's edge.

"These must be the oxygen chambers," said Andromeda, examining the dark, spiraling currents from behind their protective rail.

"Or as some call them," said the senator, "the Chambers of Life and Death."

"Why do they call them *that*?" Leo wondered.

"It's thanks to these chambers that we're all able to breathe in Luna City," Mallock explained. "If you were to somehow crack one, not only would you be sucked in to your demise, but so would be the fate of our entire delicate biosphere. That is exactly why these chambers have received such a name, and that is exactly why this door remains locked, and any attempt to revisit the chambers is strictly forbidden."

The senator gave everyone a moment to grasp the severity of this concept with a forewarning eye and then led them down to the moon's lowermost level.

"The second area off-limits is Floor Double-Z," said Mallock, as the gravity-shaft's doors reopened and the group entered a large industrial room where the waterfall began, and loud, beastly generators and trash-compacting-bots sorted through the city's recycling.

"Why would anyone want to come down *here*?" Pavo asked over the sound of the roaring trash collectors.

"My point precisely," said the senator. "So now that everyone has gotten visiting restricted areas *out* of their systems, I'll be showing you where you *can* be going."

The gravity-shaft arrived at the city's center, where Leo,

Pavo, Andromeda, and Grus stepped into an idyllic park filled with hundreds of firs and evergreens, hovering park benches, and a pond trimmed with lolling geese.

"And this must be Central Gardens!" Andromeda exclaimed, helping herself over the translucent floating bridge to get a better look at the neighboring classrooms.

"Yes, and you will find your classes through these connecting corridors," said Mallock. "The gardens should be useful for your studying and reflection between them."

"—or more like useful for stepping into goose-poo," Pavo whispered to Leo while passing a fat squawking goose.

Mallock gave Pavo a meaningful look, but before he could say another word, Grus was running off, shouting wildly in front of one of the gardens' many branching rooms:

"BY JIMMENY-JIM-JIMS!—THEY'VE GOT ROBO-PETS!"

Leo, Pavo, and Andromeda were in no time alongside Grus's spot in front of a large electronic window that read:

Madam Cebulka's WoNdErOuS Trade Shop

"BOY!" said Grus dreamily, staring over the array of robotic pets at the window's display. "I never thought I'd get to have a ROBO-PET in Luna City! Maybe I'll get a whole family of robo-kitte—er, uh,—TARANTULAS!" he adjusted, noticing Pavo's weirded-out look.

"Yes, well, I'm afraid those are all on the high-point list," said the senator, unamused by Grus's smudge mark across the glass, "alongside those atrocious Gravital posters . . ."

"Points?" wondered Andromeda aloud. But before Mallock could deter them, the door chime went off and a short, rounded woman with unruly dust-colored hair and a beguiling set of green and yellow eyes was standing in front of them.

"*Ojejciu!*" she said in a heavy Polish accent. "Fresh Luna Citizenz, have we, Senator?" She smiled eagerly at Leo, Pavo, Andromeda, and Grus, and waved them inside. "Pleaze, pleaze, come in, come in!"

Mallock watched expectantly as the four were hypnotized inside the shop, drooling over the innumerable toys, gadgets, and sweets. Grus ran off to check out the robo-pets while Pavo dug his nose into a Robotron Electron comic. Andromeda instead found herself bewitched by a real-D maze while Leo (who had hardly had the chance to look around the shop at all) stood transfixed in front of the register.

"High expectationz, have we, my dearz?" Cebulka asked, hoisting herself around the counter with the help of a robotic-hip. "That over ther' iz our top-prized item; one of a kind, made to celebrate the city'z opening!" She brought it down for Leo to take a look—it was an incredibly sleek and agile skydisk—and its ability to follow commands or shift into any shape you'd like made it a million times cooler than Gavin Jones's air-board!

Leo, however, was quick to notice the board's price:

1,000,000 trade-points. "So how do we start earning points?" he eagerly asked, running his hands across its smooth vinyl.

Cebulka smiled and went on to explain how everything worked. "Oneza quarterz, or on special holidayz, we allow shipment of Earthly goodz for our studentz to purchase via traded pointz. Pointz are earned from assigmentz and examz within your classez, and for completing variouz taskz within your Sectionalz."

She then went on to show them how the point board worked.

"You get 10 pointz for every right homework answer; 50 pointz for every right answer on quiz; 100 pointz when you complete qualifying Sectional task; and 500 pointz for every correct answer on final exam."

Everyone was excited to start earning points right away, but before they could finish thanking Madam Cebulka for her explanation of the points, or for the piece of sour-meteor candy she had given them, Mallock was escorting everyone out of the shop and to a lower level.

"This area here," said Mallock, leading the group into a greenhouse filled with every single plant, fruit, and vegetable you could think of, "is where our prized laboratories and conservatories are."

The four glanced around in amazement at the number of hover-bots busily transporting trays stacked with various herbs and flowers beneath a motion-sensing water-sprinkling drone-o-system. They followed Mallock into a neighboring lab, which was packed with hundreds upon hundreds of floating Petri dishes.

"Everything you will ever eat or drink in Luna City is all made right here in our very own labs," Mallock explained to them.

Leo, Pavo, Andromeda, and Grus watched with delight as a miniature hover-bot added a single droplet of water to a cube labeled 'Repli-Beef,' and it turned into a life-size patty before their very eyes.

"So when I'm eating a burger," said Grus thoughtfully, "I'm not really eating meat from a cow?"

"More like a super-cow," said Andromeda smartly. "Only the finest plant life has been genetically replicated to be *resemblant* of meat for our consumption." However, her attention soon turned to a distant yodeling through the lab. At first, there came an "*AHH!*" followed by a rather hefty "*OOH!*" And then, even closer, an "*EEE!*" and a "*YELP!*" Until one large and painful sounding "*OOOWWW!*" came hurtling straight past them.

"And here comes the head of our Science Department right as we speak," said Mallock airily, watching, nonplussed, as Dr. Row hopped past them, swatting his hands at his ever-balding head.

At the sudden realization of a crowd, the doctor turned a bright shade of watermelon red!

"Oh, my!" he stuttered embarrassedly, while continuously swatting. "I know how this must look; but I promise, I've not entirely lost my noodle! I've . . . instead . . . *somehow* . . . ," he went on with difficulty, "managed to . . . shrink a . . . bee!"

"You can *shrink* a bee?" Pavo asked, impressed.

"Er—well . . . not a real one," the doctor admitted. He found a remote control from the table beside them and gave it a firm click. "It's robotic! I like to call her Bumble-bot!"

Dr. Row collected the small bot and passed it around for everyone to take a look.

"It's *becredible*," said Andromeda, admiring its pellucid wings.

"It actually looks real," added Leo.

"Yes—well, that's the precise problem with it," said the doctor, desolate. "I've somehow managed to make her so realistic that I failed to remove her stinger prior to testing . . ."

Mallock looked at the bee with a skeptical eye and asked, "I do hope this is part of an *official* assignment, doctor?"

Though Leo didn't think it was at all possible, Dr. Row's ears turned even redder! "I was—ahem," Row stammered, "trying to invent a more efficient way to pollinate all the conservatory's flowers!" He looked at the senator, who didn't look convinced. "To diminish costs for Luna City, that is. Which reminds me!" he added, chuckling. "The Datura innoxia need tending to! Toodle-doos!"

Everyone giggled as the doctor scurried away, hurrying back to reclaim his Bumble-bot, which he had momentarily forgotten.

"Is he always this *louco*?" Pavo asked as soon as he left again.

"It would appear so," said the senator stiffly. And he escorted them out of the lab and up to the amphitheater for orientation.

Much like most things in Luna City, the amphitheater was unparalleled in its display of technologically advanced yet botanically diverse architectonics. Its mountain-esque stage stood suspended in the city's center, draped with upward flowing vines of ivy and a spattering of willow-hybrid trees. In its middle was a crystal podium, highlighting the backdrop of the reverse spiraling waterfall that gently flowed up toward the moon's stargazing ceiling.

"Some seats," said Pavo to Leo after the senator left them in line to claim a floating chair with no clue how to hail one.

"Do you pay attention to anything?" Andromeda said. She snapped her fingers, and her Meta at once signaled a chair to float down to them.

"See?" said Pavo lazily. "I don't even have to ask and she does things for me!"

Andromeda rolled her eyes as the boys laughed and took their seats. Then, after a moment of chairs filling, a tall, old man with dark umber skin (and what looked like an ash-covered bird's nest on top of his head) stepped up to the podium. He made one small quiver with his knobby finger and the abundant chatter ceased completely. Without introduction, everyone knew it was President Soenso.

The lunar president, however, didn't seem the slightest bit enthralled with his name badge, or title, which Leo quickly realized because Soenso had adjusted it to read "So?" He then, unhurriedly, set up his techni-reader (in which he had prepared some notes) and said in a voice that came from the very bottom of his throat, "My newest Luna Citizens, it is with great honor and privilege today that I am to announce the start of your first lunar year!

"To those of you who have won your ticket, welcome!— *and don't worry, you'll learn about stress-free economy soon enough!* And to those of you who have had your admission so generously purchased for you, my greatest thanks to your parents for their investment in us!

"Now, before we get started on official announcements—" The president stopped, readjusted his laser-specs, and went on. "I'm sure you're all eager to learn the results of your Placement Exams?"

A wave of excited murmurs filled the air.

"Very well, then! Metas on!"

And in a second, the amphitheater filled with the sound of a thousand students turning in their chairs, each eagerly announcing whichever Sectional they had been placed in to those seated beside them.

"Yay!" Grus sang as a small musical note lit across his Meta badge. "I'm in the MUSIC SECTION!"

"That's great, Grus," said Andromeda while a mathematical symbol appeared across hers.

"*Ooh*," said Grus, pointing at it excitedly. "What's *that?*"

"It's the symbol for Pi," said Andromeda, "you know, for math."

"*Not fair*," Grus mumbled, looking slightly disappointed. "I didn't know they let you eat *pie* in math!"

"They don't," said Andromeda, looking at him weirdly. "It just stands for 3.141592 . . ."

"Oh," said Grus, oblivious, "I knew *that*!"

"And what about you, Pavo?" Andromeda asked. "Which Sectional did you get into?"

"Hopefully not the same as you," Pavo muttered as a miniature coliseum lit across his.

"Nice," said Leo. "Wish I was good enough at sports to be in Athletics!"

"Me too . . . ," said Pavo, slightly embarrassed. "The coliseum is for—er—History. You?"

Leo looked down at his badge to find a small beaker symbol emerging across his.

"Science," he replied with a grin.

Everyone continued turning in their chairs, eager to meet any new Sectional mates beside them; but as Leo turned in his, his hand dropped to his side.

"Greetings, Leo . . . the *Strange*," snickered Gavin Jones, sitting alongside a thoroughly puzzled-looking Aabher Pawar.

Leo had completely forgotten that Gavin and Aabher were going to be in Luna City. If he hadn't have, he would have watched more closely where he was sitting!

"Thought you lost your ticket?" said Gavin bitterly.

"Guess I found another," said Leo coolly. Though, in the back of his mind, Leo feared what Gavin would say next. He didn't necessarily want everyone at his new school knowing he was considered the "strange" kid in his hometown. But it appeared that Gavin knew that Leo had something to throw back at him: his cheating.

Gavin, however, didn't end without saying something else. "That's really too bad you're not still in Riverdale," he jeered, sneering at Leo rudely. "Guess now my home won't have anyone at least *somewhat* reliable to patrol for tree-thieves anymore. No one can count on that stinky old dog-spit—he couldn't catch a snatch if his life depended on it!"

Leo's skin boiled at the sound of Gavin snubbing on Gudrun, but he kept his words under his tongue as Gavin continued with his air-headed comments.

"And oh! I almost forgot," he added, turning to the boy sitting next to him. "This here is my and Aabher's new room-mate, Crewt."

Leo exchanged looks with the boy with thick black hair, ghostly dark skin, and eyes a menacing lapis. If it were possible, he looked even meaner than Gavin did as he sat there without a sliver of a smile.

The boy corrected Gavin's horrible pronunciation. "It's *Crux*, Crux Mallock," he said as if bored to death with having to repeat that the "x" was silent.

"Yeah, and he practically invented Gravital," bragged Aabher.

At the sound of that, Andromeda invited herself in on the boys' conversation.

"*Mallock?*" she repeated. "As in, *Senator Mallock?* So your dad's pretty much the mediator between all of Earth and Luna City?"

"Something like that . . . ," said the boy without interest.

"Well, my name's Andromeda, An-dro-*may*-da Groves, and my cousin over here, Pavo, is a world champion at Ping-Pong if you ever need someone to play with."

Pavo turned around in horror.

"*N-o-o-o* I'm not," he stammered, sinking in his chair.

But Crux's eyes were twinkling at the sound.

"Really?" he asked, examining Pavo's lack of muscular features. "I'd love to have someone to 'play with' . . . or *beat,* rather. What do you say about a match this Friday?"

"YES!" Andromeda answered for him. "He'd LOVE to!"

But the look on Pavo's face showed he couldn't have wanted anything less.

"It's settled then," said Crux, appearing pleased with Pavo's non-response. "We'll set the match for this Friday, at the first anti-gravity gym, after final-hour. I'll take Gavin for my Pilot and . . . Aabher as my Back-up Hitter."

"Ooh! Ooh! . . . Ooh! Ooh!" Grus chirped excitedly. "Pick me, Pavo! Pick me! I can be your Pilot! Or your—"

But Pavo's voice had suddenly returned to him!

"I'll take Leo as my Pilot," said Pavo quickly. He paused, clearly speculating over who'd be a better match between his two options. "And um—" He sighed with defeat. "—Andromeda, for my Back-up Hitter."

"YES!" Andromeda shouted, pumping her fist as she swiveled back in her chair.

Though as Pavo turned in his, he nearly slipped right out of it!

"You know I've never played *Gravital* before," he hissed at his presumptuous cousin.

"Neither have I," said Andromeda in her own defense. "But you're an excellent Ping-Pong player, and you need to at least *try* to make some friends!"

"Who said anything about needing any *friends*?"

"I wouldn't worry too much about it," said Leo. "We've got a whole week until Friday to practice. And besides, I'm sure Gravital can't be *that* difficult." However, Leo was equally as concerned about how to use the Pilot remote! But before anyone had the chance to worry more about Friday's match, the president resumed his speech.

"And now for those official announcements, please welcome Senator Vladimus Mallock!"

The crowd clapped in anticipation for the senator to arrive. But as the seconds passed, it soon became clear that he wasn't going to show.

Soenso's gaze traveled to Principal Yin, but she shook her head, not knowing where he was.

"I suppose your principal could go over the Rule Book one last time . . . ," Soenso suggested after a moment of reflection. A series of moans echoed through the amphitheater, so he thought better of it and said, "But if my memory serves me right, I believe you have a long day ahead of you tomorrow. So I say, *go eat!*"

The amphitheater filled with cheers and the sound of a thousand students shuffling out of their chairs. And before Leo knew it, he was moving down a line filled with a hundred chef-bots and various cuisines, from pizzas and pastas to curries and relishes, pies, puddings, and frozen ice creams, all neatly packed into silvery meal pouches.

"Hey, guys!" Andromeda called out after Leo and Pavo (who were attempting to find a table of their own).

Pavo sighed, annoyed, and snapped at his cousin, "Can't you find someplace *else* to sit?"

"I *could* . . . ," said Andromeda with a thoughtful sneer, "but then you wouldn't hear what Grus and I just heard Soenso discussing with Principal Yin!"

Pavo eyed them reluctantly but allowed them to sit.

"*Well* . . . ," Andromeda started, lowering her voice to a whisper once realizing she had unwittingly invited some extra ears, "apparently—today—during orientation—someone tore apart the old book database of the library!"

"So?" said Pavo, uninterested in library vandals.

"*Soo,*" said Andromeda, "whoever it was unsorted every single book!—the entire place is now a disaster area!"

"Didn't the security cameras see who it was?" Leo inquired.

"That's the strangest part," said Andromeda. "Miss Genie, the library-bot, said all the books began to fly off the shelves by themselves—and the security cameras confirmed it!—there wasn't a *single person* in there!"

"That's impossible," said Pavo.

"Truth or not," said Andromeda importantly, "we won't be able to use it until everything's resorted, so Soenso suggested Principal Yin make it *our years'* detention!"

"Good thing none of us will have to worry about *that*!" said Grus with a mouthful of veggie burger.

"Let's hope," said Andromeda, giving Leo and Pavo a scrupulous look.

Leo, however, was just noticing the senator reappearing down a far-off Quickpath. Where had *he* been all that time when he wasn't there for orientation? Could he know something more about the library's vandalization? *And what would someone want to vandalize a library for?* Leo wasn't sure, but he was suddenly starting to feel more and more curious about the senator's mysterious note.

CHAPTER

10

THE GRAVITAL BET

T he first day came swiftly, and Leo awoke to his air-wave-bed deflating and Meta reading off his new class sched-ule. It was a strange feeling knowing it was morning when the same nightly sky still lingered outside his window.

Pavo was the first to wake and take advantage of the shared bathroom, while Leo (who still wasn't completely used to being scrubbed by an automatic robo-wash) took a while longer as he went in second. Grus, instead, was the last to get up, and as he took his turn singing made-up lyr-ics to one of Beethoven's final symphonies, Leo and Pavo made their break for the cafeteria, leaving Grus to enjoy his shower opera to himself.

There were a lot of classrooms at the Lunar Academy, and even more Quickpaths to get to them. Leo found his Luna Watch came in very handy in helping him find his way around, thanks to its interactive holo-map, and of course, to Meta, who made sure to bug him every step of the way on how many minutes he had left to make it to class without being late.

Leo's first class of the day was Art, with Professoressa Pittore: a tall, twiggy lady from Italy with dreaded, viridescent hair and a perpetual scent of coffee. Leo was happy to find out he shared the class with Pavo, but they both regrettably came to realize that simply painting a smiley face on their canvases was not a sufficient enough form of "Expressingz'a onez'a emotionz'a" and missed gaining their first assignment's bonus trade-points.

History of Space was after Art, with Herr Pendeluhr: a remarkably short (and remarkably hairy) man from Germany, who always seemed to have too much to say and not enough time to say it. Andromeda was in the class too, along with her new roommate, Phoebe Voiles, a drama student from France, with rich chestnut skin, short violet hair, and an even shorter temper to go along with it—a proper fit for the Theater Sectional, or so Leo supposed.

Introductory Astronomy was Leo's third-hour, with Professor Kikaren: one of the youngest professors at the academy, from Sweden, who couldn't fully see but saw via a shape-to-mind-projection-headband. Leo was super-excited for the class once he learned he'd be spending the entirety of it examining the Jovian planets from a real-D planetarium; but he was even more excited to find that the two kids he sat next to, Scotti and Ume Tokage, robotics whizzes from Japan, were more entertaining than anyone else he had yet met at the academy with their near-constant bickering in laser-sign language.

After third-hour, Leo would meet up with Pavo in Central Gardens to head to lunch. The gardens, as the senator suggested, had easily become everyone's favorite meeting spot, including the president's, who could often be found taunting the geese with non-glutenous breadcrumbs. Though with each day that passed, Leo was increasingly finding himself becoming less and less a fan of their abstract-expressionistic decorating.

Leo spent the rest of the afternoon in his Science Sectional, working under the direction of Dr. Row. Though Dr. Row did not turn out to be the most popular Sectional Director among the other members in his group (due to his never-ending lists of seemingly pointless pollen toxicity testing labs), he had quickly became Leo's favorite, due in part to his wide breadth of knowledge in all the sciences . . . and due in part to his wacky mannerisms.

Despite Leo not being thrilled about his monotonous botany work, he found his lab partner was a huge help in speeding up their tasks: Izma Nazari, a microbiology expert from

Abu Dhabi and—to Leo's surprise—a know-it-all in Gravital. And he gratefully took all the advice from her he could get in preparation for Friday's match.

"We'll toss for first-serve," Crux announced as the two teams gathered outside the anti-gravity gym that afternoon after class. He instructed his Meta to produce a holographic coin, and Gavin quickly shouted, "We call heads!"

"I guess that settles *that*," Pavo whispered to Leo.

"HA-HA!" Gavin laughed out loud the second Crux's Meta revealed the outcome of the toss. "We've got starting serve!" He ran past Leo and Pavo, sneering at them, overzealous to claim what he clearly must have thought was the better half of the court.

Leo shook his head and went over the tips Izma had given him as he hopped onto his Pilot chair. Pavo obsessively wrapped his wrists with tape while Andromeda, Phoebe, and Grus took their spots on the hovering bleachers, waiting for the game to begin. And the second the scoreboard lit, Crux tossed the gravityball in the air, and the Gravital match began!

Leo tapped away speedily at his remote as his three Hed-bots started off from the center of the court. To make any of them go faster than their automatic-set pace, they had to be individually selected; but even then, despite Leo's vigorous tapping, they inched away like snails.

Leo decided he'd take Izma's suggestion of giving each of his Hed-bots an equal lag, selecting them in intervals to keep them evenly paced. Gavin, however, had clearly chosen to focus on advancing just one of his Hed-bots, as two of them were virtually still at the starting line while one Hed-bot was halfway toward the goal.

Pavo and Crux hit the gravityball back and forth between them, for a long time, neither allowing the other any close hits. But then, Leo spotted a gap widening on Pavo's far right, leaving their most advanced Hed-bot an easy target. But to Leo's misfortune, so had Crux. Pavo hit the gravityball back toward Crux's courtside. Crux struck toward the gap, and Leo readied his fingers over his trigger; the gravityball slipped past Pavo's racquet; and Leo pulled down on his trigger, flipping his Hed-bot—to his surprise—brilliantly into the air!

The robotic scorekeeper called it: "A near Hed-hit by C. Mallock, saved by L. Gray!"

Andromeda, Phoebe, and Grus cheered with fervor for Leo's first save. But Gavin looked at Leo with an envious rage.

"Nice save . . . *LEE-WAD*," he shouted from across the court. "Bet you fifty fat trade-points you can't do that again!"

Leo, whose nerves were just settling from all the excitement, couldn't help but feel somewhat overconfident as he replied, "Deal! Fifty trade-points says I will get to flip another Hed-bot . . . and another fifty says you won't get a chance to flip any of yours!"

Gavin rolled over with laughter. "Ha! You'll lose it all today, GRAY!"

Leo ignored him, anxious for the chance to take fifty precious trade-points away from Gavin. But in the very next serve, Gavin was flipping his Hed-bot long before the gravityball had passed the centerline of the court!

Leo's eyes raced to the scorekeeper—he was certain it had to be a foul! By now, a large group of students had formed in the gymnasium to watch the match, and everyone seemed split down the middle on whether it was a legit Hed-save or not; that is, until the robotic scorekeeper called it to favor Crux and Gavin.

"*SEE?*" Gavin shouted snootily to Leo. "Told you I'd get to flip one! That's fifty FAT trade-points to me, and another fifty if you don't flip another one of yours!"

Leo tried to tune out Gavin, but it was proving increasingly difficult as Gavin continued, "And he's supposedly *GOOD* at Ping-Pong? HA! WHAT A JOKE! I bet that potbellied Dr. Row would be a better match than HIM!"

Leo's hairs prickled on his neck as Gavin chorused:

> *Fifty fat trade-points to me!*
> *Leo the Strange ain't no match for me!*
> *Fifty fat—*

But just when Leo turned to tell Gavin off, a flash of silver flickered past the corner of his eye, and before Leo could make out what it was from, Gavin was shouting triumphantly, "HED-HIIIIT!"

Leo looked to the court to find Pavo staring back at him with an expression of complete despair.

The robotic scorekeeper called it: "One hundred points won by C. Mallock! And an illegal racquet toss by P. Digbi, requiring a three-minute time-out to ready their Back-up Hitter!"

"What were you *thinking* up there?" Pavo said to Leo, as Leo hovered down in his Pilot chair. "That should have been an easy save!"

"Sorry . . . ," Leo muttered ruefully, still in disbelief that he had just let Gavin's air-headed comments get the better of him. "I swear, I won't let it happen again."

"It doesn't matter now," said Pavo as Andromeda ran up from the bleachers, thrilled to be taking her turn on the court. "You're stuck playing with *her*."

"What's *that* supposed to mean?" Andromeda snapped at him, snatching Pavo's racquet.

"*You know* . . . ," Pavo mumbled. "I mean, it's not as though you're going to be able to keep up with Crux and all with a—"

"—*Prosthetic?*" Andromeda gushed, glaring at Pavo scathingly. "Seriously, just because my leg's made of metal, doesn't mean it doesn't work!"

"*Metal?*" Leo repeated.

Andromeda sighed habitually and rolled up her legging. "There! See it?" she said. "Good. Now that everyone has, *questions?*"

Leo couldn't think of how he hadn't noticed it!

"Wait—how did it—" he started to say; until he realized the answer. "Your mom and dad weren't the only ones in that boat-jetting accident?"

"Luckily for me, I got to 'walk' away from it," said Andromeda crisply. "Now, if you don't mind, we have a game to *win*?"

"Right," said Leo readily. This time, nagging Gavin or not, there was no way he was going to let him gain another point on them now—especially as he'd have to help cover for Andromeda!

And so Leo returned to his Pilot chair, more focused than ever.

The second round started, and for Leo and Andromeda to tie with Crux and Gavin, Andromeda would need to make a Hed-hit. Even though Leo was already out one of his most advanced Hed-bots, he still had two left, and he kept his eyes locked on them, anticipating the second he'd have to flip either one of his Heds once Andromeda missed her return serve.

But as Leo sat there, waiting to save either of his Hed-bots, the gravityball never came; in fact, as Leo finally looked to Andromeda, his face slumped with surprise: Andromeda was smashing the gravityball straight past Crux's racquet, nearly taking out Gavin's most advanced Hed-bot!

The crowd rooted Andromeda on as she continued to hit the gravityball back at every one of Crux's attempted Hed-hits. Not only was she managing to hold her own against Gravital's inventor, she appeared to be an even better match against him than Pavo was!

The tension soon grew between the two sides of the court as neither Andromeda nor Crux was allowing the other an opportunity to advance with another close hit. But then, after what felt like an hour of meticulous hitting, there was a loud, deafening *POP!* And before anyone knew where it had come from, Crux was swinging at air, and Gavin was crying with defeat: Andromeda had actually done it!—she had taken out Gavin's and Crux's lead Hed-bot!

Grus and Phoebe went berserk from the bleachers, while Pavo sat there, rendered speechless by his cousin.

It was soon five minutes into the final round, and each side was now out one Hed-bot, with two drawing dangerously close to the goal line. Leo's frustration grew by the second, as each time he glanced to the other side of the court, both of Gavin's Hed-bots were just as close as his were to the goal— meaning they had an even tie.

Leo tapped away vigorously on his remote, trying to speed up his Hed-bots—but they were already going their max speed.

The scoreboard lit to the last remaining minute. Andromeda and Crux were guarding their Heds more vigilantly than ever.

If I can get just ONE of these slug-bots over the goal line before Gavin, we could actually win the match! thought Leo. He held his breath as the scoreboard lit with the final seconds. He tapped and tapped and tapped until his fingers were sore. And then, the buzzer blew, and his most advanced Hed-bot dispersed a striking green glow, double back-flipping in the air as it crossed the finishing goal line.

Leo threw his hands up with excessive delight. Though as he looked toward the other side of the court, his excitement at once faded: Gavin hadn't gotten just *one* of his Hed-bots across the goal line, but *both* of his Hed-bots had crossed it and were doing somersaults victoriously in the air.

Leo let out a depressed groan as the robotic scorekeeper hovered over to Gavin and Crux's side of the court to reveal their final points. The only way Leo, Pavo, and Andromeda could be winning now was if, by some luck, their only saved Hed-bot was the bonus bot. But Leo knew better than to bet on that! The odds that either of Gavin's Hed-bots was the bonus bot were double his.

Leo suddenly found himself wishing he hadn't made that stupid bet for a hundred trade-points against Gavin. He was now, officially, certain he had lost them.

The robotic scorekeeper finally announced Gavin and Crux's points. "Two 100-point-bots to make it across the goal line, by G. Jones," he called out while inspecting their Hed-bots, "in addition to one 100-point hit, won by C. Mallock . . . awarding team Mallock and Jones 300 points in total!"

The crowd cheered, and Gavin shot Leo a satisfied sneer.

The robotic scorekeeper hovered to Leo and Andromeda's courtside.

"One Hed-hit worth 100 points won by A. Groves . . . ," the scorekeeper continued, "and—" He paused for a second, double-tapping on their only remaining Hed-bot. "Five hundred bonus points for the goal-crossing bot, made by L. Gray . . . awarding 600 points in total to team Digbi, Groves, and Gray!"

Disbelief ran across Leo's face as cheers broke out throughout the gymnasium—he had saved the bonus-bot!—he, Pavo, and Andromeda had won the Gravital match!

That evening, in the cafeteria, no one could believe their luck at winning the Gravital match against Crux and Gavin. Leo was thrilled for having won the bonus-bot, but he was even more thrilled that he had managed to flip another one of his Heds, winning him his 100 trade-points back from Gavin.

Though however exciting the match may have been, no one could stop talking about one thing:

"You sure showed it to Crux out there today, didn't you, Andromeda!" said Grus, munching away at a floating piece of pizza.

"No kidding," said Pavo with amazement. "Where'd you learn to play like *that*?"

"I don't *know* . . . ," said Andromeda, facetious. "If I'm not mistaken, I think I'm related to a *world champion* Ping-Pong player? Of course, I had to try some sport sooner or later to match up with him; so I figured I'd try my new leg out at tennis camp over the summer to see if it was any good. But I *never* could have imagined that I'd one day be a better Hitter than him in GRAVITAL!"

"Yeah, well, you should have seen *LE CHOC* on Crux's face when you took out his lead Hed-bot!" said Phoebe, giggling as a sudden clamoring came their way.

"Hey, you!" a girl called out to Andromeda.

The entire table turned and gaped. A girl with sun-kissed skin and striking strawberry locks approached their table.

"Crux requests a rematch," the girl reported.

Andromeda looked lost.

"Well, One-leg, are you in or not?"

"Um, *yeah!*" said Phoebe on her behalf, shaking Andromeda from what she clearly must have thought was a dream. After all, it was Carina Van'ness: a celebrity in her own right back on Earth, who had apparently paid her way into Luna City from just one ad of smiling.

"And you can let Crux know that Andromeda's gonna kick his LITTLE BUTT!" Grus called out after her, folding his arms as though that settled things.

"*Um, okay . . . ,*" said Carina, looking at Grus weirdly.

Leo, however, was quick to notice Pavo's quiet state.

"You're not *jealous*, are you?" Leo asked him once they got back to their dorm room.

"No," said Pavo, staring dejectedly at the ceiling. "Just confused. How's *Andromeda* better at Gravital than *me*? If I had known, I would have let Grus be my Back-up Hitter."

"Don't worry," said Grus encouragingly, "you can always pick me next time!"

"*Próxima vez?*" said Pavo wildly. "As if there'll ever be one of those!"

Grus continued trying to cheer up Pavo, telling him *all* about his "MAD" skydisking skills. Leo took out a slice of cheese he had snuck back from the cafeteria and knelt beside his bed to feed Archimedes. But as Leo lifted the roof of the small pet-house, Archimedes, curiously, wasn't there.

"Hey, you guys . . . ," said Leo, scanning the room. "Have either of you seen Archimedes?"

"'Archimedes?'" Grus repeated thoughtfully. "He should be here somewhere. I mean, I was just playing with him before the match!"

But as Leo continued to look for him, a wave of panic flooded him as he realized: "He's not here!"

"What do you mean 'he's not here'?" said Pavo, finally lifting his sulking head out of his unibook. "Where could he have gone to?"

And for a long while, Leo didn't know . . . but then it hit him.

"It's Gavin," he answered darkly. "Gavin must have taken Archimedes to get back at me for winning our bet on the Gravital match!"

"'Gavin,'" Grus repeated (as though this made perfect sense). "Who knows what he could be doing to poor little Archimedes right as we speak!" And with that, Leo's nerves shot through him like a lightning bolt. He had promised Gudrun that he was going to take care of Archimedes, and now, he had lost him. If Gudrun ever found out, he'd never speak to him again!

"*Ei!*" Pavo shouted after Leo as Leo took off toward the door. "Where are you going?"

"To go get Archimedes," said Leo determinedly. And

before anyone could say another word, Leo was storming down the hall to Gavin's.

It was after normal hours, and the dormitory's halls were now dimly lit by incandescent computer-touch-walls. Pavo and Grus ran after Leo, shouting about how they weren't supposed to be out of their rooms past curfew. Leo hissed back at them to keep quiet and instructed them to keep watch for Floris and Japps, two of the dorm's robotic security guards, who were, luckily, nowhere in sight.

Leo reached Gavin's door. He could hear him wailing to Aabher about their defeat and about how dumb he had been for having made the bet for 100 trade-points against him.

Leo took a short breath and let himself in.

"Where is he?" Leo demanded, greeting Gavin with a piercing stare.

"*W-w-where's who?*" Gavin stuttered.

"You know who," Grus replied. "Where's Leo's pet mouse, Archimedes?"

But at this, Gavin's face flickered from confusion to cruel delight.

"So Gray has a pet rat, does he?" he said in a tone that meant he knew pets weren't allowed.

Leo's stomach sank to his feet: Gavin couldn't have stolen Archimedes—he didn't even know he existed!

"I don't have a *rat*," said Leo, trying to get himself out of the mess he had just gotten himself into.

"Yeah guys, Grus was only kidding. *Right, Grus?*" said Pavo, nudging Grus in the hope of him catching his drift.

Grus didn't catch it.

"*No, I wasn—*" Grus started to pout. But before he could finish, Crux entered the room, looking absolutely elated with Leo and Gavin's confrontation.

"Freakwheel wasn't kidding," said Crux, his lips curling into a malicious grin.

"Yeah, he wasn't kidding," retorted Aabher, sniggering out of place.

Crux snaked an arm around Leo's shoulders. "You do know pets *aren't* allowed in Luna City?"

Leo gulped.

"But don't worry," he went on, uncoiling his arm. "I won't tell . . ." And for a second, Leo was relieved that Crux didn't share Gavin's poor moral character; but Crux hadn't entirely finished.

"That is," he continued, "provided you do one thing for me?"

"What's that?" Leo asked meekly.

"Sneak into Central Gardens and . . ." Crux paused, as if debating what to do. "And kiss . . . a . . . GOOSE!"

Gavin and Aabher burst out with laughter.

"You're a GENIUS!" Aabher cackled, holding on to the side of his stomach as Gavin howled even louder.

Leo, however, was hoping his ears had deceived him.

"Do what, *exactly*?" he asked with hesitation.

"'KISS—A—GOOSE!'" Gavin repeated, laughing as though he had never laughed in his life.

Leo couldn't *believe* he had been so stupid as to have falsely accused Gavin. He normally wouldn't have jumped to such conclusions, but he couldn't continue searching for Archimedes now—he had a goose to kiss!

And so, without any other option, Leo accepted the boys' challenge. Though Leo couldn't have been prepared for what he later found out when they reached Central Gardens: Crux's plan wasn't for him to kiss a goose in front of him, Aabher, and Gavin—it was for Leo to kiss a goose in front of nearly every kid in their year!

Leo gazed nauseously into the sea of eager faces, unwillingly taking in his classmates' finger-points and laughs as he made his way over the translucent hover-bridge. He picked up one of the president's old breadcrumbs beside the pond, hoping to persuade one of the geese as quickly as possible.

Leo knelt down at the pond's edge. He held out his neck and brought the crumb to his lips. But as Leo waited there, his luck once again went missing; the fattest goose started swimming straight toward him!

The laughter soon heightened in the gardens, so much so that Leo could no longer hear his own thoughts as he stretched his neck out an inch more. The goose honked with excitement and swam closer toward him. But just before its bill reached Leo's lips, Leo noticed something shimmery at the bottom of the pond. Leo tried to make out what it was, but before he could, an exasperated shrill echoed from behind him.

"Fancy kissing *geese?*" gushed an infuriated Principal Yin.

Leo looked up, uncertain whether he should feel relieved that he hadn't actually kissed the goose, or terrified, as Principal Yin, who was now dressed in her night robe, was looking more intimidating than ever.

Leo scrambled to his feet, anxious to explain, but Principal Yin was in no mood to listen. "Back to your rooms. All of you!" she barked at the onlookers. "I'll see to it whoever is behind this gets their fair share of trade-points taken off their Metas in the morning!"

Gavin, Crux, and Aabher each shot Leo a threatening look, as if warning him about what he'd face if he ratted them out—and Leo didn't dare; he now knew what the three of them were capable of.

"This way," Principal Yin instructed Leo, directing him down a darkened Quickpath by the tug of his shirt.

Leo could feel his heart steadily losing its vigor as he followed Principal Yin up a gravity-shaft that lead them to the upper levels of the moon. The entire way, she didn't exchange a word with him, leaving Leo to imagine that he was destined for an interminable detention. But as the gravity-shaft opened, Leo's heart nearly stopped completely: they weren't going to Principal Yin's office—they were going to the president's!

Leo could already hear what sorts of terrible things Soenso was now going to think of him, having never before formally met, and now—of all things—meeting him for trying to kiss a goose! Leo had previously imagined their first meeting would have been for something far more honorable, like receiving perfect homework scores or winning a seat on student council—never had he imagined meeting the president for something like this. . .

Principal Yin pushed Leo through the doorway, where Soenso sat at his desk, perfectly distracted by a wooden spinning contraption. The office itself was nothing like the rest of Luna City; there was nothing high-tech or modern about it (except for the president's floating desk and hover-chair). Instead, the place was stacked with vintage almanacs, and its ceiling was covered with antiquated flying machines (one of which Leo recognized as being from Da Vinci; however, most of them simply looked ridiculous).

Soenso gestured for them to have a seat.

"Sherry?" he offered the principal, toying around with his spinning thingy.

Principal Yin looked more irritated than ever as she snapped, "Now is not the time for *drinks!*"

Soenso looked confused. "Oh?" he said funnily. "Then what is it that we're here for?"

"We've had an unexpected calamity in the gardens this evening," Yin hissed, gesturing toward Leo.

Leo's face turned even whiter.

"Ah!" replied Soenso, seeming without care or judgment to

Principal Yin's extremely ruffled presence in his office as he adjusted his laser-specs toward Leo.

"So, then, what is it that we've done?" he asked Leo simply.

Leo, however, didn't know where to begin.

"I, uh—" Leo started, trying to think of the best way to put it, "tried to—er—"

"Get on with it!" Principal Yin shouted.

"Tried to kiss a goose, sir," said Leo quickly.

Soenso choked a little and then turned a much more attentive gaze to the principal.

"*Cornelius?*" he muttered, taken aback. "He means to say it was Corneli—"

"Why *else* do you think I'd bother coming up here at such an hour?" said Principal Yin, looking as though the president taking his time to realize things was his usual manner.

"Oh," said Soenso, suddenly low-spirited. "Yes, yes . . . right, of course . . ."

Leo, however, didn't understand any of it. How was trying to kiss a goose such a big deal? Or maybe it was the fact that he had been out past curfew, but even then, so had everyone else! And who was this Cornelius guy they were talking about? Leo imagined they had meant Crux, but he still couldn't figure out what all the fuss was over, especially now as he was receiving deep, penetrative stares from the president.

And for a long time, Soenso sat like this, his narrow, wrinkly eyes pressing into Leo's as if reading some sort of detective book; until he said at last, "Very well then, Yin. I'll take care of it."

"Good!" she shouted rapturously and left the room.

But as the doors sealed behind her, Leo suddenly felt himself becoming even sicker. The president floated his chair beside him and said, "So, who's put you up to it?"

Leo looked at the president with disbelief; how did *he* know it wasn't his idea? Leo opened his mouth but then shut it, remembering Gavin, Crux, and Aabher's stares.

"Well?" Soenso egged.

"No one," said Leo, grimacing.

"'No one?'" the president repeated, looking at Leo with a skeptical brow. "You don't really mean to tell me that you were actually trying to kiss a goose on purpose?"

"I was just trying to be funny," Leo lied, smiling weakly.

The president, however, looked as though a whale had just been lifted from him. He shook his head and heartily laughed, "My dear boy, you had me worried you were up to much more dangerous deeds!"

"So I'm getting kicked out of Luna City?" Leo asked, worried.

"No, no," said Soenso, calming himself down a bit as he squeezed a fragrant bubble out of his pouched drink, "that is, provided you can promise me something?"

"Anything!" said Leo, desperate.

"No more kissing geese."

And with that, Leo's cheeks flushed with heat, and feeling more relieved than ever, he headed back to his room to catch up on some much-needed sleep.

DOWN THE SECRET STAIRS

T he following weeks were the busiest weeks Leo had ever experienced. He had become extremely busy studying for his first exams, documenting chemical changes of Datura innoxia plants, and searching for Archimedes whenever he had the chance.

Though Gavin, Crux, and Aabher had each lost 100 trade-points once Principal Yin learned they had blackmailed Leo into kissing a goose (thanks to two unnamed first-years informing her about the mass visi-text message that Crux had sent to everyone in their class), Leo and Pavo couldn't brag that they had many more either, having gotten caught snooping around the lab mice cages in one of Dr. Row's labs. To everyone's great relief, Archimedes wasn't among them; but after weeks of searching, Leo still didn't have the slightest clue about where Archimedes had gone.

This, of course, left Leo completely frazzled about what to say to Gudrun when Gudrun finally invited him for a visi-chat.

"What do you think I should say to him?" Leo asked Pavo while scanning in their unibook passes with Miss Genie, the library-bot, during their break after lunch.

"I don't know . . . ," said Pavo, searching for an open visi-lab. "Maybe you should just tell him you lost him?"

"'Tell him I *lost* him?'" Leo repeated, looking at Pavo as though he were completely out of it. "He'd *kill* me—remember? He still thinks Archimedes is all he has left from his 'alien'-abducted wife."

"Oh, yeah, that's right," said Pavo, having forgot. "So just tell him he's sleeping or something. That sounds like a pretty normal thing for a mouse to do."

"Yeah, but he can't sleep forever," said Leo, frustrated that neither he nor Pavo could think of a better excuse.

"Well, *I* think you should tell him the truth," said Andromeda from behind them, alongside Phoebe. "It's not fair to Gudrun for him to not know what's going on with his pet."

"*Ei*, don't you need to practice skydisking or something?" Pavo barked at his cousin.

"She doesn't *need practice*," said Phoebe, shooting Pavo a

"Hey, you two!" Gudrun barked at them. "Get those outta here!—*Don't know who they belong to*," he added, blushing wildly. "*Anyhoo*—been meanin' ta ask ya Leo, how's Archimedes doin'? Hasn't been chew'n up all your homework, I hope?"

Leo froze as Gudrun laughed at his own joke—of course a mouse couldn't eat electronic paper—but he hadn't been expecting Gudrun to bring it up so quickly! Leo hated the thought of lying, but he couldn't imagine what Gudrun would think of him if he told him the truth. But before Leo said another word, Gudrun brought up something else.

"Noticed your guys's room's gotta be on what . . . the bottom of the moon? Hopefully it doesn't get too chilly down there for wee fella?"

"*Bottom of the moon?*" Leo repeated, not knowing how Gudrun could have any idea about where his room was.

"Yeah—er—Guess I forgot ta tell ya!" said Gudrun, picking up on Leo's confusion. "Before you two left I'd done got Archimedes one of those there microchips—ta keep track of him, so he don't get lost like he always does 'round here. Just realized it was kinda sorta keepin' track of you, too! *Anyhoo*, I was meaning ta give ya the link, o' course. I know you didn't pay for your ticket up there and all that, but ya'd think, for what it was worth, you'd be able to request sumthin' a bit higher-up!"

But Leo was no longer hearing a word Gudrun was saying; if Archimedes was microchipped, that meant they'd finally be able to find him!

"Do you still have that link?" Pavo interjected, opening a holo-note over his Luna Watch.

Gudrun shuffled through the heaps of junk on his desk.

"Erm . . . hold on a sec. I'll go see if I can find it for ya . . ."

Anxious looks shot across the lab as Gudrun returned with an electronic post-it.

"Oh-key-doke!" he said, sitting back down. "It's—uh—www—dot—*Now here's a good name for a pet find'n website!*—findyourfuzzyfurryfriend—dot—now!"

"Got it," said Pavo, jotting it down.

"Oh, and his login is 11-10-06-23-04-08—in case ya wanna look him up!"

"That's great, Gudrun," said Leo, getting up readily. "Er—uh—I don't mean to cut the conversation short—" He paused, trying to think of the most polite way to hang up on Gudrun. "But I just remembered I'm late for getting something I *really* need to get!"

Gudrun's smile sank. "But I hadn't gotten ta tell—"

"I'll visi-chat you again as soon as I can," said Leo. "Thanks again, Gudrun!" And a second later the visi-lab shifted to a static black.

Pavo opened the link on his map: a small red dot appeared, blinking at the bottom.

"*Très bizarre . . . ,*" said Phoebe, tracing over it. "According to the map, Archimedes is somehow past *the lowest level?*"

Andromeda looked at Leo fervently. "Yeah, but there's *no*

way you're going down there! You heard what Mallock said—FLOOR DOUBLE-Z IS *STRICTLY* RESTRICTED!" But her shout was nothing but a wasted whisper in Leo's ears as he flew out of the visi-lab in search of his long-lost friend.

Pavo and Andromeda hurried after Leo as Phoebe headed off to her next class.

"Have you gone MAD?" Pavo shouted at Leo as soon as they caught up with him.

"*Mad?*" Andromeda repeated. "More like tri-polar! Since when did you suddenly want to get *kicked out* of Luna City?" she asked Leo.

"Didn't you guys see the map?" Leo said. "Archimedes is on the lowest level!"

"Uh—*yeah*," said Pavo, for a moment sounding just like Andromeda, "and don't you remember, none of *us* are allowed down there? You saw those trash-compacting-bots—they're extremely dangerous!"

"That's exactly why I need to find him," said Leo, determined.

Pavo and Andromeda turned to each other as if realizing there was no further convincing him.

"Fine," said Pavo suddenly. "I'll go with."

"You'll *WHAT*?" Andromeda screeched.

"With both of us looking for him, we're far more likely to actually find Archimedes," Pavo replied reasonably. "And besides, I've got the map!"

Andromeda looked as though her eyeballs were going to pop straight out of her head. "I think the only thing *you're* interested in is skipping out on our presentation in Biology!"

And Pavo did look remarkably guilty of this.

"You know I can't dissect Mr. Toad by myself!" said Andromeda hotly. "It's not VEGAN!"

"Then just say I'm sick or something," suggested Pavo without care.

"Okay—*fine*," said Andromeda, gesturing toward two bots hovering down the far end of the hall. "Then tell me: How are the two of *you* both going to sneak past the two of *them, and* turn on a gravity-shaft without an exit-pass?"

Leo and Pavo froze as they discovered Floris and Japps busily patrolling their way out at the end of the gardens. Without an exit-pass, there was no way they'd let any student take a gravity-shaft anywhere other than the confines of the academy and its dormitory floors—especially to the city's lowermost level!

Leo, however, hadn't stopped to consider any of this, and when no better plan came to mind, he looked at Andromeda and said, "That's why you're coming with us."

"I'm *WHAT*?" Andromeda blurted.

"You're going to hack through the access pad so we can get the gravity-shaft running without an exit-pass!" Leo explained.

Andromeda looked at Leo as though he had officially lost it. "Oh, right—*of course*," she moaned sarcastically. "I'll just hack into a super-complex lock system . . . tamper with city property . . . probably get caught by security—or worse—tat-tle-tale Susie! Is it just me, or am I the only one smelling DETENTION?"

Leo looked at Andromeda with pleading eyes, and it appeared at that moment that Andromeda was no longer as good as she normally was at objecting.

"*Alright. Fine!*" she groaned with defeat. "I'll help! But I'm only doing so for Archimedes," she added quickly.

"Thank you!" Leo shouted, relieved. And in the next second, he was dashing across the hall, slipping past the door of the nearest gravity-shaft.

"He's made us lose our minds, hasn't he?" Andromeda huffed to Pavo.

"Maybe he's made you lose yours," said Pavo, getting up after him, "but not me!"

But before Andromeda could move her feet, Floris and Japps turned the corner and were hovering straight toward her hiding position behind a tall potted plant.

"I'm tell'n ya, Japps," Floris was saying, showing off the four golden stars on his electro-badge, "the only reason I've got four of 'em is cause my Megabytes can beat your Kilobytes any day!"

"*Yeah-yeah,*" miffed Japps, looking down, disappointed at his one and a half. "But your hard-drive ain't got nothin' on my RAM!"

The two came to a dilly-dallying hover above Andromeda's head. Andromeda looked up, hoping they wouldn't see her, but just as she did, a leaf tickled the tip of her nose. And before she could stop herself as her nose curled and twitched, an enormously loud and terribly high-pitched "ACHEW!" flew out of her, echoing throughout the entire gardens.

Japps's eyes widened with disgust. "Ey! Not on my tin-suit, ya tin-head!"

"On YOUR tin-suit?" Floris wailed with offense. "Why, you're the one who sneezed all over ME!"

But just as the two realized the nonsense in their bickering—as robots couldn't sneeze—Andromeda made her break to the gravity-shaft.

"OH-KAY!" she exclaimed, short of breath, as the door sealed behind her. "We've got approximately one minute before it reopens . . ."

Leo and Pavo watched anxiously as Andromeda began punching in a series of codes across the keypad.

"Are you *sure* you know what you're doing?" Pavo asked, hovering over her shoulder.

"*No* . . . ," said Andromeda testily; "but if you don't mind, I can figure out whatever it is I don't know a whole lot sooner without your pizza breath all over me!"

Pavo smiled weakly and took a step back. A second later, the gravity-shaft gave a jolt.

"There!" said Andromeda, appearing impressed with her talent.

"Well," said Pavo curiously, "what was it?"

Leo looked just as curious to know.

"As if I'm going to give either of *you* the ultimate access code to all of Luna City!"

Leo and Pavo's smiles sank, and as the gravity-shaft began its descent, their previously excited air shifted into an unsettling quantity of nerves.

"Right," said Leo stressfully as the gravity-shaft's door reopened. "It shouldn't take us more than a minute to find him!"

However, as the three made their way out between the loud humming of the water generator and metal-crunching of trash-compacting-bots compacting trash, Leo's anticipated minute quickly slipped into what felt like an impossible hour.

"I don't get it," he said finally, rechecking Pavo's holomap for the hundredth time. "According to the map, Archimedes should be . . . right . . . here?"

But as Leo looked where the map was pointing, he found nothing but concrete floor.

"It probably just needs to be recalibrated," said Pavo, taking off his watch to check its mini-battery underneath a water-purity-testing microscope. "Meta, send the map's link to Leo, will you?"

"*Either way* . . . ," said Andromeda, pacing around anxiously, "it's getting late. And I know how much you want to find Archimedes, Leo, but if we don't get going back now, we're going to miss—"

"What the—?" Leo blurted out, clinging onto a recycling bin for dear life.

"*WHAT DID YOU DO?*" Andromeda shouted at Pavo, full of fright.

Pavo looked up, completely flabbergasted by what he saw: there, just inches away from where he was standing, was a massive hole, opening slowly toward them.

"Who *m-m-me?*" he stuttered freakishly. "I didn't do anything! I was just standing here, messing around with this microscope and—"

"—*That's* when it happened!" Andromeda exclaimed, running up beside him. "Right when you adjusted the left lens!"

Andromeda replayed Pavo's actions, and the hole seamlessly shut.

"*Pra caramba,*" he muttered faintly. "What do you think they need *THAT* for?"

"It's clearly here to hide something someone doesn't want any of 'us' knowing about," answered Andromeda smartly. She twisted the microscope's lens once more, which revealed a long, narrow staircase leading down to nothing that any of them could see.

Leo stared at the unwelcoming steps. And though the thought of going down them was not at all pleasant, Leo knew it was the only way he was going to find Archimedes.

"Alright," he said with a stressful sigh, "you guys, follow me!"

"*Oh, no, I won't!*" Andromeda shrieked, shaking her head emphatically. "You won't be needing my help hacking anything down some freaky stairwell! I think I'll stay right here, thank you very much!"

"Suit yourself," said Pavo, hurrying after Leo.

But after only a few short seconds of the boys leaving, Andromeda realized staying behind was equally as unnerving, and with one small, frustrated huff, she changed her mind and headed down the secret steps.

The walls going down the hidden stairwell were cold and damp and covered by an eerie dark. Not too far down them the cobbled steps became so drenched with darkness that not even the light from Leo's or Pavo's Luna Watches could do much to better guide them.

"These stairs don't end, do they?" Pavo lamented as he, Leo, and Andromeda had been traversing down them for what seemed like ages.

Leo was just about to agree when he stubbed his toe on flat ground. "Don't worry," he said, looking around hopefully, "I think we've made it!" But where they had made it to, Leo didn't have the slightest clue, as they were surrounded by a series of pitch-black cavernous tunnels.

"What *is* this place?" Pavo wondered aloud. The light from his Luna Watch trailed across the stalactites dripping overhead.

"It's probably just left over from construction," suggested Andromeda, holding back shivers.

"Well, whatever it is," said Leo, his breath dangling in the air, "it sure is creepy."

"C'mon," he added, locating Archimedes on the map, "Archimedes should be—this way . . ."

However, not more than a few steps down the tunnel's blacked-out path, Andromeda stopped everyone with a hiss.

"*Shh!* Did either of you hear that?"

"Hear what?" asked Pavo, looking around. But when nothing more came, both he and Leo were quick to dismiss whatever it was for just "tunnel wind." Only a few seconds after they had restarted down the path, Andromeda was at it again.

"*There!* Hear it?" she whispered sharply.

This time, Pavo heard it too.

"*Ei* . . . I think she's right," he said, nudging Leo to listen up.

But before Leo could make out what it was, Andromeda let out the faintest shrill. Leo and Pavo turned on the spot; and as the light from their Luna Watches reached the far end of the corridor, they were terror-stricken by what they saw: There, at its start, was a shadowy figure, pressing closer toward them.

Leo instructed everyone to "RUN!" and the three were off, dashing down the darkened tunnel.

"WHAT IN THE HECK *IS* THAT THING?" Pavo shouted, running faster than he likely ever had before in his life.

"I DON'T KNOW!" Andromeda yelled at him, panicked. "BUT LET'S HOPE IT'S NOT CHASING US BECAUSE YOU SMELL LIKE A MASSIVE PEPPERONI!"

But as Leo turned his head in the hope of catching a better glimpse of whatever it was that was gaining on them, the floor gave way under his feet. And in the next second, he was tumbling through the air, alongside the echoes of Pavo and Andromeda's petrified screams.

CHAPTER

12

THE CREATURE
IN THE CRYPT

What had once been frightful shouts soon turned into the unpleasant moans of banged-up knees and sore bottoms.

"Is everyone alright?" Leo asked as soon as he was able.

"I'm fine," said Pavo sorely. His Luna Watch flickered on and off in the distance. "But I'd be better if this stupid pine-cone hadn't busted my watch!"

It was then that Leo recognized the familiar scent filling his nostrils. "*Trees?*" he muttered curiously, trying (without success) to get himself up from the massive pile that had broken their fall.

"And what about you, Andromeda?" Leo asked. "Do you think you can get off my back yet?"

"*I'm not on your back*," she said from right beside him. But as her words slipped past his ears, Leo nearly didn't want to know the answer to what he asked next. "Then *who* is?"

Leo held his breath as he adjusted his Luna Watch to a brighter light. But as he turned, his mouth fell open at what he saw.

"PHEEEEW!" Grus Pinwheel panted, rolling himself off Leo's back. "You guys sure run FAST in spooky places!"

"*Grus!*" Andromeda shouted, ridiculously delighted to see him. "Thank *goodness* it's only you!"

"How did you know where to find us?" Leo asked, relieved that Grus hadn't been anything "monstrous."

"Phoebe told me you crazy people were thinking about coming down here when I was on my way to class," Grus explained.

"But how did you get past Floris and Japps *and* get a gravity-shaft working without an exit-pass?" wondered Pavo.

"Oh, *that?*" chuckled Grus. "It was easy. I just took those things called 'EMERGENCY STAIRS'—and BOY, let me tell YOU!—they really are for emergencies only. It took me like, FOR-EV-A to get down one flight of them! But seriously," he began laughing boisterously, "you guys were totally *FREAKED!*"

"Right," said Leo, brushing the sticky sap needles off his sleeves, "if you're going to come along then, just try to keep up."

Grus returned Leo a diligent salute; but as the four crawled down the prickly pile of evergreens, it wasn't long before Grus started muttering, "H-h-hey, y-y-you guys, I think I-I-I heard something!"

Andromeda turned to him with an unimpressed look. "*Real funny,*" she said maturely.

"No, I-I-I mean," Grus tried again, this time the wobble in his voice sounding far more convincing, "I th-think I-I-I heard—" But before anyone could express to Grus their lack of approval at his timing for a joke, the sound of footsteps could be heard, heading straight toward them.

"Hurry! Hide!" Andromeda urgently hissed. And just as soon as everyone had hid behind a mound of trees, a light was lit and footsteps stormed into the crypt.

What was once a completely blacked-out room was now fully illuminated with a warm amber hue, revealing hundreds upon hundreds of stacks of trees; some were half-sorted with trunks shredded into bits, while others were neatly organized into mounds reaching the ceiling. Leo pressed his nose between the branches, trying to see who had entered; but as soon as he did, he nearly choked at the sight of an all-too-familiar black cape.

"Where *is* it?" the cold and callous voice of Senator Mallock asked. He was speaking into what Leo was now recognizing as a holding cell at the far end of the crypt.

"Where's *what*?" a small, shrilly voice responded.

"You know what," Mallock snapped. "Where's the map?"

"The map?" the voice muttered full of innocence. "Likes I toldsid you; I never foundsid it! And even if I did findsid it, why would I keeps it from you if I couldn't even reads it?"

"Don't think I've failed to consider that you could have been better persuaded by someone who can," said Mallock scathingly.

There was a nervous gulp from the other end of the cell as the voice went on defensively, "But I've DONESID everything you've askedid of me! I've searchedid fors it throughs a million trees; received a million splinters; and how do I gets REWARDSID? WITH SHACKLES?" The voice began grumbling defiantly. "Maybe I shouldsid toldsid everything to Soenso instead. Maybe then I wouldsn't have been IMPRISONED!—maybe then I woulds've been REWARDSID!"

"SILENCE!" Mallock spat in a rage that even Leo didn't know was possible. "Only a fool would think he'd offer a pathetic lowlife like yourself any kindness. You've seen how he and his kind have treated their planet. They've abused every single privilege it has given them! They've polluted its air; sucked its waters dry; and have sentenced nearly every living creature to have graced its soil to death! And now—AND NOW!—they seek to pillage what lies beyond it!"

"But," the voice interjected feebly, "they're only doingsid what any species wouldsid in hopes of surviv—"

"There will be NO survival for their kind," Mallock venomously hissed. "Map or no map, I will find a way to destroy that precious city of theirs before the night of the lunar eclipse."

There was a wave of silent fright as Mallock turned to leave the crypt, his eyes lingering for a moment on the exact spot were Leo, Pavo, Andromeda, and Grus were hidden behind the trees. And the second his footsteps dissipated from earshot, no one could contain their shock over what they had just witnessed.

"Did you hear *that*?" Andromeda gasped, shaking tremulously. "Did you hear what Mallock said he's going to *do*?"

"He said he's going to destroy Luna City," Pavo gulped, his face blanched and sickly.

"B-b-but *how*?" Grus sputtered like a broken sprinkler.

"I don't know," answered Leo. A swirl of unknown anger and fear was flooding his entire body. "But whoever he's trapped inside that cell is going to help us find out!"

Pavo, Andromeda, and Grus each returned Leo long, trepidatious looks; but before any of them could voice their fears about approaching whoever it was behind the cell's bars, they were serenaded with an ear-piercing wail.

"IT'S ALL MY FAULT!" the small voice cried miserably to itself. "It's all my STUPID-DUMB-DUMB FAULT!

"If only I hadn't been such a STUPID-DUMMY-DOO-DOO-HEAD!—But *Nooo*," it went on pathetically, "I had to be a SELFISH dumb-dumb—I had to be a GREEDY dumb-dumb—and now looksid at me! I'm all that's LEFT! All that's leftid of the LUNAR ECLIPSE!"

Loud, pitchy sobs echoed throughout the crypt as the four stood there, suddenly more off-put than they were previously frightened.

"He sounds miserable," said Leo, covering his ears as the four crept toward the cell.

"Sounds like some major self-help issues, if you ask me," said Pavo. Meanwhile the voice continued insulting itself: "STUPID-DUMMY-DOO-DOO-HEAD!"

Andromeda pushed past Leo and Pavo, pulling out a small handkerchief from her side-bag.

"Leave it to you two to find the sound of someone crying 'repelling,'" she japed at them, reaching the cell's door and giving it a firm knock.

The sobs, in an instant, softened to a whimper.

"Excuse me," she called in, holding out her handkerchief between the gaps of iron; "I noticed you were crying—and—well—thought you might benefit from a handkerchief. *It usually helps me when I need to let it all out!*"

A sudden scuttling shot across the shadows.

"Gossypium?" the voice muttered with interest. "Sweet, succulent, Gossypium?"

Andromeda looked at Leo, Pavo, and Grus, who each shrugged, clearly just as clueless about whatever 'Gossypium' was as she was. But their puzzled expressions were overtaken with wide-eyed looks as a puny grayscale creature emerged before them. He then, much to everyone's horror, snatched the handkerchief from Andromeda's grasp and gobbled it up!

Grus's face began jiggling like Jell-o as he warbled, "IT'S A-A-A—"

"—ALIEEEEN!" Pavo shrilled in an octave far too high for him as Grus fainted into Andromeda's lap, throwing them back into a thick pile of bristly shrubs.

"You *CAN'T* be serious!" Andromeda shrieked, shaking Grus's head to get up.

Leo's knees turned to stone as he stared incredulously at whatever the thing was that had just inhaled a giant chunk of cotton: It had a long pointed nose, crescent-shaped forehead, and eyes so massive they appeared to be bulging straight out of him; its ears were also oddly shaped and reminded Leo somewhat of a rabbit's and an elf's . . . and that's when it hit him. "It's a Lunaling!" he said to himself, enchanted.

"*That?*" stammered Pavo, holding his chest as the creature bolted back into the darkness. "Or some sort of *SICK* baby humanoid chihuahua!"

"Well, whatever it is," said Andromeda, adjusting her skirt as she finally got Grus's head off of her lap, "I think you've got the 'baby' part right." She nodded toward the cell as doleful sobs stiffened the air. "Well?" she barked at them. "*Suggestions?*"

Leo and Pavo were momentarily speechless.

"You two are seriously useless," she huffed. And she returned to the cell's bars and much more gently said, "Hi there, again. We didn't mean to startle you. My friends and I had just overheard everything Mallock was saying and—" She stopped, jumping back as a large set of watery, puppy dog eyes beamed admiringly up at her. "—*And*," she continued, "we'd like to help."

The creature's pupils lit like flood lamps as he clenched the bars and squealed, "Helps us? Did you hearsid *THAT*? Someone actually WANTS to helpsid GRIMLU!"

Leo looked around for whoever the creature was talking to, but the cell was otherwise empty, except for a few dozen pinecones and some gravel-like moon rocks.

"That is," added Leo quickly, "provided you tell us what's so important about that map that Mallock felt the need to destroy all these trees to try to find it?"

The creature's excitement slumped like that of a freshly caught thief.

"*Trees?*" he muttered ingenuously. "I don't knowsid about any *trees*!"

"Alright then," said Andromeda, prompting Leo and Pavo to follow her lead out of the crypt.

"No-no, WAAAITSID!" Grimlu shouted after them. "Don't LEAVES! I'll tellsid you! I'll tellsid you what Mallock wantsid with THE MAP!"

Andromeda smiled smugly.

"Out with it then," Pavo demanded.

The creature dejectedly kicked his stubby newt-like toes across the iron bars and said:

Withoutsid the map, he'll never finds,
What's hidden acrossdid the sands of time!
Many a war's beens foughts in its name,
Many a ruler becamesid its slave,
Until one king thoughtsid it best,
To destroy the star and scatter its bits,
Across the deserts, mountains, and seas,
Alas! The Astronomer was givensid the deed!
Keeping in secrets a map for himself,
So that one day the pieces could be again founds,
But he met a tragic fate,
And his map was STOLENS away!
And with it, will surely come EARTH'S DOOM,
As once was to Jupiter, Mars, and THE MOON!
The portal will open and the great ones will wake,
And now I fear it's much TOO LATE,
To gather the shards of the sacred star,
And keepsid the Mleckorgs very far,
For the eclipse is onsid its way . . .
And I've STUPIDLY givensid THAT MAP away!

The creature's eyes swelled into something of a torrential monsoon.

"Well, that went as expected," said Leo as Andromeda rummaged through her side-bag.

"Here," she said, tossing the creature another handkerchief, "take this."

Grimlu took it, gratefully, and smeared his tears over his face. He then, after blowing his nose into it like an out-of-tune trumpet, crumpled it into a ball and ate it.

The three stood there, muttering words of sheer disgust as a pained moaning rattled from the shrub beside them. Grus had finally lifted his groggy head up, but at the sight of the creature's belly glowing a bile-shaded florescent while it digested the cotton cloth, he instead mumbled something that sounded like "Mumba-wumba," and passed out again.

"Better?" Andromeda asked the creature as he released a large, rippling burp.

"Betters," he replied between sniffles.

"So you lied to Mallock then," said Leo shortly. "You had found the Astronomer's Map and you gave it away?"

"But I didn't KNOWSID then what I knowsid now," Grimlu explained. "I didn't knowsid it was IMPORTANTS! I WAS TRIXED!" He broke off, shaking his head madly at the ground. "And now," he went on, "it's too latesid . . . The eclipse is nearly here and—"

"*An eclipse?*" said Andromeda. "Wait—what can be so bad about an eclipse?"

"It's not the eclipse that's bad," said Grimlu, his eyes glistening at them with dread, "it's what travels withins its shadows!"

"Matter?" guessed Pavo.

"DARKNESS!" Grimlu bellowed gruffly. "Pure, unthinkable, DARKNESS!"

"Well, penumbral shadows do tend to be a bit dull," said Leo lightly.

"NO!" Grimlu snapped at him, furious. "You don't getsid it! You Earth Peoples NEVER GETSID IT!"

"What's *that* supposed to mean?" said Andromeda, affronted.

"It means you only ever seesid whats you wants! You foolishly thinksid you're the center of the universe and can do whatever you pleasid without consequences—but there are consequences!—terrible, terrible CONSEQUENCES!"

"*Like . . . ?*" urged Pavo.

"Like—" said Grimlu, his eyes now wide with foreboding, "—the return of THE MLECKORGS!"

The room filled with silence as the three stood there, bewildered by the bug-eyed little creature.

"*Mleckorgs?*" Pavo repeated, as though it sounded silly. "And what are those supposed to be? Some sort of giant flesh-eating aliens?" He let out a half-suppressed snort and contorted his hands into a monstrous shadow figure.

"Only they don't eatsid flesh," said Grimlu darkly.

"Well, that's a relief," said Leo. He wasn't *entirely* ready to imagine anything else out there in the universe more frightening, let alone more bizarre than a Lunaling.

Only Grimlu was now looking at him much more severely. "That's whatsid the Martians said . . . ," he muttered, his voice filling with an ominous regret, "and now looksid at them—ALLS OF THEM DEAD!—Nothing left but ASH AND DUST!"

"*Wait* . . . are you saying," said Andromeda, "that there was actually *life* on the red planet?"

"*No* . . . ," said Grimlu, sarcastic; "obviously you Earth Peoples are the ONLY species in the ENTIRE UNIVERSE!" He then threw his long four-fingered hands over the tips of his ears and began pacing the cell, mumbling to himself grumpily, "I can't believesid the Elderlings were RIGHT! They really are a bunch of stupid-dummy-doo-doo-heads—such STUPID-DUMMY-DOO-DOO—"

"OKAY-OKAY!" Leo shouted. "We get it! We're all a bunch of 'stupid-dummy-*doo-doo-heads*' . . . so there really was life on Mars, then?"

"One of the most advancedid civilizations of their day!" said Grimlu very matter-of-factly, "except for us Lunalings, that is. They were the ones responsible for all those bones you keep diggings up and mislabeling. Nasty beasts them dinosaurs were . . . brains no larger than a pigeon's head!

"*Though I would givesid a pretty moonstone to revisit the colosseum days*," he said in a moment of reflection. "I never didsid lose a dino bet!"

"As in *dinosaur* battles?" asked Pavo, amazed.

"Only they shouldn'ts have been callsid '*battles*,' per se," said Grimlu poignantly. "Most weren't very fair. The weak were always pairsid up against the most vicious of breeds. But even then, the most vicious dinosaur was no match for the Mleckorgs . . ."

"How can that be," said Andromeda, "if you said they don't eat flesh?"

"What they eatsid is far, far worsid than skins and bones!" replied the Lunaling.

"What can be worse than *that*?" guffawed Pavo.

But Grimlu's eyes were flooding with distress as he stuck his pointy nose through the gaps of the bars and said, "TIME! The most worsid, darkest, EVILEST thing onesid can do in all the galaxy is feedsid off someone elsids TIME!" He took a deep breath and grasped his tiny stump of a neck. "To completely sucksid away all traces of one's life—" He exhaled, wheezingly. "Not a happy memory, or a sorrow leftdid—just life converted back to the way it was before their prey's existence . . . leaving any that gotsid away with a shiver of constant worry and nowheres to pointsid their fingers as to what caused it!"

"Er—um—I don't mean to interject or anything," said Leo, "but I think you may be meaning something else. I mean, I don't think it's entirely possible for someone to *consume* time."

"Such big heads and yet they don't THINK!" Grimlu shouted brashly. "You're consuming time rights as we SPEAK!" He took another deep, demonstrative breath. "With each inhale, a little times is gainsid! And with each breath out—" he blew out dizzily, "—a little times is lostdid! Until, one day, you've breathed out more energys than you could ever consume back again and you—"

"—die," Pavo finished for him.

"Only the Mleckorgs have foundsid a way around that death by stealing the energys trapsid within the remnants of fallen stars—" He picked up a small rock from the ground and pressed it between his fingertips, illuminating it like a golden lightning-bug. "—Star Stones!" he muttered mistily, as the three stood there in a complete trance of the glowing rock. "The most rarest, powerfulestid element in all the universe; giving out life wherever it landsid, collecting energys with every death passedid!"

"So these Star Stones . . . ," said Andromeda, "are sort of like some super-galactic tape recorder?"

"Until one chooses to hit erase," said Leo, watching as Grimlu reverted the energy he had transferred into the ordinary pebble back into his fingertips.

"Only now," Grimlu went on, "it's too lates to stop the reversal that's onsid its way! On the night of the lunar eclipse, the portal between our galaxy and the Mleckorgs will opensid once more, and whensid it does, where do you thinksid they'll go?"

"Mars?" guessed Pavo.

"No . . . ," said Andromeda, suddenly quiet. "They'll go straight to where they left off. That means they're coming to—"

"—Earth," Leo finished for her.

"But they can't!" Andromeda shouted. "I mean, isn't there a way to stop them? To keep the Mleckorgs from waking up?"

"It'sid impossible," said Grimlu, lowering his head. "As long as all the pieces of the Star Stone are on Earth, that's exactly wheresid they'll goes searching for them. And now, withoutsid the map—" He broke off, shaking his head madly at the ground. "—the Earth IS DOOMED! DOOOMY-DOOMED-DOOOOOMED!"

Loud nauseating sobs ricocheted off the walls as Grimlu sprawled himself out over the floor, crying like an out of control two-year-old.

"Great," said Andromeda, searching for another handkerchief. "Not only is the Earth 'doomed,' but so are all my handkerchiefs!"

"How *many* of those do you keep in there?" Leo asked, bewildered.

"Clearly not enough," answered Andromeda. "If he starts in again, we're out of luck—this is my last one!" But this time, as Andromeda held it out, Grimlu didn't take it; in fact, he didn't even look at it: he was, instead, too busy lamenting all his woes to a pinecone.

"I knowsid I PROMISEDID I wouldn't letsid anyone takesid you," he said, caressing the pinecone's edge, "but sadly, not all promises can be KEPT!"

"How long do you think he's been locked in *there*?" Pavo whispered to Leo.

"Clearly long enough," Leo replied, finding it hard not to view the creature as anything other than insane—that is, until Andromeda grabbed at his wrist.

"Leo, look!" she shouted, pointing to a small thread of white jutting out from the side of the pinecone.

Leo caught sight of it just as it disappeared behind the cone; or had it disappeared into *the wall?*

Pavo let out an unexpected gasp as the object of Grimlu's attention came into view: Grimlu hadn't been talking to a pinecone, but rather—as he slid it aside, just visible through a small crack in the wall—revealed he had been speaking to—

"ARCHIMEDES!" Leo shouted, trying to squeeze himself through the gaps of the bars. His heart gave an enormous bound as Grimlu held the small white mouse between his hands. Archimedes was safe, and just as full of life as ever.

"I can't *believe* he's alright!" said Andromeda.

"Archi-*who-doo?*" inquired Grimlu.

"Archimedes!" Leo repeated. "The mouse you have in your hands—he's my pet!"

But Leo's elation was suddenly fleeing him as Grimlu grasped Archimedes and protectively said, "*Your* petsid?" His bulbous yellow eyes were now narrowing with a vivid offense. "This isn't YOUR petsid! This is MY very special, very littlestid friendsid . . . And her *names* is not Archi-DOO-DOO!—Her namesid is Priscilla!"

"*Priscilla?*" Pavo repeated. "What kind of name is *that?*"

"C'mon," said Andromeda sensibly, "it's not nearly as archaic as Archimedes. What's worse is that he thinks *he's* a *she!*"

"What her or his name is, is *not* what's important," said Leo, watching with resentment as Grimlu coddled 'Priscilla' like some sort of baby doll. "What's important is that—that *thing* thinks he *owns* Archimedes!"

"How DARESID you calls her such FOULSID names!" spat Grimlu.

"I swear, if you don't give him back to me," Leo threatened, but Grimlu had already taken a retractive step into the shadows.

"Or you'll whatsid?" the creature asked him. "You'll findsid the key and comes in here and BEATS ME?"

"He didn't say that!" Andromeda gushed.

"But I just might," replied Leo, trying harder than ever to wiggle himself through the gaps of iron.

Pavo grabbed Leo's shoulders, pulling him back as the baby alien charged menacingly toward him.

"YES!" Grimlu shouted, looking devilishly delighted. "That's what you'll DOSID!"

"You actually want him to *beat* you?" said Pavo, incredulous.

"*No . . .*," said Grimlu, as though Pavo was well below his own intelligence level. "I wantsid him to *findsid* THE KEY!"

"Fat chance!" said Leo, as Pavo and Andromeda held him back from what they clearly feared was a certain strangling of the baby alien. "Why would I do anything for you when you won't give me back my pet?"

"Because," said Grimlu flatly, "if you findsid the key, I'll givesid you Priscilla. That way we BOTH getsid what we wants!"

"No," said Leo sharply, "you'll give her back to me now!

She was never yours to begin with . . . and her name is not PRISCILLA!"

"Er—um, Leo," interjected Andromeda, tapping on his shoulder while the Lunaling retreated into the darkness. "I don't think we're *really* in a position for negotiating. I mean, if you want to get Archimedes back, I think you're just going to have to do what he says."

Leo folded his arms with frustration. Then, after a long moment of scowling and a kick of a twig, he said, "Fine. I'll do it! I'll go find you that stupid key!"

Grimlu sauntered toward them, beaming.

"I KNEWSID IT!" he shouted with glee. "I KNEWSID you'd helpsid me findsid THE KEY!"

"Now give me back Archimedes," Leo demanded, shoving his hands through the cell's gaps.

"Uh-uh-uh!" Grimlu tutted. He slapped at Leo's fingers. "Not until I'm *freed* first!"

"Fine," Leo agreed. "I'll first go and 'findsid' you that key! So where is it then that we're supposed to find this key, anyway?" he inquired.

"I don't know . . . ," replied Grimlu. "Where do you thinksid he would keeps it?"

"Probably his office," said Andromeda.

"*In Mallock's OFFICE?*" Leo and Pavo repeated.

"Of course, if you don't *wantsid* Priscilla?" said the creature.

"Of course, I 'wantsid' Priscilla!" said Leo. "And, of course,

I'll go find that stupid key for you; but I do expect one more thing in exchange for your freedom."

Grimlu looked at Leo inquisitively.

"We'll need your help in stopping Mallock from doing whatever it is he's planning on doing before the night of the eclipse."

Grimlu's lips curled agreeably. "Deal!" he said, his nubs of piranha-like teeth glimmering at them through the darkness. "I'll helpsid you stopsid Mallock!"

"Great," said Pavo readily, "then, um, if you don't mind, I think we're gonna get going now." He turned to Leo and hissed in his ear, "Did you hear what you just *said*? What are you doing making a deal with that *THING*? You know there's no way we're going to get that key if it's in Mallock's office!"

"I know . . . ," said Leo, following Andromeda to a nearby bush to help get Grus out of it, "but it's better that than—well—you saw what he did with all her handkerchiefs."

"*Hey!*" Andromeda shouted, "those were my grandma's! But if you don't *mind*—" she added with difficulty as they hoisted Grus up over their shoulders, "—put some *BACK* into it!"

The boys gave another heave, and Grus Pinwheel finally wobbled onto his feet.

"Let's just hurry out of here before we miss check-in," said Leo while Grus mumbled something of which none of them could distinguish and cuddled Leo's arm like a stuffed koala.

But this time the four made sure to take the same route the senator had taken as their exit.

"So now what are we supposed to do now?" Pavo asked as soon as they reached the top of the stairs.

"We have to tell Soenso about Mallock," said Andromeda.

"Oh, right, like *that's* gonna work," Pavo replied. "We'll just run into his office and casually say, '*Olá, Senhor Presidente*, did you know that Senator Mallock is secretly trying to destroy Luna City and that he keeps a FREAKY little baby alien locked up in the basement'?"

"He wasn't *that* freaky," said Andromeda. "And, actually, now that I think of it—for my first time meeting an alien—I'd say he was pretty cute!"

"Your preferences change fast," Pavo mumbled.

"That's *not* what I meant," said Andromeda.

"Either way," said Leo as a glimmer of light emerged from the tunnel's end, "none of us are even supposed to know this place exists, so Pavo's right: We're just going to have to find that key and figure out how to stop Mallock on our own."

But as the four exited the gravity-shaft, eager to reach their dorm rooms before check-in, they were instantly wishing they had taken the stairs, as Floris and Japps were hovering outside it with wide triumphant glares.

CHAPTER

13

THE SEARCH FOR THE INVISIBLE KEY

The following morning Leo, Pavo, Andromeda, and Grus were all informed by their Metas that their day of detention was scheduled for Halloween. Though Grus wasn't entirely sure what he had done to deserve it—or why they had been caught outside their rooms past curfew to begin with—he made sure to enlighten everyone's breakfast with tales of his "super-realistic alien dream." No one, at the moment, felt up to explaining to him the reality of it.

The walls throughout the academy were now aglow with images of darkened graveyards and decrepit haunted houses. And despite everyone knowing they were only holographic, the occasional ghost would pop out and cause an unsuspecting teacher or student to jump or scream in an embarrassed panic. It was also the week of the Hallo-ball: a masquerade dance filled with goblins and ghouls, zombies and werewolves, and one too many witches on makeshift hovering broomsticks. Though most first-years went together in a group of friends, the upperclassmen were busy decorating drone-o-invites into scary-faced jack-o'-lanterns to send to their prospective dates. Naturally, detention was scheduled to start at the precise moment the Hallo-ball was set to begin.

Leo, Pavo, Andromeda, and Grus waited in Central Gardens the day of the Hallo-ball after their Sectionals for Mr. McNaught, the detention-bot, to arrive and take them to their punishment. However, they soon learned that they weren't going to be the only ones late to the festivities, as Gavin, Crux, and Aabher were following right behind him.

"Tut, tut, tut," McNaught hummed disapprovingly, looking over the two groups as though they were disobedient puppies. "Not even past the first semester, and we already have MISBEHAVING MISFITS in our tranquil society!

"Well—what are you waiting for?" he barked at them like a deranged drill sergeant. "Follow me!"

Gavin, Crux, and Aabher laughed as Leo stumbled to his feet under the wind of Mr. McNaught's shouting in his face. Though as they entered the old book database of the library, no one could laugh at what they were seeing: books were scattered tempestuously across the shelves; there were stacks upon stacks of encyclopedias piled into heaps on the floor; hundred-year-old dictionaries had their pages ripped and torn in two—it looked as though an actual tornado had stormed right through the place!

Mr. McNaught smiled a pleased, slithering grin, unveiling his rusted, micro-chipped teeth after examining everyone's distraught faces. "Here is where you'll do your time," he said, escorting them around the sea of tattered dictionaries.

"Each of you two groups will need to scan in a hundred of them!—*that* ought'a make ya think twice about being out past curfew . . ." He looked meaningfully at Leo, Pavo, Andromeda, and Grus. "And copying each other's homework answers!" he said looking at Gavin, Crux, and Aabher.

Gavin appeared completely outraged to be anywhere where so much reading took place as he complained, "But it would take an entire CENTURY to scan in twenty!"

"Well, you'll have all night to do so," said McNaught. "So chop-chop!"

"But what about the dance?" Andromeda called out after him as the hover-bot fluttered toward the exit.

"*The dance?*" repeated McNaught. "Don't think you'll be

doing any sort of dancing in here. *Noise is strictly off limits in the library!* So if you're hoping to make it to your Halloween ball before it's finished, I suggest you get a move on; these here books aren't going to magically sort themselves!"

The detention bot left with a devilish cackle.

"It's even worse than I was expecting," moaned Pavo, walking around an avalanche of scattered dictionaries.

"We've got this pile over here!" said Gavin, running over to claim the stack of books closest to a scan-o-bot before Leo, Pavo, Andromeda, or Grus could reach it.

"Of course you have," Leo muttered. The second closest stack to a scan-o-bot was halfway across the room!

Despite everyone's disappointment, they began scanning in books straightaway; but it wasn't long before the two groups realized they had set an undeclared race. And Leo, Pavo, Andromeda, and Grus quickly split up, with Leo positioned at the scan-o-bot to scan in books, and Pavo, Andromeda, and Grus, busily relaying them to him.

"*Seriously!*" Andromeda exclaimed while passing Leo an almanac, "I don't know how people even *read* these things if the pages don't illuminate?"

"Or collapse into a small enough size that you could reasonably take with you somewhere *without* breaking your back!" said Pavo, dropping off a heap of encyclopedias.

"I'm pretty sure they didn't bring *THIS* baby anywhere," shouted Grus, wobbling over with a book that was nearly the same size as him.

"That's gotta weigh more than a hippo," said Pavo with amazement.

"*Whatever that is . . .* ," said Leo, opting for Andromeda's much smaller book instead.

"Only fifty-three left!" he called out after adjusting the scan-o-bot's settings. But as Leo inserted the book, the scan-o-bot began to beep and erratically buzz: "ERROR: PLEASE TAKE OUT AND INSERT AGAIN!"

"Great," Leo said under his breath as the scan-o-bot shot the book back out at him. He, at once, returned it; but the error code went off again . . .

"I wonder why that is?" said Andromeda, setting down a pile of paperbacks.

"I don't know," said Leo, taking the book out and passing it to Andromeda in exchange for another.

Though as Andromeda flipped through its pages, she at once realized why the scan-o-bot couldn't read it.

"Of course . . . ," she said, showing Leo its pages. "The scan-o-bot can't read this book—*it's illegible text*!"

Leo looked at Andromeda strangely. But as he took another look-see at the book, his eyes widened at what he saw.

"That's the same handwriting I found on a note dropped from Senator Mallock!" he exclaimed, bewildered by the familiar, bizarre style of writing. "This must be Mallock's journal!"

Leo, however, was quickly wishing he had said it more quietly, because as soon as he had, Crux turned to him and said, "You have something that belongs to my dad?"

"Oh, no! We were only joking!" said Andromeda as Crux approached the two of them and snatched the journal from their hands.

"What *is* this junk?" Crux muttered, flipping through the journal's pages.

"Like Andromeda was saying," said Leo, "we were only *joking.*"

"Well, if you think you've slowed us down," said Crux, thrusting the book into Leo's chest, "then the joke's on you—we're already finished."

"HA!" Gavin laughed from across the room as their scan-o-bot announced: "ONE HUNDRED BOOKS SORTED! YOU HAVE FINISHED YOUR DETENTION!"

"See ya, LOSE-AAAHS!" Aabher shouted awkwardly.

"*After* the dance, that is," added Crux.

Leo sighed as Gavin, Crux, and Aabher exited the library. Their scan-o-bot's meter was only at "52." Though Leo, Pavo, Andromeda, and Grus still had plenty of books to sort before they could be finished, Leo was at least relieved that he had gotten Mallock's journal back from Crux.

"So now we know who messed up this place during orientation," said Andromeda cleverly.

"Yeah," said Leo, "but why?"

"Maybe," said Andromeda, waving the leather-bound book in her hand, "if I can decode *this*, it will give us our answer!"

"Or maybe it will give us all of Mallock's girlfriends' visi-numbers," said Pavo.

"Hey, you guys!" Grus called out a moment later, heaving over another ginormous dictionary. "Check out this WHOPPER!"

"You do know it's not the *size* that matters?" said Andromeda, looking at him sillily. "It's the *number*!"

"I knew *that*," said Grus, though he clearly didn't. "That's why I picked this one: volume three-hundred-and-fifty-three!"

Leo, Pavo, and Andromeda let out an expectant chuckle as Grus flopped the larger-than-life book over the scan-o-bot. The four quickly got back to their scanning and then, after twenty endless minutes of sorting, the scan-o-bot announced their finish.

"*Finalmente!*" exclaimed Pavo with delight. "Now let's get to the *festa*!"

But as the four reached the gymnasium, decorated with a hundred strands of drone-o-skeleton lights and glittery glow-in-the-dark confetti bats decorating its entrance, Leo stepped off to the side. "You guys go ahead," he said. "I think I'm going to skip out on the dance this time."

"What do you mean you're going to '*skip out*' on the dance?" Andromeda repeated while pulling out a series of masks from her side-bag. "I did *not* spend all free-hour decorating these things for nothing!"

"With Mallock there chaperoning, it's the only chance I'll have to sneak into his office and find the key!" Leo explained.

"What key?" wondered Grus.

"It's nothing," said Andromeda quickly. "And *no*," she reiterated to Leo, "it's *not* the only chance we have of finding it. *I* have a better idea than risking another hour of detention from getting caught breaking into Mallock's office! But this time, you're going to have to follow me."

Leo grimaced as Andromeda pulled a wolflike mask over his face. And as soon as she finished putting a mask on herself, one on Pavo, and one on Grus, Leo laughed as he found himself surrounded by three little pigs.

"I had intended for Pavo to be the wolf," said Andromeda, "but since you're so *dogmatic* . . ."

"Thanks," said Leo, blushing underneath the papier-mâché.

"Now come on," she said, "you've got a house to blow down!"

"I've got a *what?*" Leo asked.

"Just come on!—you'll see!"

And the three followed Andromeda into the gymnasium, where their ears were submerged in a wave of electro-pop and their eyes were flooded with a rainbow of strobes bouncing off the armor of one too many Roman soldiers doing "the robot" with ancient Egyptians.

"They're having a first-century costume competition," said Andromeda over the music, brushing past Cleopatra at the floating appetizer stand, "*BCE*, that is . . ."

"*Ooh!*" Grus chirped excitedly, ogling a plethora of pouched treats. "HORS D'OEUVRES!"

"*HEY,*" called out a creepy deep voice from beside him. "ARE YOU LOOKING TO GET PUNCHED?"

Grus let out a girlish shrill as a headless man leaned over him, and then—to Grus's surprise—passed him a pouched drink.

"Don't worry," said a voice from below, "it's only us!"

Grus looked down, relieved to find the heads of Scotti and Ume peeking out of a robotic contraption from within the headless man's jacket.

"Nice costume!" said Andromeda.

"Thanks!" said Ume, adjusting her bangs with the help of Scotti's leg. "But it'd be even better if Scotti didn't lose our head!"

Scotti signed something up at her sourly.

"*I* didn't lose our head," Ume retorted, singing back at him and declaring, "it was *your* turn to hold on to it!"

Scotti shook his head as though it wasn't.

"Yes, it was!" Ume insisted.

Scotti, too, insisted it wasn't.

"*Ei,*" said Pavo to Leo, nodding toward the far end of the gym, "have you seen *that*?"

Leo turned and spotted a haunted holographic abode with a row of students lining up outside in its graveyard.

"*That!*" said Andromeda, "is where we're going!"

"W-w-we are?" Grus stammered, looking uneasy.

"Um—yeah!" said Andromeda. "Unless you *don't* want a chance at winning a *robo-pet*?"

"ROBO-PETS!" Grus shouted. The handful of pouched treats he had been trying to cram into his pockets fell to the ground. "Well, what are you waiting for, *people?*—LET'S GO!" And the four took off toward the haunted abode, where they were then greeted by a robotic skeleton guarding its entrance. In its hand was a holo-sign that read:

ENTER, ENTER, BUT BEWARE,
THIS HOUSE IS FULL OF TRICKS AND SCARES!
A MAZE OF TERRORS TO THRILL THE MIND,
WHO KNOWS WHAT MONSTERS LURK INSIDE!
SO IF YOU'RE SMART YOU'LL TURN AROUND,
AND LEAVE THE DARE FOR THOSE LESS SOUND!
BUT IF YOU SEEK TO STILL GO FORTH,
I SUGGEST YOU TAKE A TORCH,
FOR ONLY A LUCKY FEW WILL FIND,
A PRIZE FOR MAKING IT OUT ALIVE!

"Er—uh—" said Pavo, suddenly looking more squeamish than Grus as a shrill echoed past the haunted house's door, "I think we better take the skeleton's advice and *vamos.* I mean, he looks as though he was a nice enough guy, doesn't he?"

"*Actually . . . ,*" said Grus, staring over the skeleton with a discerning eye, "I think he's just painted plastic."

"*C'mon!*" said Andromeda, passing them each a laser-torch. "We're going in!"

The haunted house was almost completely lightless, less the outlining of illuminated cobwebs and spiders dangling from its ceiling. There were old-fashioned rocking chairs that rocked back and forth without anyone sitting on them, and cupboards that would open and close on their own as you passed them.

"Why *exactly* are we doing this again?" Leo asked Andromeda, catching his breath after nearly losing his cool over a holographic cat that ran past his leg.

"*Because*," said Andromeda, calming herself down as a ghost popped out of the hallway's mirror, "if we can get to the other end, we'll get a spider-pet!"

"'*A spider-pet?*'" Leo repeated. He turned the corner only to jump at a colony of robotic bats fluttering past his eyes. "Why *in-the-moon* would we want to go through all *THIS* for a SPIDER-PET?"

"Isn't it obvious?" said Andromeda, leading their way into a room filled with coffins that were slightly cracked opened, revealing pale-green, decomposing hands. "We can use the spider-pet to sneak into Mallock's office instead of us . . . you know, it can go through the vents! That way we eliminate all the—AHHH!—" she shouted, stumbling back as a faux spider dropped onto her face, "—all the RISK!"

"Hey, uh, you guys," Pavo chimed in, "I know you're having a really *interesting* conversation and all, but maybe now is not the best time to be talking about sneaking *into* places when we should be trying to figure out how to get *OUT* of this *casa!*"

"Um, *yeah*," said Andromeda, "that's what we're trying *to do* . . ."

"No, I mean," Pavo went on, "can we try to do it more *rápido*? Because I don't think those zombies back there behind us are holographic."

Leo, Andromeda, and Grus turned to find a herd of zombies heading their way.

"HOLE-E-CRAPPER-BAPPERS!" Grus yelled with fright, and he took off running at full speed ahead of everyone. "Like Pavo said, 'VAMOOOS!'" And the four were dashing through the haunted halls, screaming as the zombies followed swiftly after them.

"NEVER—AGAIN!" Andromeda shouted the second she, Leo, and Pavo finally figured out which of the haunted house's doors was not a fake exit.

"Now let's get that spider-pet," said Leo, readily.

"But where's Grus?" Andromeda asked, looking around for him.

"Probably being munched on by a zombie," Pavo suggested.

"He can't be," said Leo. "He ran up in front of—oh, there he is! He's at the prize-claiming station."

"HEY, YOU GUYS!" Grus called out, running up to them with a shiny black robotic kitten. "Look what I got! Isn't he *A-DOR-ABLE*? I think I'm going to name him Snickers. Say 'Hi,' Snickers!"

The robo-kitten meowed robotically.

"Yeah, he's, um—*real* cute," said Andromeda, giving the

cube-shaped robotic cat with massive googly eyes a weird look, "but what about the spider-pets?"

"They just gave the last one away," said Grus, indifferent. "But don't worry, they have *PLENTY* more robo-kittens left. Apparently, nobody wanted them, but I can't see why? THEY'RE *SOO* CUTE!"

Grus went off to show Snickers to Phoebe and Izma while Leo, Pavo, and Andromeda ran over to the prize-claiming station.

"Grus was right," Andromeda groaned with frustration. She looked furiously into the box of robotic felines. "Now what are we going to do?"

"You mean, you *don't* have a plan?" said Leo while staring at a cat that was twirling around, batting its dumb googly eyes at him.

"No . . . ," Andromeda replied. "I was *certain* we were going to get one of them!"

"So all *that!*" said Pavo, "was for *NADA?*"

Andromeda nodded.

"I knew I shouldn't have come," said Leo. "Now when are we ever going to get another chance to sneak into—"

"Sneak into where?" Phoebe interjeted from behind him. She was dressed as a purple-caped witch, alongside Izma, (who was dressed as her typical self, but joked that *that* wasn't going to stop her from observing a good party!).

"*You!*" Pavo shouted at Phoebe, his mouth opening with surprise. "You have a—*spider-pet?*"

"Yep!" said Izma coolly. The group watched in amazement as the small metallic spider crawled up and down Phoebe's finger on a thin silvery rope, then dropped, and dangled like a yo-yo.

"It was the last one," said Phoebe, "—and *no*—I'm not going to trade it for a stupid robo-kitten. I mean, have you seen those things? They're virtually lethargic!"

"Um—yeah, we've seen them," said Leo, his eyes landing ravenously on Phoebe's spider-pet. "I really like your spider-pet. I was wondering if I—" He stopped for a second. "I was wondering if I could, possibly . . . borrow it?"

Phoebe looked at him with a suspicious brow.

"What for?"

"Nothing bad!" said Pavo quickly. "We just need it to—er—check on something—"

"—in someplace you're not allowed?" Izma finished for him.

"Um—yeah," said Leo with defeat.

"That's fine," said Phoebe. "You guys can borrow Two'eyes."

"'*Two'eyes?*'" Pavo repeated.

"Well, he's not anatomically correct. He should have eight of them, but if you borrowing Two'eyes means you *won't* be getting my roommate into trouble again, then that's cool with me! *But*," she went on, "I do expect one more thing . . ."

"What's that?" Leo asked.

"I think the two of you should dance," she replied, smiling.

"The two of *WHO*?" Pavo repeated as he and Leo turned to each other.

"Not the two of *you*," said Phoebe. "The two of *you*!" She pointed toward Leo and Andromeda.

Leo gulped.

Andromeda's cheeks flushed a vibrant pink.

"The—two—of—" Leo mumbled nervously. Suddenly dancing with Pavo sounded far less terrifying!

"Yep!" said Phoebe, chuckling. "I think it's about time someone got this party started! Now go on," she said, pushing Leo and Andromeda toward the dance floor, "*DANSE*!" And the two were soon swung into the pack of werewolves and fairy princesses jumping up and down to an energetic beat. But just as soon as Leo and Andromeda steadied their feet, the song shifted to a much slower beat.

"Er—uh," Leo muttered as the lights dimmed to a soft candlelight hue, "I'm not really good at dancing . . ."

"Me neither," said Andromeda quickly, nodding toward her leg.

"*What do you mean?*" said Leo, looking at her in disbelief. "Your leg's incredible! Did you forget how good you are at skydisking?"

Andromeda's cheeks went even more pink.

"Thanks," she said, hiding them behind her tawny locks.

Leo looked over his shoulder to find that Phoebe was looking impatient.

"Right, then," he said. And he took a deep breath and placed his arms around Andromeda. "For Archimedes!"

"For Archimedes," Andromeda agreed, folding her hands around Leo's neck. And for three whole minutes, they danced to a song called "Hollow Moon."

The next few days Leo did not catch a break from Pavo asking him question upon question about dancing with his cousin: "Did you look deeply into each other's eyes? . . . Did you see cute chubby angels flying around with bows and arrows? . . . Or did you *really* step on her toes?" Meanwhile, they were both busy keeping track of the senator's every movement, having navigated Two'eyes into the vent inside his office after Scotti and Ume rigged its ocular configurations and added a remote control.

Mallock took his breakfast at exactly 7:30 each morning, though he did not eat it in the cafeteria with the other staff, but rather, in the solace of his office. He would then take a brief break at nine and return to brood over paperwork up until lunch. His lunch, too, was eaten alone in his office, and he did not leave again until thirty minutes after noon for a two-and-a-half-hour meeting with city officials.

Leo and Pavo initially thought that this would have been the ideal moment to send in Two'eyes to find Grimlu's key, but instead, as soon as Mallock left, a robotic secretary took his place, sorting through piles of electronic documents.

"*Que vida*," Pavo said to Leo when Mallock returned to

his office for dinner over their visi-screen. "I swear, other than that one meeting he had earlier, he never leaves!"

"Let's just hope he doesn't sleep there again," said Leo, stretching out a yawn. However, a second later, Leo was straightening himself up. "Hey! Someone's just walked in!"

The two watched as Principal Yin approached the senator.

"What are they saying?" Pavo asked, watching the officials exchange inaudible words.

"I don't know," said Leo, adjusting the volume with no luck. "They're not speaking loud enough for us to hear from the vent!"

"We need to get Two'eyes closer," replied Pavo, carefully sending the spider-bot down the office wall until he was close enough to remain invisible to Principal Yin and Mallock, yet close enough to pick up on their conversation.

" . . . I know all this has been especially hard on you, Vlade," Principal Yin was saying, "but you can't continue on like this—I mean, look at yourself!—all cooped up in here, all hours of the day as if no one else is doing anything—"

"They're *not*," said Mallock bitterly.

"Everyone's doing all that they—"

"What everyone's doing is NOT enough," said Mallock. "They've built a city with impenetrable walls and speak of it as though it's an accomplishment—as though it's a fair wager to save a select few while *millions* are down there—*SHE* is still down there!"

"And at peace, Vlade," said Principal Yin. "She is one of the lucky few who will never know what happened!"

"'At *peace*?'" Mallock repeated with revulsion. "How can you speak of peace knowing what will become of her—of what will become of the millions of people who are down there right now?"

"You're right, Senator, forgive me. I have spoken out of turn. But you can't go on pretending we can change the sentiments of fate. We've known for centuries now that they'd be returning—the Egyptians knew it—the Romans knew it—for crying out loud, Vlade, even the Nazis knew it! It's only been a matter of time for them to wake . . . At least now we know when that is! You should feel grateful that we've at least been able to accomplish this small piece of freedom before then!"

"'*Freedom*'?" Mallock repeated, his voice quavered with rage. "We will never know freedom if it lies in the wake of another lifeless planet!"

Principal Yin placed a comforting hand on Mallock's shoulder.

"And no one," he continued, brushing Yin's hand briskly off, "in this city deserves to live as an exception!"

"*Pra caramba,*" Pavo muttered the second Yin left the room.

"They've always known," said Leo, staring blank-faced at the screen.

"Who's always known what?" Pavo asked.

"The government!" said Leo. "The government's known

this entire time that the Mleckorgs would be returning . . . so they built Luna City as a safe house—they built Luna City to save us!"

"So why's Mallock so pitted against this place?" Pavo wondered. "I mean, he's safe, right?"

"Maybe *he* is," said Leo with sudden clarity, "but not *her* . . . " Leo pointed out a real-D photo on Mallock's desk portraying a beautiful young woman with striking dark skin, silky white hair, and eyes a magnetic blue.

"Is that . . . *Crux's* mom?" said Pavo, amazed.

"It must be," said Leo. "And she must be back there." He nodded toward Earth.

"That would explain why he's so *feliz*," said Pavo sarcastically.

"And it would explain why Mallock's trying to find all the pieces of the Star Stone before the next eclipse!" said Leo in a moment of revelation. "If Mallock can somehow find all the pieces of the Star Stone and bring them here . . . the Mleckorgs won't go to Earth: They'll instead come to Luna City!"

"So . . . does that make him a bad guy, or a hero?" wondered Pavo. "Because, technically, here only a few thousand lives would be lost, versus billions—"

"Neither, in my book," said Leo, watching as Mallock, at last, left his office. "Not if there's a way to save everyone—and there has to be; we just have to hope that Grimlu knows it!"

The boys didn't waste another second to send Two'eyes in on his search; and to their relief, Mallock did not return to his office. Leo and Pavo spent all evening into the night, sorting through Mallock's desk and his electronic filing cabinets in search of Grimlu's key. They even managed to slip Two'eyes inside the drawers and between the cushions of Mallock's hover-chair. But the more they searched for the key to release Grimlu and get back Archimedes, the more obvious it became that the key wasn't there.

Days went by . . . weeks went by . . . and despite Leo having persuaded Phoebe to let him and Pavo borrow Two'eyes for the rest of the month, by the time Thanksgiving rolled around, they were no closer to finding the key than they were when they started their search for it.

"I can't *believe* you guys had that thing for an entire month and still couldn't find the key," said Andromeda to Leo and Pavo, while nibbling away at her floating tofu salad.

"If you could just get her to agree to let us borrow Two'eyes for *one more week*," Pavo pleaded.

"No," said Andromeda flatly. "If you couldn't find the key while you had him, you're not going to have any better chance of finding it now . . . Obviously, Mallock's hidden it somewhere no one would think to look."

"But how else are we going to free Grimlu?" wondered Pavo.

"Yeah, and get back Archimedes?" added Leo.

"I don't know . . . ," said Andromeda, "but *I,* at least, have some news. Though I don't think you're going to like it."

Leo and Pavo stared hungrily at Andromeda.

"Well . . . ," she continued, pulling out Mallock's journal from her side-bag. "I've decoded part of it." She pushed it over for the boys to take a look.

"*And?*" said Pavo. "What's it say?"

"That's the part you're not going to like . . . It's just a bunch of integers, which for now, don't mean anything."

"So a whole month and all you got are lousy *números?*" Pavo exclaimed.

"At least it's something," said Leo.

"Yeah, well, it's not that easy," said Andromeda. "I mean, maybe it'd be easier if a whole page wasn't missing, but even then, I doubt that would—"

"Whoa," said Leo, as it suddenly dawned on him. "I never gave it to you?"

"Gave me what?" Andromeda asked.

"Mallock's note!" said Leo. "That's the page! That's the page that's missing from the journal!"

Leo didn't know why he hadn't thought of it before. "Wait right here," he said, springing from the table. And as soon as he returned, Andromeda's eyes bulged at what she saw.

"*SERIOUSLY!*" she shouted at him. "An entire MONTH of gritting my teeth, and you've had the legend THE ENTIRE TIME?" Andromeda dug into her side-bag, pulled out her notes, and started flipping through the journal madly.

"I didn't know what it was," said Leo, watching Andromeda in amazement.

"Just—SHUSH!—for a second," she snapped, scribbling away.

"Okay—the sideways V is an A . . . ," she mumbled, " . . . the Z-squiggly-thingy must be an S . . . , then there's T . . . , and R . . . ; and oh! The dotted circle is an O! *Obviously it's an O—I should have guessed that!* Then N . . . , and M . . . , and—" She stopped for a second, her eyes twinkling like bright hazel agates. "—THAT'S IT! Leo, look!" She flipped her notes to face him. "These numbers aren't just numbers—they're coordinates! This book isn't Mallock's journal—it's the Astronomer's Map!"

CHAPTER

14

THE CHAMBERS OF
LIFE AND DEATH

The month of November went by even quicker than October, and before Leo knew it, the large fir in the middle of Central Gardens was being dressed with hundreds of silvery ornaments, layers of shimmering tinsel, and glimmering nano-drone lights. The walls around the academy had also changed. Instead of autumn scenes of oaks losing their persimmon-colored leaves, lush wintery forests, projecting a holographic snow that fell over students as they walked to class.

But the change of seasons also brought about a change in course load, and Leo and Pavo soon found themselves spending more hours in the library than they had ever imagined possible, busily preparing for the end-of-semester exams and plotting over where to search next for the key to release Grimlu and get back Archimedes.

"It doesn't seem real, does it?" Leo said to Pavo, staring dispiritedly out the library's window at the green and blue globe. "Today it's here—tomorrow it could be gone . . ."

"Maybe it'd be better that way," said Pavo, slumping in his chair. "I mean, maybe we're not supposed to find the key to release Grimlu or help him find all the pieces of the Star Stone. Maybe the Mleckorgs would be doing everyone a favor—you know, cleaning everything out so we can start fresh again."

"How can you *say* that?" said Leo, looking at Pavo incredulously. "I mean, your parents—your family—they're still down there!"

"And they don't *care* about me . . . ," said Pavo, suddenly distant. "The second my mom opened her birthday present from her new boyfriend last year and discovered a Luna City ticket with my name on it, she went completely berserk—"

"You mean," said Leo funnily, "you didn't *win* your way in?"

"*I wish!*" Pavo exclaimed. "I just told Andromeda I had won my ticket at a Ping-Pong competition, you know, to not look like a total loser compared to her."

"But you're not," said Leo.

"Yeah, well, if you haven't noticed from my lack of skills

in Gravital, I'm not exactly 'pro' at Ping-Pong, either. Anyway, none of that matters now—it's not as though we're actually going to find that key to free Grimlu, let alone be able to help him find all the pieces of Earth's Star Stone before the next eclipse. I've figured out when it is." Pavo pulled up a series of lunar charts on the holographic computer desk. "The next one," he went on, scrolling through the various real-D crescents, "is December . . . the twenty-second."

"That's just *three days* before Christmas!" Leo shouted.

"Like I was saying," said Pavo, "maybe we should try to make the best of it—you know, like actually try to have some fun before the holidays are over? I mean, two weeks doesn't give anyone much time to *salve o mundo*—and I doubt we'll get to do much celebrating after it."

"You're right," said Leo, shuffling his things into his bag, "that isn't much time. And this picture of an aloe vera plant"—he held up his not-so-very-well-shaded drawing assignment—"is *not* making the best use of it. We need to find those pieces of the Star Stone before anyone else gets to them!"

"Yeah, but how are we going to do that without Grimlu?"

"Who said we need Grimlu—when we've got Gudrun!"

An invisible lightbulb lit over Pavo's head, and he at once put away his things and followed Leo.

Leo instructed Meta to send Andromeda a visi-text to meet up with him and Pavo in the first open visi-lab as soon as she was able; and in a moment's time, she arrived with the map in hand (and a plethora of electronic notes).

"Oh-kay!" she said importantly, spreading everything evenly onto the desk. "So you do know, Leo, for this to work, that you're going to have to tell Gudrun everything that's happened?"

Leo nodded.

"I mean," she went on, "you're fine telling Gudrun that you lost his pet, and that he's currently trapped in a dungeon that's not very easy to get to, with the same creature he blames for abducting his wife?"

Leo's readiness to dial up Gudrun suddenly faded.

"Actually, I hadn't thought about it *that* way," he replied.

"Well, I still think it's the best idea you've had," said Andromeda. "We haven't found Grimlu's key yet, and with the next eclipse happening in just a couple short weeks, that doesn't give us much time to find it, either. And from everything we know about Gudrun, he seems like someone who'd believe us. I say we give it a go."

Leo took a breath and tapped in Gudrun's digits. The visi rang for a few seconds, and then Gudrun's face emerged.

"Happy Hanukkah! Happy Ramadan! Happy Kwanza! And Meeerry Christmas! *And any of those there other holidays I left out,*" he hiccuped, smiling over a tall glass mug with a thick layer of foam dripping off his mustache. "Off to me mother's house for some better seasonal cooking . . . *and more eggnog!*" he added, looking slightly disappointed at what was left in his mug. "I tried ta do Thanksgiving on me own this year, but that—er—didn't exactly work out . . ." He directed the camera toward an enormous dog bowl, in which sat a king-sized turkey, scorched a deep velvety black. "Don't know why Muffin an' Princess won't touch the thing—that bird cost me a hefty zozo, it did!

"*Anyhoo*, if you're getting this message, I'll be back shortly after me old lady passes out on Christmas—which will be after the roast . . . and the stuffing . . . and the nummy nummy cranberry sauce . . . *but luckily not the cake*!" He winked mischievously at the camera. "Which I will, *o' course*, be sneaking home with me! So until then, wishing you all a Happy Hanukkah! Happy Ramadan! Happy Kwanza! And a MEEERRY—"

Leo shut the visi off.

"Well, that cancels out that idea," said Pavo, as Leo sat there, beyond disappointed.

"So now what?" Andromeda asked.

"I don't know," said Leo, "but I'll think of something."

But that something never came. Instead, days went by with Leo doing none of his homework, spending all day and into the night trying to think of ways to free Grimlu and get back Archimedes. He asked Scotti and Ume if they would help build a robot using various tools he had collected to try to crack a lock, but they refused on the premise of having too much studying to do and not enough time to create something worthy of the acclaimed "Tokage" name. Leo even attempted sneaking back to the secret stairwell on his own, but after their last excursion, Floris and Japps were not letting any space get between them and the main gravity-shafts, each eager to claim a new star on their electro-badges for catching another student trying to trespass.

The entire city was celebrating the season—that is, everyone except Leo, who couldn't stand to think of what little celebrating there would be if he couldn't think of a way to set Grimlu free quickly. And then, without realizing how the time had passed, Meta was waking him up, announcing the long-awaited week of Christmas festivities.

"There will be Christmas cookie decorating and a gingerbread house competition in the cafeteria on Monday," Meta said cheerfully. "On Tuesday, Madam Cebulka will be having extra-special discounts in the trade shop on select items, including complimentary robotic gift wrapping and change-your-color bowing. There will be real-D holiday films playing in the visi-theater on Wednesday and—"

"—No Earth on Thursday if someone doesn't do something," said Leo miserably while Meta continued with his announcement of Christmas Eve caroling and Christmas Day feasts.

Leo sat through classes that day like a ghost whose life had long ago passed. He received his month's worth of incomplete and failed homework assignments back from Professoressa Pittore, who told him she had expected "much'a more'a" than him scribbling in large letters *I CAN'T DRAW* or *WHAT'S THE POINT OF THIS?* or titling one of his blank canvases *PHANTOM*, which he argued was his most "artistic" work of art of the year.

Though Leo had the luxury of knowing Professor Kikaren couldn't fully see his downtrodden emotions, Kikaren, too, stated his dismay at Leo's sudden lack of enthusiasm for the class and hoped that whatever was bothering him would pass before the next semester.

Herr Pendular, on the other hand, was determined to make Leo a half hour late to his Sectional work, having yapped his ear off about how "he must not let his history of poor efforts repeat itself in the future" and that "the future of mankind relies on its youth to care about the years and years of effort put forth by man to get him where he is today."

"History!" Pendular told him, "is in the future of tomorrow's yesterday!" Though at this point in the conversation, Leo couldn't help but feel sorry for the guy, as it was clear that he (like everyone else) was not aware that Earth's history, in a few short days, would be depleted.

The only person who did not seem entirely upset with Leo—despite Leo's equal slack with his botanical recording efforts—was Dr. Row.

"Erm, Doctor?" Leo said to him, stepping up to the scientist's desk after finishing documenting his thousandth Datura innoxia plant.

"Oh—hmm—yes?" said the doctor, distracted by a vial of noxious green gas.

"I was wondering if I could ask you something?" Leo ventured.

The doctor nodded approvingly.

"Well, I was wondering . . . ," Leo continued, then stopped and shook his head: He knew what he was about to say was going to sound ridiculous. Dr. Row, however, encouraged his question with an eager brow.

"I was wondering what *you* think the probability of extra-terrestrial life actually existing is?"

"'*Extraterrestrial life*'?" Dr. Row repeated, looking at Leo curiously. "Why, that's a rather funny thing to ask: Everyone knows the universe is crawling with trillions upon CENTILLIONS of little microscopic bacterium!"

"I guess I was meaning, more like . . . *intelligent* life," Leo articulated. "You know, like the kind that could be more advanced than humans."

"Oh," said the doctor, suddenly apprehensive, "you mean, like the kind that use their limbic systems for things other than *spontaneously reproducing*?"

"Um," said Leo, hesitant, "yeah, like *that* kind . . ."

"It doesn't exist," answered the doctor stiffly.

"But I was thinking—" Leo started to say.

"You clearly have *not* been thinking!" Dr. Row laughed heartily. "*Intelligent* extraterrestrial life?" he cackled even louder. "*Ha!* Now don't go making me reconsider your intelligence level, Leo. You're a smart boy; you should know by now there's nothing more intelligent than mankind—*especially aliens!*" The doctor began laughing without reserve, and Leo took the hint and left the room.

Dinner was about as enjoyable as the conversation Leo

had attempted with Dr. Row, when Grus merrily listed off all the holiday activities he had signed up for and did not get off Leo's case when Leo replied that he had signed up for "none."

"I don't get it," said Grus emotionally, "out of all these fun and exciting and FESTIVE festivities, you don't even want to try just *one?*"

"No," said Leo firmly.

"But it's Christmas!" Grus cried. "It's the holidays! It's that special time of year! You know . . ." And he broke into song:

> *Christmas is here,*
> *It only comes once in a year!*
> *The snow falls;*
> *The ground chills;*
> *And children dream of reindeer!*
> *Christmas is here,*
> *So full of holiday cheer!*
> *The tree is dressed;*
> *The stockings are stuffed;*
> *And carolers sing of the year!*
> *Christmas is here,*
> *"But where is Leo's good cheer?"*

"Oh," Grus muttered, noticing Leo's idle stare was directed toward the magnificent orb outside the cafeteria's window, "you miss your family, don't you?"

Leo didn't respond.

"Well, if it'd make you feel better," Grus went on, "you can always borrow Snickers. He's nearly just as good as family, and he's really good at making you feel all warm and fuzzy, especially when he purrs and kneads his tiny little robotic paws all over your tummy!"

"Thanks," said Leo, "but no thanks."

"How about some hot chocolate with itty-bitty star-shaped marshmallows in it then?" Grus asked.

"No," said Leo again.

"Your loss!" sang Grus, getting up to go claim seconds. And as Grus went off to the hot cocoa stand, Leo sat there, feeling more depressed than he had ever felt before in his life.

"You really should try to lighten up," said Andromeda. "It's not healthy, and Grus is right, it's the holidays! We really should try to have some fun . . . And we have the Astronomer's Map now, so you don't have to worry anymore about Mallock somehow finding all the pieces of the Star Stone and bringing them here to destroy this place, too—at least we're all safe!"

"That's easy for you to say," said Leo, "you're not going to be losing somebody you weren't already going to be losing soon anyway."

Andromeda looked at Leo with pain-filled eyes.

"Hope you have a Merry Christmas too, Leo," she snapped at him. And she stormed out of the cafeteria.

"Nice one," said Pavo, looking at Leo crazily. "And I thought *I* was the one with *problemas*?"

"Yeah, well you're not being much help either," said Leo, as he, too, picked up his tray and left the table.

"*EI!*" Pavo shouted after him. "SHE'S MY GRANDMA, TOO!"

The rest of the lunchroom turned to face him.

"Grandmas," Pavo muttered uncomfortably, "are *cool* . . ."

That evening, after the rest of the city had fallen asleep, Leo awoke with a start; his chest was pounding as he lay in bed, trying to convince himself he was alright. He had just had the most terrifying dream: A veil of darkness had fallen all around him, and a deep, pulsating pain penetrated his wrists, so life-like that he grabbed at them, sweating profusely—and then there was a laugh: a cold, malevolent laugh. Leo tried shaking it out of his head, but it was so realistic, he could have sworn he had heard the laugh from right beside him.

Leo pulled on his robe and slipped out of his room for a drink at the globule-releasing drinking fountain; some H2O, he hoped, would help erase the nightmare from his brain.

The hall was still and silent, though it was much brighter than it usually was for that time of night as the tall fir tree was adorned with thousands of slightly swaying glimmering nano-drone lights. Leo had always loved everything about Christmas: the food, the trees, the presents; but this year, despite his not wanting to be anywhere else, he couldn't help but think of home.

He remembered the scent of his mother baking sugar cookies, and his father lacing strands of multicolored bulbs around their shrub, Spruce. He remembered his sister, Lily, crying about not getting to open her presents early, and how happy she had been when he had given her her now headless doll, Poofie. He even missed Misses Kisses hissing around the house while trying to scratch her faux antlers off . . .

Though as Leo stood there, remembering Christmases past, he realized for the first time how fast the semester had gone and how different his life had become; he had left Earth for a new home inside the moon; he had made (though he now regretted his poor behavior earlier in the cafeteria) real friends for the first time in his life; he had learned that his crazy neighbor wasn't entirely crazy after all (having stumbled upon Riverdale's missing trees and having met an actual Lunaling); and he had done a pretty good job of showing it to Gavin when he had won their bet in Gravital (though losing Archimedes and having nearly kissed a goose in front of his entire class had quickly offset his excitement from that). And just as Leo was thinking about the goose he never kissed, it was as though someone gave him a kick.

"The pond!" he thought aloud, staring down incredulously at it. "I never thought to check the pond!"

Leo dashed down the hall and hopped into the nearest gravity-shaft. And as he approached the tall fir tree in the center of the gardens, it became even more impressive in size, with its bright silvery ornaments glimmering in the reflection of the pond.

"Now, where was it I saw you?" Leo muttered, kneeling on all fours. His eyes shifted back and forth between the pools of light. But just as Leo was starting to think he hadn't actually seen anything glittering in the pond when he had tried to kiss that goose, a golden speck caught his eye.

"There you are!" he murmured, kicking off his slippers and stepping into the tepid pond. "Please be what I'm hoping you are . . ."

However, as Leo went to pick it up, his appearance inside the pond was announced by the fattest goose. And just as it had done before, it began flapping its wings, swimming excitedly toward him.

"Great," Leo groaned, overhearing Floris and Japps in the distance.

"I swear, this time, Floris, I'm gonna find out who keeps bothering that goose!"

"Not if I find out first, ya blubbering lunch-box!"

Leo took a deep breath as his fingers wiggled themselves between the slippery rocks, until, at last, they caught hold of something solid.

Without a second to give the object a look, Leo dashed out of the pond, grabbed his slippers, and ran, skidding across the park grounds toward the nearest gravity-shaft.

"C'mon, c'mon!" he said under his breath, anxiously waiting for his get-away-lift to arrive.

Floris and Japps turned the corner, but the gravity-shaft's doors opened and shut just in the nick of time!

Leo released a grateful sigh as the gravity-shaft started its ascent. But as he loosened his hold on the object wrapped in his fist, his heart did a double jump: A small golden key was nestled underneath his fingertips!

Leo sprinted to his room.

"Get up! Get up!" he hissed at Pavo, shaking him vigorously to wake.

"What . . . is . . . it?" Pavo yawned, rolling over and looking alarmed.

"I've found it!" Leo whispered. "I've found Grimlu's key!" He showed Pavo the prize he had in hand, and as Pavo's eyes fell upon it, he sat straight up.

"*Pra caramba!*" he muttered. "Where did you find it?"

"The only place we didn't think to look," answered Leo. "The pond!"

"You mean," said Pavo, "with all those *geese?*"

Leo nodded.

"Andromeda really was right," said Pavo. "Mallock did hide it someplace no one would want to look! . . . But how are we going to get back to Floor Double-Z?" he asked Leo. "You've seen how those two metal-heads have been guarding the main gravity-shaft ever since then?"

"Easy," Leo replied. "We just go the same way Grus did."

"You don't mean—" said Pavo.

Leo nodded yet again. And a short second later, the two were creeping across their dormitory floor and traversing down the emergency stairwell.

"Here it is," Leo announced once he and Pavo reached the door marked "Double-Z."

"And you'd think, before gravity-shafts existed, all the people who had to climb up and down these things would have evolved with winged-knees!" said Pavo.

The boys let themselves through the door and went directly to the microscope. They gave its lens a good twist, and at once a familiar hole reemerged. Only this time, as Leo and Pavo journeyed down the secret steps, they knew exactly which tunnel *not* to take to avoid falling into a massive pile of Evergreens.

"*Tick . . . tock . . . tickedy . . . tick . . .*" Grimlu's squeaky little voice echoed throughout the crypt.

Leo, however, had a good excuse for interrupting the Lunaling's singing. "We've got the key!" he called out, as he and Pavo ran up to Grimlu's cell.

Grimlu's eyes turned as large as radishes as he held on to the cell's bars, jumping up and down with excitement.

"I KNEWSID IT!" he squealed with glee. "I KNEWSID you'd findsid the KEY!"

But as the iron bars at last creaked open, the small gray creature's expression sank.

"What's the matter?" Pavo asked.

"Here . . . ," said Grimlu, picking up Archimedes from his small bed of twigs and passing him to Leo. "As I promisedid, *you* takesid Priscilla . . ."

"You can still hold him—or um, *her*—for now," said Leo. "As *you* 'promisedid,' we're still going to need your help!"

"With what?" Grimlu asked, evasive.

"With finding all the pieces of the Star Stone before the next eclipse!" answered Pavo.

"BUT I CAN'TSID!" Grimlu shouted. "Likes I toldsid you: I don't havesid THE MAP!"

"But *we* do," said Leo with a cunning grin. And Grimlu's eyes suddenly turned a fiery topaz, and the three were off, running out of the Evergreen Crypt and sneaking themselves back to the boys' dormitory floor.

"WHERE *ISID* IT?" Grimlu demanded the second he, Leo, and Pavo entered the boys' room.

"*Shh!*" Leo hissed at him, taking "Priscilla" out of his hands as the alien creature proceeded to hop onto the boys' desk, messing up a stack of electronic papers.

"You need to keep him *quiet*," Pavo whispered to Leo; but Grus had already woken up and was staring, his eyes bulging, at what was going on below him.

"H-h-he w-w-was *REAL*?" Grus stuttered, gasping with fright at the sight of Grimlu's beady little eyes beaming intensely up at him.

"No," said Leo melodically. "This is just . . . a . . . dream— go . . . back . . . to . . . sleep!"

"Okay," Grus agreed. And he threw the covers over his head, and a few seconds later, was snoring.

"*Ei*," said Pavo, "that actually worked!"

"Yeah, well, now we just need to get the map back from Andromeda *without* Grimlu waking up the rest of the city . . ."

"You go," said Pavo, taking hold of the unruly baby alien, who was not abating his writhing and squirming in attempts to set himself free. "We'll wait here for you."

"Thanks," said Leo. And he took off down the hall to wake Andromeda.

Andromeda was already waiting outside her room when Leo got there. "Seriously, who sends someone twenty-eight visi-texts *in a row?*" she yawned, folding her arms sleepily. "One was all that was needed to wake me. Anyway, you're not supposed to be here; Bertha, our robotic hall monitor, should be passing by any minute—you know boys aren't allowed on the girls' side of the dormitory!"

"I know," said Leo, "but like I was telling you, *I found the key!* And we have Grimlu! All he needs now is the map!"

"And what? I'm just supposed to give it to you?" Andromeda guffawed as she repeated, "It's not as though *I* care if the world ends and I lose someone I'm already about to lose soon anyway . . ."

Leo's stomach sank.

"Listen, I'm sorry, really . . . that was stupid . . . *and* selfish of me. I didn't mean it . . ."

"Oh, really?" said Andromeda. "I'd like to see you prove it!"

And it was just as though someone was giving Leo another kick that he quickly leaned in and gave Andromeda a kiss.

"*Oooh!*" sang Phoebe from beside the door. "I knew I felt *l'amour* in the air!" She took the leather-bound book from

Andromeda's desk and passed it to Leo. "Here!" she said with excitement. "She forgives you! Now go!—*Allez!*"

Andromeda stood there, rendered speechless, as she placed her hand on her suddenly rosy cheek.

"Thanks," said Leo. And he took the map and ran away.

"That was fast," Pavo said the moment Leo returned.

"Yeah," Leo replied, catching his breath, still thinking about what he had done seconds earlier, "it really was!"

"The only problem," Pavo continued, "is that it wasn't fast enough . . ." He nodded toward Grimlu, who was sprawled out, drooling in the currents of Leo's air-wave-bed.

"Well, wake him up!"

"I've tried," said Pavo, "but he doesn't budge. The thing sleeps like a rock!"

"It must have been all the excitement," Leo suggested.

"Yeah, that, or all the stairs!"

Leo placed the map on his desk. "I guess we'll just have to wait until tomorrow, then, to figure out what Grimlu's plan is . . . that is," he added with difficulty, trying to move the creature over, "provided I can get him to the . . . other . . . side!"

Leo pushed and pushed, and Grimlu, at long last, rolled a slight inch to the right. And despite Leo not wanting to sleep anywhere near the baby alien, he maneuvered himself to the bed's edge, and, in a moment's time, was fast asleep.

But not long after Leo's mind slipped back into a familiar dark, his heart began to race and he was once more greeted with a malevolent laugh.

Leo awoke, his palms sweating as he turned over, trying not to think of it; but as his gaze fell to the side, his eyes popped wide open: Grimlu wasn't there!

"He couldn't have," Leo muttered, his eyes turning toward the desk; but the map, too, was gone!

Leo bolted up and flew to the door. And as he stepped into the hall, he immediately spotted a speck of gray shooting up the main gravity-shaft.

"Where *in-the-moon* is he going?" Leo muttered to himself. He leaned over the balcony's edge, following the gravity-shaft higher . . . and higher . . . until, finally, it reached the moon's uppermost floor.

"The oxygen chambers!" Leo gasped with panic.

Without a second to spare, he leaped into the nearest gravity-shaft and took it as far up as it would allow, racing up the remaining floors via the emergency stairs.

But as Leo pushed open the final floor's door, he froze when he found Grimlu alongside a figure dressed in an all-black cloak.

"*Mallock?*" he wondered aloud, but then he realized: "No, it can't be Mallock . . ." Whoever it was, was too short.

But just as Leo said it, the figure turned to face him.

"*Doctor Row?*" Leo stammered.

"W-w-who—who's there?" Row stuttered. He cautiously doubled back to where Leo was, hidden behind the stairwell's door. At the sight of it being just a student, he let out a great sigh of relief.

"Oh, Leo, it's only you!" he said, chuckling. "You gave me a real scare there, you did!"

Leo looked to Grimlu, who was clutching a sizable bag of cotton balls, stuffing them one by one, like a chipmunk, into his ever-stretching cheeks.

"Ah, so you two are acquaintances?" the doctor inquired. "Yes, well, as I was saying, Leo, I've yet to meet another creature in the universe smarter than a human being! Though I suppose now I stand corrected, as it appears a ten-thousand-year-old baby Lunaling has outsmarted you!" Dr. Row chuckled a bit more to himself, as Leo stood there, dumbstruck by what he saw—Dr. Row had the map in his hands!

"He's—he's given the map to *you*?" Leo asked, puzzled.

"He most certainly has," answered the doctor, patting Grimlu cordially on the head. "Lunalings will do anything for Gossypium hirsutum—colloquially referred to as cotton. I, of course, offered to pay him handsomely in it if, when he found the map, he'd give it to me instead of Senator Mallock.

"The only problem was when I finally got ahold of it, I couldn't read it. So I figured I'd scan it into the Universal Decoder in the library. However, I knew better than to let myself be seen, or else Mallock would have discovered me!"

"So *you* were the one who ransacked the old book database?" Leo asked, though it wasn't really a question.

"Well, technically, my fleet of shrunken bees did all the dirty work for me," Row explained. "Only the blasted bots were still in the rudimentary stages of prototyping, and instead of doing what they were *supposed* to do, they destroyed half the library instead!

"I, naturally, suggested that Soenso have all the students do the resorting—as a means of disciplinary reform—so that I could spy on them with the help of my bots until someone finally found it. Though I must say, I was not expecting your girlfriend to do all the decoding work for me; or for Grimlu, for that matter, to be so thoughtful as to bring it back to me!"

"So . . . you're trying to *help*, then?" Leo asked. "You've been after the Astronomer's Map to try to stop Mallock from getting to any of the Star Stone pieces before the next eclipse?"

"Of course I'm trying to *stop* Mallock!" Row wittily laughed. "If Mallock had found the map and destroyed any of the shards of the sacred star, then Master's plan would fail and I"—he broke off, suddenly convulsing—"would fail to EXIST!" His face began to drip with beads of alarming purple sweat. "But now," he went on, breathing with difficulty as his face rapidly twitched, "now that I have the Astronomer's Map, Master's plan will not be ruined, and all of Earth's time will at long last be OURS!"

Leo fell over with terror as Dr. Row's face began to rip and tear in two. And as the synthetic skin peeled itself back, from underneath emerged a dark, skeletal beast: Its cheeks hollow and sunken to the bones; its eyes, a bottomless pit filled with a never-ending black. And this time, there was no questioning what Leo was seeing: The creature's veins were glittering, just as Leo thought he had once seen the Senator's at the competition!

"Your—your veins," Leo gulped with horror, "they're—glittering?"

"Ah, *yes* . . . ," growled the creature that was once Dr. Row, his voice suddenly low and scratchy as he obsessively stroked the back of his wrist. "Funny souvenir of consuming time: The molecular strands of DNA in the body begin to twist and contort when you're running out. And so I must apologize"—he began to wheeze heavily—"for my brevity . . . in this . . . little . . . conversation . . . but as I do not . . . wish . . . for my own . . . strands . . . to BLOW UP . . . I must get . . . going back . . . to the . . . task . . . at hand!" He reached into his cloak and took out a large, lumpy bag.

"Datura innoxia!" he said ravenously, pulling out a robotic bumble-bot from within it, "the rare and delicate moonflower—hallucinogenic in small doses, but lethal in high quantities! And this . . . little stinger . . . has just enough . . . tropane alkaloids in it . . . to put every . . . human . . . in this . . . city . . . into an eternal slumber!

"Pity about your . . . girlfriend, though! Such a waste to see . . . a . . . similarly . . . intelligent mind . . . go . . . But alas! I can spare no chances . . . to have Master's plan . . . impeded!"

"Andromeda," said Leo fervently, "will *never* be like you!"

"You're right," said the creature evilly, "because she'll soon be dead . . . as will you! So with that"—he held the bag of bumble-bots over the balcony's edge—"TOODLE—DOOS!"

Leo pushed himself up, his knees trembling as he lunged toward the beast, throwing himself onto the creature's chest as he reached for the bag of poisonous-bots.

"LET . . . GO!" the creature growled, digging its razor-sharp nails into Leo's wrists.

Leo only tightened his grip. "NEVER!" he shouted with all his might. But in the next second, a stinger was penetrating his arm's skin and a blazing heat was seeping through his veins. The creature threw Leo back, pushing him over the balcony's rail.

"GRIMLU—PLEASE!" Leo gasped, clinging to the railing for dear life. "GO—GET—HELP!"

By now, the heat was so strong, Leo imagined there was an actual fire ablaze inside him. And then there was a soft breeze flowing across his face, and Leo felt as though he were back home, flying in the go-kart with Gudrun; he saw Muffin and Princess rolling around in the front yard, and his mom and dad and Lily waving at him. He even spotted Misses Kisses chasing Archimedes up a tree! . . . And then he saw Pavo and Grus . . . and Andromeda . . . they were all there, too. But just as soon as their faces appeared, they vanished, and the gentle breeze came to a stop, and all that surrounded Leo was a deep, unthinkable dark.

CHAPTER

15

GLITTERING VEINS

The days that followed were the grimmest days the Lunar Academy had ever seen: Notices flooded the halls, along with hundreds of gifts that lay untouched underneath the tall fir tree. Those days, no one could stop talking about what had happened; but those days would too quickly be forgotten as the simulated snow came to a stop and Luna City's winter turned to spring.

Pavo, Andromeda, and Grus were hit the worst by the changing seasons, as they no longer had their best friend by their sides to help them get through the end of the semester and the start of a new. Though Andromeda had lost her rematch against Crux—having not been entirely in the mood for games—when the entire school demanded an End-All match between Gravital's creator and the girl with one leg, Andromeda was left with no option but to accept.

And nearly just as soon as spring announced its arrival, it, too, reached its end. There was just one week left until the final semester would be over, and the halls were buzzing with excitement for the Academy's break. But Pavo, Andromeda, and Grus were aloof among the other students; it simply didn't feel right knowing they'd be ending the year without Leo there beside them.

"You don't have to go through with it," said Phoebe to Andromeda during lunch in the cafeteria.

"Yes, I do . . . ," said Andromeda stressfully. "Anyway, I don't know what the big deal is for the match this Friday if everyone knows I'm going to lose."

"It's still worth a try," said Grus, chomping away at his veggie burger faster than anyone had ever seen.

"You're right," said Andromeda, getting up suddenly. "I probably *should* try to squeeze in some practice."

"Which reminds me!" said Pavo, jumping to his feet, "I need to get going, too. You know, to check on Archimedes!"

"Didn't you just get back from that?" Phoebe asked, suspicious.

A puzzled look replaced Pavo's eager grin. "Oh, uh, yeah . . . that's right." He sat back down.

"Anyway, I'll see you guys later, then," said Andromeda; and she left the cafeteria.

"PHEEEW!" Grus blurted out a second later while holding on to his stomach. "These onions sure are SPICE-E! I think I better get going to the bathroom before I get caught making some MAJOR air pollution!"

Pavo—who still didn't get Grus's sense of humor—wasn't offended by the loss of company. "See-ya," he replied and he stretched his legs underneath the table as Grus, too, exited the lunch room. But as Pavo finally looked at his watch, he sprang up from his seat: He knew exactly where Andromeda and Grus were going!

"Good afternoon, Miss Groves," said a robotic nurse to Andromeda, smiling at her kindly as she entered the waiting area of the city's hospital. "There are just another thirty minutes left of visiting hours, so you'll need to make it quick this time, okay?"

Andromeda nodded and followed the nurse into Patient Room Two. A floating chair greeted her and brought her toward a long glass tube in the center of the room. A small tear formed in her eye as she pressed her hand to the cold, rounded glass; the glass tube had been the home of her dearest friend, Leo Gray, ever since that terrible night in December.

"If only you'd wake up," she scolded him softly, wiping a tear as it rolled down her cheek.

But, as expected, no response came.

Leo lay there, his eyes shut and his body motionless as he breathed the forced oxygen being pumped into his healing chamber. If his eyes were open, he'd see the table next to him overflowing with holocards, flowers, and bags of Luna-sweets. Andromeda was quick to notice a newly placed card on the table with a holographic heart and a pouty-faced puppy on it. She knew it wasn't hers to open, but she couldn't resist the temptation to take a peek.

"You don't mind, do you?" she asked Leo, who remained as responsive as a rock.

Andromeda swiped the card open and read:

Dear Leo,

Please wake up. Luna City misses you.

Love,
Carina Van'ness ♡

Andromeda's nose crinkled at the bubbly font dancing around the card. She wasn't exactly *fond* of Carina, especially now with her sudden liking of Leo. She had never even seen Carina speak to him before, and now she was writing "*Love*" to him in her letters?

"Pathetic," Andromeda huffed. She returned the card to

the table, but then, spotted the trash bin next to it. Andromeda smiled to herself cleverly, extended her finger, and gave the card a good flick; but just before it reached the canister, someone else's hand caught it.

"Not a fan of Miss Van'ness?" asked the president.

Andromeda's cheeks went scarlet.

"No-no, I—" Andromeda tried to explain, but Soenso stopped her.

"I don't think someone like you really needs to worry much about a girl like her," he said, taking a chair next to Leo. "She doesn't hold a laser lamp to your intelligence!"

"Thanks," said Andromeda, "but I wasn't meaning it *that* way."

"Nor was I," replied the president with a wink as the sound of another hover-chair echoed toward them.

"Guess you're not at practice then," said Grus grumpily, swinging in between Andromeda and the president, looking highly disappointed that he hadn't gotten there first.

"Yeah, and I guess you're not off to the *banheiro* either?" said Pavo.

It appeared that each of them had tried to sneak off to get a moment with Leo by themselves. Every day, for the past few weeks, Leo's visiting slots were stuffed with teachers and students from their first-year class, hoping to get a glimpse of him. Leo had become so popular after having fallen from the top of the moon that even Gavin felt obligated to get him something; though, of course, he swore up and down the only reason he had done so was because Crux had, who also insisted the only reason he had gotten Leo a gift was because the rest of their year had.

"Anyway, I had wanted to ask you," Andromeda said to Soenso, "when do you think he'll wake up? I mean, I've read that comas can last longer than weeks or months—"

"For *YEARS* even!" Pavo blurted, stressed.

"Yeah, and then for some," Grus went on, looking as though his watery eyes were going to burst at any moment into Niagara Falls, "they never wake up AT ALL!"

"You have to understand," Andromeda pleaded, "the nurses won't tell us anything!"

Pavo and Grus nodded as the president replied with a heavy sigh, "Well, I guess that's up to Leo to decide, now, isn't it? I suppose if he wants to wake up, he'll wake up. But until then, I think he would want each of you to stop worrying so much."

Pavo, Andromeda, and Grus all knew the president was correct—they had been worrying an awful lot about Leo after everything that had happened—but, given the circumstances, it was exceedingly difficult to try to focus on anything else when their best friend lay like a corpse inside a healing chamber.

"It's time," announced the robotic nurse from beside the door.

The three each took a moment to say their goodbyes and headed, unwillingly, back to their Sectional work. Then, after a long and demanding week of exams, finals were over, and Andromeda was off to the End-All Gravital match.

"Winning comes from within," she was saying to herself importantly. She watched her fellow classmates fill in the floating bleachers from the side of the court. "From believing that you're capable of winning—you must think like a predatory creature—you must think like a scorpion!—you must fully believe that you're capable of crushing your opponent . . . *crushing . . . crushing . . . crushing . . . How he could have been CRUSHED by that terrible fall!*"

"Ready?" asked the robotic scorekeeper.

Andromeda twisted her lips. It was impossible to feel "ready" when all she could think about was who had helped her win her first Gravital match: *What was the point of winning if you didn't have all your friends there to celebrate your win with you?*

"Miss Groves?" the scorekeeper tried again.

"Ready," Andromeda said at last—though on the inside she felt far from it.

Andromeda hopped on her skydisk as Izma took her spot as Pilot over the court. Crux had reselected Gavin as his Pilot, but in an End-All match there were no Back-up Hitters; it would be just one last defining round. In the event of a foul, the non-fouling team would instantly be declared the winner.

If only Leo was here, Andromeda thought to herself the second the buzzer sounded and the game began—*then maybe, just maybe, I'd feel like winning!*

Though right as Andromeda was thinking it, she couldn't possibly have known that, at that very same moment, someone's eyes had started to open. Leo Gray had finally woken up—though not fully—but he was moving and breathing on his own, and as he lifted his head, he was greeted with a nice solid *WHACK* from the top of the healing chamber.

"Oh, you're awake!" a robotic voice chirped beside him, though it did not *at all* sound like chirping to Leo, but rather, like some sort of sonorous gong! "What wonderful news!" she exclaimed, fluttering toward the door. "Wait here, just one minute, dear—I have strict orders to inform the president straightaway!"

Leo adjusted himself, turning around to catch the fuzzy outline of the nurse hovering outside the door. He was still in a fairly good haze about where he was, or what was going on. His head hurt pretty badly—that was for sure—and his vision was definitely blurred . . . But then he spotted the pile of gifts and holocards on the table next to him, and he realized it.

"*I'm in . . . the hospital?*" he said to himself wildly. He hadn't a clue about why he would even be in one! But as the president appeared at the doorway, a wave of panic washed over Leo as he remembered, "*THE OXYGEN CHAMBERS! . . . DOCTOR ROW!*"

"Shh, shh . . . it's all been taken care of," said Soenso gently, taking a seat next to Leo and opening the chamber's lid to give Leo some fresh air. "Mallock told me everything that happened."

"Mallock?" Leo repeated, his elbows wobbling as he tried to steady himself upright.

"You were very lucky he caught you when he did," said the president sternly. "That was a very high height to fall from!"

"You mean," said Leo, looking at him funnily, "*Mallock* was the one who saved me?"

"Apparently a little bird informed him of your predicament . . ."

It was then that Leo remembered how he had so terrifyingly hung from the top of the moon, and how he had so desperately cried out for Grimlu to go get help. Grimlu must have gotten Senator Mallock—Grimlu had, beyond Leo's belief, actually saved him!

"BUT THE BUMBLE-BOTS!" Leo spluttered out. "DID THEY—"

"No," said Soenso calmly. "Thanks to you, not a soul—other than yourself, that is—was hurt."

Leo released a grateful sigh.

"So . . . you *know* then?" he asked the president. "I mean, you've known all this time about Mleckorgs existing?"

Soenso nodded. "I'm afraid this city wasn't built solely for fun."

But then, in another wave of panic, Leo blurted out, "Wait!—THE ECLIPSE!—has it?—"

Soenso nodded yet again and Leo's heart plummeted.

"So then—" Leo gulped.

"Not yet," replied the president. "There's still time—travel between galaxies does not happen instantaneously."

"But they will still come, won't they?" Leo asked. "The Mleckorgs, that is. They're still going to come to Earth to try to find all the pieces of the Star Stone and destroy it?"

"Only time will tell," said Soenso, "but now that the map has been returned to safe hands, we can all sleep a bit more soundly knowing that *you've* made it much more difficult for them to achieve their task.

"Mleckorgs live off borrowed time, time consumed by the deaths of others—and without the map, their time to find any piece of the sacred star will be extremely limited.

"That said," he went on severely, "I can assure you all of Earth's military will do their best to repel them. And with that, I don't think it's something that an *eleven-year-old* should feel the need to worry over?"

Leo nodded at the president's reproachful brow.

"So . . . how long has it been?" Leo asked, glancing at the massive pile of gifts.

"Only the entire second semester," answered Soenso.

"'The ENTIRE second semester?'" Leo repeated.

"Ah, yes, well, at least you got your sleep in!" replied the president. "But, for the record, Leo, no one else knows what actually happened that night—that is, other than you and me.

And it's my greatest hope that you will be wise enough to keep what happened *secret*."

Leo looked at the president strangely.

"As I'm sure you can imagine, if either of us told anyone that an alien had penetrated our city's walls and was trying to destroy it, I doubt they'd think of either of us as sane or normal-minded people ever again. And, given that I'm rather *fond* of my position . . ."

"I understand," said Leo, squinting a bit as he held on to his forehead, which was, at the moment, throbbing more than he desired.

"So for now," continued Soenso, "the rest of the city simply believes you went to the Oxygen Chambers on your own accord and jumped."

"'*JUMPED?*'" Leo repeated.

"As a science experiment, to test your gravity belt, of course," said Soenso. "Naturally, as Dr. Row was the one who approved of your ridiculous proposal for such a dangerous stunt, he's been dismissed from his teaching job at the academy."

"So *that's* what everyone thinks of me now?" said Leo, embarrassed. "That I'm some sort of . . . *scientific daredevil?*"

"Well, not everyone," said the president. "I believe a few of your friends know more about what happened that night than they're letting me know. And though I must say what you did was incredibly foolish, it was also, remarkably, brave."

"Thanks," said Leo, "but I don't think I'd call it *that*."

"You're right," said Soenso. "Risking your life to save the lives of everyone else in this city is much, much more than heroic—it's selfless—and for that, I would like to give you a little something."

The president pulled out a long silvery electro-wrapped package from underneath Leo's healing chamber.

"You didn't need to," said Leo, taking the parcel gratefully.

"But I wanted to. And after a fall like *that*, I do think a little extra flying support is more than deserved."

Leo pulled back the shimmering paper, his eyes at once returning to those of the president as he discovered a stratospheric skydisk underneath it.

"But how did you—" Leo muttered.

"Madam Cebulka informed me you had inquired about it when you first arrived. And, evidently, your friends have informed me that you're very fortunate for that, because I had been previously debating between a nice blue or red robotic kitten!

"Now, let's see if your legs are ready to try it, shall we?"

Soenso gave Leo a helping hand out of the healing chamber, and as Leo wobbled to his feet, Andromeda dove in hard on her own two limbs, nearly missing her return of the gravityball.

"TIME-OUT!" Izma shouted from above the court. The robotic scorekeeper sounded his whistle to allow for it.

"*Seriously!*" Izma snapped at Andromeda, hovering down

from her Pilot Chair to the court. "Do you even *want* to win this game?"

"I'm trying," said Andromeda unfairly, "but—" She broke off, spotting the rest of her friends' dismayed faces: Grus appeared as though he had actually been crying; Phoebe's electro-flag sat lifelessly in her lap; Pavo didn't even seem to be paying attention to the match, poking around at his watch; and not a line of color was streaming out of Scotti or Ume's electronic laser phalanges. And as Andromeda's eyes trailed up and down the rows of disappointment, she thought she saw Leo in the crowd, at the very top of the bleachers, right next to the president.

Andromeda chuckled to herself.

"Um, *hello?*" chimed in Izma. "Do you mind telling me what it is about *losing* that you find so funny?"

"Oh, no—it's not that!" said Andromeda. "I was laughing about something else—or, rather, someone else that I thought I saw—*who clearly couldn't be there . . .*"

"You mean, Leo?" Izma asked, redoing her long black and red color-shifting electro-headscarf.

"Yeah?" said Andromeda, looking at her perplexed. "How'd you know?"

"It's only because he's right there"—Izma pointed him out—"sitting next to Soenso. So happy to see he's finally woken up! I can't believe he was in that coma for over three months!"

Andromeda froze, thinking she was mishearing things, but as she turned toward the crowd, her mouth dropped with surprise: Leo was right there, waving to her, alongside the president. And as the reality of it finally hit her, the smile on her face couldn't have stretched any wider. There was *no way* she was going to let Crux get one up on her now—not with Leo watching!

And so Andromeda dove in more forcefully than ever. Crux, meanwhile, clearly hadn't been expecting Andromeda's change in pace, and as she sent the gravityball toward his most advanced Hed-bot, cheers echoed throughout the gym as Andromeda smashed it back! And then, in the next serve, she took out Crux's second lead Hed-bot . . . and then his third! And the crowd roared louder than ever as the robotic scorekeeper called the end of the match.

Crux and Gavin looked at Andromeda, completely stupefied, as the scorekeeper announced that Izma's and Andromeda's last remaining Hed-bot to have crossed the goal was the 500-point bonus bot. But Andromeda couldn't have cared less about winning the match; the only thing she could think of was how happy she was that Leo Gray was no longer stuck inside that healing chamber!

Andromeda threw on her gravity belt and dismounted her skydisk, dashing up the floating bleachers. Pavo, Grus, and Phoebe all passed each other weirded-out looks as Andromeda ran past them.

"I can't *believe* you're OKAY!" Andromeda squealed, throwing her arms around Leo's neck.

"*Hey,*" Leo croaked. "I'm still . . . a bit of . . . a vegetable!"

"Oh, right, sorry!" said Andromeda.

And then Grus Pinwheel shared her realization. "HOLE-E-CRAPPER-BAPPERS! HE'S AWAKE!"

Pavo, Grus, and Phoebe all ran up to greet Leo, while Scotti, Ume, and Izma followed behind. And before Leo knew it, he was surrounded by classmates asking him question upon question:

"What was it like falling?"

"How long have you been awake?"

"Did you open my gift yet?"

"Yeah, what about mine?"

"What's it like being in a coma?"

"Do you actually think about things . . . or is it just like sleeping?"

"Could you hear us when we were speaking to you?"

"How many fingers am I holding up?"

"Would you ever jump again?"

Leo's head buzzed with which question to tackle first, but luckily the president put an end to all the questioning as he said, "I believe there will be plenty of time for questions *after* we eat."

Everyone was quick to agree, and as Leo entered the cafeteria, he felt more fortunate than ever as he sat down at the floating table alongside all his friends. Though it had only seemed to Leo as though he'd been away a short day, he could not deny the surge of happiness he felt knowing that everyone had actually "missed" him.

But as Leo started in on the first real meal he had had in weeks, he suddenly found it hard to swallow his bite, as Gavin, Crux, and Aabher were headed straight toward him.

"Hey, Leo!" Gavin called out, for some reason beyond Leo's comprehension, smiling at him. "Did you get the gift I gave you?"

"Yeah, and mine too?" Aabher asked with interest.

"By the way," said Crux to Leo as Leo noticed Carina Van'ness waving to him from their table, "we have an extra seat, if you'd like to sit with us. Everyone's *dying* to hear what it was like jumping!"

"Yeah, we think you're really *cool* now that you jumped," added Aabher.

Gavin elbowed him dumbly. "I mean, we think it must have been really COOL falling!"

"Thanks for the offer," Leo replied, looking around as the entire cafeteria seemed to be awaiting his response, "but I think I'd rather sit here and tell the story to my friends first."

Gavin, Crux, and Aabher's grins embarrassedly flipped, and as they returned to their table, Leo, Pavo, Andromeda, and Grus couldn't help but laugh. They were all, simply, glad to have their friend back.

The next morning Leo sat in his room, trying to cram all his gifts into his suitcase when there was a knock at the door.

"Come in," Leo allowed, wondering where he was going to fit his new skydisk.

The president entered and took a seat on the edge of Pavo's bed.

"So," he said, "you're *certain* then that this is what you want to do?"

"Yes," Leo replied, nodding. "I want to go home."

"And you do understand that—"

"—That I can't come back?" Leo finished for him. "Yes, I understand—I just want to be home with my family."

"Very well," said Soenso, getting up. "I'll send Weathers in for you as soon as the departure shuttle's ready."

"Thanks," said Leo, and the president left. Though not more than a minute after he had, the door was swinging back open and Pavo, Andromeda, and Grus were rushing in, each with terribly distressed looks on their faces.

"You're not *really* going to leave us, are you?" Grus cried out, throwing his arms around Leo and sniffling into his chest.

"Er—yeah," said Leo, peeling Grus off of him. "Like I told you guys, I don't know what it is yet, but something's not right. No one's seen Mallock, or Grimlu since what happened that night . . . And it doesn't sound like the president has any plans to try to stop any future invasion . . . And though I don't want to leave—*at all*—I can't just sit around here and wait for something more to happen. I have to get that map to Gudrun!"

"Here," said Andromeda, passing Leo a thin rectangular box. "The copy I made of it is inside. Luckily, I was able to piece together all my notes, so everything's essentially decoded for you. As long as you can figure out where the coordinates actually lead to, you should be able to find all the pieces of the Star Stone."

Andromeda let out a small, frustrated sigh. "Are you *sure* you want to do this, Leo? I mean—" She broke off, trying not to cry. "You only just got better . . . and you really shouldn't be pushing yourself. And what if something goes wrong? What if the Mleckorgs get to Earth before you find anything . . . or you—"

"Don't *worry*," said Leo to Andromeda as she gave him a hug goodbye. "I'll be fine. And I've got Meta now, so I can at least keep in contact with you guys to let you know what's going on over the summer."

Andromeda released her hold as another knock sounded at the door.

"The shuttle's ready," Weathers announced, hovering in to help with Leo's bags.

And as the four followed the bot to the loading dock, Leo's eyes widened with surprise as he found nearly the entirety of his year there, all waiting to tell him goodbye. The president and Principal Yin were there too, along with all of Leo's instructors—well, that is, all except for one, who had turned into a Mleckorg!

"Well, Leo," said Principal Yin, passing him an enormous stack of electro-papers. "These are for you."

"*What's all this?*" Leo asked, his knees buckling as he accepted the heavy load.

"Your homework, naturally," answered Herr Pendular. "Just because you slept through a good portion of history, doesn't mean you get to let History pass you!"

"Right," Leo mumbled, shaking his head as though he should have known.

Weathers fluttered over to help with the weighted stack.

"You will want to finish it all as soon as you can," Principal Yin added. "If you want to continue going to school on Earth, you won't be allowed into the next year without them completed. When you're finished, you can simply send them in to me, and I'll arrange a virtual final for you."

"Thanks," said Leo, who, though he was grateful for the special accommodations, had been privately hoping that his teachers would have forgotten about his entire semester of missed homework!

"So then, I guess this is farewell," said Soenso finally. "Or how is it Principal Yin so beautifully says it?"

"*Yìlù shùnfēng,*" she said, smiling.

"Yes, yes, though Chinese is a beautiful language, I still prefer a good Germanic *Gute Reise!*" belted Herr Pendular.

"*No, no, no!*" Professoressa Pittore shrieked, shaking her head dramatically. "*Buon viaggio* is the only'a way to'a wish someones'a safe travels!"

"I think *bon voyage* is a bit more universal," said Phoebe.

"Yeah, but *boa viagem* sounds the coolest," said Pavo.

"Don't forget Professor Kikaren," added Andromeda, who she helped come forward to say, "*Trevlig resa!*"

"Or *yoi ryokō o!*" said Ume while Scotti laser-signed in unison.

"Or *riḥlat saʿīdah!*" echoed in Izma.

"Or *szerokiej drogi!*" boomed Madam Cebulka.

"In whatever language," said Soenso, "we all wish you a safe trip."

"Thanks," said Leo. And he started up the shuttle's steps. "Oh, and President Soenso?" he added, turning around.

"Yes?" Soenso granted with interest.

"Who's Cornelius?"

The president chuckled for a long moment at this before he replied, "My goose!"

And with that, Leo made his way into the shuttle, and as its doors sealed, he was left smiling. The year had turned out more spectacular than he could have ever imagined . . .

But there was one more thing Leo wished he had thought to have asked the president before he left; though it wouldn't come to him until he was on the airjet, finally on his way back to Riverdale, when he noticed, for the first time, that his veins were mysteriously glittering.

And so the story's finished now,

The pages will turn blank,

Perhaps we'll meet another time,

And for that, I thank:

You, of course, the reader who reached the very end!

The people of facts and figures,

The knights of the red pen,

The paperboys and papergirls of all of my requests,

The muses, yes, the muses—for never making any sense!

And finally, the universe, for allowing it all to be,

For I suppose things could have gone quite differently,

If I were, instead, a bee!

ABOUT THE AUTHOR

K.J. KRUK is an award-winning visual artist and is both the author and illustrator of *Leo Gray and the Lunar Eclipse*. Kruk is also well-known in academia for the discovery of a spiral galaxy, the identification of coordinates leading to a verifiable rip in the fabric of time, and most recently, for the excavation of bones from an unknown alien species dating back to 9,600 BCE. For more information on the author's most recent endeavors—or to purchase a rather nifty t-shirt—simply visit leograybooks.com.